R. Arthur Arnold

Through Persia by Caravan

R. Arthur Arnold

Through Persia by Caravan

ISBN/EAN: 9783743317734

Manufactured in Europe, USA, Canada, Australia, Japa

Cover: Foto ©Andreas Hilbeck / pixelio.de

Manufactured and distributed by brebook publishing software (www.brebook.com)

R. Arthur Arnold

Through Persia by Caravan

THROUGH PERSIA

BY CARAVAN

By ARTHUR ARNOLD,
AUTHOR OF "FROM THE LEVANT," ETC.

NEW YORK:
HARPER & BROTHERS, PUBLISHERS,
FRANKLIN SQUARE.
1877.

Inscribed

TO THE

EARL AND COUNTESS GRANVILLE.

PREFACE.

During the summer of 1875, my wife and I left London, intending to travel through Russia and Persia. In the following chapters I have transcribed our notes, commencing at Warsaw. From Poland we passed to St. Petersburg, and from the Russian capital southward to Astrakhan. We traversed the Caspian Sea from extreme north to south, and, landing at Enzelli, rode through the whole length of Persia—a distance of more than a thousand miles. Leaving the Caspian Sea early in October, we arrived at the Persian Gulf in February. In March we were in Bombay; in April at Alexandria.

Had I chosen a Persian title for these notes of travel, I would have taken "Zil-ullah," which is assumed by the two great sovereigns of the Mohammedan world. Nazr-ed-deen, Kajar, Shah of Persia, and Abd-ul-Hamid, Sultan of Turkey, are styled, in the high official language of their own countries, "Zil-ullah" (Shadows of God). In Christendom there is one sovereign, and only one, the Tsar, upon whom is imposed the awful burden of representing the ideal of wisdom, justice, mercy, and goodness.

Civilization — the extension of civil rights — has taught the Western world to look with some contempt upon this assumption of supernatural dignity. It is a pretension which is doomed to fade away, and to become extinct. It dies unlamented, because it lives by force — by withholding from mankind, or, at best, by holding in trust for mankind, their birthright of liberty and responsibility; never deigning to admit that the sources of its power are other than divine.

A. A.

CONTENTS.

CHAPTER I.

The Vistula.—Warsaw.—French Sympathies.—Partition of Poland.—Passport and Local Regulations.—The Three Imperial Courts.—The Turkish Capitulations.—The Ideal Pole.—The Real Pole.—Religion in Poland.—Hôtel d'Europe.—Statue of John Sobieski.—Lazienski Palace.—Russian Government.—Napoleon at Warsaw.—Grodno.—Wilna.—"Tronfolger's Namstag"..Page 17

CHAPTER II.

Russian Railway Carriages. — Russian Ventilation. — Dunaburg. — White Sand.—Droschky Tickets.—St. Petersburg.—Exaggerated Praise.—Newski Prospekt.—The Hermitage.—Winter Palace.—St. Isaac's Church.—The Old Cathedral.—Tombs of the Romanoffs.—Down the Neva.—Cronstadt.—Droschky-driving.—The Gostinnoi Dvor.—The Kazan Church.—The Russian Language.—The Road to Moscow............................ 29

CHAPTER III.

Moscow. — The Native Capital of Russia.— The Kitai-Gorod.— Lubianka Street.—The Kremlin.—The Holy Gate.—The Redeemer of Smolensk.—Bell-tower of Ivan.—Church Bells.—Church of the Assumption.—Dean Stanley's Description.—The Coronation Platform.—The Virgin of Vladimir.—Corner Tombs.—The Young Demetrius.—John the Terrible.—The Tsar Kolokol.—The Foundling Hospital.—Nurses and Babies.—"Nés avant Terme."—Moral and Social Results.—Cathedral of St. Basil.—John the Idiot.—The Lobnoć Mèsto.—Iverskaya Chasòvnia.—How the Metropolitan is paid.—Virgin from Mount Athos.—Tsar and Patriarch.—Motto from Troitsa.. 36

CHAPTER IV.

The Road to Nijni.—Rivers Oka and Volga.—Nijni.—The Bridge of Boats.

—The Heights of Nijni.—Lopachef's Hotel.—A Famous Landscape.—Prisoners for Siberia.—Their Wives and Children.—The Great Fair.—The Last Bargains.—Caravan Tea.—Persian Merchants.—Buildings of the Fair.—Gloves and Furs.—Russian Tea-dealers.—Mosque at Nijni.—Shows and Theatres.—Russia vs. Free Trade.—Russian Hardware.—Articles de Paris.—Melons and Grapes.—The Governor's Palace.—Picturesque Nijni..Page 50

CHAPTER V.

Leaving Nijni.—The *Tsarevna Marie*.—Tickets for Two Thousand Miles.—Our Fellow-passengers.—The *Alexander II.*—Kazan.—Mohammedans in Russia.—Our Lady of Kazan.—"No Sheets!"—Oriental Cleanliness.—Russian Climate and Clothing.—Orientalism in Russia.—Persian Prayers.—A Shi'ah's Devotions.—Shallowness of the Volga.—The River Kama.—Hills about Simbirsk.—Samara.—Mare's-milk Cure.—Volsk.—Saratof.—Tartar Population.—Prisoners for the Caucasus Tsaritzin.—Sarepta.—Gingerbread and Mustard.—Chorney Yar.—A Peasant Mayor.—Tartar Fishermen.—Astrakhan.—Mouths of the Volga.—Raising Level of the Caspian... 63

CHAPTER VI.

Louis XIV. and the Tsar.—Russian Church and State.—Empress Anne's Buffoon.—Prayers for the Tsar.—The Russian Press.—Censorship.—Press Regulations.—The *Moscow Gazette.*—Difficulties of Journalists.—The *Wjedomosti.*—The *Russki Mir.*—Russia not Russian.—Foreign Races.—New Military System.—The Emancipation of the Serfs.—The Communal System.—Bad Farming.—Ignorance of the Peasantry.—The Corn Trade.—Complaints from Odessa.—Resurrection of Sebastopol.—Corn from Russia and the United States.—The Artel of Odessa.—Demands of Odessa Merchants.—A Viceroy wanted.—English Interests in Russian Corn.—The Soil of Russia.—The Conquests of Russia.—Contrast with Persia.—Borrowed Money.—Unprofitable Railways.—Revenue of Russia.—Produce of Poll-tax.—Privileged Citizens............................ 80

CHAPTER VII.

The Delta of the Volga.—Persian Passengers.—The *Constantine.*—Petrovsk.—Derbent.—"Le Feu Éternel."—Persian Merchandise.—Persian Clothing.—A Colored Deck-load.—Russian Trio of Spirits.—"Un Knut Russe."—Baku.—"Dominique."—Dust of Baku.—The Khan of Baku.—The Maiden's Tower.—Russian Naval Station.—Petrolia in Asia.—Baku

Oil-carts. — The Petroleum Wells. — Kalafy Company. — Fire-worship. — Parsees and Persians. — The Indian Priest. — The Surakhani Temple. — Manufacture of Petroleum..Page 99

CHAPTER VIII.

Bathing in the Caspian.—The Way to Europe.—A Tarantas.—The Baku Club. — Mihailovski Gardens. — Leaving Baku. — Lenkoran. —Astara.— Petroleum on Deck.—Enzelli.—Persian Boatmen.—Mr. Consul Churchill, C.B. — Enzelli Custom-house. — Sadr Azem's Konak. — The Shah's Yacht.—Lake of Enzelli.—Peri-bazaar.—Province of Ghilan.—Resht.— Bazaar and "Green." — Women of Persia. — Their Street Costume. — Shopping in Bazaar.—Riding in Persia.—Chapar and Caravan.—Kerjavas.—A Takht-i-rawan.—Leaving Resht.—Charvodars and Gholams.— Lucky and Unlucky Days.—Whips of Iron.—"Ul-läh."—The Bell Mule. —Houssein Mounted.—The First Station.—Our Camp Kitchen.—A Mud Hovel... 113

CHAPTER IX.

The Month Ramadan.—Mohammed's First Wife.—Ramadan in the Koran. —The Nocturnal Kalian.—Loading Up.—A Persian Landlord.—Persian Money: Tomans, Krans, and Shihees.—Counting Money.—Persian Mints. — Rich Provinces. — Kudem. — Chapar-khanah. — Bala-khanah. — Constructed to Smoke. — Caravanserais.— Unfurnished Apartments. — Our Bell-mule.—A Traveled Khan.—The Safid-Rud.—Rustemabad.—Village of Rhudbar.—Parchenar.—Khan offers his Tree.—A Night in the Open. —Mistaken for a Thief.—"The Bells!"—Camels in the Path.......... 132

CHAPTER X.

How Hills are Made. — Kharzan. — Mazara. — A Persian Village. — John Milton and Casbeen.—The Plain of Kasveen.—The Mirage.—Gardens of Kasveen.—Dervishes.—Decay of Kasveen.—A Persian Town.—Women of Kasveen.—Persian Costumes.—"Allahu Akbar."—Mosque of Kasveen. —Telegram from Teheran.—Visit to the Khan.—His Love Affairs.— Lost in Kasveen.—Abdulabad.—An Alarm and an Arrival.—"Gosrozink."—Native Plows.—On to Karij.—Lodged in the Shah's Palace.— The Imperial Saloon.—An Imperial Bedroom.—Approach to Teheran.— Population of the Capital.—The Kasveen Gate.—Mud Houses and Walls. —The Imperial Theatre.—Entrance to the "Arg."—Neglect of Public Works.—British Legation.—Mirza Houssein Khan.—Teheran Bazaar.— Caravanserai Ameer...148

CHAPTER XI.

Teheran.—Street of the Foreign Envoys.—The British Minister.—Lanterns of Ceremony.—The English in Teheran.—The Shah's Palace.—Mirza Houssein Khan.—The Sipar Salar.—An Oriental Minister.—Persian Corruption.—Mirza Houssein Khan's Policy.—His Retinue.—Brigandage in Persia.—Saloon of Audience.—The Jeweled Globe.—The Shah's Throne.—The Old Hall.—Persians and the Alhambra.—The Shah receiving Homage.—Rustem and the White Devil.—Reports in Teheran.—The English Courier.—Character of Persian Government.—The Green Drawing-room.—The Shah's Album.—Persians and Patriots.—The Shah's Jewels.—The "Sea of Light" ....Page 168

CHAPTER XII.

The Shah.—The Kajar Dynasty.—Boxes of Justice.—Persian Soldiers.—Their Drill and Pay.—Military Supper in Ramadan.—Jehungur Khan.—The Shah's Presents.—Zoological Garden.—View from Teheran.—Demavend.—Persian Fever.—Persian Honesty.—Europeans and Persians.—Caps and Galoches.—A Paper War.—The Ottoman Embassy.—A British Complaint.—A Turkish Atrocity.—Persian Window Law.—English in Bazaars.—The Indo-European Telegraph Stations in Persia.—The English Clergyman in Persia 183

CHAPTER XIII.

Teheran.—Snow in November.—Our Servant, Kazem.—Getting a Takht-i-rawan.—Abd-ullah, the Carpenter.—Preparing for the Road.—A Charvodar's "Beard."—Black Monday.—Trying the Takht-i-rawan.—Loading the Caravan.—Servant's Merchandise.—"Zood! Zood!"—Leaving Teheran.—The Road to Ispahan.—Seeing the Khanoum.—Shah Abd-ul-Azim.—Moollahs on the Road.—On to Kinaragird.—The Great Salt Desert.—Pul-i-delak.—A Salt River.—A Negro Dervish.—Salt-water Soup.—A Windy Lodging... 195

CHAPTER XIV.

Koom.—Approach to the Holy City.—The Golden Dome.—Koom Bazaar.—The Governor's Procession.—The Itizad-el-Dowleh.—Mirza Teki Khan.—Disgraced by the Shah.—Order for his Assassination.—The Shah's Contrition.—A Visit to the Governor.—A Coat of Honor.—Pipes of Ceremony.—Mesjid-i-Juma.—Tomb of Feth-Ali-Shah.—The Shrine of Fatima.—A Pretended Pilgrim.—Reception at the Mosque.—

Not allowed to Enter.—A Temperance City.—Takht-i-rawan in Bazaar.
—The Road to Sin-sin.—View from the Chapar-khanah..........Page 208

CHAPTER XV.

Kashan.—Visit to the Governor.—Kashan Bazaar.—The Governor's House.
—The Governor on Railways.—Tea, Pipes, and Sherbet.—A Ride round
Kashan.—A House pulled down.—Present from the Governor.—Presents
from Servants.—Manna.—Leaving Kashan.—Gabrabad.—Up the Mountains.—A Robber Haunt.—Kuhrud.—In the Snow.—A Persian Interior.
—A Welcome Visitor.—Kazem as a Cook.—The Takht-i-rawan Frozen.
—Pass of Kuhrud.—Soh.—"The Blue Man."—Beauties of the Road.—
Province of Ispahan.—Moot-i-Khoor.—Ispahan Melons.—Village of
Gez.. 222

CHAPTER XVI.

Ispahan.—Approach by Road.—Suburbs of Ispahan.—A Ragged Bazaar.—
Departed Greatness.—The Grand Avenue.—The Great Madrassee.—
River Zayinderud.—Pipes on the Bridge.—Djulfa-by-Ispahan.—Russia
and the Armenians.—Gate of Djulfa.—The English Missionary.—Mr.
Bruce's House.—Armenian Women.—The British Agent.—Church Missionary School.—Armenian Priests.—Enemies of the School.—Visit to
the Governor.—The Prince's Carriage.—"The Forty Columns."—The
Prince's Anderoon.—The Shah's Eldest Son.—His Estimate of the
Army.—Zil-i-Sultan.—His Hope and Fears.—His Court at Ispahan.—
His Carte-de-Visite.—The Princess's Costume......................... 238

CHAPTER XVII.

The Zil-i-Sultan.—Order about the School.—Not Responsible for Murder.
—Telegraph to Teheran.—Reports and Rumors.—Excitement in Djulfa.
—Closing the British School.—Relapse of Fever.—Letter from the Prince.
—Persian Compliments.—Prescriptions by Telegraphs.—A Persian Doctor.—Persian Medical Treatment.—Persian Leeches.—The Prince's Hakim.—His Letter of Introduction.—His Newspaper and Autobiography.
—The Prince and the Province.—A Son of a Moollah.—"The Sticks."
—How Punishment is Given.—A Snow Torture.—A Persian Dinner-party.—Before Dinner.—An Englishman's Legs.—A Great Khan.—The
First Course.—Les Pièces de Résistance.—Going Home............... 256

CHAPTER XVIII.

Ispahan.—Zil-i-Sultan and the British School.—Church Missionary Society.

—The "Crown of Islam."—A Ride through Ispahan.—The Meidan.—Runaway Horses in Bazaar.—"Embassador Lilies."—New-year's-eve.—Severe Cold.—Sufferings of the Poor.—A Supper in Ispahan.—Kerbela and Nedjif.—Houssein and Ali.—Imām Juma's Court.—Confiscation of Christians' Property.—Bāb and Bābis.—Execution of Bāb.—Attempted Assassination of the Shah.—Punishment of the Conspirators.—Revenge of the Koran.—Bāb and Behar.—The Followers of Behar........Page 271

CHAPTER XIX.

Getting out of Persia.—Northern and Southern Roads.—Advantage of Russia.—Russian Goods in Persia.—English Interests in Persia.—Mr. Mackenzie's Plan.—Navigation of the Karun River.—From Ispahan to Shuster.—A Subsidy required.—Price of Wheat.—East India Company's Survey.—Letter to Lord Derby.—Baron Reuter's Concession.—Traffic in Persia.—Mules and Railways.—Difficulties of Construction.—Intercourse between Towns.—Estimates of Population.—Traveling in Persia.—Mountain Scenery.—Plains covered with Snow.—Persia and "The Arabian Nights."—No Old Men.—The Lady and the House.—The Greatest Power in Persia... 281

CHAPTER XX.

Leaving Ispahan.—"The Farewell" Hill.—Opium Manufacture.—The Telegraph Superintendent.—Punishing a Servant.—Khadji Josef's Tea-party.—Marg.—Kum-i-Shah.—The Baggage lost.—Neither Ispahan nor Shiraz.—Ahminabad.—English Doctor robbed.—Doubt and Danger.—Yezdikhast.—A Vaulted Chamber.—A Black Vault.—Telegram from Shiraz.—The Abadeh Istikbal.—A Traveling Pipe.—Display of Horsemanship.—Abadeh.—The Governor's Present.—Bread from Teheran.—Letter from Abadeh.—An Ill-looking Escort.—Khanikora.—Miserable Lodging.—Soldiers refuse to March.—Up the Mountains.—Houssein Khan.—Dehbid.—Shooting Foxes.—Khanikergan.—Meshed-i-Murghaub.—Robbers about.—Persian Justice.—Tofanghees... 292

CHAPTER XXI.

Classic Persia.—The Tomb of Cyrus.—Date of the Ruins.—Passargardæ.—Columns of Cyrus's Tomb. — Color of Ruins. — Neglected by Persians.—Kawamabad.—Takht-i-rawan in Danger.—Houssein Khan and the Sheep.—Village of Sidoon.—Ruins of Istakr.—Situation of Persepolis.—Araxes or Bendemeer.—Staircase at Persepolis.—Darius and Xerxes.—Cuneiform Inscriptions.—Study of Cuneiform.—Chronology of Assyria.—

Great Hall of Xerxes.—The Persepolitan Lion.—Hall of a Hundred Columns.—Professor Rawlinson on the Ruins.—Tomb of Darius.—"The Great God Ormazd."—The Bringer of Evil.—Dios and Devils.—Errors in Religion and Art.—Pedigree of Architecture.—Persians, Medes, and Greeks.—Origin of Ionic Architecture.—Leaving Persepolis.—Plain of Merodasht .... Page 314

CHAPTER XXII.

Kinara.—A Family House.—A Troublesome Cat.—Houssein Khan and the Sheep.—Soldiers and their Debtors.—Zergan.—Persian Scenery.—A Persian Funeral.—Zergan to Shiraz.—Pass of Allahu Akbar.—Snow-storm at Shiraz.—The English Doctor.—Gate of Shiraz.—A Good Persian House.— A Present from Firman Firma.—Letter from His Excellency.—A Dervish at the Gate.—Meidan of Shiraz.—Visit to Firman Firma.—Widow of Teki Khan.—Firman Firma's Character.—Poverty of Persia.—Passion-play in Mohurrem.—Bazaar of Shiraz.—Tomb of Hafiz.—Odes inscribed on Tomb.—Translation of Hafiz.—The New Garden.—Tea in an Imaret 334

CHAPTER XXIII.

Literature of Persia.—Hafiz and Sa'di.—Contemporary of Dante.—Mr. Bicknell's Translation of Hafiz.—Consulting Hafiz as an Oracle.—Nadir Shah and Hafiz.—Hafiz's Fragments.—"Tetrastichs" of Hafiz.—Sa'di's "Bustan."—Sa'di's "Gulistan."—Extracts from "Gulistan."—Sa'di's Wit and Wisdom.—Gardens of Shiraz.—Slaves and Slave-brokers.—English Surgeons and Persian Patients.—Influence of Russia.—Mr. Thomson and Mr. Bruce.—Indo-Persian Telegraph.—Major Champain's Reports.—A View of the Neighbors.—Persian Homes.—Government of Shiraz.—Eeliats in Fars.—Attack on a Caravan.—A Vengeful Government. —Cruel Execution of Robbers.—Firman Firma superseded.—Taxation in Persia.—The Shah and Shiraz... 352

CHAPTER XXIV.

The Road to Bushire.—Yahia Khan's Portrait.—To Cinerada.—Last View of Shiraz.—Difficult Traveling.—Khan-i-Zonoon.—A Caravan in Trouble.—A Cold Caravanserai.—Murder of Sergeant Collins.—Death of Sergeant M'Leod.—Advantage of an Escort.—Dashtiarjan.—"Eaten a Bullet."—Plain of Dashtiarjan.—Ghooloo-Kojeh Pass.—A Lion in the Path. —Mr. Blanford's "Interview."—Up a Tree.—Wounded Horse.—Kaleh-Mushír.—Mount Perizan.—Kotul Perizan.—View of Mian-kotul..... 372

CHAPTER XXV.

Mian-kotul Caravanserai. — Tofanghees on Guard. — Feuds between Villagers. — Kotul Dochter. — Traveling on the Kotul. — The Mushir-el-Mulk. — Lake Famoor. — Encampment of Eeliats. — Ruins of Ancient Persia. — Plain of Kazeroon. — Songs of Persian Soldiers. — Kazeroon. — Anniversary of Houssein's Death. — "Ah, Houssein!" — Fanatical Exercises. — Orange Gardens. — The Sheik of Kazeroon. — Plain of Kazeroon. — Attack on Major Napier's Caravan. — Village of Kamaridj. — Plain of Khan-i-Takhte. — Hospitality in Persia. — Kotul Maloo. — A Difficult Path. — Daliki River. — Arabs in Persia. — Palm-leaf Huts. — A Loop-holed Bedroom. — Petroleum at Daliki. — Barasjoon. — Rifle Practice. — Indian Officers in Persia. — Functions of Political Resident. — Sowars from Bushire. — Caravanserai at Ahmedy. — Arrival of Captain Fraser. — The Mashillah. — A Wet Day's Ride. — Bushire .... Page 387

CHAPTER XXVI.

Bushire. — The Residency. — Arab Towers and Wooden "Guns." — Government in Persian Gulf. — The Arabian Shore. — Arabs and Arabs. — The Sultan's Power in Arabia. — Oman and the Ibadhis. — Pilgrims to Mecca. — Destiny of Rotten Steamships. — Pilgrims' Coffins. — Six Hundred Arabs Drowned. — Persian Land Revenue. — Collecting Customs Duties. — Trade and Population. — Commerce of Bushire. — Cultivation of Opium. — Opium and Cereals. — Export of Opium. — British Expedition in 1857. — Occupation of Persia. — Persian Army in 1857. — Interests of England. — The Indo-Persian Telegraph. — Persia Ripe for Conquest. — Persia and India 406

CHAPTER XXVII.

The Province of Fars. — Memorandum by Colonel Ross. — Boundaries of Fars. — Government of Fars. — Six First-class Governments. — The Districts of Bushire. — Karagash River. — Eeliats. — Nomad Tribes of Fars. — Numbers of the Tribes. — Eel-Khanee and Eel-Begee. — Chief Routes in Fars. — Taxation and Revenue. — A Revenue Survey 421

CHAPTER XXVIII.

British India Steam Navigation Company. — Crew of the *Euphrates*. — Pilgrims in Difficulty. — Streets of Bushire. — German Archæological Expedition. — Sermons in Bricks. — Leaving Bushire. — Slavery in the Persian Gulf. — Fugitive-slave Circulars. — The Parsee Engineer's Evidence. —

Ships searched for Slaves.—Pearl-fisheries of Bahrein.—Anglo-Turkish Ideas.—Lingah in Laristan.—Bunder-Abbas.—Landing at Cape Jahsk.—"Pegs" and Pale Clerks.—A Master Mariner's Grievance.—The End of Persia.—Coast of Beloochistan.—Shooting Sleeping Turtles.—Harbor of Kurrachee.—Kurrachee Boat-wallahs.—The Orthodox Scinde Hat.—Faults of Indian Society.—English Ladies in India.—Intercourse with Natives.—Unmannerly Englishmen.—Exceptional Behavior.....Page 428

CHAPTER XXIX.

Bombay.—The *Serapis* in Harbor.—Suburbs of Bombay.—Parsee Dead.—Towers of Silence.—Hindoo Cremation-ground.—Cotton Manufacture in India.—Report of Indian Commission.—Neglect of Indian Government.—A Bombay Cotton Factory.—Hours of Factory Labor.—Seven Weeks' Work. — Natives of India. — Expenditure of Indian Government. — The Great Absentee Landlord. — Grievance of Cultivators. — Their Enemies, the Money-lenders. — English and Native Equity. — The Suez Canal. — Landing at Ismailia.—English at the Pyramids.—Alexandria.—"Cleopatra's Needle."—Proposed Removal to England.—Condition of the Obelisk.—Recent Excavation.—Captain Methven's Plan.—Removal in an Iron Vessel.—Cost of Removal.—Egypt and the Khedive.—Preparing for Mr. Cave.—Sham Civilization.—The Horse-trampling Ceremony.—English *en voyage.*—Egypt and Persia.—Customs Officers at Alexandria.—Egypt and Turkey................ 443

CHAPTER XXX.

"From the Levant."—Sunnis and Shi'ahs.—Turkish Government and Turkish Debt.—Fuad and Midhat Pashas.—Not a "Sick Man."—"Best Police of the Bosphorus."—Religious Sanction for Decrees.—The Council of State.—"Qui est-ce qu'on trompe?"—Murad and Hamid.—Error of the West.—Precepts of the Cheri.—Authority of the Sultan.—Non-Mussulman Population.—Abd-ul-Hamid's Hatt.—A Foreign Garrison.—Hatt-y-houmayoun of 1856.—Failure of Promises.—Fetva of Sheik-ul-Islam.—Non-Mussulmans and the Army.—Firman of December, 1875.—Sir Henry Elliot and the Porte.—Conscription in Turkey................ 458

CHAPTER XXXI.

Islam in Persia.—Mohammedans of India.—Ali of the Shi'ahs.—Abu-Bekr Successor of Mohammed.—Imāms of the Shi'ahs.—Réza and Mehdee.—Religion in the East.—Mohammed as a Soldier.—War with Infidels.—Christianity of the Middle Ages.—Stretching the Koran.—Mohammed's

Marriage Law.—Status of Mohammedan Women.—Women and Civilization.—Special Privilege of Mohammed.—Mormonism and Mohammedanism.—Consequences of Polygamy.—Protection of Polygamy.—Mohammed and Ayesha.—Scandal silenced by the Koran.—Mohammed's Domestic Difficulty.—Law for Men and Women.—Women in Mohammed's Heaven. — The Mohammedan Paradise. — Mohammed and the Jews.—Birth of Christ in the Koran.—Miracles of Christ.—English Leaning to Islam.--Mohammedanism and Christianity.—Christians of the East.—Moslem Intemperance. — Wine and the Koran. — Superiority of Christianity..Page 471

THROUGH PERSIA BY CARAVAN.

CHAPTER I.

The Vistula.—Warsaw.—French Sympathies.—Partition of Poland.—Passport and Local Regulations.—The Three Imperial Courts.—The Turkish Capitulations.—The Ideal Pole.—The Real Pole.—Religion in Poland.—Hôtel d'Europe.—Statue of John Sobieski.—Lazienski Palace.—Russian Government.—Napoleon at Warsaw.—Grodno.—Wilna.—" Tronfolger's Namstag."

By the waters of the Vistula we sat down and talked of the historical wrongs of Poland. We were on the lower bank of the river, near where the bridge of latticed iron connects the suburb of Praga with the city of Warsaw. From this point of view the situation of the capital of Russian Poland is picturesque. It was a beautiful evening in September of last year, and the rays of the setting sun gilded the stately lines of the palace, once that of Poniatowski, which stands from fifty to a hundred feet above the level of the water. The queer old houses of one of the most ancient parts of Warsaw are scattered on the slope, and the background is filled with yet higher objects—the lofty roofs, towers, and spires of Polish churches, and the five golden cupolas of the Russian Cathedral.

Rafts of pine timber, cargoes of ruddy apples and dark-green melons, float before us; the river has nearly the width of the Thames at Putney, but nowhere the beauty of our metropolitan stream; it comes to where we sit, visible afar in its course through flat, sandy lands, a silvery streak; and as we mount the rising ground into Warsaw, we can trace its flow, burnished by the dying sunlight, as it passes away through a country equally destitute of charms or of high cultivation.

Arrived at the top of the slope leading to the bridge, we are in the principal street of Warsaw, which, indeed, in its entire length is composed of two streets—the Krakowski Przedmiesci, or Faubourg de Cracovie, as the French-loving people of Warsaw call it, and the Nowy Swiat, or Rue de Nouveau Monde, as the more fashionable shop-keepers at once inform any stranger. There must be thousands of people in Warsaw who would be glad to see the defeat of Sedan and the annexation of Metz avenged and reversed. There is an air as well as a natural gayety in the manner of the people which makes one almost ready to forget that the broad expanse of the German Empire lies between this city and France, to which, of all foreign lands, the Polish sympathies are given. With the exception of the tram-way cars, which look like English second-class railway carriages, the vehicles have caught this gay and lively air. The queer-shaped omnibuses, like a landau and small omnibus pressed together, are as bright as red and yellow can make them. Occasionally one sees dashing through the crowd the equipage of some Russian official, the flat-capped and petticoated driver holding the reins *à la Russe*, one in each hand, steering his fast-trotting horses with marvelous skill and address, and with no need of whip.

There are some populations which it seems impossible to fancy as living in apparent happiness and gayety together with their conquerors. For my own part, I can imagine the Battle of Dorking a reality, and conceive the occupation of London by foreign soldiery; but I can not picture to myself holiday-making Londoners in the Tower of London by permission of alien sentries, nor merry parties on the hills of Hampstead and Sydenham and Muswell cracking nuts and jokes as they looked down upon London, the prey of a foreign foe. I can better frame for the mind's eye the debonair populace of Paris disporting in the Bois, under the guardianship of Germans, than Berliners happy in the Thiergarten, while the Unter den Linden was patrolled by French. The Italians would be lighter-hearted in such circumstances, and the Poles exhibit their affinity of race by all that the traveler sees in Warsaw.

The partition of Poland is now something more than an accomplished fact — it is part of the settled distribution of the Continent of Europe. Nearly a hundred years have passed away since "Freedom shrieked" at the fall of Kosciusko and of Warsaw. Generations have matured to which the independence of Poland is but a dim tradition—generations which have followed the road to comfort and prosperity, by subservience to the Russian power. Yet the rule of Russia has been harsh, and there has been no disposition, at least until the last few years, to conceal the character of the claim by right of which Russia rules in Warsaw. The insurrection of fourteen years ago is outwardly forgotten, yet in many a Polish heart there must be rankling memory of the cruel time when the ferocious tyranny of the Russian General Mouravieff evoked remonstrance from England. The older rebellions are commemorated in Warsaw. The insolence of conquest could not look more grim than in the blunt and stunted obelisk, supported on lions, which was erected in 1841 upon the Saski Place, in memory of the "loyal" Poles and of "their fidelity to their sovereign."

We have been visitors in Paris and in Rome during a state of siege; but when the Germans were at St. Denis, and the army of Versailles at Neuilly—when Garibaldi was in arms at Mentana, and the newly invented Chassepot had "*fait merveille*" upon the bodies of men which were yet unburied, it was easier to enter or quit either of those cities than it is to find acceptance in time of peace as a visitor in Warsaw. The penalties are dreadful for those who receive a stranger without at once giving notice to the police of his country and his quality. No hotel exists without a passport bureau; and travelers are not "ushered," as reporters say, into their apartments, but are rather "interned" to await, on Polish food, the good pleasure of the Russian police as to their liberty within the city, and the time of their departure. If their passports do not bear the *visé* of the Russian Legation in their country, they will be required to spend a good deal of time in a shuttlecock existence between the police-office and their hotel. They will be teased with formalities, which of course a well-informed conspirator would easily avoid.

In fact, the inhabitants, temporary and resident, of Warsaw live in a fortress, under special license from the police and the governor-general. One notices in the streets that not only for convenience, but "by order," every shop-keeper must inscribe in Russian whatever name and business he chooses to set up in the native language. If on the right hand of his shop-window he writes, in the letters which are common to most of the languages of Europe, "Konicz, Tailleur, Chapeaux de Paris, la Dernière Mode, Style Élégante," he must on the left side, or elsewhere, communicate to all whom it may concern the same announcement in the semi-barbarous characters of the Russian language. One is everywhere reminded that Warsaw is Russian, not Polish; that Russian soldiers form the garrison; that Russian is the official language; that the Russo-Greek Church imparts the official religion of this essentially Roman Catholic Poland. There would be little, perhaps, to recall to mind the fact that here is a suppressed nationality, were not the vital difference of religion ever present to remind the stranger of the history of this part of Europe.

The partition of Poland is the fundamental bond of union, drawing together the alliance of "the three imperial courts," "who," in the language of the Berlin Memorandum, "believe themselves called upon to concert among themselves measures for averting the dangers of the situation" in Turkey; "who," when united, are absolutely masters of that situation, and can be subject to the interference of other great powers only in their dissensions. The three emperors, who, if they agree, can, without reference to any other power, impose their own solution of the Eastern question upon the world, are first of all united in that transaction which gave to Prussia her Roman Catholic provinces upon the Baltic; to Russia, the central district, of which Warsaw is the chief city; and to Austria, Cracow and Galicia. No more effectual mode of insuring the extinction of Poland as a separate state could have been devised; and in fact Poland has ceased to exist. There is not even a quiver in the divided limbs; Poles must be Prussian, Russian, or Austrian, if they wish for a successful career. He who climbs toward the prizes must wear the colors of the sovereignty; and so it usually happens that acquiescence and contentment follow conquest. This was manifest even in the short-lived annexations of the First Napoleon. I have heard of Garibaldi that he, an Italian of Italians, was in fact born a Frenchman; that in Nice, under the First Empire, it was the wish of prudent parents that their children should talk French, and that the tongue of Molière, rather than that of Dante, was the language in which he first learned to speak.

Poland is dismembered, but in religion she is united; and undoubtedly the preservation of peace in the North of Europe has some assurance in the circumstance that her religion is not that of Russia nor that of Prussia. Austrians have always had a hold on the sympathy of Poles, which neither

Russia nor Germany can attain, in the fact that both turn to Rome as the fountain of their religious faith. Perhaps it is owing to this communion in religion that the rule of Austria in her Polish dominions has been milder; although there can be no doubt that in part this has been the result of policy—of a desire to engender envy on the side of Russian Poland—so that, in the event of war, Austria might rely upon the detention of a large Russian force in and around Warsaw. The Austrian Poles have neither Falck laws nor a schismatic Church connected with the Government to which they are subject; and in a conglomerate empire, in which there is unavoidably some confusion of tongues, the Government is not impelled by that irritating desire to impose the official language which marks the rule of Russia and of Prussia. The Tsar is doubtless aware of the leaning of some among his Polish subjects toward his Austrian brother, who is, to a certain extent, protected in his ambition upon the Danube by the probability that he could raise revolt in Warsaw by promising Poland autonomy like that of Hungary. Indeed, the more we examine the condition of Poland, the more convinced shall we become that it is the centre upon which reposes the concord of the three imperial courts; and that but for the present settlement of Poland we might have less ground for confidence in their pacific resolutions.

As for ourselves, and in connection with the politics of the East of Europe, it will possibly surprise not a few Englishmen to learn that for the peculiar privileges, "capitulations," as they are called, by which our intercourse with the Ottoman Empire is regulated, and under which Englishmen live and carry on business in Turkey, we are as much indebted to the Poles as to any other people. These concessions, the existence of which has always proclaimed the infirmity of Mohammedan rule, were not made to us or at any bidding from our Foreign Office. They date, as we learn from Mr. Hertzlet's compilation,* from a time when England was not a great power in the East. Two hundred years ago—in 1675—" an extension to British subjects of privileges granted to French, *Poles*, Venetians," was conceded, " by command of the Emperor and Conqueror of the Earth, achieved with the assistance of the Omnipotent, and with the special grace of God—We, who by the Divine Grace, assistance, will, and benevolence now are the King of Kings of the World, the Prince of Emperors of every age, the Dispenser of Crowns to monarchs, and the Champion;" and it is in right of this extension of privileges originally granted to " French, Poles, Venetians," that our consular courts exercise judgment and authority in Turkey and in Egypt. Every historical student must have noticed how the use of such high-sounding titles, such pretenses to a quasi-Divine sovereignty, fade away at the dawn and in the increase of civilization; but perhaps there is no more remarkable example on record than that which is afforded by a comparison of the Sultan's style and titles in the treaty above referred to, with the simple designation of a successor in the Caliphate, Abd-ul-Medjid, in the Treaty of 1856, where the Sultan is, in French fashion, merely styled " Emperor of the Ottomans."

Having thus connected Poland with ourselves, especially in our relations with the chief of Mohammedan powers, let us turn again to that shadow of her former self, which is seen in and about her ancient capital, of which the history mounts to the twelfth century. Those who were young children thirty years ago had at that time perhaps very much the same conception of an ideal Pole, an ideal which has possibly lingered in their thoughts through life. My notion of a Pole was of one who passed his time in the severest practice of the most noble exhibitions of personal honor and patriotism; of one who was generally in chains, often in Siberia, who had a most

---

* " Treaties, etc., regulating Trade between Great Britain and Turkey."

romantic visage, an elegant figure, a very picturesque costume, a coat all frogged and braided, a brilliant scarf, very high boots, as suitable for dancing as for striding over the corpses of his oppressors, and a painful, oft-renewed acquaintance with the knout, as wielded by Russian executioners. I will venture to add that, in my own case, Mr. *Punch* is responsible for perverting this idea. In the days of the late Lord Dudley Stuart, that zealous friend of Polish refugees, Mr. *Punch*, by the pencil of Leech and others, gave me to understand that a Pole was an alien creature, who inhabited London in the neighborhood of Soho and Leicester Square, chiefly with the object of stealing the hat or overcoat of paterfamilias upon the front door of an English house being opened to his petition, and whose loftier vocation was that of making love upon the smallest opportunity to any eligible young lady, with a view to an elopement, and to enjoying after marriage any patrimony which might fall into the lap of the bride. Mr. *Punch*, it may be observed, is never very kind to people who are dissatisfied with the government of their country. But let that pass. There was another circumstance in the life of the Pole of my childish imagination which has long since been dispelled. I thought him an inhabitant of craggy hills and lovely dales, living always in sight of high mountains and deep forests, a country like that in which dwell the insurgents of the Herzegovina, like those countries with which, from the almost invariable success of insurrection in mountainous regions, it is perhaps natural for untaught intelligence to surround the ideal insurgent. The Pole is in fact the laborious cultivator of a sandy plain, which would be a desert if it were in a rainless country two thousand miles south of Poland; he is pinched and poor — as a tiller of sand is likely to be — and, to say the truth, he is very ignorant and terribly bigoted — a neglected child in education and a priest-led fanatic in religion.

Standing not long ago beside the open door of the Roman Catholic cathedral of Warsaw, I noticed that all who were neither Jews nor Russian soldiers uncovered as they passed, while not a few prostrated themselves upon the damp and dirty pavement, making humblest obeisance to the distant altar. A droschky-driver, whose restive horses and nervous "fare" demanded all his attention, would not pass but with bare head; the country carter doffed his cap; the porter dropped his load; even the school-boy paused to make his mark of homage; some kissed the sacred threshold of the door; all who had leisure seemed to enter. Quite a common sight in the Roman Catholic churches of Poland is a prostration like that of the Moslems, with the knees and forehead resting on the pavement. The Papal religion and national sympathies have always been close companions in Poland, and it is probably true that many a fanatic has also been what is called a rebel. Looking to the intensity and superstitious character of the devotion in these Polish churches, one is almost surprised that there are not miracles à la mode in Warsaw. Perhaps the Tsar and Prince Gortschakoff do not approve of Roman Catholic miracles, though they would hardly put the seal of their authority to the French couplet—

"De par du Roy, défense à Dieu,
De faire miracle dans ce lieu."

Warsaw is one of the cities which "have been." It wants "cleaning up," as I heard an English lady say in the Nowy Swiat. It is nearly as foul as some parts of Berlin in regard to open drains coursing beside the pavements of the streets, and we noticed, not as a sign of progress, that men were watering a principal thoroughfare with the familiar pot and "rose" of our English gardens. But the people who invented the polka and the mazurka are, perhaps, lifted above sanitary considerations and a policy of sewage. The streets of Warsaw will certainly match those of any city of the world for pretty names. Some British novelist will be indebted to me for suggesting as the name of his next heroine that of a chief street—"Dluga;" or, "Freta," that of another main street. But the great, new, unpeopled way is called after a lady who has consented to become English—"Alexandrovna." Except in the houses of the very poor, there is great liberality of space in and about Warsaw. Of the hotels in Europe older than the second half of the nineteenth century, the Hôtel d'Europe of Warsaw must be one of the largest. It is quadrangular in plan, and upon each of the floors there is an utterly unfurnished corridor at least ten feet wide.

The gardens in and about the city are pretty well kept; I know of no town which has in its midst a more pleasant and ornamental garden than that which adjoins the Saski Place in Warsaw; and the park surrounding the Lazienski Palace is more wooded and undulating than Hyde Park or the Bois de Boulogne. This suburban palace, in a most charming site between a lake and woods, was built in 1754 for King Poniatowski. In style, it is an Italian villa, and the decorations include mosaics from Rome and Florence. In the grounds, which are studded with summer-houses and pavilions, perhaps the most notable object is an equestrian statue of John Sobieski by a native artist.

If an Englishman discusses the past and present condition of Poland with a Russian, the latter is sure to introduce the state of Ireland by way of comparison, and will undoubtedly believe and maintain that the manifestation of political opinion is no more free in Ireland than in Poland. Apropos of this well-worn comparison, the sight of the statue of John Sobieski reminded us of what we had seen a few weeks before in Dublin. Some days after the termination of the inharmonious proceedings in connection with the O'Connell Centenary, we noticed, in riding through the streets of Dublin, an uncared-for, neglected remnant of the Home Rule procession in the shape of a green handkerchief which still encircled the neck of the statue of Mr. Smith O'Brien. Fancy what would happen to the daring enthusiast who should venture to tie the colors of revolutionary Poland around the collar of John Sobieski, or to the officer who, seeing this manifestation accomplished, should fail for one unnecessary moment to remove the irritating symbol! What a rattle of swords, what a jingling of spurs, there would be among the long-coated Russian officers, who are omnipresent in Warsaw, smoking always, and in nearly every street! What a flutter of paper there would be at the head-quarters of Russian government, in the city palace of Poniatowski, that dull quadrangle of stone which we looked at from the Praga side of the Vistula, where the Russian viceroy lives! The hapless man would soon meet the forms of Russian justice, administered in a language incomprehensible to him, and punishment proportioned to Russian estimate of his offense. I can see him, as I have seen others, marched off, chained in company with base criminals, to Siberia, his wife and children being permitted, if they please, to accompany him at the expense of the Government to that inhospitable region, the rigors of which can not be understood by those who have only seen the northern plains of Central Asia during the transient brightness of the brief summer.

At Warsaw, in a back street, stands the hotel in which the First Napoleon is said to have rested in his flight from Moscow; of that great tragedy we were reminded again, when, after crossing the sandy plain from Warsaw, the name of Grodno was shouted by Russian railway men. It was dark and late when we arrived at Wilna, where Napoleon deserted the remnant of his army, and galloped off toward France— and Elba. Between the railway station and the principal street of Wilna the wall of the town intervenes, and high over the gate-way, which forms the main entrance, is a small chapel dedicated to the mother of Jesus Christ, which is an object of worship quite, in its way, as superstitious as was ever paid to the gods of ancient Greece or Egypt; with the difference that this guardian of the town is in herself, and in the ornaments with which she is surrounded, an exhibition of art in forms at once mean and base. This tawdry shrine faces the street, which descends rapidly from the gate-way; and through all the hours of the day, and through many of the night, the sloping pavements are crowded with worshipers, gazing, some with the touching, tender, wistfulness of anxious maternity, some with the doubting, half-despairing hope for spiritual aid to be rid of deadly clinging vice; some with the look of prosperity upon them, whose desire is evidently to make the best of both worlds, and who especially wish to have the savor of piety in this world; others with the misery of neglected old age, blinking and muttering their formulas, their hopes and wants, with their ideas of the Infinite subdued and compressed within the lines of this vulgar image.

Our Polish driver, like every one else of the same nationality, held his hat in his hand as he approached, passed through, and descended from this chapeled archway. Within the town there was a curious and by us quite unexpected illumination. At regular intervals of two or three yards, there were lighted lanterns placed in the gutter on both sides of the streets. We drove a long distance through this curious manifestation, which was further exhibited by lighted candles placed in a few of the windows, without knowing the event which it was intended to honor. At the hotel, a German-speaking waiter replied, "*Tronfolger's Namstag.*" It was the birthday of Alexandrowitch, heir to the throne of all the Russias.

CHAPTER II.

Russian Railway Carriages. — Russian Ventilation. — Dunaburg. — White Sand. — Droschky Tickets. — St. Petersburg. — Exaggerated Praise. — Newski Prospekt. — The Hermitage. — Winter Palace. — St. Isaac's Church. — The Old Cathedral. — Tombs of the Romanoffs. — Down the Neva. — Cronstadt. — Droschky-driving. — The Gostinnoi Dvor. — The Kazan Church. — The Russian Language. — The Road to Moscow.

A RUSSIAN railway carriage resembles a gypsy wagon, in having a stove-pipe issuing from the roof, and a succession of these chimneys attracts the notice of any one who is for the first time traveling in the dominions of the Tsar. Fortunately, the stoves were not lighted on the mild September evening in which we set out for St. Petersburg—I say fortunately, because the Russian notion of a fire is to enjoy its warmth without ventilation. Russian climate is the coldest, Russian rooms and railway carriages the hottest, in Europe. Our train staid a few minutes at Dunaburg—time enough to eat one of the excellent veal-cutlets which are always hot and ready for travelers. But at day-break, when we took coffee at Luga, in the raw and foggy morning, the guard needed the warm gloves in which he took the tickets. One notices, as a sign of the severity of the climate, how kindly people take to gloves whose equals in England would be unable to do their work with their hands so covered. White sand, gray sand, the face of the country is covered with sand in the North of Russia; flat sand, hidden for the most part with scanty crops, and with wide forest patches of fir, the sombre hues of which are occasionally varied with the more tender green and the silvery bark of birch-trees.

There is nothing interesting or picturesque in the approach to the Russian capital. One looks out to see the golden domes and spires, and is not disappointed. There from afar shines the gilded cupola of St. Isaac's Church, and there, like golden needles, glitter the spires of the Admiralty, and of the old cathedral in which all the greatest of the House of Romanoff lay buried. Soon we are at the station, where the uninformed or incautious traveler, who rushes at the nearest droschky-driver to secure his carriage, will be disappointed. They manage these things otherwise in Russia. One must look out for the official on the steps of the station, whose hands are filled with numbered plates, and the only cab the traveler can engage is that of which the number is received from this person.

St. Petersburg has been often described, but generally in language of exaggerated admiration. It certainly possesses that feature, without which there can be no grandeur in town or city—that feature of space which we are slowly and successfully, though at an enormous cost, giving to London. I should say that the clear and flowing waters of the Neva, sweeping in ample width through the city, form the chief advantage and ornament of St. Petersburg. But for that overpraised pile of stucco, the Winter Palace, I have no admiration; and as for the treasures of the Hermitage Museum, they can not bear comparison in richness or interest with those of more Southern cities. The streets are wide, the pavement in the roads is execrable, the shops are gay only in the Newski Prospekt, and there is no more antiquity than in Boston or New York. St. Petersburg is not a handsome city, after the manner of Vienna and Paris, for those cities have at every turn the results of high civilization and a genial climate, which are lacking in the Russian capital.

Before entering the Winter Palace, one must visit a den somewhere about the foundations—a place reeking with tobacco-smoke—in which Russian officers sit to deliver the necessary permission; and the glories of this florid wilderness of stucco are supposed to culminate in the semi-barbaric resplendence of the golden boudoir of the Empress—a small apartment, of which the ceiling, the walls, and even the doors are gilded. No wonder the Emperor Nicholas took refuge and comfort in his plain apartments, the furniture of which remains as it stood in his life-time. So entirely is the *status quo* preserved that his majesty's cloak and hat, his sword and gloves, are in the places they occupied in his life-time.

There is one exception to the buildings of St. Petersburg which, if we overlook some of its internal decorations, appears worthy of all praise. The Church of St. Isaac is, in my opinion, the noblest building of modern times, and one of which not half enough has been said in Europe by way of eulogy. Perhaps it is not difficult to account for the misplaced adulation of Russian palaces. The "special correspondents," who are sent to St. Petersburg on great occasions, have their eyes fixed upon the ceremonies of the court, and there can be no doubt that the Russian court is seen to great advantage by the soft glare of thousands of wax-candles. It is unquestionably true that the Winter Palace "lights up well," better even than the White Hall of the old Schloss of Berlin, and with far finer effect than the comparatively small apartments of English royalty. It must be owing to the effect of wax-lights on the brain that, in accounts of St. Petersburg, the stuccoed gewgaws of the Winter Palace, and the veneered lapis lazuli and malachite of the Hermitage, have obscured the grand and solid magnificence of St. Isaac's—a building most worthy of the golden crown which, with vast circumference, domes the centre of this splendid edifice, which has been completed during the present reign. The style is Byzantine, that mixture of Greek and Romanesque architecture which is perhaps the best suited to the Northern climate; and though smaller than

St. Paul's in London, or St. Peter's in Rome, St. Isaac's is more massive in construction.

St. Peter's has some monoliths, pillaged from temples of the ancient city, but none that can compare with the polished columns of Finland granite which support the four porticoes of St. Isaac's; and there is nothing in the elevation of either of those world-famous churches more admirable than the bronze statuary with which the tympanum of each one of the pediments of these porticoes is adorned, or than the compositions which, placed upon the wings of these pediments, vary with excellent effect the outlines of the church. In solidity, the masonry is not surpassed by any ancient work, and the splendid interior is only disappointing because its permanent decorations are somewhat too substantial, and its religious ornaments out of harmony with the grandeur of a building in which the spectacle of crowds smacking their lips upon the trumpery portraits of persons, some of them obscure, and sanctified after a narrow-minded life, spent for the most part in dirt and asceticism, is especially ridiculous, if not irritating.

The church in which the predecessors of the Tsar are buried is comparatively insignificant, and the tombs of the emperors are simple parallelograms, built with plain slabs of white marble, with not the least attempt at artistic style or ornament. The young soldier who acted as our guide in this church pointed to the graves of Peter the Great, of Nicholas I., and of the eldest son of the present Tsar, as those most interesting. The Romanoffs rest beneath trophies of battle in the shape of flags, including those of most nations, the Union-jack among the number — a flag, perhaps, taken from the *Tiger* when that unfortunate vessel, having grounded in a fog off Odessa, was, during the Crimean war, surrendered by Captain Giffard to the Russian General Osten-Sacken.

From all that we saw in steaming down the Neva, and at Cronstadt, I should suppose Sir Charles Napier could see the highest pinnacles of St. Petersburg while he was forced to respect the range of those ugly fortresses. But that was in the unarmored, muzzle-loading days. What would happen now in a real fight between floating fortresses of iron and stationary fortresses of stone it is not for me to say; but at least this much is certain, that the conditions of naval warfare are entirely altered since the time when Sir Charles made his famous speech, ending with "Sharpen your cutlasses, lads, and the day is your own!" It seems that in our time the "Shiver my timbers!" of Marryat's age would be as little out of place as the "Sharpen your cutlasses" of 1854. "Ram often, and ram home!" is more likely to be the watchword of the future.

From the front of the Admiralty House in St. Petersburg one can look down the whole length of the Newski Prospekt, a mile and a half or so, to the Moscow Railway Station. Among the many "cures" which English physicians now prescribe, including mud-baths and grape cures, and the diligent drinking, as in Russia and Germany, of mares' milk fermented, I wonder no one has suggested driving up and down the Newski Prospekt, or, better still, the back streets of the Russian capital, in a droschky as a "cure" for a sluggish liver. Such a shaking can be obtained nowhere else. The ride has other advantages for gentlemen whose hearts and hands are free. Convenience and obvious custom may be pleaded for encircling a lady's waist with an arm when the jangling, rattling vehicle is occupied by one of each sex; this mode is indulged in not only from occasional necessity as the only means of keeping a light body on the seat of the droschky, but it is further almost obligatory, on account of the smallness of the seat, which, though often occupied by two, is probably constructed only for one person.

The journey down the Newski Prospekt may be broken at the Gostinnoi Dvor, or great bazaar, an institution in Russian towns, a reminiscence probably of Tartardom, that bygone state of Muscovite existence which, it has been said, may easily be rediscovered by scratching a Russian.

The Gostinnoi Dvor of St. Petersburg is a well-built quadrangular arcade of shops, of which, perhaps, the most interesting to a stranger are those of the furriers; for, as a rule, there are but few native products or manufactures in Russian shops, or it would be more correct to say, few possessing any uncommon interest or original character. There is plenty of bad hardware, that of Birmingham being excluded by high tariffs; but where there is seen a rich display of taste in any of the St. Petersburg shops, the work is sure to be French. Russian garments of fur are little suited for English wear, because of a radical differences in the usages of the two countries. In England fur is worn partly for ornament, and consequently the hair is turned outward; in Russia it is always reversed, and the fur concealed beneath the outward cloth of the garment. And it is noticeable that the fur mostly used in England—seal-skin—is not met with in the St. Petersburg bazaar. If any one wishes to put as much money as possible into a fur-coat—a "shuba," as this indispensable part of the wardrobe of a gentleman is called in the Russian language—let him order in the Gostinnoi Dvor one of the fur of the "blue" fox; it will be worth much more than its weight in silver rubles.

Close by is the Kazan church, another pile of stucco, concerning the silver altar rails of which the guide-books make a terrible, unwarranted fuss. As these famous rails are short, hollow, and plain as a pikestaff, their glorification is somewhat absurd. That which is much more curious in this church is the collection of keys of surrendered towns and the gilded and jeweled screen—the Ikonostas—standing between the rails and the sanctuary of the church, that ecclesiastical threshold which no woman may cross.

But we had better leave the eccentricities of the Russo-Greek Church for the present, and get on from St. Petersburg to Moscow—a journey which, owing to the railway arrangements, English travelers usually make by night. Every one who has wandered much in the South of Europe will have met with Russians unable to speak the language of their country; and from the number of these it might be inferred that in Russia the use of the vernacular was exclusively confined to the lower classes. It remains true, however, that in Russia there is no language so useful as Russian, though from Cronstadt to Sebastopol the traveler who can speak German is never in great difficulty. By many of the higher classes, and at a few of the most fashionable shops, French is spoken, but German is unquestionably more useful in traveling. When morning dawns upon the mail-train, as it approaches the more ancient capital of Russia, there is very much the same landscape in the neighborhood of Moscow as that which meets the eye in coming to St. Petersburg from the west: the same sand from which laborious peasants scratch a scanty crop; the same forests of fir and birch in which princes and nobles delight to hunt the grizzly bear. All is flat and uninteresting. One shivers in the cold of May or September, and begins to comprehend what a reservoir of warmth is the tossing sea, how bitterly cold in winter are those vast, sandy, waterless plains, which, with the aid of rain, are coaxed to cultivation in the North, but in the extreme South of the Empire are seen and known as barren steppes, yielding nothing but a sense of bigness to the Russian Empire.

CHAPTER III.

Moscow.—The Native Capital of Russia.—The Kitai-Gorod.—Lubianka Street.—The Kremlin.—The Holy Gate.—The Redeemer of Smolensk.—Bell-tower of Ivan.—Church Bells.—Church of the Assumption.—Dean Stanley's Description.—The Coronation Platform.—The Virgin of Vladimir.—Corner Tombs.—The Young Demetrius.—John the Terrible.—The Tsar Kolokol.—The Foundling Hospital.—Nurses and Babies.—"Nés avant Terme."—Moral and Social Results.—Cathedral of St. Basil.—John the Idiot.—The Lobnoé Mèsto.—Iverskaya Chasòvnia.—How the Metropolitan is paid.—Virgin from Mount Athos.—Tsar and Patriarch.—Motto from Troitsa.

Moscow is unlike any other city, not only in its walls, its towers, its cupolas, its churches, but in its streets and houses, its hospitals and its populace. He has not seen Russia who has never been to Moscow. Of countries more advanced in civilization—of constitutional Spain and Greece—he too has seen little who knows but the capital. Modern Athens is a reproduction of Munich; and to see the chief Spanish town one must go to Seville, not to Frenchified Madrid. The human heart of Moscow lies within the walls of the Kitai-Gorod—the Chinese Town, as it is called—"Kitai" being Chinese for "centre," just as the Orthodox and Imperial heart is found in the Kremlin. The encircling walls of the latter exclude the town, just as the walls of the Kitai-Gorod shut out the suburbs, where wealthy Moscow lives, sometimes in pretty villas. After the fire in 1812, which did not efface these girdles, Moscow dragged herself up again without regard to any great improvement of plan; and the streets are so irregular that the easiest thing in the world is to lose one's self in the narrow limits of the Kitai-Gorod, in which nearly all the shop-keeping and the whole of the mercantile business of Moscow are carried on. From the Kremlin, or Acropolis of Moscow, which stands on a bank rising steeply about a hundred feet above the river from which the city takes its name, the ground slopes gently through the Kitai-Gorod to the Lubianka Street, from his house in which Count Rostopchin announced to the terrified people that the Russian garrison would make way for the French army. In passing to the Kremlin from this street, one enters the "Chinese Town" through a gate-way in the massive wall of brick, and, if he is a Russian, uncovers before the little church on the left hand, which is one of those curious edifices that are seen nowhere beyond the pale of the Greek Church—a tiny building, the roof of which, with eaves that scarcely escape the hats of those who are passing by, is tortured into the most unexpected shapes and angles; here a little cupola, and there a crocket—a confusion of the architecture of a pagoda and of a Lombard church, with tiles colored, red, blue, green, and yellow, in tints sobered and softened by age into a curious beauty. The ornamental little windows are not needed, for the diminutive church is ventilated only by the frequent opening of the door; and as for light, there is that of the lamps and candles, which are constantly burning.

In point of superstition, I see no superiority in the lower classes of Russia over those of Spain. With the latter, their religion is, for the most part, symbolized by wooden dolls, blackened with age, such as "Our Ladies" of Atocha and Montserrat. With the Russians, solid images are not permitted; and the symbols of their faith are generally worthless pictures, made to resemble images as much as possible by having robes, wrought in thin gold or silver, placed over the painting upon that part of the person where such garments would be worn in life. The celebrated gate in the wall of the Kremlin, to which one ascends by the slope leading from the Kitai-Gorod, is famous because a picture of this sort—"The Redeemer of Smolensk," as it is called—is suspended over the high archway of brick. With an opera-glass, one can discern a representation of the typical face of Christ, decked in golden garb and nimbus. It is barely permitted, even in these days, that any one may pass under this archway except uncovered. Jews and Mohammedans generally find some less sacred portal, and the Tsar himself never enters the Kremlin by this "Redeemer Gate" with his hat upon his head. The tower above the gate-way—a Gothic structure upon Italian fortifications—is suggestive of much that one sees in Russia. The traveler who expects to find grand buildings upon the Kremlin will be grievously disappointed. They are interesting because they are national, because they are unique and curious; but that is all. Highest rises the octagonal bell-tower of Ivan the Great. The bells, as is usual throughout Russia, are, as the French would say, *montés au jour;* so that bell, and tongue, and beam, and machinery are seen from the ground, with no intervening wall or window.

The importance attached to bells in the Greek Church has been curiously illustrated in the Blue-book, containing "Correspondence respecting the Affairs of Turkey, and the Insurrection in Bosnia and the Herzegovina." Consul Freeman reports that orders have been received at Bosnai Serai to construct a second minaret to the chief mosque. It is to be much higher than the existing one, that it may command the Orthodox church and steeple. "The execution of this work at the present time," says the consul, "when, notwithstanding the proclamation, the Christians are refused the permission, so ardently desired, to have bells in their churches, can not be regarded otherwise than as a demonstration of Mussulman fanaticism and superiority." Sir Henry Elliot communicated with the Turkish Minister for Foreign Affairs, and reported to Lord Derby that, "before granting the permission to put up bells in the churches—which is now about to be granted, and which may create some soreness on the part of a portion of the Mussulmans—the Government considered it prudent to authorize the erection of a minaret, which should be higher than the steeple."

In Russia, as in Rome, there is a saint to be invoked upon every thought or purpose in life; and happy is he or she who remembers the right one when a handkerchief is mislaid or a sweetheart lost. Every one knows the church in Rome close to the basilica of Santa Maria Maggiore, to which pet lambs and dogs, and the horses of the Pope and of the cardinals, are taken for the blessing of their patron, St. Antonio Abbate. The chapel in the basement of the tower of Ivan is, or ought to be, frequented by ladies about to marry; for it is dedicated to that particular St. Nicholas who is their appointed guardian in a country of many saints, and where the rude forms of the Anglo-Saxon action for breach of promise are, happily, unknown.

But pass within the commonplace iron railing which shuts off the tower from the Church of the Assumption, enter, and there is no disappointment. One is dazzled and charmed with the spectacle. Let us hear Dean Stanley (who is disposed to look more kindly on the antics of the Greek Church than the present writer) upon the first view of this truly remarkable interior. "It is in dimensions," he says, "what in the West would be called a chapel rather than a cathedral. But it is so fraught with recollections, so teeming with worshipers, so bursting with tombs and pictures, from the pavement to the cupola [the dean would not have been less accurate had he used the plural number, as there are five cupolas, though that in the centre may be called *the* cupola], that its smallness of space is forgotten in the fullness of its contents. On the platform of its nave, from Ivan the Terrible downward to this day, the Tsars have been crowned. Along its altar-screen are deposited the most sacred pictures of Russia: that painted by the Metropolitan Peter; this sent by the Greek Emperor Manuel; that brought by Vladimir from Kherson."

The platform to which Dean Stanley thus refers is a square daïs of wood, raised by one step from the floor of the church, in the centre of which it is placed. The church has no "long-drawn aisles," nor any of the solemn beauty which is so admirable in the dean's own Abbey of Westminster. The interior is a blaze of color from floor to ceiling. The walls are gilded in all but the frescoed representations of "The Seven Councils" and "The Last Judgment;" and the five domes are upheld by four tall circular pillars of almost unvarying diameter, which are richly gilded from pavement to arch, except where they are adorned with quaint and highly colored portraits of martyrs.

"Time was," wrote Cardinal Wiseman, with a well-pointed sneer, "when it needed not a coronation to fill the aisles of Westminster." Since that was written, we have seen those aisles thronged with eager listeners to the eloquence of a Wilberforce or a Stanley. A coronation in the Uspènski Sabòr of Moscow is probably a grander sight, because of the awful power with which the new wearer of the Russian crown is—*not* invested, but invests himself. Possibly Dean Stanley was present at the coronation of Alexander II. "The coronation," he writes, "even at the present time, is not a mere ceremony, but an historical event, and solemn consecration. It is preceded by fasting and seclusion, and takes place in the most sacred church in Russia; the Emperor, not as in the corresponding forms of European investiture, a passive recipient, but himself the principal figure in the whole scene; himself reciting aloud the confession of the Orthodox faith; himself, alone on his knees, amidst the assembled multitude, offering up the prayer of intercession for the Empire; himself placing his own crown on his own head; himself entering through the sacred door of the innermost sanctuary, and taking from the altar the elements of bread and wine." The Tsar is at once priest and king, pretending to be that which the Persian poet Sa'di describes as the kingly office—"the Shadow of God."

The picture of "The Holy Virgin of Vladimir" is saluted by the devout as the work of St. Luke, and by the careless as bearing nearly fifty thousand pounds' worth of jewels, including an emerald of enormous size. The faithful, when divine service is over, walk along the altar-screen, on which this and other sacred pictures are placed, kissing them one after the other with marks of deepest devotion. These and other treasures were, of course, removed before the evacuation of Moscow, in 1812. It is quite impossible, without the aid of a series of colored plates, to convey to the mind of any one who has not seen it an accurate notion of the interior of this church. The principal architectural feature is the appropriation of about one-third of the area to the sanctuary, the altar-screen reducing the interior space from a parallelogram to a square, in which the four frescoed columns stand equidistant from the centre. No part of the walls is unadorned with paint or gilding; and with the head well thrown back, one can see a gigantic face of Christ painted upon the inner surface of the central dome.

There are many points, and those of great and significant importance, in which, to a Protestant mind, the Russian churches might be improved by following the example of any mosque. There can be nothing more opposed to the method of Islam than the constant exhibition of pictures, and the monstrous devotion and salutation of which these—for the most part daubs—are the object. Dean Stanley, however, notices one matter in which this great church of Moscow has followed Oriental custom—the assignment of its four corners as the places of most honored sepulture.

The adjoining church, the Cathedral of Michael the Archangel, is more celebrated for its tombs. There lie the remains of John the Terrible, and of his murdered son Demetrius. As we entered this church, we noticed that all persons appeared to direct their steps, in the first place, to a low tomb not far from the centre, and that there they bent with utmost reverence to lay their lips upon a small opening in a golden framework, a brown, parchment-like patch, which is actually the forehead of the young Demetrius. This prince achieved his present position of saintship and adoration, involving neglect of the shrine of his "Terrible" parent, in consequence of his having been murdered by order of Boris Godunof, the Tsar of that turbulent period which preceded the settlement of the Empire by the election of young Romanoff, son of the Metropolitan of Rostof, in 1613. There happened also a "miracle" which led to the discovery of his sainted remains. Above the shrine his portrait hangs in a massive setting of gold.

Externally the architecture of the buildings of the Kremlin is neither grand nor pleasing. It is possible that the uncommon aspect of the gilded domes, of which there are five on each of the churches above referred to, and several on other buildings, has led to the general impression, which certainly prevails, that these plain edifices are externally remarkable. The big bell, "Tsar Kolokol," claims attention as a fractured apartment (it is big enough for habitation) in bell-metal; and if the day is fine, the view from the front of the Palace of the Kremlin will command admiration. The massive wall is at this point sunk beneath the brow on which the Kremlin stands; and across the river, in the foreground of a very extended prospect, there stands a huge white building, the Foundling Hospital, to which we descended, fortunately upon the day when strangers are admitted to this vast nursery for Russian infants.

To those who know any thing of the statistics of infant mortality, there is something sad and ominous in entering a huge barrack such as this, devoted to the care of willfully deserted infancy. The chief officer, a Russian exquisite, who conducted us over the building, spoke, and appeared to feel, like a showman. As for the inmates, he was quite unpitying. He looked for our deepest sympathy as he informed us that every day it was his duty to walk through the well-kept wards. There is nothing to be seen like the dramatic cradle in which, at dead of night, the tearful, frightened mother deposits her new-born babe, and reels, swooning with terror and agitation, into the dark background, after she has sounded, with feverish grasp, the knell of her maternal joys and anxieties. In Moscow we find the State encouraging the increase of population, and, with the least formality and utmost openness, relieving all who choose to bring their infants, from the burden, the cost, and responsibilities of parentage.

Two women, friends, as they said, of the mother of the babe which one of them carried, entered the building shortly after we arrived. The child was not six hours old. According to the usual rule, there were but two questions asked—one to learn whether the child had been baptized, and if so, by what name. It was not officially a member of the Orthodox Church, and therefore was only described in the books by the number which it would from that time bear in the Foundling Hospital. This was the twenty-ninth child that had been received that day, and ten more would probably be registered before midnight. The baby was washed in a room adjoining the place of reception, dressed in the swaddling-clothes of the establishment, which, unlike the long clothes of English infancy, are swathed almost tightly about the limbs, and carried up-stairs to a large, long ward, where it was placed, feet to feet, with another baby, in a curtained cradle, about the centre of the ward, its number being hung round its neck, and also fixed on the cradle above its head. Downstairs we had seen a number of robust peasant-women seeking employment as nurses in these wards. The pay and rations are so good, and there are such substantial advantages in obtaining babies as boarders when they and their wet-nurses leave the hospital, that these places are eagerly sought; and it is said that a mother not unfrequently leaves her infant, or sends it to the hospital, and then applies for the position of nurse, in order that both may be maintained by the State.

The inspecting officer informed us that these women receive seven rubles a month and a gratuity, as a reward for good behavior while they are serving in the hospital; and that when they leave it is usual for them to take away a baby, to be boarded out in their family, for the care of which they are paid two rubles per month. If the children are healthy, they are usually sent out, after vaccination, when they are ten days old. Each nurse has the care of two infants lying in the same cradle. In the wards the nurses wear a becoming uniform, with caps of scarlet. The arrangements, temperature, and cleanliness of the wards are admirable. It struck me that a little noise would have sounded more healthful and natural than the painful silence of these regiments of, for the most part, dumb cradles. Especially was this sad feature noticeable in the sick ward, where there were many cases of ophthalmia. But the most curious of all was the ward devoted, as the foppish officer said, to "*les enfants nés avant terme;*" those which had come prematurely into the world, and were now in wadded and flanneled cradles of copper—hot-water cradles, in fact, the heat of which was maintained and regulated with the most careful precision.

There may be, even in England, differences of opinion as

to the morality and advantage of an institution such as this, which deals in the manner I have described with nearly fifteen thousand infants every year. To me it appears to be an approach, dangerous to the morality of a people, to that form of Communism which is especially to be dreaded. It rewards, at the cost of all, the deliberate desertion of the most sacred duties and obligations of parentage. It tends to degrade women by relieving them and the men with whom they associate from the responsibilities of childbirth: it places upon the careful, affectionate, and dutiful parents, in their capacity as tax-payers, the burden of maintaining the offspring of those who have none of these virtues. On the other hand, we can not doubt that it prevents infanticide in many cases, and promotes the peopling of the vast wastes of Russia. But it can hardly be denied that, while thus encouraging population, it is indirectly responsible for the deaths of thousands of infants, because it is on record that the mortality of this hospital is terribly high, and that scarcely more than twenty-five per cent. of the infants committed to its care lived to learn, as men and women, the circumstances of their childhood.

We will return to the heights of the Kremlin, from which we made this digression, and descend through the holy gate to that part of the space before the Kitai-Gorod in which stands the Cathedral of St. Basil the Blessed, a church far more remarkable in its architecture than any other in Moscow. It is said that when the First Napoleon saw this miniature cathedral, with its grotesque irregularities of outline, he ordered the commander of his artillery to "destroy that mosque." But indeed the Cathedral of St. Basil has little resemblance to a mosque. It is perhaps the best example of that queer admixture of Indo-Persian, Tartar-Chinese, and Græco-Byzantine architecture, which may fairly be called the Russian style. The Cathedral of St. Basil, of which only the crypt is used for divine service, is all towers and domes. These cupolas, or domes, in their colors of red and green, as well as in shape, resemble huge inverted onions, the upturned "root" finished with a gilded cross. Of the eleven domes, no two are alike in superficial ornamentation; one or two are painted in bands, which will certainly suggest the vegetable comparison above mentioned. One is indented like the surface of a pine-apple, others are decorated with patterns that are decidedly arabesque, and the highest of all is elongated with a multiplicity of ornament into something like a spire; yet perhaps the cupolas are not the most curious part of the church, of which every portion is colored. One is hardly surprised to find the maze of small chapels above the crypt unused; they are too intricate.

The whole building does not cover more ground than the Albert Memorial in Hyde Park. Dull red and green seem to be the prevailing colors; but the church is so bewildering that one can hardly feel certain about any part of it. It is just such a church as one might suppose had been built by or for a lunatic; then it appears not inappropriate. The riddle of its architecture seems to be solved when one learns that St. Basil, though regarded by many as a prophet and worker of miracles, was probably one whom in these degenerate days we should call a harmless simpleton; and the church, fortunately uninjured by the French, was finished in the latter part of the sixteenth century by a Tsar, who, to the bones of Basil, added those of John the Idiot. In religion, the Russian people have a tenderness for lunacy and idiocy which I suspect has now and then taken ultimately the form of canonization. John the Idiot is certainly a saint—a religious mendicant who in his life-time, we are told, was known as "Water-carrier," or "Big-cap," because he was ready to bear others' burdens of water, and from the iron cap he wore. St. John the Idiot's cap was lost during the Napoleonic invasion; but the weights and chains which he and St. Basil are supposed to have used for the mortification of their life are preserved in the chapels. At all events, their reputation is fitly enshrined in the most bizarre and fantastic church in Europe.

Of about the same date is the circular rostrum, or pulpit of stone, about four yards in diameter, with a surrounding seat inside, which stands in the large open place near the Church of St. Basil. This was the platform from which the Tsars made solemn promises, and the patriarchs administered blessings to the people. It is called Lobnoé Mèsto; and at other towns in Russia there are similar tribunes. Passing this uninteresting monument in a line from the Cathedral of St. Basil, and entering the Kitai-Gorod, one is in front of the principal entrance—the Voskreneski gate—of the "Chinese Town." Just outside that gate there is to be seen one of the most remarkable sights in Moscow—and, indeed, in all Russia. In no other European country is there such an exhibition of what is called religious devotion. Before the stout wall of brickwork, which separates the outcoming from the ingoing way, is the Iberian Chapel (Iverskaya Chasòvnia), architecturally nothing but a large-sized hut of stone, or a platform raised by two steps above the road-way. From morning till night this platform is thronged, and the chapel overflows with a crowd, chiefly composed of men, pressing, all bare-headed, and all with money in their hands, toward the narrow door-way of the little sanctuary.

We were some time getting into the chapel, which will hold about ten people abreast, and is lighted by the flickering glare of a score of candles. There is a step at the farther end, and the wall opposite the door is resplendent with shining metal, except where the object of this extravagant devotion looks grimy through its frame-work of gold. On the left side of "The Iberian Mother of God"—which is the name given to this commonplace daub, supposed to possess miraculous powers — stands a long-haired priest, now and then relieved by another long-haired, deep-voiced priest, who, hour by hour, in the name of the jeweled and tinseled picture, and with blessing, consecrates the prayers and offerings of the faithful.

Only the face of the Madonna is visible, and in the candlelight it is not easy to distinguish the features beneath the dust of years. But not a minute passes in which the rattle of money, falling to the uses of the Russian Church, is not heard, or in which lips are not pressed upon the frame-work, or upon the rudely wrought robes of beaten gold, which conceal the picture to the neck. Surely no lower depth of superstitious degradation was ever reached in connection with Christian worship! One can not be surprised that to a Turk a Russian seems to be an idolatrous worshiper of pictures. The refining explanation which the most enlightened fathers of the Greek Church could offer concerning this disgusting exhibition is precisely of the sort, and differs only in degree, from that which might be offered on behalf of the idol-worshipers of more Eastern and Southern lands. The picture has no historic reputation. It was brought from Mount Athos, that pleasant wooded hill, peopled with monkish drones, who so distrust their masculine instincts that not only may no woman enter their charming territory, and enjoy the lovely view seaward over the blue Levant, but no hen may be brought to their table; though it is not on record that they refuse eggs which, if hatched, would produce female birds. About twelve thousand pounds a year is collected in coppers at this chapel, and from this sum the salary of the Metropolitan of Moscow is paid. Time has been when, in the ceremonies which precede Easter, the Tsar of Russia used to lead the donkey on which the Patriarch of Moscow rode, carrying a sacred chalice and a copy of the Gospels. Nowadays that ceremony is neglected; but we are given to understand that the Tsar never enters Moscow without assisting the revenues of this distinguished ecclesiastical officer, by praying at the shrine of the "Iberian Mother of God." In reading Dean Stanley's "Lectures on the Eastern Church," I am disposed to wonder at the patience with which he tolerates degrading and grossly superstitious observances. I can not pretend to equal moderation in sight of these things. It may be that he has taken to heart, as I can not, the archiepiscopal inscription near the famous monastery of Troitsa: "Let not him who comes in here carry out the dirt that he finds within."

CHAPTER IV.

The Road to Nijni.—Rivers Oka and Volga.—Nijni.—The Bridge of Boats.
—The Heights of Nijni.—Lopachef's Hotel.—A Famous Landscape.—
Prisoners for Siberia.—Their Wives and Children.—The Great Fair.—
The Last Bargains.—Caravan Tea.—Persian Merchants.—Buildings of
the Fair.—Gloves and Furs.—Russian Tea-dealers.—Mosque at Nijni.—
Shows and Theatres.—Russia vs. Free Trade.—Russian Hardware.—Articles de Paris.—Melons and Grapes.—The Governor's Palace.—Picturesque Nijni.

THOUGH it is only the 20th of September, the air is keen and frosty, as we drive to the Moscow station of the Nijni-Novgorod Railway. We have a sleepy recollection of the comfort of some hot soup at Vladimir. When we awoke in the morning, at no great distance from Nijni, the window-glasses of the railway-carriage were covered with hoar-frost, and the ground was hard as iron. We soon beheld the Volga, flowing in a broad, yellowish stream past the height on which the official town of Nijni stands; and from the opposite side of the carriage, as we approach the buildings of the world-famous Fair, we can see the lesser stream of the river Oka in its course to the point where it gives itself to the Volga, the site of the Fair being upon the angle between the two rivers. The sun was shining warmly, and the rugged pavement in the main street of the Fair was ankle-deep in mud, which our rattling droschky threw up on all sides. The driver, like all Russian coachmen, had his coat gathered at the waist, and sat upon the ample skirts with a rein of rope in each hand, "p-r-r-r-ing" his horses along at a rate which would be punishable in London. It is, however, done at Nijni, though there upon the road are crowded carts loaded with cotton, tea, and melons, and people of every Eastern nation, many of whom come from lands where a wheel is never seen, where merchandise is of necessity carried by mules or camels.

What a thundering the scampering hoofs of our horses and the rumble of our wheels seem to make as we pass on to the planked bridge of boats by which we must cross the Volga to reach the town of Nijni-Novgorod! From this point the view of the town is very picturesque. Close to the bridge the ground rises abruptly to a height about two hundred and fifty feet, and the summit is crowned with the chief buildings of the place. Overlooking the river, the united stream of the Volga and the Oka, there is the white-walled Kremlin, inclosing not only the governor's residence, a pleasant garden, and the barracks of a considerable garrison, but also the principal church, the emerald-green cupolas of which show in pleasant contrast to the unvarying white of the walls. Along the ridge, and from the banks of the Volga up the slope, is placed the town of Nijni. We rattle along the street, past the stalls where men and women are selling huge water-melons, cut in radiating slices at something less than a farthing for a pound-weight of the fruit, which looks delicious in the rapidly increasing heat of the day; past tawdry shrines of St. Nicholas and St. Isaac, before which long-haired and heavily booted peasants are bowing their bare heads nearly to their knees; past a church built very much after the style of that of St. Basil in Moscow; mounting always and at last through a deep, grassy cutting, which has the Kremlin on one side, and on the other a group of prettily colored villas, the palest blue or green, soft red and primrose yellow, all with bright-green roofs of wood or metal, to the high table-land, where we are first in the great "place" of Nijni, and then in a wide street, in which is Lopachef's Hotel.

There is a terrible smell of stale tobacco inside Lopachef's closed door; but we have only to choose between Lopachef and Soboref, and the latter is Russian vapor bath as well as hotel. We are, without doubt, in the best hotel in Nijni, though there are no carpets on any of the floors, no sheets on the beds, and nothing but the invariable *hors d'œuvres* of a Russian dinner—arrack, uncooked sardines, caviare, and radishes, to relieve our immediate hunger. There is, of course, a picture of a saint, all but the head covered with tinseled robes, in one corner of the dining-room; a lamp burns beneath it, the light hardly discernible in the brightness of approaching noon. Soup and cutlets, with something more drinkable than the alcohol of Russia, are, however, soon before us; and in an hour or two we are strolling to the front of the high ground to enjoy the famous prospect—a view so extensive as to be limited only by the clearness of the air and of one's eyesight. From left all round to right, the foreground appears flat; the windings of the Volga and the Oka can be traced, like those of ribbon on a vast table, flowing through miles of sandy plain, varied with patches of pine forest, and smaller areas in which cultivation has reclaimed the soil. The steamboats move like elongated dots. We can trace the ground-plan of the Fair, which is more than a mile distant, and see its myriad life moving to and fro like that of ant-hills. An unceasing stream of carts and droschkies pours, during the months of the Fair, across the bridge of boats. The scene is one to be remembered in company with that from the Kremlin of Moscow.

The usual quiet of this part of Nijni was broken, as we returned to the hotel, by the tramp of armed men. They were guarding a long procession of prisoners, who were making forced marches to Siberia. The soldiers slouched along, looking hardly less miserable, dusty, and travel-stained than the wretched people whom they watched with fixed bayonets and drawn swords. The prisoners marched, some four and others six abreast, between the files of soldiers. Some were chained in couples, others tramped alone, and all were apparently of the lower classes. There were three or four hundred convicts, as nearly as I could count. Very little talk was passing among them, and the soldiers, with sword or bayonet, rudely kept off any one who approached within their reach. All traffic was suspended while the long line passed. The prisoners were followed by twenty-seven wagons, loaded with the poor baggage of their families, upon which the women and children were uneasily mounted, among whom lay a few elderly or sick men. These women were the wives who were willing to accompany their condemned husbands, and to settle in Siberia at least for the term of their husbands' sentence, which in no case is less than four years. If the wives choose to go, they must take their children, and all submit to the degradation and rigors of surveillance and imprisonment. The pavements of Nijni are the worst imaginable; and as these springless vehicles (which were not really wagons, but simply four fir poles fastened at obtuse angles on wheels) jolted over the uneven bowlders, the poor children were shaken high out of their wretched seat at nearly every yard of the journey. Soldiers with drawn swords walked beside these cart-loads of weakness and childhood. It was very touching to see the old men and the sick painfully lift themselves whenever they passed a church, and with the sadness of eternal farewell, uncover their miserable heads and cross their breasts devoutly as they were borne along in their terrible journey to Siberia. For another month or six weeks these wretched people, or such of them as survived, would be traveling to their dreaded settlement, which, however, I believe, is somewhat better than the Siberia with which our novelists and playwrights have made us familiar.

A pleasanter sight was that of the great Fair. Now is the time for the last bargains in the greatest Fair in the world—an international exposition half a dozen times as large as that which in 1851 set us all thinking the millennium had arrived when Prince Albert's ideas and Paxton's plans were realized in Hyde Park. What shall we buy? There is a sharp-eyed tea-merchant watching our movements, hoping to get rid of yet one or two more of those square seventy-pound bundles of tea piled at the door of his store. The tea is in a light chest, which has been cased before it left China in a damp bullock's hide, the stitching of which has been strained and hardened in the long caravan journey over Central Asian deserts. Thinking that we may perhaps purchase, he makes a sign of encouragement, and forthwith rams an iron bodkin, three feet long, and shaped like a cheese-scoop, but with a solid, pointed end, into the tea, twists it, and produces a fragrant sample. He is one of hundreds of tea-merchants who have hired a stall in the Fair; and, in compliment to the commodity, the roofs in this part are built pagoda-fashion, but, like all the rest, the tea-stores are sheds of timber and brick, placed together in long parallel lines, sheltered from sun and rain by a rough arcade, upon the brick pavement of which purchasers and idlers pass along.

More attractive, perhaps, than the tea-dealer is the Persian opposite, whose dark eyes gleam with desire to sell any thing in his store. He has carpets of soft colors, such as the sons of Iran best know how to blend, carpets heavy as himself, to cover large rooms; small carpets; mere handfuls, on which the faithful may kneel in orthodox Mohammedan fashion five times a day, fixing their eyes in the direction of Mecca. He has books; here is a copy of the Koran, bound in Tabriz, marble-backed, with yellow-edged leaves, like some of our older editions — a book which, for two rubles, any one, no matter whether his faith is centred at Mecca or Jerusalem, anywhere or nowhere, may put in his pocket. This bright-eyed merchant might be shown in London for the Shah, whom he much resembles; and if, in his high-standing cap of black lamb-skin, his grass-green tunic, and his scarlet-lined overcoat, he were to appear at Charing Cross surrounded by two or three of his own traveling-trunks, which are also for sale, by way of luggage, he would be sure, as a traveling "sensation," to achieve legitimate success. He presses, with a gay smile, upon our attention one of the chests, which is painted bright vermilion, cross-barred, like Malvolio's legs, with bands of black; but he has another of green and black, and a third of yellow, with blue bands of iron; and if one had the boldness requisite for traveling in such illustrious company, these trunks would certainly obviate all difficulty as to recognizing one's luggage in the customary and truly British scramble at any London terminus.

We see at a glance that any one who wishes to have a true idea of Nijni must get rid at once and forever of any notion of an English fair, by way of comparison. On the Volga they mean business, not pleasure; and the Fair is held in buildings infinitely ruder and simpler in construction, but quite as permanent as those of the Lowther Arcade. For about half the year these are closed, and the straight lines of the parallel streets of the Fair are only tenanted by sparrows, picking up the last traces of the great gathering. The site is flat, but in Fair-time the roads between the long rows of sheds are worn into rivulets of filth, or into heaps and hollows of dust. Not one man in five wears a leather shoe; the rest, those who do not go barefoot, are for the most part content with sandals made of dried grass, bound over thick woolen stockings with wisps of the same vegetable.

There is a great deal of genuine barter going on. In one sense, indeed, it may be truly said that no one at this gathering has "ready" money. Here are two Persian boys bargaining for a ring which has surely come from one of the *fabriques d'imitation* of Paris. The process is long. Twenty copecks, perhaps, divide seller and buyer, and it may be that part of this difference will disappear in talk to-day, and the remainder to-morrow or the day after. Three Tartars, dressed in ragged sheep-skins, have their slanting eyes, that unmistakable mark of race, fixed upon the gay glories of a cotton handkerchief, which I hope is Manchester, but fear is Moscow, work. And so it goes on all through the busy town, or commercial camp, which is called the Fair of Nijni-Novgorod. Not rarely does a bargain take three days in the making. What Adam Smith calls the "higgling of the market" is a tremendous business at the Russian mart. "Small profits and quick returns" is not the Nijni motto. Prices are all "fancy." It is not easy to get at the relation of supply and demand. The dealer asks twice or three times the legitimate value, and then engages in a wordy duel with the purchaser, in which by-standers are quite at liberty to "jine in," as a Yankee would say.

Out from his perpetual throne upon the bergs and amidst the fogs of the North, the Ice-king will come in a few weeks, sealing, as he passes, the land and the rivers of Russia; and consequently no small portion of the work of the Fair is directed toward providing for his reception. Thick woolen and leather gloves are largely bought by the hairiest peasantry in Europe—men whose long back-hair and beards run into and seem intermixed with the wool of the dirty sheep-skins which cover them from head to foot. All these gloves have that well-known peculiarity of shape (common also to the gloves of English infancy) which Charles Dickens so happily described as made up with a parlor for the thumb and a common tap-room for the fingers. Of course there are furs —piles upon piles of fur—but this article of dress or ornament is not cheap at Nijni, and the kinds of fur most worn in England are not to be seen. There is no seal-skin, and but little sable or ermine. Black fox and silver fox, wolf and bear skin, and commoner furs for lining, are much sold.

Desperately anxious upon these last September days of the Fair, which opens in May, are the dealers to sell their remaining stock of cloth coats lined with fur—the shuba—so much worn in Russia. The prices rise from eight pounds to one hundred pounds, according to the sort of fur.

A Russian will be warm, at any sacrifice of elegance in his person or of ventilation in his home; but he has another requirement not less imperative—he must have in his ill-ventilated house a tinseled picture of the head of Christ, or of some saint; if a saint, then it is generally the one after whom he is named. There is not a baptismal name in common use throughout Russia which is not that of a saint—which has not a saint to father it; and so it happens that when all the Alexanders or Alexises in a village celebrate, with all the arrack they can get, the return of their name-day, a sort of brotherhood often becomes established between people who have received the same name at the ecclesiastical font. A roughly built country cart has just passed carrying off a purchase, a large head of Christ, the conventional face looking out from a setting of tawdry ormolu, the whole framed in vulgar, gaudy gilt. Two men are holding the frame, to keep it from contact with the sides of the cart, which rumbles and tumbles along the uneven way; and as it goes, peasants and dealers uncover their heads and make most reverently the sign of the cross upon their bodies before this article of merchandise.

It is ten o'clock, and here are two men swinging back the iron doors of their shed to begin business for the day. They are Russian tea-dealers. With feet placed close together, with cap in hand, they bow in deep obeisance three times toward the nearest church, crossing themselves, as they bend, before they unfasten the padlocks; and then, on gaining the floor of their shops, they repeat the religious bowing, which in the Greek Church never takes the form of genuflection, the knees, in fact, being almost the only joint that is not bent.

Last summer we met with a cottier farmer in Ireland who had given two hundred pounds toward the building fund of a Roman Catholic chapel, which was being erected in the parish wherein he lived. The sum was immense for a man in his position, and people were naturally inquisitive on the subject. To one who asked why he had subscribed so largely he said, "I want to have a claim on the Almighty;" and I am sure I do these Russians no wrong in believing that these ostentatious shop prayers of theirs are in part a demonstration, and in part concerned with averting the influence of the devil of the Greek Church from their till.

The "religious difficulty" is nicely settled at Nijni. In the interest of Russian trade, the Crescent is lifted to the skies high as the Cross. Raised somewhat upon an artificial mound, near the centre of the Fair, is a mosque, probably the most Northern mosque in Europe. In the small court-yard, a stalwart moollah was making signs of direction to a Tartar dwarf—a hunchback, and in rags; a deaf-mute, whose glittering eyes fixed greedily upon us as we advanced to visit the mosque. Perhaps the moollah in charge had not done well at the Fair; he looked sad as we walked with him over the floor of his church, which was covered with clean matting, on which a few of the commonest sort of Persian carpets were laid. Probably he was sad at the thought that the glories and the work of the great Fair were nearly over.

One finds no trace whatever, on entering a mosque, of the anti-human principles which are taught there from the words of the Koran. In the air of a mosque there is no taint of vengeance, of slavery, of polygamy, of deadly animosity toward dissent. One contrasts rather the purity and simplicity of the place of worship, the grateful absence of any stupid attempt to personify the Infinite in mortal forms, with the degrading and meretricious attractions of a Greek or Roman church, with the trumpery, vulgar images of saints and virgins, images of persons, some not only without real claim to reverence, but rather deserving, as repressors of civilization, the forgetfulness, if not the contempt, of mankind; objects of conventional regard, which not one worshiper in ten thousand could explain or account for by any well-informed statement of the saint's claim. The mosque of Nijni was, like all mosques throughout the world, a temple without trace of sect. We passed from it into the adjacent church for the people of the Fair who are of the orthodox Russian faith; and there a priest in sumptuous raiment was bringing bass notes apparently from somewhere about the region of the stomach, after the most admired manner of priests of that communion, and, as he paused to take breath, kissing pictures on the screen, gluing his worship and praise with his lips to the framework of these daubs, and to the sham jewels in the cover of the copy of the Gospels which lay before him. Over the way stood an Armenian church, a nearer approximation to Rome. No limitation to pictures with flat robes of gold or silver in that place of worship! There they may go the whole animal, so far as images are concerned.

Not distant from the churches is the principal theatre of the Fair, a wooden building, in which, at the time of our visit, one might see—so the bills said—"the unapproachable Hickin Family." These were the only words in English (and perhaps Mr. Hickin would tell us these words are "American") which we observed within the Fair. There was, however, one unquestionable exception. The heap of "Three-cord Knitting" on a stall near the governor's house must surely have been of English manufacture.

If I remember rightly, Mr. Cobden made a tour in Russia, and then formed no very high opinion of the solidarity or strength of the Empire, especially for external warfare. I never heard that he visited Nijni, and I hardly think it possible that he could have been there in the Fair-time, without leaving such a record of his visit as it would not have been easy to forget. Had he been there, his patriotic soul would surely have poured over with contempt for the commercial policy of Russia, and with longing for the universal reign of free trade. We passed scores of stalls covered with hardware of all sorts—knives, padlocks, door-locks, tools, nails, household cutlery and utensils—all of miserably inferior manufacture, the blades and fastenings bearing the mark of Warsaw, but most often of Moscow, or some other Russian town. Tens of thousands of these useful articles had passed within the four preceding months, and were passing daily during our visit, from Nijni into Asia. What a trade might Mr. Bright's constituents do in this way if it were not for the prohibitory rates of the Russian tariff! and how soon would Russians, of Europe and of Asia, learn to appreciate the difference between a Sheffield or Birmingham blade and the home-made knives of coarse iron, which are forced upon them at a price for which they could obtain English manufacture, from a mistaken belief that this provision of inferior articles to the many for the benefit of the few is advantageous to the general welfare of the Russian Empire! Of the vast quantity of cotton goods in the Fair, some look like Manchester pieces, but much is certainly the inferior work of Russian hands. There is no mistaking the "Nouveautés de Paris," which are to be met with on all sides; buttons, especially ornamental buttons, gayly ribboned slippers, pictures of women beautiful in face and very much *décolletées* as to dress, figures in lewd attitudes, some representing the performance of the *cancan*—very salable in Persia—parcels of scent, toys of all kinds, and musical instruments. The large and open demand for Parisian pictures of the lascivious sort in Mohammedan countries is worth volumes of printed commentary upon the teaching of the Koran. These pictures, which a garçon of the Quartier Latin would think it bold and roué-like to display upon the walls of his garret, are, in Persia and Turkey, paraded in the family apartments, and treasured in photographic albums in recesses which answer to the drawing-room tables of Western Europe; nor is it common for any father to hesitate in illustrating conversation carried on in presence of his sons by indecent reference to these erotic productions, which are usually the work of Frenchmen, unless the taste of the khan or effendi leans to the less veiled and coarser indelicacy of German work. But this is premature; we are not yet in Persian houses. In the Nijni Fair, Parisian spoons seem to tickle most successfully Asiatic fancy, while prosaic and solid-working Germany contributes stockings and *strümpfbände,* less elegant than the *jarretières de Paris.*

Floating through the Fair are the sellers of water-melons, shouting " *arbus,*" *a-r-r-r-r bū-ū-s,*" at the top of their voices. But they are silent often when the glistening red inside of the huge fruit attracts thirsty buyers of slices at one copeck each. Others, armed with scale and weights, vend luscious grapes just arrived by steamboat from the shores of the Caspian. One can not go far without meeting a man loaded with furry caps, much worn in Russia. About the centre of the Fair is the governor's " palace," in which the Duke of Edinburgh lately staid. It has an unusual, and, I believe for a palace, unique feature, in the emblazonment of " Café Restaurant" upon the wall of the ground-floor. This is in Russian letters, of course, and it tempts one to enter. Being a Russian café, it is without ventilation, and the fumes of smoke—to say nothing of the mingled smell of soup, of oily fish, of tea, and of greasy people in heavy costumes bearing the dirt of years—prevent any immediate certainty as to whether it is the governor in person, or a young lady of

Nijni, to whom so many guests on leaving are paying their addresses and their copecks. It is a young lady; and there is no connection between the café and the apartments of the first floor, which lately sheltered the illustrious son-in-law of the Tsar.

The lively aspect of the Fair spreads upward to the roofs, which, as one sees from the top of this building, are all painted red or green. One sees, too, the "life" of the Fair, not only coursing over all the land between the two rivers, but extending to the barges, the steamboats, and the shallow-bottomed vessels of every shape which are moored upon the sandy shores.

Nijni is, as I have said, very picturesque and very dirty. One way of making a picturesque town is to take a site somewhat irregular and rocky, and to plant houses washed with different colors, including blue, yellow, and salmon color, in gardens; cover these habitations with roofs painted red or green, let the intervals be filled in with trees and shrubs, most of them old and large, the leaves showing varied tints of autumn; raise here and there a green or gilded cupola of some Byzantine church; secure over all a blue sky, made bright with the genial warmth of the shining sun; the result will be pleasing, and will much resemble Nijni as it appears toward the end of September.

CHAPTER V.

Leaving Nijni.—The *Tsarevna Marie.*—Tickets for Two Thousand Miles.—
Our Fellow-passengers.—The *Alexander II.*—Kazan.—Mohammedans in
Russia.—Our Lady of Kazan.—"No Sheets!"—Oriental Cleanliness.—
Russian Climate and Clothing.—Orientalism in Russia.—Persian Prayers.
—A Shi'ah's Devotions.—Shallowness of the Volga.—The River Kama.
—Hills about Simbirsk.—Samara.—Mare's-milk Cure.—Volsk.—Saratof.
—Tartar Population.—Prisoners for the Caucasus Tsaritzin.—Sarepta.—
Gingerbread and Mustard.—Chorney Yar.—A Peasant Mayor.—Tartar
Fishermen.—Astrakhan.—Mouths of the Volga.—Raising Level of the
Caspian.

It was not at all an easy matter in Nijni, a town of forty-five thousand inhabitants, to find a person who could speak even a few words of any language other than Russian, or the Arabic *patois* of the Russian Tartars. But the captain of the *Tsarevna Marie,* a rather high and mighty man, in fur coat and fur-lined boots, could talk German, and with his assistance we obtained, for one hundred and twenty-six rubles, two tickets, entitling us to a separate cabin from Nijni down the Volga to Astrakhan (a river journey of about fourteen hundred miles), and from Astrakhan, again south, for the whole length (more than six hundred miles) of the Caspian Sea to the Persian landing-place of Enzelli. The steamboats of this part of the world, in waters which have neither ingress nor exit for shipping, are the pride of all the mooring-places, though they are not of native manufacture. They are built in other countries by foreigners, and brought in pieces to the banks of the Volga. It has always been so in Russia. The first vessel of war ever built in Russia was put together this way at Nijni by a company of merchants from Holstein, who in the seventeenth century obtained permission to force a trade with Persia and India by way of the Volga and the Caspian.

From the considerable town of Twer to its largest mouth in the Caspian Sea, the Volga carries steamboats for about eighteen hundred miles, into such a change of climate that one sees passengers who are wrapped, chrysalis-like, in furs and rugs at Nijni, transformed into a butterfly lightness and gayety of costume at Astrakhan. We left Nijni at the time of year when the boats are most crowded, and the deck saloon of the *Tsarevna Marie* was not exactly delightful. Though female as well as male passengers were at liberty to smoke in every part of the vessel, and certainly did not neglect the privilege, there was a prejudice against open windows which one finds nowhere so strong as among the stove-grown people of Russia. Literally, the Russian women of the richer classes are reared in hot-houses, and have the characteristics of fruit so produced. They have less vitality than women of other countries, and their beauty—exquisite as it sometimes shows itself—fades more quickly. We struggle, and at last resign ourselves to the disagreeable accompaniments of the journey.

We travel with the stream. We are all returning from the Fair of Nijni—a heavy boat-load. Our fellow-passengers are Russians from the least civilized parts of the European Empire, Persians from Resht and Teheran, Armenians and Georgians from the Caucasus, Tartars from the Lower Volga. We are the only English on board. Our neighbors' clothes are of many colors and shapes, and this many-colored variety is the striking feature of their luggage. The Christians of the superior class eat royal sturgeon in cutlets, and delicate sterlet mostly in soup; while the more picturesque Mohammedans on the deck are content with unleavened bread and grapes, or water-melons. All of us, without distinction of creed or country, drink tea; the engine boiler has a tap on deck from which the Mohammedan kettles and those of the poorer Christians are supplied with hot water. In the saloon we take tea *à la Russe*—in glasses, and amazingly weak. I venture to abuse the Russian mode of taking warm water with the faintest coloring of tea, which at once brings down the national wrath of a passenger, who declares that the English "boil" their tea, and will have it no other way but "cooked" like broth or soup.

When it was wet and cold, on the way from Nijni-Novgorod to Kazan, the poorer Christians on board the *Tsarevna Marie* drank corn-brandy largely, while the Mohammedans hid themselves beneath their carpets and muttered hopes of reaching a better land. At Kazan, we were transferred to the *Alexander II.*, a very large vessel, her white hull towering five-and-twenty feet above the water. She is built upon the plan of those Hudson River and Mississippi steamboats which have so long made river traveling in America most comfortable. She has two floors or stories above the water, into which she presses nowhere to a greater depth than four feet, and the first and second class saloons and sleeping-cabins, with their surrounding galleries, are entirely shut off from the under story or main deck, where are the third-class passengers, and where the cargo is received, and the crew are busy in making the vessel fast at the numerous stations on the river. In September, no vessel drawing four feet of water can get up the river to Nijni, and, for our parts, we were by no means sorry to quit the narrower limits of the *Tsarevna Marie* for the splendid saloon and ample space of the *Alexander II.*, which, after assuring us that she is "the first ship on the river," the captain said was built in Belgium, sent in pieces to Russia, and put together on the banks of the Volga. There is time to drive to Kazan, of which, though it is three miles distant, we might see something from the river if the banks were not so high as to render this impossible.

The first sight of Kazan, a town of eighty thousand inhabitants, impresses one with a sense of the error of supposing that Russia in Europe is exclusively inhabited by Christians. We had, in 1868, seen mosques at Eupatoria, and Tartars in other parts of the Crimea, but we hardly expected to find so large a proportion of the population of one of the principal towns in Central Russia composed of Mohammedans, of whom, perhaps, there are not less than twenty thousand in Kazan. There is a tower in Kazan which some assert is a relic of times when the Tartars held their own in this region. But Kazan has been "reduced to ashes," as the historians say, more than once, and there is so much that is Tartaresque in Russian buildings of the fifteenth and sixteenth centuries, that this may as well be a monument of the conqueror Ivan the Terrible as of any Tartar Tsar. There is "Our Lady of Kazan"—she is Russian every bit of her. She is "miraculous," and a church has been built on purpose to receive her. Her "miracle" consisted in escaping destruction when the building in which she was suspended was consumed by fire. Doubtless she was removed by some priest and placed in a miraculous position after the fire, or she may easily have been preserved by the accidents of the conflagration. It is probably true that many "miracles" of this sort happened in the Pantechnicon to articles of furniture stored there before the fire. From a picture she was transformed into a revenue by the miracle. Catherine II. placed diamonds of enormous value above her head; and orthodox Russians, who bow down before her, feel entitled to look with contempt upon their heathen fellow-townsmen, the Tartar Mussulmans.

"No sheets!" I hear the one English lady exclaim, as we are leaving the moorings at Kazan; and it does strike one as odd and uncomfortable, to see nothing but a bare couch provided for a five days' voyage—not a single article of bedding. *Prostenia*—*i. e.*, bed-linen—is perhaps the Russian word which

English travelers pronounce with most energy. Muscovite civilization has not yet attained to sheets; indeed, Russians are generally prepared to maintain that theirs is the better mode of sleeping. The Russians have in this, as in many other matters, the Oriental rather than the Occidental fashion. In Western Europe, it is the cleanly, wholesome custom to lay aside entirely the garments of the day. In Eastern Europe and in Asia, the opposite plan prevails; and, for the most part, people sleep in some, if not all, the clothes in which they have tilled the land or walked the street. In the house of a Persian, a man's bed is anywhere upon the carpets in any one of the rooms. There are always pillows lying about, on which to rest the arm or back by day and the head by night. He takes his sleep by night as an Englishman does his nap after dinner, except that the Englishman is generally raised from the floor, and the Persian is not. Britains will humble themselves metaphorically to the dust, in asking a friend to "give them a bed." In Oriental lands, neither host nor guest would understand such a phrase; for every traveler, whether he be visitor or voyager, carries all that he requires for sleeping, except shelter from inclement weather; and a man's hospitality is not limited, as with us, to the confines of his "spare bed," nor is there any of that sense of indelicacy in sleeping in company with others which is the natural consequence of the bedroom arrangements of Western Europe.

When people make their bed anywhere, and are in the habit of carrying all that they deem requisite in this way from place to place, they dispense with articles which would require frequent washing. It is otherwise when the bed becomes a fixed institution, as in England; and there can be no doubt that the more cleanly practice is that which brings as much as possible of the bedding most frequently to the wash-tub, and with regard to the person, that which suggests by most complete removal of garments of every-day life the most complete and thorough ablutions.

It is quite a mistake to suppose that Oriental peoples are the most cleanly because they observe the washings directed by the Koran. These are certainly performed, and not without good effect; but this is done in the perfunctory manner in which religious obligations are generally undertaken, and it is done while wearing clothes which may not have been removed for weeks. The face is smeared with water before prayer and before eating, but there is no washing such as will remove the dust from eyes already menaced, as a consequence, with chronic ophthalmia; and if it were not the custom among Mohammedans to shave their heads, their matted hair would become a preserve for noxious vermin.

The worst of the Russian is that he has carried some of these customs rather too far north. He does not shave his head, nor clean it. His food of oily fish, or the most greasy preparation of meat, the demand of a cold climate, is not so cleanly as the rice saturated with meat gravy and the fruit of the Oriental. At six months after date, the clothes of the Russian are not so tolerable as those of the Oriental of the South. The climate being so much colder, the Russian sleeps in a less pure atmosphere, and indeed the air of Russian bedrooms, even of the higher class, is, in winter, often disgusting. Russians, whom English people meet in Italy during winter, are often heard to say that they have never experienced the miseries of cold until they came south of the Alps. On board the *Alexander II.*, though there were yet more than three months remaining of the year, and though the weather was by no means what English people would call cold, the cabins were heated with hot-water pipes. Two Russian gentlemen complained of loss of appetite, from headache, and of sleeplessness. They were astonished when we asked how they could expect any other result after lying for hours in a small cabin with the door and window closed, and with their pillows all but resting upon a huge pipe filled with boiling water. To their surprise, they were cured next day by changing their pillows to the opposite ends of their beds, and by leaving two inches of their window open. The day on which we left Kazan was such as in England would have been called and enjoyed as "a mild autumn day;" but being in Russia, the cabins were warmed to a stewy heat, and we noticed through the day that our cabin was the only one of which the window was open.

It would be possible to enumerate, almost to weariness, the points in which Russians, differing from the people of Western Europe, resemble those races whom we call Orientals. Except Turkey, Russia is the only European country in which women smoke tobacco habitually. Turkish women are, as a rule, delicate, owing to their customary seclusion in houses (some do not pass the threshold for months, or even years), and to the substitution of narcotics and sweet-meats for wholesome and nutritious food. Russian women are often not less feeble, owing to similar habits, and to the unnatural, enervating temperature of their houses. We have seen at Moscow and elsewhere how, after the manner of the mosque, Russians make the place of honor for interment in the corners of their churches. In the Cathedral of the Assumption, the resting-place of the most revered dead, the tombs of SS. Theognostus, Peter, Philip, and Jonah, all Metropolitans of Moscow, are enshrined in the four angles of that wonderful church; and there also are the remains of SS. Photius and Cyprian, of Philaret and Hermogenes, Patriarchs of the Russo-Greek Church. Some confusion of manners and customs is perhaps inevitable in an empire which extends through thirty degrees of latitude, and includes Finns and Persians, Germans and Calmuck Tartars, with people of many colors and creeds—the fair-haired girls of Hango and Helsingfors, and the ebonized descendants of Tartar slaves; followers of Luther and worshipers of Buddha.

As the setting sun and the flat horizon draw together in the reddening light of evening, representatives of millions of the Tsar's subjects mount the highest places in our vessel, and turn their prayerful eyes toward Mecca. But whether the view was clouded with pitiless rain, in our journey from Nijni to Kazan, or brilliant at Kazan and onward to Astrakhan, never did some of the Persian and Tartar traders omit, about the hours of sunrise and sunset, to stand with uncovered feet and make their prayers and obeisance toward the East. How could man, we thought at the time, be more picturesque than one of these merchants of Russian Persia, to whose naturally great stature was added a conical fur hat, high as the bear-skin of an English Guardsman! Pressing this high crown of curling black lamb-skin tightly on his brow against the wind, he stripped off his outer robe, lined with the yellow fur of the marmot, which he spread as a prayer-carpet upon the high deck. Observed, yet seeming utterly unconscious and unnoticed by all around, he laid aside his boots, and stepped in his stockings upon his coat of fur. Then, drawing his bright green tunic more tightly within his silver-mounted waist-belt, he placed both hands upon his loose trousers of black satin, and gazed in rapt attention upon the eastern sky. Soon he fell upon his knees, and pressed his forehead several times upon the deck. He rose, and with new motions, designed to clear his thoughts from things of earth, and to make him receptive of ideas of Allah the all-merciful, he continued and concluded his devotions. We know that there is hypocrisy among men of every creed, and in Mohammedanism, as in others, a frequent seeming unto men to pray; we know how much higher and nobler in morality and justice, as in every other valuable attribute, is true Christianity; but there can equally be no doubt in our minds that the outward aspect of this Mohammedan prayer is far nobler than the ceremonies of the Greek Church, than the religious exercises of Russians, with their farthing tapers, their bowings, their kissing of books and of tinseled pictures.

No river of Europe so much resembles the Nile as the Volga, and, especially in its southern course, the sandy likeness is very remarkable. For hundreds of miles the country upon the Volga is low and uninteresting. Like the Danube, and like the Nile also, the right bank is the more elevated; and, as upon the African river, the stream is occasionally crossed by sandy shallows, and the crew are summoned to sounding by the ringing of the captain's bell. Upon a river of such majestic breadth, one is at first amazed at the figures which are called out by the man who, from the head of the vessel, sounds the depth with a pole, colored alternately black and white, in lengths rather less than a foot; "eight," "six," and sometimes "five," he calls. It is demonstrated that the *Alexander II.*, with excellent accommodation for thirty first-class, as many second-class, and any number of third-class passengers, to say nothing of cargo, draws no more than four feet of water. Her furnaces are fed with the fuel of the country, cleft logs of pine, each about two feet in length; and twice or three times in every day a fresh supply of wood is taken in, which is invariably carried on board from the shore by women.

Half a day's journey after leaving Kazan, we arrive at the point where the bluish Volga receives the yellowish waters of the Kama, the highway into Siberia. We pass on toward Simbirsk, at which we touch in the hours of night. The lights of the town look down upon us from a height of five hundred feet, and the right bank of the river rises still higher as we proceed the next day toward Samara. Just as upon the Rhine one is told to reserve admiration for the famous view of the Siebengebirge, and upon the less picturesque

Danube for the scenery of the Iron Gates, so upon the Volga it is between Simbirsk and Samara that lovers of the beautiful are supposed to reach the acme of delight. The brief beauties of the Volga could be seen to no greater advantage than when we passed them in the last days of September; and the green firs set in the golden coloring of autumn-tinted birch leaves are very refreshing and attractive for the short distance in which there is any thing approaching the picturesque in the scenery upon the Volga.

Near Samara, where the right bank, like the unvarying left, is once more flat, we observed the commencement of an important public work of a character most truly Russian—a work to which, I should hope, the poll-tax, rather than British investors in Russian railways, will contribute in every stone and girder. In this century, the undertaking will never "pay," from the investor's point of view. We saw the beginning of a viaduct across the Volga, a viaduct which will be the longest in the world, forming a connection by railway between St. Petersburg and Orenburg. The procureur-général of the latter town was standing beside us as we approached the preparatory works. He and his townsmen rejoiced greatly at the proposed expenditure of a million sterling, apparently for the benefit of Orenburg, as it is not in contemplation to push the railway farther to the east. But they all understand very well that this is the high-road to Khiva, and that the Government, by constructing this viaduct and railway, will vastly increase the security of their hold upon Central Asia, and the facilities for extending conquest in that direction.

At Samara we have passed eight hundred and forty versts from Nijni. In all these towns of the Volga there is a large Mohammedan population; but the most curious circumstance about Samara is in the mare's-milk cure, which is carried on in several of the best houses near the river-side, these establishments being superintended by medical men, just as hydropathic cures are in England. At Samara, mares' milk is made into an effervescing and fermented drink by the admixture of an acid; and the result, not very unlike one variety of cheap Champagne, in flavor as well as in appearance, is taken as a cure for diseases of the lungs and kidneys. At Volsk we are nearly seven hundred miles from Nijni. We landed at this "large, handsome town," as Murray's "Hand-book for Russia" calls it, upon a sand-heap littered with refuse of all kinds. There were several carriages waiting for hire; but these were nothing better than dirty baskets, originally of great strength, containing a handful of dried roots and grass, of the roughest sort, for the "fare" to sit upon. One or two had a seat covered with leather; but it needed the education of a life-time to keep one's self on this perch, when the vehicle moved over the deep and filthy ruts of the main streets. The streets of Volsk are straight and wide; the houses are, with very rare exceptions, built like a log-hut, of fir poles, tenoned and mortised together, just in the same style as the houses in a Norwegian village.

The Mayor of Volsk and his wife, who came on board as passengers to Saratof, were full to overflowing with happy anticipation of the gayeties of the latter town, where, they told us, an Italian opera company were giving a series of performances, some of which they hoped to witness. I asked his worship how the Tartars, of whom there are a great number in Volsk, agreed with the Russians. He said that difficulties constantly arose, and that recently Tartars had complained to him, alleging that Russians would not let them use the public wells. When we arrived at Saratof, we were almost inclined to laugh at the notion of Italian opera in such a place, where the rickety wooden sheds of the Tartar bazaar occupy the neighborhood of the Opera-house. Probably one-third of the ninety thousand inhabitants of Saratof are Mohammedans, and live in kennels in the outskirts, or in their wooden shops. Some of these people, with a store in the bazaar, which is perhaps ten feet square, have a bundle of dried grass in a corner, which they cover with a carpet. This serves them for bed, and the place is at once home and shop. But the streets, like those of other Russian towns on the Volga, though their surface is the public sewer, and is without any attempt at paving, are generally straight and wide; and a house which would be thought good in a second-rate German town stands side by side with a wooden hovel neither water-tight nor wind-proof.

The Tartars in these towns have probably a hard time, and suffer much oppression. Their religion is tolerated; and though they rarely have mosques in the shape of buildings designed and erected for the exercise of their religion, they have houses which, though with none of the outward appearances of a mosque, are set apart for their religious ceremonies. All this region, where they now take the lowest place, was once their own. They have schools, but only those attached to their mosques, and there nothing beyond the poor art of reading a few sentences from the Koran is taught. Many of them steal away into the Turkish Empire, in order to avoid the operation of the new military law, which has put thousands of these Mohammedans of Europe into the uniforms of the Russian army.

On the Volga, about Saratof, in autumn, one sees boats loaded with melons, the fruit stacked high upon the decks, just as the old-fashioned sixty-pound cannon-balls were piled in former days at Woolwich. Third-class passengers rush on shore at every station, buy a melon as big as one's head for copecks of the value of threepence, a large loaf of brown-bread for as much more, and there is provision for a man for a whole day. At Nijni we had seen a procession of prisoners on the way to Siberia; at Saratof we saw a number of men, women, and children, in similar circumstances, on the way to the Caucasus. They were marched on board a passenger steam-vessel, in build resembling the *Alexander II.*, between two files of soldiers, and secured in two large cages placed near the paddle-boxes. The front of each cage overlooking the water, and the sides, which faced the stern of the steamboat, were barred with iron, so that every part of the interior could be seen, just as in the lion-houses of the Zoological Gardens, with this difference, that in the case of these prisoners there was no overhanging roof to prevent rain or sunshine from pouring in upon their wretchedness. At the back of each cage there was a lair common to all, without distinction of sex or age. When all were secured, including the guiltless wives and children, fights occurred for places least exposed to the cold wind. The Tartar prisoners were alone. No wives had elected to go with their Tartar husbands into the snows of the Caucasus. The greater criminals wore heavy chains, linked to their ankles and wrists, the loud clanking of which, as they walked to and fro in the cage, seemed to be enjoyed as a sort of distinction in the miserable crowd. There were three soldiers in undress uniform, one of them wearing chains of this sort. But the saddest sight was the exposure of the innocent children in a criminal cage, and the inevitable injury to them of being thus associated with criminals, and exhibited for days to the population of the Volga, in a company where there could be no doubt that he appeared the greatest hero whose chains clanked heaviest.

Saratof is the largest town upon the Volga, and its site is so hilly that from one point of view nearly the whole of its buildings may be seen. It has an immense trade in fish and agricultural productions. The description of Saratof as "handsome," in Murray's "Hand-book," is ridiculous and misleading. It has a few official buildings which would pass muster in a second-rate German town, and it has the prime element in the formation of a handsome town—that of liberal space in the plan of its roads and streets. Compared with a purely Tartar village, it may seem handsome; but Saratof is, to a great extent, itself Tartar. So is Tsaritzin, the next railway station upon the Volga. Tsaritzin is usually the place of debarkation for travelers from Persia and the Caspian who are bound for Western Europe. With the next place, at which the *Alexander II.* stops, we are disappointed. We had hoped to find the little town of Sarepta upon the water-side. It is known throughout Russia as an exclusive colony of the German "Herrnhüter"—the Moravian Brethren, and spoken of as a model of social welfare and successful industry. Instead of the town, there was only a wooden stall in sight. This was painted green, and stood at some little distance from the landing-place on the sandy bank of the river. The captain declared he did not intend to wait more than two or three minutes, but it was clear that, whatever happened, half a hundred at least of the passengers were resolved to reach that wooden stall. Behind the little counter, which was spread with gingerbread cakes and neatly fastened packets bearing the word "Sarepta" in large letters, stood a tall, solemn-looking German, who, if he had been born with ten arms in place of two, could not have delivered gingerbread fast enough to satisfy the eager and hurried passengers. Seeing that the cakes looked good, several people bought the mysterious packets, of whom one at least was ignorant, as we were, that these contained not cakes, but condiment—the mustard of Sarepta, for the manufacture of which the German colony is famous. The Sarepta community have a shop in St. Petersburg for the sale of their mustard and gingerbread.

The Volga widens to a noble stream. Gazing on its broad and resplendent surface at any point between Kazan and Astrakhan, one would hardly suspect its real weakness — its shallowness. At Chorney Yar, we were more than sixteen hundred miles from Twer, and yet our four-feet-deep ship grated on the sandy bottom of the shallows at that point. To be sure, we were there in the time of year when the waters of the Volga are at their lowest; in May the river has twice the breadth to which it dwindles in September, and there is then more movement and life upon the stream. We passed hours without seeing a vessel of any description. At Chorney Yar the mayor and his deputy ushered the governor of the province of Astrakhan to a cabin in the *Alexander II.* They, in their official costumes, afforded an interesting exhibition of the personnel of Russian local government. The mayor, evidently a peasant, wore a gilt-laced coat, very like a Windsor uniform, and over his shoulders a massive chain — of brass, I should think — which at odd moments, when his worship fancied himself unobserved, he adjusted to a nice diagonal upon his wide chest. He looked as comfortable, in his gorgeous apparel, as the Shah did in his diamond-breasted coat when seated upon a high chair at some of the London entertainments.

We glide on over the stream, running between low sandy banks across the steppe of Astrakhan. The water of the Volga pales from the appearance of burnished gold to that of molten silver, as the lovely tints of the Southern sunset gave place to the cool twilight. What a picture those four Calmuck fishermen, with their immense circular caps of white fur, their swarthy faces, with the clearly marked Mongol features, their pink, blue, and white garments would make! Their rudely constructed boat, with a bow rising from the water and sharpened to the shape of a pike's mouth, is grotesquely painted. On the high, square stern is a cartoon representing a yellow lion, with face averted from the object of pursuit, chasing a lady in short costume among a grove of trees. The evening sun bathes them in splendor; their squalor looks like glory; a pelican, whose natural color is a dirty white, flaps its yard-long wings, and projects its pouched bill over the water before them — a gilded bird; even the misery of their reed-roofed hut, with walls of crumbling sandy mud, is metamorphosed into beauty; and far in the distance, across the unvarying level, the sunlight marks the green cupolas of the Orthodox Cathedral of Astrakhan—a town mainly Mongol, partly Russian, where the Volga at last pours its waters through many and long mouths into the Caspian.

Within a week we have passed in the same boat from one of the best bear-hunting grounds in all Russia, a forest of fir near Kazan, to this strange town, to which Russian gentlemen come for the Indian sport of "pig-sticking," which is much practiced in the neighborhood of Astrakhan—a town in which the scanty mixture of Russian houses with the mud-built huts of Calmuck Tartars proclaims the remotest borders of European civilization. There is nothing very strange to see in Astrakhan, except the houses of the Tartars and the curious worship in their pagodas. Perhaps the best thing in the place is the caviare, for which Astrakhan is famous. This delicacy is, however, being obtained at cruel and ruinous cost to the sturgeon-fisheries of the Volga. Russians say that caviare is nowhere so good as in Astrakhan, and certainly the damp turnip-seed, or that which looks like turnip or rape seed, sold in London as caviare, has very little resemblance to the greenish, fresh dainty which one obtains, though not very cheaply, in Astrakhan. Each particle of the caviare of Astrakhan is three times as large, apparently from mere freshness, as that sold in London; the color is different and the flavor as unlike as that which distinguishes fresh grapes from raisins.

Moored at Astrakhan after six days' journey on the river, we can not but reflect how vastly greater would be the Russian power if the Volga had the uniform depth of the Thames; if, instead of flowing through two thousand five hundred miles of the poorest land in Europe, it watered such soils as those of Berks and Bucks; and if, in place of emptying itself into a closed and shallow sea, it were a highway for the commerce of the world. Even here at the quays of Astrakhan, the steamboat, drawing only eight feet of water, which is to carry us down the whole length of the Caspian, can not approach; we must be tugged in a flat-bottomed barge for sixty miles or more through the delta of the Volga to where the vessel lies anchored in the sea, and when we have boarded her we shall pass yet another sixty miles over the Caspian before we shall get into five fathoms of water. Six months after we had quitted this region, we read in *The Times* the scheme of an American engineer who proposed to raise in forty years the surface of the Caspian five-and-twenty feet, to a level with the waters of the Black Sea, by cutting a small channel, which in that long period would be scooped by the effluent water to the size of a ship-canal. Our recollection of various heights of the shores of the Caspian is not, in an engineering sense, precise, but we would suggest to this "American engineer" the practical consideration whether his plan, if carried out, would not submerge Astrakhan and a large part of Southern Russia. It would certainly obliterate the Russian station of Ashurade, so important for the maintenance of Russian influence in Persia, and it would conceal forever the Persian landing-places on the Caspian, together with the town of Resht, and much of the most productive land in the dominions of the Shah.

CHAPTER VI.

Louis XIV. and the Tsar.—Russian Church and State.—Empress Anne's Buffoon.—Prayers for the Tsar.—The Russian Press.—Censorship.—Press Regulations.—The *Moscow Gazette.*—Difficulties of Journalists.—The *Wjedomosti.*—The *Russki Mir.*—Russia not Russian.—Foreign Races.—New Military System.—The Emancipation of the Serfs.—The Communal System.—Bad Farming.—Ignorance of the Peasantry.—The Corn Trade.—Complaints from Odessa.—Resurrection of Sebastopol.—Corn from Russia and the United States.—The Artel of Odessa.—Demands of Odessa Merchants.—A Viceroy wanted.—English Interests in Russian Corn.—The Soil of Russia.—The Conquests of Russia.—Contrast with Persia.—Borrowed Money.—Unprofitable Railways.—Revenue of Russia.—Produce of Poll-tax.—Privileged Citizens.

In the great library of St. Petersburg there is preserved a writing exercise—a calligraphic study—done in the days of his childhood by Louis XIV. of France. Six times, at least, the little hand of the future sovereign was instructed to pen the following sentiment: "*L'hommage est deue aux roys ; ils font ce qu'il leurs plait*"—("Homage is due to kings; they do as they please"). We shall be more kind to the memory of monarchs when we remember how they have been trained by sycophants. Nowhere is the royal office exalted higher than in Russia, where every human creature holds life and liberty at the good pleasure of the Tsar. Except the Sultan, the Tsar has no peer in Europe; and it is no wonder if the solemn loneliness of his elevation impairs the nervous system and menaces the sanity of members even of the stalwart race of Romanoff.

Sprung from the Church of Russia, the Tsars are never dissociated from it. They are divine as well as imperial;

the Tsar is priest as well as king; he is a miracle-worker upon the Neva; he administers the sacramental bread and wine with his own hands at his coronation; in short, like the Shah and the Sultan in their respective dominions, the Tsar is, in the theory of Russian Government—which stands for the present in place of a constitution—"the Shadow of God." Members of other imperial houses may change their creed to win, or even to share, a throne; but it is not so with a Romanoff. In Russia, an empire by no means homogeneous in population, this thorough and personal association of Church and State is the centre of the centripetal force which is grinding foreign races into Russians.

The grand ambition of the Emperor Nicholas, and the high moral character and qualities of his successor, have in our time cleared the Russian court, and the exercise of its autocratic powers, from the vagaries of a period when there was no responsibility to a dumb people, or even to the more enlightened opinion of Western Europe. The days in which, according to respected authorities, the Empress Anne married one of her buffoons, himself a prince of the Empire, to a Calmuck dwarf, and made them pass the first night after their wedding upon an ice couch in an ice house upon the Neva, are gone forever. So, too, is the issue of such ukases as that by which Peter the Great sought to subdue heresy and the obstinacy of hairy sectaries by a decree prohibiting the wearing of beards, when every one who dared to present himself at the "Redeemer Gate" of the Moscow Kremlin with a beard upon his chin was caught and fined; or that by which the Emperor Paul, in 1799, with the same object, forbade the use of shoe-strings and the wearing of round hats. All this is gone, but the personal power of the Tsar continues. In all Russian churches the most earnest prayer —that without which no service is complete—that during which heads are most bowed and crossings are most frequent, is the prayer in which the welfare of the Tsar and of his house is implored. It has been said that a venturesome diplomatist once asked the Emperor Nicholas who was the most distinguished of his majesty's subjects? And, according to report, the Tsar replied that the most distinguished Russian was he whomsoever the Emperor honored by speaking to him. Even Alexander II., the mildest and most modern of his line, could declare, "*La Russie c'est le Tsar*," more truly than the young copyist with whose name I commenced this chapter could say, in after-days, of himself and France, "*L'État c'est Moi*."

The Russian Press is a sham, inasmuch as its existence leads the outside world to suppose that there is within the Empire a widely based expression of public opinion. I am not now alluding to the censorship which forbids the utterance of progressive sentiments, or the full expression of hope for a constitutional régime, but to the initial fact in the just comprehension of this important matter, that the productions of the Russian Press are not open to more than one in a hundred of the Tsar's subjects, because of their ignorance of the meaning of letters. Every reader of a newspaper in Russia, of the most loyal, and even servile, of the issues from the Press, is, we may say, a marked man, because as a rule journals can only be obtained by subscription through the post-office. Many visitors from our own country must have learned by irritating experience the truth of this statement, when they have found their English newspapers sequestrated, day after day, because they were not subscribed for in this manner. In 1870, including printing of every sort and kind, there was but one printing-press in Russia for every sixteen thousand of the population.

The life of a journalist in Russia must be, to say the least, uneasy, if we may presume that he has any opinions of his own. There are two newspapers published in St. Petersburg which are not designed for the Russian people—the *Journal de St. Pétersbourg*, printed in French, and the *St. Petersburger Zeitung*, printed in German; the latter being the organ of the German-speaking people of Russia, as the former is of the Russian Foreign Office. These journals are, of course, valuable rather for information relating to external than to internal affairs.

A writer long resident in Russia, one who has already attracted the unfavorable notice of the Tsar's Government for his too accurate and well-informed acquaintance with imperial arrangements, has lately described Russian newspapers, and the régime to which they are subject. He says of the censorship that "it appertains to the department of the Minister of the Interior, and is carried out either by special committees, as at St. Petersburg, Moscow, Warsaw, and Odessa, or by individual censors in such towns as Kief, Kazan, Riga, Dorpat, Mittau, Revel, and Wilna, who have to report their decisions for confirmation to the Chief Board of Censors at St. Petersburg. The committees are composed of a president, and three senior and six junior censors, with an inspector of printing-offices and book dépôts, and his assistants. The president and three chief censors meet at least once a week, when the various manuscripts and journals are registered, and either licensed or prohibited. All writings which are directed, first, against the dogmas of the National Church; secondly, against the form of government existing in Russia, and especially against the person of the Emperor, or any member of the imperial family; thirdly, against morality; and, fourthly, those containing offensive attacks on any private person, or calumnies of any kind, are prohibited by the censorship. No communication respecting the imperial family may be printed until permission has been obtained from the Minister of the Imperial Court. Not only writings, but pictures and music, are subject to the censorship; and care is taken to prohibit the latter when any thing resembling the airs of the Polish insurgents is discovered to have been introduced. It is left to the discretion of the editors whether they will place themselves under the preliminary preventive censorship or not. In the latter case, they are subject to the control of the Press Director—an official also belonging to the Ministry of the Interior. Under this régime, articles are not subject to official examination and revision before they make their appearance in the columns of the paper; although in cases where the Government has had an inkling of some more than usually dangerous effusion, the whole issue has been seized as it left the printing-machine. The usual method of proceeding—which in its main features appears to have been borrowed from the Press Laws of the second French Empire—is, for the head authority of the particular branch of the public service that considers itself unwarrantably assailed to lay a complaint before the Press Director, should he indeed not have already taken the initiative. In either case, he gravely cautions the offending printer to be more careful for the future. A repetition of the offense is followed by a repetition of the warning; but should three such remonstrances prove ineffectual, the offending periodical is suspended for a period not exceeding three months. If, on its re-appearance, it obstinately persists in its former course, it receives three further warnings, and is finally suppressed. A preliminary caution, too, is sometimes sent round to the different editors, forbidding them to mention a certain subject at all, or enjoining them to take only a particular view of it. This was especially the case with regard to the Khiva expedition. For accidentally disregarding a similar injunction, the *Moscow Gazette* (*Moscauer Zeitung*)—the organ of the German element in Central Russia, and most ably conducted by M. Katkof—recently underwent a temporary suspension."

This system is not calculated to give a fresh, progressive, vigorous, and independent tone to the Press of Russia. The Press Director is, under this régime, virtually the editor of the whole Press. The writer above quoted says: "The larger St. Petersburg and Moscow papers are almost all under his control." If an English statesman were in friendly talk on this subject with such men as Prince Gortschakoff or the Grand Duke Constantine, men of liberal mind and large acquaintance with the forces that mold and govern the actions of mankind, I am sure he would be told that the Russian Press is not injuriously controlled; that the Government of the Tsar would not only sanction, but that it desired, that reforms and even radical changes in the mode of government should be discussed and examined. But how? It can not be doubted that a journalist desiring, say the spread of education, and convinced that it will never come until representative institutions are established, which shall in some measure control and determine the action of Government, may express an opinion " that if it should seem good to his Imperial Majesty, our august Imperator, in the progress of the century, and when to the wisdom of his Government it shall appear that the Russian people are fitted to bear the burden of so great responsibility, then, if it please the Tsar to establish representative institutions, these will further the work of civilization." But he dare not say that such institutions are good, and ought to be established, without showing that he regards the existing order of government as the very best that human hands, assisted by celestial influences, could construct, and that he desires nothing except through the bounty of the Tsar and his majesty's Government.

Occasionally the Russian papers exhibit their differences from each other in a leaning to Germany or to France, either tendency not being sufficiently strong or external in its aims, or offensive to the Government, to bring down upon them the interference of the Press Director. A Russian journal which desires a successful, untroubled existence must turn its eyes from the acts of Government, bestowing now and then indiscriminate praise without scrutiny.

The writer to whom I am already indebted gives a fine example with reference to the *Wjedomosti*, a paper founded by Peter the Great, and which used to represent the Russian Liberal party. A few months ago "its editor, M. Korsch, who by his sympathy in the cause of reform has helped to raise it in public opinion, was summoned before the Minister of the Interior and told that the paper was of such radical tendencies that he must resign the control of it. The editor sought to mollify the ministerial anger by offering to make certain changes in his staff, but without effect; and as in Russia, in matters connected with the Press, a ministerial has all the force of an imperial ukase, nothing remained but to quietly obey, when the paper was placed under the immediate supervision of the Ministry of Public Instruction, and supplied with an entirely new staff, appointed on the express condition of publishing as leading articles all communications which the Ministry may think proper to forward, and of defending the Ministry itself on all occasions through thick and thin." One is not surprised to learn that even in Russia, under these circumstances, "influence and circulation alike have been dwindling away." Only those who have nothing to lose can afford to attack the Government in Russia. M. Korsch, the denounced editor of the *Wjedomosti*, "endeavored to buy the *Russki Mir*, or *Russian World* [the organ of General Tchernayeff], at that time under suspension. It seems that its proprietor, finding he was losing money, hit upon the expedient of attacking the War-office, both with regard to the administration of Turkistan and the Kirghiz rebellions of a few years ago, until he succeeded in getting his paper suspended, hoping that things would take a turn for the better in three months, when he proposed to start afresh with all the prestige pertaining to a martyr—always a certain advantage under a despotic form of government."

There can be no question that the neglect of social improvement and reform, when the work is much less conspicuous than the emancipation of the serfs (which no power but that of the Tsar could decree, as it affected the nobles in their property), is in no small degree due to the misdirected training of Russian statesmen. In the absence of representative institutions and of a free Press, politicians find in the line of diplomacy and the field of foreign affairs the only road by which it is possible to arrive at a great reputation. The eyes and thoughts of Russian statesmen are in consequence averted from their country, and their ears are closed to appeals in the language of Russia. There is no free and widely studied debate in which they can hope to win influence by making a great name throughout the Empire; the only path to distinction is by successful manipulation of Russian influence upon external politics, by wielding the pen which is weighted, at the advice of the writer, with the armed forces of Russia, or the sword which leads those forces to battle and conquest.

And it must be acknowledged that the work of leading Russia from a system of government which has resemblance in system more to that of the Sultan than to any other Government of Europe, is beset with many and great difficulties. Russia is not yet Russian. All the pressure of the superincumbent machinery of Government, exercised in the name of God as well as of the Tsar, has not as yet resulted in a fusion of the diverse populations of the Empire. To Germany, and to her war with France, from which he wisely held aloof, the Tsar is indebted for the establishment of a military system which, in spite of its obvious faults in diverting productive labor and diminishing the wealth of Russia, is, in fact, the most powerful agency which, perhaps, in the circumstances of that Empire, could have been devised by the Tsar, not only for the amalgamation of his heterogeneous subjects, but also for securing progress in general education. In Russia in Europe there are Mohammedans speaking dialects of Turkish and Arabic; Poles clinging to their national language; and German-speaking people of whom probably one million are actually natives of *Vaterland* and aliens in Russia. In the towns, the Mohammedan, the Pole, and the German keep, as far as possible, aloof from each other and from the Russian. They do not intermix or intermarry. The poor of Warsaw do not understand the Russian language. The German colonies upon the Volga are distinguished not only for the general superiority of their houses, but throughout their life for a higher standard of comfort than is common in the Russian towns—a result of their superior education. And in the densely populated Mohammedan quarters of towns such as Kazan and Saratof, there are multitudes of people preserving their religion, their customs, and their race unmixed, though they are regarded, like the Jews of Odessa, with dislike and contempt by their Muscovite masters, who do not forget or forgive the barbarities practiced by the forefathers of these Tartars upon the persons and the buildings of their own ancestors. There is no pretense or affection or sympathy between the German-speaking people and the genuine Russians. This is perhaps most conspicuous in the Baltic provinces, where in line with the treatment of native Germans there is always a train laid which may be exploded at any moment into a *casus belli* by the chancellor of either Empire. Germans in the North and Jews in the South are hated, not only because their presence is inharmonious with Panslavonian ideas, but rather for their superior success in trade and commerce. The poor Mohammedans have no such guilt, but it is traditional policy with the faithful of the Eastern Church to trample upon Islam.

The new military system of Russia, which excepts neither

creed nor race, which carries the youth of all, German, Polish, Mohammedan, as well as Russian, far away from home, to make all alike soldiers of the Tsar, is the severe but effectual school in which these distinctions are being most effaced. One can see this in the streets, in the comradeship of oblique-eyed Tartars with bright Armenians from the Caucasus, of golden-haired boys from Finland with native Russians from the South, all speaking, or trying to speak, the language in which they are drilled, and by the knowledge of which they can alone hope to win higher pay and improved position. In every branch of the military service there are some educational facilities and even requirements. To these the troops are led by self-interest, and in some cases by stern punishments. Every impulse in the direction of personal advantage suggests to them to make the Russian language their own, and to direct their spiritual ideas toward that truest index of national loyalty—the Russian Church. The Russian military system is probably accomplishing as great a social reformation as that which was achieved by the abolition of serfdom.

That grand measure, the main glory of the present reign, has not yet effected all the improvement of the Russian peasant and his tillage which the most sanguine of its advocates expected would immediately follow the operation of the great ukase of 1861, and the belligerent power of Russia is reduced because of the unimproving condition of agriculture. Primarily, this is due to the general ignorance and poverty of the peasantry; and, secondarily, to the land system and the onerous taxation of Russia. It was very absurd to expect that twenty-two millions of people would, at a stroke of the Tsar's pen, advance by a leap from the display of the characteristics of slavery to the exhibition of the virtues of people who have for ages sustained the ennobling cares and the responsibilities of personal freedom. It may be said, without fear of contradiction, that the Russian peasantry will never be as the rural population of Germany or Switzerland, or even of less educated France, until they too are instructed, and until they, like those, are accustomed to the exercise of a substantial and duly responsible share in the Government of the country. In many villages or communes of Russia, the peasant is disposed to say that the Emperor's benign policy has done him no good, inasmuch as it has resulted in giving him a harder master in the commune than he had in the proprietor. The advances which the Government has made to the peasantry for the enfranchisement of their lands, as well as the revenue resulting from taxation, are secured by making each commune equally with each individual responsible for payment. In 1872, the State had advanced no less than eighty million pounds in respect of sixty-six million acres; and if the peasant fails to pay to the commune his due share of the interest and sinking fund upon the aggregate sum which stands against the name of the village and its local government in the books of the Empire, he is of course not unlikely to meet with severity from his fellows, who must make good any deficiency on the part of lazy or dissolute defaulters.

Perhaps at this point we may usefully make a brief, and therefore necessarily imperfect, reference to the Russian land system, merely in order to exhibit the blighting effect of the communal system upon agriculture. In the primitive state, the Russian people used land, and, when that was exhausted, went farther afield for more. By degrees, in fertile places, when there was no more land to be had, this method began to assume the aspect of private property by right of possession. But the community increased, the land did not; the fulfillment of the obligations of individuals to the State and to proprietors was demanded, and could not be met, according to Russian ways of agriculture, unless every man had land from which to earn his contribution to the general liability. So it came about that the system of periodical redistribution of the cultivated land by each commune was established, and under this system the Russian peasant has no security of tenure, no certainty as to his payment to the commune, and through the commune to the State, for these things are determined by the circumstances of his neighbors. Mr. D. M. Wallace, who has lived in Russia, says: "The allotment of the land is by far the most important event in Russian peasant life, and the arrangement can not be made without endless talking and discussion. After the number of shares for each family has been decided, the distribution of the lots gives rise to new difficulties. The families who have plentifully manured their land strive to get back their old lots, and the commune respects their claims so far as these are consistent with the new arrangement; but it often happens that it is impossible to conciliate private and communal interests, and in such cases the former are sacrificed in a way that would not be tolerated by men of Anglo-Saxon race."

This will account in a great measure for the inefficiency of Russian agriculture where the communal system prevails; but that is not universal, and greater intelligence would bring about a reform in the method of Russian agriculture, which is much needed. A three-course system of farming — one field of rye or wheat, one field of spring-corn (oats, etc.), and one field fallow—obtains over nearly the whole of European Russia.

This inferior condition of the Russian people affects not only their agriculture, but also their foreign trade. Odessa is perplexed because the corn trade from that port is dwindling; and we are told, upon official authority, that "a peculiarity of the bills in circulation in South Russia is, that ten per cent. of them are given or indorsed by persons who can not sign their own names, but get it done by proxy at a notary's; and from twenty to thirty per cent. more are omitted, and indorsed by parties who can only just sign their names, and are not able to write any thing in addition." The Odessa Committee on Trade and Manufactures have reported to the Council for Trade and Manufactures in St. Petersburg that the commerce of their town, by far the most important in South Russia, "is not only undergoing a temporary crisis, but is actually entering a period of absolute decline." The "temporary crisis" is due to the failure of the two last harvests; and Vice-consul Webster reports from Kherson that "nearly every body in South Russia will be bankrupt" if the harvest of this year be not sufficient. "The commercial banks," he writes, "whose principal occupation now is renewing or prolonging old bills, have been assisted by the State bank, and will be able to make way till the probable result of the harvest of 1876 is known. Should the harvest fail, a financial crash is inevitable." The Odessa Committee find that Nikolaief and Sebastopol, having become places of export, are drawing away their trade, and that much of the produce in the fertile district of Kief, which was formerly brought for shipment to Odessa, is now conveyed by railway to the ports of the Baltic, the freight from Königsberg to England being less than half that to Odessa, or in the proportion of three to seven.

"But it is not in the opening of these new outlets for Russian grain that the committee see the danger to Odessa." "The competition of Nikolaief, Sebastopol, or even Königsberg, could not prevent Odessa continuing to be the natural outlet for a tract of country quite sufficient for a large remunerative trade." The danger is one which threatens, not Odessa only, but all Russia; and it comes from the valley of the Mississippi—from the United States of America. Of the nine million to fourteen million quarters of foreign wheat required by England, the proportions supplied by Russia and the United States have been as follows during the last seven years:

	Russia. Per Cent.	United States. Per Cent.
1867	44	14
1868	32	18
1869	32	18
1870	38	21
1871	40	23
1872	51	24
1873	21	44

The committee say they have no positive information for 1874, but they have reason to believe the result is less favorable to Russia than that of 1873. The figures given above show that in seven years Russia and the United States have, in this very important matter, changed positions. In 1867 Russia supplied 44 per cent. and the United States 14 per cent. of England's demand for foreign wheat; in 1873 the United States supplied 44 per cent. and Russia only 21 per cent. The Odessa Committee have no illusions; they indulge no hope that even a most prosperous harvest in Russia will turn the scale; but rather believe that the United States will take a still higher position among the grain-producers of the world. Congress has granted 2,000,000 dollars for deepening the mouths of the Mississippi, and on the completion of these works the cost of the transport of wheat from Chicago to England will be diminished by more than 50 per cent. The Odessa Committee see in a near future the United States " so absolutely the controller of the prices of the London market that we shall be utterly unable to compete with her." And in this race it must be admitted that they, in common with all Russian enterprise, are heavily weighted by the official system of the Empire. The Artel (Association of Workmen) has a monopoly of Custom-house work; and the committee find that the cost of the necessary Custom-house formalities is, on the average, seven times, and for some classes of goods, eleven times, more than before this association was formed. It is estimated that the annual sum paid to the Artel of Odessa amounts to 400,000 rubles, "and this for no service rendered, as the Artel in no way dispenses with the necessity of employing the workmen who were employed before the institution of the Artel." The committee further complain that the inspection of goods commences at eleven and closes at two, which they think a somewhat absurd indulgence of Russian bureaucracy. That powerful caste—for the official class has a tendency to become such—is, of course, directly interested in maintaining the troublesome system by which "the declarations required for the formalities of clearing goods pass through twenty-nine different hands."

But impartial critics must admit that, while stating nothing untrue, the Odessa merchants have not been careful to relieve their picture, and that they employ the very dark coloring of their foreground to show up the remedial measures which, with the natural dependence of people living under a despotic and protective system, they hope for from the Tsar. Such tactics are natural. When Marshal MacMahon was Governor-general of Algeria, a disastrous earthquake occurred, by which hundreds of houses were destroyed, and many people impoverished. I shall never forget the scene, nor the spectacle of the emigrants crowding round his excellency, and declaring that if the emperor did not rebuild their houses, they would return to France. In like manner these *enfants d'état* of Russia want the Tsar to make Odessa a manufacturing centre, in spite of the facts that it is bounded on one side by the Euxine, that fuel is scarce, and that water must be paid for. Very characteristic of the evils of Russian Government is their proposal to exempt manufactures from all taxation, and their belief that the appointment of a viceroy instead of a governor-general "would be the best guaranty for the effectual carrying-out of the measures they have suggested." They want the State to help them to wash wool, and to make dépôts for colonial goods, regardless of the fact that the proprietor of the only wool-washing establishment in Odessa lately hanged himself, a suicide which was followed by that of the principal importer of colonial goods.

But perhaps England has most direct interest in the statements which have reference to the export of wheat. From a thoughtless glance at the figures, held up by the Odessa merchants, it might be supposed that our supply from Russia had in seven years fallen off by more than one-half, from 44 per cent. in 1867, to 21 per cent. in 1873. But this is not so. To say nothing of the increase from Sebastopol and Königsberg, the export of cereals from Odessa in 1867 amounted to 2,674,978 quarters, and to 2,648,000 quarters in 1873; while the value of the export in the latter year was greater by 15,200,169 rubles than in 1867. In 1874 there was an increase in quantity as well as value; and while we learn from these facts that the Russian supply is not declining, we can not escape the conviction forced upon us by the table of figures given above, that Russian agriculture is stationary in comparison with the boundless and successful activity of the United States.

In all this there is much that may be amended with advantage; but Russia is not a fertile country. We hear of it as a great corn-exporting land, and are apt to compare it, as a whole, in fertility with such rich soils as those of the Danubian provinces, or the alluvial valleys of British India and of the United States. In this important matter it is hardly possible to make a greater error. The present writer has visited Russia twice, in north and south, has passed leisurely through the length and, to a great extent, the breadth of the European Empire, and has also seen something of the Asiatic dominions of Russia. In these travels no fact is more constantly impressed upon the mind than the unequaled poverty of its soil. From the frontier of Russia west of Warsaw to St. Petersburg, and from the capital, through Moscow and Nijni, to Astrakhan, is a journey of about three thousand miles. The constant feature of that route is white sand, the worst and most hopeless, thankless soil for cultivation. There is no natural fertility; and this is exhibited by the surest proofs. There are none but stunted trees other than the pine and fir, and the landscape is therefore without a charm which is present in every English county. It may well be doubted whether the scrubby wastes of the Crimea would repay the cost of cultivation, if that were attempted; but there can be no question that, taking the Empire from north to south, and east to west, Russia is, and will remain, the poorest country in Europe. There are rich lands in Russia in the south-west; but the existence of these, to which the Emperor Nicholas would gladly have added the territory now known as Roumania, does not neutralize the fact that, for the most part, the Empire consists of plains of white sand, which, if Central Russia were rainless as Central and Southern Persia, would be arid and irreclaimable desert, because there are no mountains in which water might be stored for irrigation. It is noteworthy, also, that the recent conquests of Russia in Asia have been of the same quality, and, so far from adding to the wealth of the Empire, are probably burdensome to the revenue. Except where Persian territory borders upon the Caspian in its southern extremity, Russia is sole owner of the shores of that sea; but there is hardly a mile of her large frontage upon the Caspian which for agricultural purposes is worth the cost of occupation.

These facts augment the anxieties of her neighbors. Not only on the Pruth, but east of the Black Sea, where her Georgian and Persian conquests border upon the Shah's province of Azerbaijan, and again east of the Caspian, where the Attrek marks her off from the Persian Province of Astrabad,

Russia looks upon territory of great natural fertility which is not her own. And in her approach to the northern borders of India she occupies a position wherein this contrast of her own poverty with her neighbor's wealth is even more remarkable.

In spite, however, of the terrible weight of her increasing debt and unproductive expenditure, her people appear to be cheaply governed, if we compare them with other populations of Europe. But as they are poorer than any other people of that continent, the comparison would be unfair. It would be a very nice question to decide how far they have been enabled to support their burdens by the largely unproductive expenditure upon railways and other public works, the cost of which has been chiefly provided for by English capital. The revenue gathered from a population which approaches (including the Asiatic dominions of Russia) 90,000,000, does not amount to £77,000,000 — much less than £1 per head. Great as is the cost of the Russian army —£23,716,000 in 1874—they "drank themselves out of it" with the exhibition of a surplus; for this people who, in company with all their Northern neighbors to the extremity of Ireland, are among the most drunken in Europe, contributed £27,609,000 in 1874 to the revenue by means of excise duties on spirits and other intoxicating drinks. By this means, and by the poll-tax, nearly three-fifths of the revenue are provided, the poll-tax yielding in the same year no less than 122,000,000 rubles. To what extent Russian ability in the matter of taxation has been assisted by the annual expenditure of £12,000,000 to £15,000,000 of borrowed money, I shall not attempt to determine. But it is clear that Russia has borrowed about £70,000,000 for the construction of railways, and I can not accept the argument of the *Economist* that this great sum "is at least no more than can be afforded, even if the railways are directly and indirectly unprofitable, because the interest of these loans is charged in the accounts, and there is still a balance of revenue and expenditure, or even a small surplus." To uphold this proposition, it would be necessary to prove that Russia can maintain this equilibrium when the annual expenditure of £15,000,000 of borrowed money is discontinued; and, from all that I have lately seen of Russia, I have no confidence in the statement that this outlay, which now produces an income of only £2,132,000, will be remunerative. Of course, I do not deny that railways are necessary to the existence of the Russian Empire.

The Government of Russia rewards distinguished citizens and successful traders who are loyal and respected, by making them free from all taxation. There are probably four or five thousand of these privileged untaxed citizens in Moscow, and it is not ordained that, paying nothing, they shall have no voice in the general expenditure. Quite the contrary. Owners of a hundred arpents of land, which is the qualification for one who has the legal privileges of a "proprietor," elect in great part the provincial assemblies, which elect the provincial judges; and perhaps it would be impossible for any system to be more strongly marked with injustice than one in which all those most able to pay are exempt from taxation, and have a powerful voice in the election of judges who can not afford to disregard the claims of important constituents because their tenure of the judicial office is only for three years, at the expiration of which they must, if they desire to continue their functions, again submit their candidature to the provincial assemblies. It should, however, be said that these provincial judges can not sentence a prisoner to more than one year's confinement, and can not deal with civil cases in which the amount claimed is over five hundred rubles.

CHAPTER VII.

The Delta of the Volga. — Persian Passengers. — The *Constantine.* — Petrovsk. — Derbent. — "Le Feu Éternel." — Persian Merchandise. — Persian Clothing. — A Colored Deck-load. — Russian Trio of Spirits. — "Un Knut Russe." — Baku. — "Dominique." — Dust of Baku. — The Khan of Baku. — The Maiden's Tower. — Russian Naval Station. — Petrolia in Asia. — Baku Oil-carts. — The Petroleum Wells. — Kalafy Company. — Fire-worship. — Parsees and Persians. — The Indian Priest. — The Surakhani Temple. — Manufacture of Petroleum.

WE quitted the line of our travels at Astrakhan for this digression into the general affairs of Russia. The delta of one great river is very much like that of another, and there are no peculiar features about the delta of the Volga. For fourteen hours, the long barge in which we sat, in company with nearly a hundred passengers (mostly Persians, many from the provinces of Old Persia, which have long been Russian, and a few from the dominions of the Shah), was tugged by a small steamboat from Astrakhan to the steamship *Constantine*, which was moored in the shallow waters of the Caspian. We were along-side about two in the morning of the last day of September. There was a dreadful pell-mell: the Persian passengers being anxious to secure the most sheltered places on the deck for their bales of pillows and carpets, their caged canaries and pipe-cases. Bags and bundles were hastily lifted from the barge, and descended like a shower upon the decks of the *Constantine;* and in the cabins of the first-class the pressure of Armenians of doubtful cleanliness was so great, that we had difficulty in obtaining attention. When at last our cabin was lighted, there was, of course, no bedding, and, to our horror, the walls and roof were covered with crawling creatures of small and suspicious form. They vanished at the candle-light; and observing the preference of these insects for darkness, the sleep we had upon the *Constantine* was consequently accomplished by illumination of our cabin.

The *Constantine* is not a Russian-built ship; she, like all the vessels of the same line, came from Great Britain in pieces, and was put together upon the shores of the Caspian. After steaming about fifty miles from her moorings near the entrance to the Volga, the *Constantine* lay to in twenty-four feet of water, on account of a strong east wind, which in the deeper sea would have caused the ship to roll so as to jeopardize the piles of Persian baggage upon the main-deck. The carpets and rich silks would certainly have been soaked with the very salt water of the Caspian. In two days we reached the harbor of Petrovsk, a straggling town upon the edge of a mountainous country, from which there is a good road to Tiflis; and at the next station we could see the high walls of Derbent, as we anchored beneath them in moonlight. This is a fortress which Peter the Great wrested from Persia in 1722.

When travelers are told in Russian, French, and German that on their way down the Caspian Sea it is absolutely necessary, for their information and advantage, that they should stay at Baku and see the "everlasting fire," they are naturally inclined to yield to this concurrence of advice. So it happened that when the *Constantine* rounded the promontory on which Baku stands, and, facing suddenly northward, approached the long range of bare, brown hills which shelter this chief town and port of the Caspian from the coldest winds, we were prepared to make Baku our home for a week at least.

I am sorry I am not a painter, and can not render in colors the aspect of the vessel we were about to leave. What an Oriental picture the after-deck would have made! There was not a foot of space which was not covered with Persian carpets. The deck had been quartered out among themselves, with fair regard to the balance of power, by the Persian traders returning from Nijni; and in groups of three or four they lay intrenched beneath their gorgeously colored saddle-bags and bundles, stuffed with rich shawls, with finely worked saddle-cloths, and with silks of most beautiful colors. The barricades between each group were sometimes four or five feet in height, and there were many curious boxes and cages containing canaries, whose yellow plumage and sweet song are much esteemed both at Baku and in Teheran. There was not a man among them who did not wear a fine turquois set in a leaden ring, though all were third-class passengers; not one without the tall hat of black fur or felt, or without robes of those soft colors which the Western world of fashion has but lately learned to love. They were the same Persians—at least in manners and appearance—as those whose acquaintance we all made years and years ago in "The Arabian Nights' Entertainments." A patriarch, with nails and beard dyed red with khenna, stood blowing out his water-pipe—the Persians call it "kalian"—in preparation for the shore. Three young men sat near us in outer robes of black, which, like the covering of some tropical insect, heightened the effect of the bright coloring of their bodies, which were covered with tunics of red, green, and purple, decorated with silver and gold. They were on a coverlet of red silk, quilted upon a thick lining of cotton wool, and behind each man lay a richly colored pillow. The three were pecking, like fowls in a yard, but with their fingers, at the half of a water-melon, the inside of which had been slashed into pieces with a knife. In another "encampment," one who might, as he wore the green turban, be a descendant of the Prophet of Islam, was reading to the others from the Persian version of "Joseph and Potiphar's wife." In the Persian, the encounter of virtuous Joseph with the amorous Zulaikha is worked up into a tale of infidelity, passion, and revenge, and, for obvious reasons, is very much in vogue in Persia—as popular as a book can be in a country where publication in finely written manuscript is still common, and where there is virtually but one book—the Koran.

The passage from Astrakhan has been a very rough one; and we may add, that all Byron has said of the fate of the traveler in the "Euxine" might be told with equal truth of the nauseous swell of the Caspian. We ventured, as members of Mr. Plimsoll's committees, to ask the captain why he allowed his main-deck to be so loaded and encumbered that the sailors could only pass to the wheel by walking upon the bulwarks of the vessel. "Ah," he replied, "these Persian people won't give up their baggage. They would cry if I sent it down into the hold. They think every body is going to rob them, and that nothing out of sight is safe. As a fact, I believe they do rob each other whenever they get an opportunity. They would rather risk having their carpets and things washed with sea-water on deck than put them safe in the hold." Certainly our fellow-passengers were foolish as to their baggage; but as to themselves, almost any corner of the open deck was better than to endure the vile atmosphere of the cabins, where the smells of a Russian dram-shop and of an unventilated Spanish prison seemed to be mingled in almost suffocating odor. Early in the voyage we had paid the penalty of opening our cabin window, in having our bedding soaked by a huge wave; and, to the indignation of the steward, the waters from our window had passed beneath our door into public view. There was the alternative of the deck-saloon, where no one would suffer a window to be open; where every body smoked tobacco, and spit in every direction except that of the neglected spittoon; where there was suspended a tinseled image of St. Constantine, patron saint of our vessel, whose fixed eyes stared upon the invariable Russian trio of bottles, containing spirits, brown, green, and white, all ardent and intoxicating. Both captain and passengers seemed much more devoted to the spirits than to the saint. The presence of English names upon every part of the ship betrayed the backwardness of mechanical skill in Russia—a country which seems to be full of kindly, good-natured people, steeped, for the most part, above the ears in superstition, but loyal to their Church and Tsar to a degree almost fanatical, and quite beyond comparison with the sentiments of the less simple-minded people of Western Europe.

"Voilà un knut Russe, monsieur," laughed a Russian officer in my car. We were approaching the wooden quay, where the police of Baku were thrusting the crowd of too urgent porters back from the gangway, and threatening them with short but terrible whips, a representation in miniature of the "knout," of which we read in childhood with so much horror at the barbarity of Russian punishments. The porters, some with huge pads on the back of the neck, others carrying cords in their hands, with which to balance or secure their loads, were a body of strong men, twenty or thirty, at least, whose bare limbs of every shade, from the ebony of Africa to the copper of Southern Persia, and the redder tinge of native Baku, protruded from rags which seemed to have neither shape nor fastening. The Baku policemen are a most peculiar institution. They wear a Circassian costume, with huge muff-shaped hats of white or black sheep-skin; and, besides their lash, carry a long sword and a dagger. One must, however reluctantly, admit that something more than the "Move on" or "Stand back, can't you?" of our own Policeman X is needed to maintain order among Baku boatmen and porters. The former have a very savage appearance, which indeed is common to the boatmen of the Caspian. Waving aloft their spade-shaped oars, propellers as primitive as those of any Sandwich Islanders, they invoke with smiles and shouts, rising to screams and shrieks, if their overtures do not receive attention, the descent of passengers into their boats; and the porters, who unite the powers of the camel to the pertinacious appetite — for baggage — of hungry jackals, are not easy to manage. We were about to engage three, when one seized upon our trunks, and, piling two together upon a high seat, passed a cord round the load, and with a face beaming with satisfaction at the prospect of a good job, bent almost double, and took the pile, like the howdah of an elephant, upon his back. Along the wooden jetty he led us to the street, and delivered his burden to the turbaned driver of one of several two-horsed carriages, better and handsomer than any which stand for hire in London, or in Paris, or St. Petersburg. These carriages were all open barouches, clean and bright, as things may be where there is no rain or mud for many months. In Baku, when, as often happens, these carriages are drawn by white or gray horses, the manes and tails are dyed pink, after the Persian manner.

When a stranger—a European—arrives in Baku, nobody seems to have any doubt as to his destination. In the first place, he, with all his luggage, must desire to go to "Dominique." If a European landed at Baku and said nothing, he would be taken to Dominique. No one ever alludes to "the Hôtel d'Italie," though that is synonymous with Dominique, who is, in fact, the landlord of that hotel. Along the quays, past the baths floating in the clear, bitter-salt sea, through the dusty place, we drove to Dominique, where, after surmounting the ground-floor, occupied with casks and stores, by a lengthy flight of wooden stairs, we were shown into rooms with floors thickly sanded by the sea-breeze, each "furnished" with a bare bedstead and a chair. At our request, Dominique slouched in, a man with a cigar in his mouth and ear-rings in his ears, spitting now and then as he approached—a man with the appearance of a Levantine sailor who had once been an Italian of Leghorn or Genoa. Dominique has none of the deferential manner of the average hotel-keeper. No fear of rivals haunts his mind. He is Dominique; and if any one comes to Baku with sufficient money in his pocket, a room in Dominique's house is his by a sort of right which Dominique does not question, but to the exercise of which he seems profoundly indifferent. The rooms are sandy, but so is all Baku, except where the streets are spread with a mixture of water and the dregs of petroleum; and if bedding is required, Dominique keeps a little in store for eccentrics from Western Europe, and will produce a scanty supply of linen for a consideration in the bill.

Dominique is a quaint, pleasant fellow, and, from the spacious balcony, points out, between puffs of his cigar, the chief objects of interest in Baku. Peter the Great, he says, built that strong wall which surrounds the old town when he had captured Baku from the Persians. But Russia, he adds, lost it again; and it was not till the beginning of the present century that Baku became a part of the Russian Empire. He directs our eyes to the sombre, solid building, placed in a station of command where the town rises highest—the old palace of the Khans of Baku—now used as a military store-house; a building, in its fluted arches and in other features thoroughly Persian or Moorish, but, though very similar in style, infinitely inferior in design and workmanship to the palaces of the Deys of Tunis and Algiers. A merchant (an Armenian) joins us—there is much freedom and fellowship at Dominique's—and kindly volunteers a recital of the legend concerning "The Maiden's Tower," the most prominent building in Baku, a huge cylinder of masonry rising in the lower part of the town, which is somehow connected at present with the water supply of the place. The khan, it appears, had a daughter—lovely, of course, like all the ladies of all the legends—whose will he desired to coerce—matrimonially, we need not say. The daughter, whose inclinations were opposed to her father's commands, ascended the tower, which the khan was then building, and soon afterward her lifeless body was carried from its foot.

Dominique ejaculates the Italian equivalent for "rubbish!" and points, as more worthy of attention, to the farther side of the bay, to the white buildings of the Russian naval station, in front of which there are two steam corvettes lying at anchor. One looks with interest on these ships of war, imprisoned on this isolated, land-locked sea, destined never to meet with their equals or superiors under other flags, for Persia has no ships of war—can not, must not, by treaty with Russia, have them in the Caspian; and where is the possible enemy who will bring ships of war in pieces from the Tigris or the Black Sea to be put together in a hostile country? They have, however, a useful function in preventing piracy in the Caspian, and at no very distant day these vessels may be called upon to cover and protect with the fire of their guns the landing of Russian troops upon the Persian shore. The harbor of Baku is not only the best in the Caspian, but it is the only capacious, sheltered port in that sea.

At Baku rain rarely falls; the sky is generally cloudless; but if a man has the fixed popular belief that his life will endure until he has eaten the proverbial "peck of dirt," and no longer, then he will only expedite his end by coming to Baku. It is more dusty than San Francisco or Odessa, the dustiest towns of Europe and America, and one must be careful, or he may swallow "the peck" in a month.

Baku is part of Old Persia. Nine-tenths of the population are descendants of subjects of Shah Abbas. The manners and customs of the bazaars are thoroughly Persian. The old men, in striking contrast to their high hats of black fur, dye their beards bright-red with khenna. Very few women of the superior class are to be seen. We arrived in company with many men who had been absent from their homes in Baku for months, trading at Nijni-Novgorod, but no wives met this "husbands' boat" from Europe. The Persian women in Russian Baku rarely leave their homes. There were three or four shuffling along the quay with slippered feet, closely covered from the sight of man, and groups of washerwomen labored in the ripples of the shore, who were careless as to any other exposure, so that they could clap something over their faces at sight of a passing stranger.

There is not a tree or shrub to be seen upon the arid hills and stony steppe, and the odor of naphtha is never out of the nostrils. Baku has for ages past been celebrated in the Eastern World for that which every one in the town who can speak three words of French calls *Le Feu Éternel;* and in these days — when her native population is sprinkled with sharp Armenians who would rake profits out of this or any other fire, and some streets are bordered with houses of European style — Baku presents the aspect of an Oriental town, conscious of coming greatness and higher civilization under a different system, when her subterranean riches shall have become better known, and be more largely brought forth. Baku has "struck oil;" and before many years are past, the world will hear much more of this obscure town — this Petrolia in Asia. The engines of the *Constantine* — the ship in which his imperial majesty the Shah traversed the Caspian — were driven with petroleum. Coal, the captain told us, costs eighteen and a half rubles per hour, while petroleum costs only one and a half rubles — a reduction from fifty shillings to four shillings. In three years Baku will be united by railway with Tiflis and the Black Sea, and then probably all the Russian steamships on the Euxine will be supplied with the same disagreeable but inexpensive fuel. The machinery for combustion reminded us of one of those pretty contrivances for blowing the spray of liquid scent about a drawing-room. As the coarse residue of the petroleum—for it is the dregs or sediment only which is burned—pours in a thin, muddy stream from a tap near the door of each furnace, a jet of steam, generated by a coal fire, blows it into spray, and thus it is consumed, with an even heat, throughout the furnaces of the engines.

All day long petroleum rolls into Baku in carts of the most curious pattern imaginable. A Neapolitan single-horse, two-wheeled carriage for fifteen people is unique, but it is commonplace in comparison with an oil-cart of Baku. Few men would have the courage to import a Baku oil-cart, and drive it, even for a very high wager, through Regent Street or Pall Mall. Where is the man who would dare to pose himself there, perched and caged in a little railed cart, big enough to hold one barrel of petroleum, and lifted so high on wheels seven feet in diameter, that another huge tub can be slung beneath the axle, the whole thing being painted with all the colors of the rainbow, and creaking loudly as it is drawn by a diminutive horse, the back of which is hardly up to a level with the axle? Yet the *exploiteurs* say that already they pay collectively not much less than one hundred thousand pounds a year for the cartage of oil in carriages of this sort. They were eager to show us the oil-wells, and hopeful, as they are much in want of capital, that we should send them some meek and moneyed Englishmen. We set out to visit the "everlasting fire" and these mines of liquid wealth, in a dust-storm, with horses so active that we might suppose they too were fed with naphtha.

In the outskirts of Baku, where we saw a scorpion for the first time, the country is all dust and desolation—a desert in which every one with an original turn of mind may make his own road. For two or three miles along the shore of the bay, the many buildings in which the petroleum is refined by itself as fuel pour forth dense smoke, and at eight miles from the town are the springs. The average depth at which the oil is touched seems to be about a hundred and fifty feet. The wells are, for the most part, nine inches to a foot in diameter. From the first well we visited, a small steam-engine, with most primitive gear, was lifting about four hundred and fifty thousand pounds' weight of petroleum in a day. The oil is of greenish color, and, as it is drawn from the earth, is emptied into a square pit dug in the surface soil, from whence men take it in buckets and pour it into skins or barrels, the charge at the wells being at the rate of one and a half pence per fifty pounds' weight of oil. At the works of the Kalafy Company, an Armenian concern, when their well was first opened, the petroleum burst up in a fountain nine feet in diameter, a part of which rose forty feet in the air. At all the wells the oil is now raised in circular tubes about nine feet long and as many inches in diameter, with a valve at the lower end which opens on touching the ground, and closes when the tube is lifted. This cylinder is lowered empty, and raised again when filled with oil, in less than two minutes. A man pulls the full tube toward a tub, into which its contents are poured, and through a hole in the tub the oil runs into the pit from which the skins and barrels are filled. We were assured that the Baku petroleum is of better quality than the oil of Pennsylvania, and that it is less dangerous, because its flashing point of temperature is from thirty to forty degrees higher than that of the American product.

It is certainly very wonderful, upon a sandy plain, with not a tree nor a blade of grass in sight, to look upon a reservoir of liquid fuel thus drawn from this stony soil; yet to our thinking there was a spectacle much more curious, about twelve versts farther from Baku, when we came to one of the oldest altars in the world, erect and flaming with its natural burnt-offering to this day. Surakhani is an ancient seat of probably one of the most ancient forms of worship. For unnumbered ages, the gas which is generated by this subterranean store of oil, identical with that which caused the Regent's Park explosion, has escaped through long-established and inaccessible fissures in the limestone crag of which the hills in the neighborhood are composed, and the fire of this gas has lighted the prayers of generations of priests, as it blazed and flared away to the heavens.

Fire-worship in Persia, of which until the eighteenth century Baku formed a part, is older than history. When we have passed about a thousand miles farther south, between Ispahan and Shiraz, we shall come, at the ruins of Istakr and Persepolis, upon authentic traces of the reigns of Cyrus, of Darius, of Xerxes and Artaxerxes. But the fire-worshiping period is older than Cyrus. We do not know when the remnant of the fire-worshipers was driven southward, nor precisely how far we are justified in assuming the Parsees of India to be their descendants. But we find the Parsees using as sacred books the "Zendavesta" of the Zoroastrians; and we know that at an obscure town between Kurrachee and Bombay there is a Parsee temple, the fire in which is regarded with peculiar reverence as the "oldest" fire in the world, the tradition among the Parsees being that this fire was originally brought in charred wood from a temple in Persia, and that it has never since been suffered to expire. It may be that the fire in this temple has been unextinguished for a period extending from before the time of Cyrus. "It is," says Professor Westergaard, "to this ante-Achæmenian period that I refer Zoroaster; and I find it therefore quite natural that he could have belonged to a remote and uncertain antiquity so early as in the fourth[*] century before Christ, when his name is first mentioned by Greek authors. The main accounts of his lore date,

---

[*] This may be a misprint in the preface to Westergaard's translation of the "Zendavesta."

I think, from the period which they intimate; and their language, two cognate dialects of very distinctive character, possesses a greater store of grammatical forms, and has an appearance less worn, and consequently older, than the old Persian, in the descriptions of Darius, the nearest cognate branch."

For long, long ages, the worship of these flaming issues of petroleum gas at Surakhani has been maintained by delegations of priests from India, who have died and been buried upon the spot, to be succeeded by other devotees from the same country. It would, of course, be possible to extinguish the blaze, if one were to choke the fissures; and the people about the place say that sometimes, when the wind rises to a hurricane, the fire is actually put out. The gas, however, can then at once be relighted with a match. We saw this done, not, as of yore, with mysterious incantations, and the terrified awe of superstitious worshipers, but—to what base uses may gods come!—in order to burn lime for Baku, and to purify the oil raised from the natural reservoir in which the gas is generated. We thought that never, perhaps, had we seen a man more to be pitied than the "poor Indian," who is the successor of a long line of religiously appointed guardians of this once wholly sacred spot. There the light of this lamp of Nature's making flared on its formerly hallowed altar-place, maid of all work to half a dozen degenerate Persians, now subjects of the Christian Tsar, who thought of nothing but making lime, and of warming their messes of sour milk and unleavened bread. In another place the gas was conducted from the surface of the ground into a furnace, where it flamed beneath vats of petroleum, in the process of refining the native oil by distillation. Surely there never was such a pitiful *reductio ad absurdum!* Before us stood the priest of a very venerable religion, which has always seemed to me to be one of the most noble and natural for a primitive people. There he stood, ready for half a ruble to perform the rites of his worn-out worship, and there also was the object of his life-long devotion set to work as economic firing. Such a rude encounter of the old and the new, of ideality and utility, of the practical and the visionary, was surely never seen elsewhere.

I suspect that, as a Yankee would say, the worship of *Le Feu Éternel* at Baku is almost played out. Of course, the enlightened Parsee worships God in the fire, and not the fire as God; his theory being, I believe, that the God of Nature can not be truly adored unless the worshiper has his attention fixed upon one of the elements—fire, air, earth, or water. Failing fire, a Parsee may pray in open air, or beside a tree or stream. The "poor Indian" of Surakhani complains bitterly that he is robbed of every thing by the Persian workmen, of whom probably not one now sees any mystery at all in these flames issuing from the earth. They are every day engaged with an inflammable material, and not a few have made perilous acquaintance with the explosive properties of the gas which is emitted from petroleum; yet but few accidents seem to occur.

CHAPTER VIII.

Bathing in the Caspian.—The Way to Europe.—A Tarantas.—The Baku Club. — Mihailovski Gardens. — Leaving Baku. — Lenkoran.—Astara.—Petroleum on Deck.—Enzelli.—Persian Boatmen.—Mr. Consul Churchill, C.B. — Enzelli Custom-house. — Sadr Azem's Konak. — The Shah's Yacht.—Lake of Enzelli.—Peri-bazaar.—Province of Ghilan.—Resht.— Bazaar and "Green." — Women of Persia. — Their Street Costume. — Shopping in Bazaar.—Riding in Persia.—Chapar and Caravan.—Kerjavas.—A Takht-i-rawan.—Leaving Resht.—Charvodars and Gholams.— Lucky and Unlucky Days.—Whips of Iron.—" Ul-lāh."—The Bell Mule. —Houssein Mounted.—The First Station.—Our Camp Kitchen.—A Mud Hovel.

WE had bathed every day in the buoyant waters of the Caspian; we had sailed two miles across the natural harbor to visit the Russian naval and military station, which will become still more important as a base for operations in Central Asia when the railway from the Caucasus is complete. We had become known to many of the Armenian exporters of petroleum, who continually implored us to send them a few British capitalists (as if such people were to be picked up in London for the trouble of stooping), so that their works may be extended, and the oil produced more cheaply. We had made acquaintance with a "tarantas," and with the members of the Baku Club, before we prepared to quit that rising town.

If we had decided to return to Europe by Tiflis, we must have taken a tarantas, or, rather, we must have purchased a tarantas; for no one lends or lets a suitable carriage for that five days' journey, over a road which is impassable for carriages of lighter construction than a tarantas. Where the return journey would cost more than the value of any vehicle in the country, hiring is of course out of the question. A tarantas is simply a stronge carriage, securely fixed upon half a dozen horizontal fir poles, the pliancy of which (and, being small trees, they are not very elastic) stands for springs. The wheels are small, and very strong. To the carriage, sometimes three and sometimes seven horses are attached, according to the view which the postmaster at each station takes of the pocket of the traveler, of the engagements of his horses, and the condition of the road. The body of the tarantas is quite unfurnished. Some travelers from Baku make a seat by plaiting rope across from side to side of the carriage; but it is more usual to make a seat of some box or bundle, inasmuch as the traveler is expected to carry his luggage inside. A tarantas costs about fourteen pounds sterling, and at the end of the journey will probably be found unsalable. In Dominique's yard, at Baku, there was a tarantas in which a British consul in Persia had traveled with his wife from Tiflis. Dominique had been told to sell it for the owner; but there it stood, rotting away with years of waiting for a purchaser.

As seen by light of the oil of petroleum, the Baku Club is a pleasant institution. There is a sea-side garden at Baku in which a few shrubs are dragged through life by copious watering applied daily. They look dusty and unnatural by daylight, and so do the gayly-painted wooden pavilions; but at night, when the rippling sea can be heard between the pieces of music, the club meets in the highest of these pavilions. The garden is then full of people, and there is no stint of the light of petroleum oil. None may mount the steps of this pavilion who are not of the club. The pavilion is open to the garden, and is set out with refreshment and card tables. In this place the Russian officers of the station and the wealthier of the towns-folk of Baku, together with their wives and families, appear to spend the happiest hours of their existence.

The aggregated babble of their talk, a good deal of it real "coffee-house babble," and the strains of the music from this Mihailovski Garden, fell not unpleasantly on our ears, as we embarked late one evening for the realms of the Shah. There was a strong wind blowing; and the captain, who could speak German after the manner of a Finlander, said that if it continued, which he did not think likely, we could not be landed in Persia, which has no port or harbor on the Caspian. Any body may take a ticket entitling the bearer to travel by the boats of the Caucasus and Mercury Company (which is heavily subsidized by the Tsar's Government) from Baku to the Persian town of Enzelli, the usual landing-place for Teheran; but if, when the vessel arrives in the roadstead of Enzelli, the wind is blowing strongly from the north-north-east, there will be a surf rolling in which not all the power of Shah or Tsar can enable passengers to land. Who that has read the "Diary" of the Persian "Shadow of God" can forget the pathetic record of imperial and grand-vizierial sufferings when the *Constantine* rolled so fearfully off Enzelli that her yards nearly touched the waves, and the Shah, with the hand of apprehension placed on the stomach of discomposure, feared he would never again touch the soil of his own Persia!

The scenery in the south of the Caspian is magnificent. At Lenkoran—a famous place for tiger-hunting—the sea is bordered with high mountains. We see the last of Russian territory at Astara, where a narrow river of that name limits for the present the conquests of Russia from Persia. We had four immense hogsheads of petroleum on board for Astara, but our steam-vessel rolled so heavily that it was impossible to land them. They must be carried to Astrabad and back, more than five hundred miles; and possibly upon the return journey there would be the same difficulty, and the enormous tubs must then be returned to Baku. On personal grounds, we were sorry not to be rid of this part of the cargo. The hogsheads were lashed to the funnel upon the main deck, and the Persian passengers used them frequently as a support for their kalians, from which the lighted charcoal rolled sometimes on to the deck. It seemed to me that we lived in momentary danger of an explosion, which would have destroyed the vessel, with all its passengers and cargo.

Possibly it was for a fair wind that the Persians were praying at sunset upon the last evening of our voyage. There was hardly a man of the score or so upon the after-deck who had not, either in a bag hung round his neck or hidden in the top of his tall, brimless hat, a circular lump of sacred sun-baked clay, about the size of four half-crowns, taken from somewhere near the tomb of Houssein at Kerbela, in Turkish Arabia. When the supplicant knelt in prayer, this was laid before him upon the deck, so that he could press his forehead upon the holy clay; and an elderly man who was not possessed of such precious fruit of that pilgrimage, which ranks next in importance to a religious journey to Mecca, borrowed the treasure from one of the company, and performed his devotions, with his face toward Mecca, while the previous supplicant was engaged in preparing the sugary tea-water, the "chiŭ," which rich and poor in Persia seem to prefer to any other drink.

Is it owing to their vegetable diet that Eastern people appear so rarely to suffer from sea-sickness? Those who have endured such sufferings, for which the Caspian offers much opportunity, will have passed Astara, and approached the shore at Enzelli with gladness. If the sea is moderate, as it most fortunately was when we arrived, they will not be sorry, even though there comes through the cabin windows a Babel of screams and shouts, varied with the cracking of wood, as the surf-boats are dashed by the waves against each other and upon the side of the steamship. While the bundles of reeds tied upon the bulwarks of the frail craft are crunching together, with what skill the half-naked rowers avoid tumbling into the sea, or suffering injury to their hands and arms! "Pedder sec!" ("Son of a dog!") shrieked a melon-seller with nothing upon him except a skull-cap of many colors, a beard dyed bright red, and a tattered pair of blue-cotton trousers. "Son of a dog!" he raved, as he saw his chance of early approach to the gangway diminished by the stealthy advance of an ingenious rival. To impute that a Persian's progenitor was canine rouses still more indignation than is evoked even when the average Briton is told that he may trace his pedigree to an ape; to say "Pedder sec!" to a son of Iran is as bad as calling a Frenchman "cochon," or a German "dummkopf." But the triumph of the melon-seller's enemy was momentary; a Russian sailor, leaning over the bulwarks of the steamboat, snatched the skull-cap from the head of the ingenious intruder and flung it into the sea, exposing the shorn pathway from forehead to neck, which is the mode of "hair-dressing" common throughout Persia.

In the terrific din caused by this exploit, there rose from another boat a tall Persian of melancholy aspect, with dark, dreamy eyes and handsome features, clad in a robe of sober green — a man with air and aspect very superior to those of the eight rowers before him. He had been looking long at us; he laid his hand twice on the front of his fur hat as he bowed in salutation, and then handed up a card, which I gladly saw was that of Mr. Henry A. Churchill (who won the C.B. for his share in the defense of Kars during the Crimean War, with Colonel Fenwick Williams and others), the British consul at Resht. I had written to the consul—ignorant that Mr. Churchill, whom I had met in Algiers during his residence there as consul-general, held the office, and he had kindly sent this man (who accompanied us as chief servant to Teheran) to guide us to Resht. Seeing me read the card, on which Mr. Churchill had written a recommendation of "Houssein, the bearer," the melancholy Persian placed his hand once more upon his head to indicate that he was Houssein, and at a sign from me he ordered our baggage to be lowered to the boat.

The oars of our rowers reminded us of "the eight of spades;" they pulled with short, sharp digs in the water as we moved slowly to the place where the Lake of Enzelli pours the muddy waters of the Peri-bazaar (I have adopted throughout the ordinary English spelling of this word) River into the Caspian. In front of the wooden building which serves as a custom-house at this northern gate of Persia, there is no landing-place; some ragged, and more than half-naked, boys laid a plank from the bundle of reeds which formed the gunwale of our boat to the shore, and we landed, following Houssein into the only two-storied house in the place, the first floor of which was neatly spread with mats of grass. There were a few colored tiles over the door-ways, but the whitewashed walls were as bare as the mud-cement of the exterior, and on the matting there was not an article of furniture.

We had fasted for many hours; and in that simple freemasonry of signs, familiar to all the world, I made known that on landing in Persia we wanted something to put in our mouths. Houssein had left us to attend to the baggage, and the bearded attendant seemed at once to understand and appreciate our wants. He hurried off, as I supposed, to bring some food, and soon re-appeared with a blue-glazed pitcher of water. The pitcher was pretty in design and coloring, but water was not quite all that we needed. It was not till we arrived at Resht that we discovered the full meaning of this watery provision; the house which we had supposed to be a Persian hotel, where we could call for any thing—the kababs of the bazaars, the cakes of Noureddin Hassan, or the sweetmeats of the harems—was indeed a villa, a "konak," belonging to the acting Sadr Azem, the Prime Minister of Persia, in which, by special favor, we were allowed to take shelter for half an hour from the sun while a boat was being prepared to carry us twelve miles across the Lake of Enzelli. It was the first suggestion of that which is almost universal throughout Persia. The traveler will have no difficulty in finding a bare room in the towns. At a palace the servants in charge will cheerfully, if he looks likely to give them a present, put apartments at his disposal, and the floors may, perhaps, be covered with matting; but for all other requirements he must depend upon himself or his own attendants.

The white awning and cushions of our boat gave promise of comfort. The Shah's steam yacht, also white, was moored close at hand, and soon we had rowed past her to enter the shallow lagoon or lake which lies between Enzelli and Resht. A pensive, slender lad, with features of exquisite form, took his place behind us at the helm. His flowing robe of light stuff, resembling cashmere, appeared hardly suited for his occupation, but he had evidently a skillful knowledge of the currents and shallows of this muddy lake, upon which the sun was glaring. The banks were hidden from us by tall reeds, their tops waving ten feet above the water; and rising behind this rustling fringe, we could see the highest trees of the rank, dense jungle, which is famous as the home of tigers, and of the huge water-fowl, which screamed and fluttered among the reeds as we passed. It was very slow work getting across the lake with oars shaped like a baker's "peel," and three hours had passed before we reached the oozy banks of the Peri-bazaar River. Then the spades were shipped, and a long rope, attached to the very top of the mast, was handed to the shore. The rowers landed, and disappeared among the reeds. On the muddy bank they harnessed themselves to the rope, which, descending to them from the mast, touched only the heads of the reeds as they moved swiftly along the river-side. The scene was as purely natural as if we had been exploring some country never before trodden by the foot of man. The brown stream was not more than sixty feet wide. The current seemed to be silenced by the weight of mud suspended in the water; the air was still and oppressive between the high walls of reeds. Sometimes, where, for a few yards, there were no reeds, we could see the heads of our crew, who were pushing their way through the grass of the jungle; and now and then there was a buzz, or a loud rattle among the reeds, and a gorgeous pheasant, or a wild turkey, or a long-legged stork sailed over our heads to the other side of the river. After being tugged in this way for an hour, we arrived at a landing-place, to which there was a stony foot-path leading from a large house partly in ruins. By the river-side there was a group of people, excited at the approach of our boat. This was Peri-bazaar, from whence we had to ride seven miles — is it not written in the Shah's Diary?—to Resht. We bought some of the only food to be obtained at Peri-bazaar, a few grapes, and about a foot square of the brown flabby bread of the country, in thickness and general appearance very like soaked leather. Our boxes were hoisted on to the backs of mules, and secured with cords of camel's hair neatly plaited; the melancholy Houssein then grandly waved us to a carriage which it appeared he had specially retained for our advantage.

We were told at Resht that this was the one and only carriage in the whole province of Ghilan, recently imported from Russia by a khan of high degree, who, it seems, was not above letting it out to Houssein for our use. It was, in fact, a superannuated Russian droschky of the meanest kind. We planted our feet with utmost firmness, and grasped the sides for safety as it moved off, uneasy as the waves of Enzelli.

But for the dignity of the thing, as the Irishman said of the bottomless sedan-chair, one of us would as soon have walked; but any exhibition of contempt might have been the death of the gloomy Houssein, so proud was he of this chariot. The admiration of the people of Peri-bazaar, who had probably not seen a wheeled conveyance since his Imperial Majesty the Shah rumbled that way in a carriage, was an insufficient consolation. As we rattled along, sometimes between rice-fields, from which the crop had been lately gathered, at others between thick groves, there was water always on both sides standing high in the ditches.

The province of Ghilan, of which Resht is the chief town, must be one of the most fertile areas in the world. From Enzelli to Peri-bazaar, and for miles beyond Resht, the country is a flat marsh, perennially manured with rank and rotting vegetation. Yet in places the richly green lane through which we approached Resht resembled parts of Devonshire. The verdure was so bright, the climate so agreeable, we might almost have fancied it to be a day of early autumn in England, save that at every turn we met some Persian, long-robed in blue, or yellow, or russet-brown, sometimes perched between the humps of a sententious camel, sometimes upon the hinder extremity of a very good-looking donkey, a most awakening object to one who was dreaming of distant England. Wherever there was a hole, it was filled with stagnant water, which the sun lifted in unwholesome vapors. The undrained approaches to Resht reeked with filth, and people were picking their way close by the walls of the houses and gardens, in order to avoid the abyss of muddy slush which awaited them in the centre. The day was hot, but our horses' hoofs were hidden in mud as we passed through the bazaar, in which there was hardly room for our miserable carriage amidst the crowd which pressed to see the strangers.

The way was so narrow that any one of the stall-keepers

on either side could have handed goods to us from his seat. But they themselves appeared far more attractive than their wares; than their gaudy horse-trappings of reddish leather, decorated with strips of carpets or pieces of bead-work, and hung with red and yellow tassels of silk or wool, and bells of silver or brass; their bowls of sour cream, their eggs (many of them colored red, a common practice in Persia), pomegranates, Russian candles, figs, and cotton prints, some of the last from Manchester, of those special patterns which are never to be met with in the home markets. They all squat upon their heels, in a position peculiar to the Persians—a posture which no man could assume whose joints had not been trained to it from childhood. From the bazaar we drove across a large open space, resembling the "green" of many an English village. It was dotted with trees, and boys were playing in costumes which made the sylvan scene, one extremely pretty and effective, appear to our eyes almost theatrical.

A few women are seen. We met one sitting astride on horseback, as all Eastern women ride. We believe them to be women because of their costume and size; but we can see no part of them, not even a hand or an eye. They are shrouded from the head to the knees in a cotton or silk sheet of dark blue or black; the "chudder," it is called, which passes over the head, and is held with the hands around and about the body. Over the "chudder" there is tied round the head a yard-long veil of white cotton or linen, in which, before the eyes, is a piece of open work about the size of a finger, which is their only lookout and ventilator. The veil passes into the "chudder" at the chin. Every woman before going out-of-doors puts on a pair of loose trousers, generally of the same stuff and color as the "chudder," and thus her outdoor seclusion and disguise are complete. Her husband could not recognize her in the street. In this costume, Mohammedan women grope their way about the towns of Persia. Their trousers are tightly bound about the ankles above their colored stockings, which are invariably of home manufacture; and slippers, with no covering for the heel, complete the unsightly, unwholesome apparel of these uncomfortable victims of the Persian reading of the Koran.

In the East the appearance of guests is, we may say, never the first announcement of their arrival. From the "green" of Resht, Houssein galloped off at a wild pace, and we were soon very kindly welcomed by Mr. Churchill, whom, as I have said, I had met in Algiers, when he was consul-general in that pleasant colony. He and Mrs. Churchill hospitably entertained us for a day while we were hurriedly preparing for our ride to Teheran. On the way to Persia, one learns, if ignorant before, that in traveling there one must be self-dependent for all but fruit and the plainest and coarsest of uncooked food; yet with the experience of Europe, and even of Palestine and Egypt, where dragomans abound, and of Algeria, with its Arab-French caravanserais, a traveler is slow to believe that this can really be the fact. The roughness of Russian travel, especially the absence of bedding, prepares one for worse in Persia, and at Resht the whole truth becomes evident. It is well to be forewarned and forearmed. We were fortunate in meeting, at any price, with camp bedsteads and bedding of English make, and into the dirt of the Resht bazaar we plunged to obtain other necessaries for the journey to Teheran. The noise of wooden hammers upon metal pots led us to the department where we had to purchase a whole *batterie de cuisine*. Intended for use over what is known in England as a gypsy fire, none of the Persian pots are provided with handles. The Persian smiths seem to have no faith in solder; perhaps they do not know how to prepare it. And all Persian pots are of copper; so that after buying what Houssein thought requisite, we left the saucepans to be tinned upon the inside—an operation which in all Persian households is renewed at intervals of about three weeks. Houssein and the servants of the Consulate kept off a curious crowd, who appeared to be deeply interested in watching our selection of innumerable yards of cotton for sheets and other purposes. Later in the evening, our servant brought in, with an air of triumph, a folding-table, which bore the name, roughly carved upon its surface, of an English officer of Royal Engineers, who had been traveling the previous year in Persia; and to Houssein, when we grew tired of shopping, we left the purchase of candlesticks and glasses, saddle-bags and bridles, and the necessary stores of food.

There is but one mode of traveling in the interior of Persia. Even from Resht to the capital, on the most frequented road in all the empire, no carriage can travel except with a sufficient number of men to lift it over places which are otherwise impassable. It was with the help of such bearers that the Shah was able to accompany his "carriage." Yet perhaps it would be more correct to say that there are two modes. The traveler may buy horses and mules; the average cost will be about ten pounds sterling for each animal. He will then have to provide pack-saddles as well as riding-saddles, and gholams, or grooms, to feed and load his horses and mules; or he may hire all the animals he requires from a muleteer, or "charvodar." In the latter case, the horses will not be so good-looking, but they will probably know the road, and be quite as safe in riding over rough paths which are sometimes dangerous. The charvodar and his gholams will be responsible for the stabling, feeding, and loading of the animals. The cost of a mule hired in this way, from Resht to Teheran, is about fifty krans, or two pounds English, for a ten days' march. It is usual to give the muleteers a present at the end of the journey if they have behaved well—a toman, about eight shillings, each. One may travel "chapar" or "caravan;" the latter being to the former as goods-train to express. In traveling "chapar," or, as the Anglo-Persians say, in "chaparing," saddle-horses are taken from one post-house or station ("menzil" is the Persian word), and galloped twelve, twenty, or sometimes five-and-twenty miles, to the next station. Those who travel with bedsteads and bedding and boxes can not travel "chapar." They, with their baggage-mules, must form a caravan, and march from station to station at a rate of about three miles an hour, which is as fast as mules can walk. Those, in fact, are described as riding "caravan" who travel at the pace of loaded mules.

For men and women who suffer from being in the saddle for so many hours, there is a choice between the "kerjava" and the "takht-i-rawan." The kerjava, in its best appearance, takes the form of two very small gypsy tents made of light bands of wood, the top bent circular, and covered with shawls or carpets. In each of these tents a man or woman sits after the kerjavas have been slung, like panniers, across the saddle of a strong mule. In the kerjava one must sit cross-legged, or with one's feet hanging out. The open side is sometimes turned to the tail of the mule, and the rider can not see where the animal is going. The kerjava may be suspended over a precipice, on the edge of which the feet of the mule have but dangerous hold; or by sudden collision with another mule—and this often happens,—one kerjava is thrown over the mule's back upon the other, and both fall heavily to the ground. Sometimes kerjavas have no roof, are simply strong panniers of wood, in which the riders (there must be two, or, if one, then an equivalent weight will be required in the second kerjava) are doubled up, their heads and feet only being visible, the body lost to sight in the kerjava, amidst a substratum of pillows and carpets. Although but one mule bears the burden, those who ride in kerjavas are very properly made to pay for two mules; and although two mules carry a takht-i-rawan, those who employ this, the superior form of carriage, pay for four mules. The takht-i-rawan is used by great ladies of the Shah's court, by the aged and infirm, and by the ladies of the foreign embassies. It is not a sedan-chair, because the bottom is usually quite flat, level with the shafts, and the occupant sits cross-legged, or lies down during the journey. But the shafts are like the four poles of a sedan-chair, and the two mules are harnessed in them—one between the two poles in front, the other, with its eyes close to the body of the carriage, between the two hinder poles. The takht-i-rawan is a carriage built of wood, and placed upon a strong frame-work, of which the two long poles, forming the four shafts, are the principal parts. The sides are generally paneled, in order to obtain strength without weight, and the roof of thin boards is covered with coarse cotton or canvas to keep out rain. There is usually a small square of glass in the side doors to give light when these are closed. One can rarely find a takht-i-rawan when such a carriage is wanted; they are usually built to order, and cost from six to ten pounds sterling. We were in a hurry to leave Resht, and not disposed to wait while a takht-i-rawan was being built. We were anxious to escape to the mountains, away from the deadly atmosphere, the feverish swamp in which the British consul at Resht is doomed to live.

On the second and last morning of our stay in Resht, we sat in Mr. Churchill's room, the whole side of which was open to the garden, transacting business with muleteers and sellers of articles of every description. We had little trouble in agreeing with the charvodar for horses and mules. He was a man about middle age, whose hair and mustache, naturally dark, were made the color of a raven's wing with a dye compounded of indigo with khenna. Like all Persians, he was shaved across the poll, the side hair being led in a curl behind the ear. He wore a red turban, wound around a buff skull-cap; his legs were bare to the knee, and his socks and sandal shoes bore marks of much travel. A green tunic of cotton left but little of his loose drawers of blue visible, and over all he wore a long garment of pale yellow, lined with red cotton, and bound about his waist with a scarlet sash. He was anxious to get back to Teheran, a distance from Resht of two hundred miles, and fortunately the day was not an unlucky one for setting out. It is of no use whatever to engage with Persian muleteers for commencing a journey on a day which they consider unlucky. They may fear to displease or disobey openly; they may consent, but they will be certain to find some means of delay. Once off, all days are alike to the charvodar, except that day of the month Mohurrem on which the death of Houssein is celebrated.

There is another rule which the charvodar always desires to establish. On the first day of a march, it takes a great deal of trouble and a strong will to get a caravan farther than two hours' ride, or eight miles, from the town. Time is not a costly consideration in Persia; and as for space, the meanest and poorest possess that great boon. It is better always to avoid Mondays and Fridays in arranging for a march.

Fortunately, the day we selected was Thursday, and there was no objection. We paid half the price of the hire of the horses and mules, and the charvodar departed, to prepare for setting out in the afternoon. It is usual for consuls' wives and for people of such quality in the East to have the shops brought to them; they lose a good deal, both in pocket and in amusement, by not visiting the bazaars, and certainly they have a more limited choice of goods. Persuaded not to visit the bazaar a second time, we had in this way to give audience to the "butcher, the baker, the candlestick-maker," and to receive their slaves, loaded with goods, from which, assisted by Houssein, who, however, could not speak a word of any language but Persian, we made very satisfactory selections.

At last every thing seemed ready, and the mules arrived, saddled and festooned with ropes, to be loaded for the first time. It is a work of great moment. Every thing must be nicely balanced; so much on one side, and about an equal weight on the other of the high, heavy pack-saddle, which the mule wears day and night, and which for weeks together is never removed, except during the very few minutes when the rude process of grooming is performed at the end of a day's march. The charvodar, whose waist was now encircled, not only by a sash, but also by a thong of leather wound twice round his body, ending in about a foot of iron chain, eyed every box and package, and with skillful hands adjusted the loads. The iron chain dangling from his waist is the ordinary whip of the Persian muleteer. It was worn bright with handling and with cruel application to the legs of his animals. The gholams, who were to accompany us, were also provided with thongs and chains of the same sort. The charvodar was engrossed with two of our trunks, which were obviously unequal in weight. He laid an iron bedstead, folded in very small compass, upon the lighter one, bound each of the trunks in coarse cloth, then placed stout cords of plaited camel's hair across the saddle of a mule, and, summoning assistance, had the two packages lifted simultaneously, one on one side and one on the other of the saddle. This is done with many an "Ul-lāh"—an invocation without which muleteers rarely engage in any signal effort. "Now, by the grace of God, let's do our best," is contained in a liberal translation of "Ullah" when thus employed; and if there is a box to be lifted, or a fallen mule to be reset upon its legs, or when the tired animals are to be urged to a quicker walk, it is invariably with an "Ul-lāh" that the effort is called for.

When the second mule was loaded, we see it is intended that he should lead the caravan. He is covered with bells, which are always ringing, and they are not the "drowsy tinklings" which may "lull the distant fold;" those upon his head, and a score more suspended round his shoulders — all these might be said to "tinkle;" but suspended from the saddle this animal carried two bells almost big enough for a steeple, the clangor of which is terrific. I object, and urge, in English so emphatic as to be comprehended by any Persian, that bags of fodder, to say nothing of camp-stools, and carpets, and half a dozen saucepans are enough; but the charvodar will not leave the bells behind him. He assures me, with a pleasant smile, that "he," and "he," and "he," pointing to the other mules, like the bells; that, in fact, they won't go without this perpetual ding-dong. Houssein, who, in spite of his melancholy appearance, is strongly recommended as a very good cook and chief servant, now made his appearance in full traveling costume. He was girt with a short, straight sword, and his long legs were incased in yellow leather. He loads his mule with saddle-bags, and upon these places a large cushion made of his pillow and overcoats; then, in the true Persian fashion, he throws himself on the neck of the mule, and struggles to the high seat, from which his legs dangle in a way that seems pleasing to Persian riders of his class. He had not forgotten brooms, which Mr. Churchill warned us were very requisite in traveling. It had been arranged that Houssein was to ride forward in advance of our arrival at a station, and look to the cleaning of our sleeping-place.

When at last we set out from Mr. Churchill's yard, our string of horses and mules carried beds and bedding, carpets, tables, folding seats, cooking utensils, and all the glass and crockery necessary for simple meals in a land where any provision beyond an empty room and a pillow of straw is absolutely unattainable, and where the comforts of such a service of dragomans and tents as may be had on the deserts of Syria and Egypt have never been heard of. Twenty-four miles in a day of eight hours, or nine, with an hour for rest in the middle of the march, is the ordinary caravan rate of traveling; and at this pace we passed out from the miserable town of Resht into the deliciously green forest which, for about forty miles, lies between Resht and the barren ground, rising ruggedly toward the Elburz Mountains, which we must cross by the Pass of Kharzan, on the way to Teheran.

Near sunset, in a small opening in the forest, we approached a building with not a soul in it, which looked like a brick-built barn that had long been deserted and had fallen into ruin. At either extremity there were the remains of a brick staircase, which led, by steps that by ruin had become very difficult, to a loft or apartment opening upon a wooden platform. Our servants informed us that this was a station, that there was none other for many miles, and that, in fact, this was to be our resting-place for the night. Both apartments had walls and floor of clay. There were window-frames, but they were broken, and the glass had fallen out. One room was full of brambles, collected for firing by some former occupant, and in the other there were holes in the floor nearly large enough for a guest to fall through into the mule-shed beneath. Like the roof, the floor was of mud, dry, hard, and dusty, laid upon sticks and straw, which covered the rude cross-beams cut from the forest. It was more than half an hour's work to clear the better room of the brambles, to collect bricks from the ruins with which to stop the holes in the floor, to sweep the place thoroughly, to spread the floor with our Persian carpets, to fill the empty window-frames with green boughs, and to set up our beds. A stream of water ran near, and a limitless supply of fire-wood was at hand; nor could any one be more skillful than Houssein in making a stove of bricks.

The crackling of our fire soon brought creatures around us, men and children in rags, who seemed to be drawn from the very ground by the smell of mutton and chicken in the stew-pots. We sat on the wooden platform enjoying the first-fruits of the fire in a cup of tea; the horses and mules were feeding in a patch of luxurious grass; and as the stillness increased at sunset, the forest seemed to grow into life with the noises of insects and animals. Our camp-kitchen upon the grass would have made an interesting picture. The grand form of Houssein stalked now and then before the flames. On one side stood an animated bundle of rags, who no doubt saw happy prospect of participation in the remains of the feast, from the fact that he was permitted to hold the cover of a stew-pot while our major-domo stirred the contents with a wooden spoon. I shouted for the kettle which occupied a corner of the fire, and other forms started up in willing service. Their joy was unbounded when we indulged a hopeful opinion that there would be pillau enough for every body to have some. But the flies in their thousands insisted also upon their share when the savory mess arrived on our platform.

Not "the worst inn's worst room" could present an appearance of abject poverty so striking as the mud-walls, the broken roof and walls, and rough rafters of the room into which we retired for the night. But our beds were excellent. The air was sweet, and the moonlight so bright that we could see all the rich colors of our Persian carpets upon the floor. There were no locks or fastenings on the door. Afterward we learned how rare it is to have a wooden door in a country where the craving for fuel is with many stronger than the respect for property. We barricaded the entrance with trunks, and slept for some hours during the first night of our ride through Persia.

CHAPTER IX.

The Month Ramadan.—Mohammed's First Wife.—Ramadan in the Koran.
—The Nocturnal Kalian.—Loading Up.—A Persian Landlord.—Persian
Money: Tomans, Krans, and Shihees.—Counting Money.—Persian Mints.
— Rich Provinces. — Kudem. — Chapar-khanah. — Bala-khanah. — Constructed to Smoke. — Caravanserais. — Unfurnished Apartments. — Our
Bell-mule.—A Traveled Khan.—The Safid-Rud.—Rustemabad.—Village
of Rhudbar.—Parchenar.—Khan offers his Tree.—A Night in the Open.
—Mistaken for a Thief.—"The Bells!"—Camels in the Path.

It is the month Ramadan, the great Mohammedan fast. Our servants, as good Mussulmans, have to do all their eating and smoking between sunset and sunrise; and, unfortunately for our repose, they do much talking at the same inconvenient time. In every great town throughout Persia a cannon is fired in the evening and morning, to signalize the moment when the fast ends and is to be resumed.

Mohammed ordained that the month Ramadan should be thus held sacred, because it was then that he first conceived his prophetic mission. He had lately risen in the world, as other leaders of men have done, by an advantageous match. Mohammed, at first the servant, the manager of her caravans, became the husband of the rich widow of Mecca, Khadijah, a woman who appears throughout her life to have commanded his affection and respect. She was his elder in years, and Mohammed was forty when, in a cave beneath Mount Hara, he disclosed to Khadijah, with all the nervous energy of his temperament, his visions, and, as he alleged, the promise of God that through his mouth should be poured out the laws of mankind. Khadijah was Mohammed's first convert. This occurred in Ramadan, and therefore it was written in the

Koran that "in the month of Ramadan shall ye fast, in which the Koran was sent down from heaven." All lawful enjoyments, including eating and drinking, may be taken during the night, "until ye can plainly distinguish a white thread from a black thread by the day-break; then keep the fast until night. These are the prescribed bounds of God."*

Sleeping in the wood near Resht, I was awaked several times in the night by the ceaseless stream of talk going on beneath our resting-place; the intervals being audibly filled with the gurgling of the narghileh, or hookah, the "kalian," as the Persians call their social pipe, which is the inevitable accompaniment of every long rest on the road, and of every hospitable reception or entertainment. Correctly speaking, this can only be called "narghileh" when the water-bowl is the shell of a cocoa-nut, for which I believe the Arabic word is "narghil." The Persians smoke but little, and no man seems to regard a pipe as entirely his own. On a march, a great prince receives his jeweled kalian on horseback; and when the lips of his highness are satisfied, the tube passes to those of his followers and servants. Among the lowest classes of the people, a reed pipe, with an earthenware bowl, is commonly used in traveling, and this passes in like manner from hand to hand. The smoke is always and at all times co-operative. To prepare the kalian, the tobacco is damped and placed in the pipe beneath a thick layer of live charcoal.

For my own part, I prefer the smell of a wood fire such as that the odor of which easily found a way through the many holes in the walls and floor of our room, and awoke us with a pleasant sense that the sun would soon rise, and that a kettle was about to boil for the purposes of breakfast. In the morning air, which in these Persian lowlands was somewhat too dewy, an hour passed quickly while the horses and mules

---

* Sale's "Al Koran," chap. ii.

were being caught and loaded. Then from beside the ashes of our camp-fire arose a personage dressed in a long, blue robe of ragged and dirty cotton, who appeared to claim the rights of a landlord over the remains of the ruined shed in which, thanks to our purchases at Resht and our other possessions, we had slept not uncomfortably. The landlords of Persian "chapar-khanahs," or post-houses, do not present a bill with a bow and a grimace, in the European method; all their accounts are, the same with Mohammedans and with Christians, discharged verbally. This one, after the invariable manner of his kind in dealing with a European, lifted his joined hands to the sky and muttered something about "Allah" and the "sahib." Then he presented both palms laid together, hollowed large enough to hold five hundred krans. The order of payment is of the "what-you-please" character; but whether you put five or ten silver pieces into those khenna-dyed hands, you will get no word of thanks; the Persian language has no equivalent for "thank you." Such an expression could only be conveyed in Persian by words glorifying the giver. But in any case the action will be the same; the "landlord" will stare at the coins, exhibit them to the by-standers, and extend his joined palms again to the giver for any addition.

The Persian money is not the least queer thing in the country. Every body talks of "tomans," which are gold coins of the nominal value of ten krans. But the small remnant of this gold coinage is sold as a curiosity in the bazaars at twelve or thirteen krans for each gold toman. Virtually, there are but three coins in the currency of Persia: the silver kran, the half kran, or penabat, and the shihee. The value of the kran, which is of pure, unalloyed silver, is about equivalent to that of a franc. It is a small piece of metal, intended to be circular, upon which the Shah's stamp may have fallen fully, or may have left but half an impression. Krans are often ragged at the edges, as pieces of dough would be if subjected to the same process, and every important town in Persia has a mint. The gold coinage has been exported, to pay for imports of foreign manufactures; and it seems that the silver is following the same course, and that Persia is being drained of the precious metals. It is a hard morning's work to count a hundred pounds sterling in the silver currency of Persia. The labor is generally shunned by employers, and trusty servants become skilled in the business. The method is always the same. The money-changer and the receiver sit upon the floor; the changer throws down from his hand the krans by fives, and both payer and payee keep in mind the number of tomans by repeating it all the while in an audible mutter. Thus, while the first ten krans are being poured out, they say "yek [one] yek—yek—yek;" then, while the "ties" are mounting to twenty, they say "du [two] du—du—du," and so on. It is very rarely that such a servant as Houssein makes an error in counting.

As to coining, that is carried on in all manner of ways. During our stay in Persia, the Shah had two Austrian officials, who were engaged, to the disgust of the Persians of the court, in arranging for the issue of money. They had been a year in the country, and were so successfully thwarted that nothing had been accomplished by these detested Europeans. A clever khan, whose acquaintance we made in the capital, had a coining-machine sent from Paris at his own expense; and with the aid of this he last year presented the Shah with some specimen coins, remarking at the same time upon the dilatoriness of the Austrians. The consequence was that he received orders to proceed with his manufacture; and now new krans and penabats are occasionally to be seen. But base money is becoming more and more common, I am told, in Persia. People who affect to know, and who are certainly in a position to be well informed, declare that most of the bad money comes from the imperial mints; and if, say, a master of a mint has a salary of a thousand tomans, and is able and willing, in order to retain his office, to give presents to the value of twenty thousand tomans—which I am assured is the case with at least one of these officers—the fact would, to say the least, throw much suspicion upon his issue.

There is a copper coinage, the shihee, of which twenty make a kran. But there are no shihees, there are only half-shihees; and it seems to be the abiding and unvarying conviction of Persian servants that this coinage, which is for the most part stamped with the well-known Persian combination of the lion and sun, is not sufficiently valuable for Europeans to handle. The odd shihees in any purchase or any settlement of expenditure are never forthcoming; the real value is much greater than the nominal worth, and perhaps Persian servants do not like to see the premium lost by unthrifty masters. Possibly this is the reason why they collect and sell them wholesale for their private advantage, at about twenty-five per cent. increase upon the nominal value of the coins.

No other part of Persia is so fertile as the wooded borders of the Caspian Sea, through which we passed from Enzelli to the Elburz Mountains. Every need of a large population might be supplied from this marvelously prolific soil; the export of silk would provide foreign produce in abundance; and the malarious fevers, from which nearly every one suffers, would disappear, if these low lands upon the coast were properly drained. The rivers are full of fish, including sturgeon and salmon. The field would produce tea, tobacco, and rice, while the forests, swarming with game, supply food for myriads of silk-worms. Silk is the chief article of commerce in this province of Ghilan, and both the quantity and value of the export are capable of great extension. But it is in harmony with all other things in Persia, to find in this a rapid and serious decline. Mr. Churchill, the British consul at

Resht, in an elaborate report upon the silk-trade, addressed to Lord Derby, has shown that within the brief space of seven years the value of the silk produced in the province of Ghilan has fallen from seven hundred thousand pounds to one hundred and four thousand pounds.

Through the green and winding path of the forest, which would seem interminable but for the glimpses of the gray mountains we catch from time to time, and which we know we have to cross, we approached Kudem, the end of our second day's march. When we alighted in the door-way of the "chapar-khanah," one of the best post-houses in Persia, in front of the brick stairs leading to the "bala-khanah," the raised apartment we were to occupy, we insisted upon having the heavy pack-saddles removed from off the backs of our mules—an order which was regarded by the charvodar as the silly whim of ignorant eccentrics. Perhaps, as like other Eastern peoples, Persians do not lay aside their own clothes at night, they suppose their mules prefer to carry a high and heavy structure composed of wood, straw, carpet, and leather, on their backs through all the hours of repose. Our mules seemed to express their own opinion by enjoying a prolonged roll on the grass. For our own refreshment, the invariable chicken was soon boiling in one of our traveling stew-pots. I should have looked forward to the result with greater pleasure if I had not seen the chicken running about an hour before it was reduced to this condition. Our apartment, though not very clean, was large, and had a boarded floor. It was placed over the archway leading to the stable-yard, and the question of ventilation was easily settled by the existence of a large hole in the floor, which, after the manner of ice-men in the parks, we thought it desirable to mark with a flag of white paper as decidedly "dangerous."

The chapar-khanah of Kudem is, I think, the best in Persia, but in outward form it resembles the usual construction.

The chapar-khanah is always inclosed with a wall built of mud-bricks, brown, sun-baked, and friable, plastered over with a coarse cement of mud mixed with broken straw. The entrance archway is secured by a strong gate. In the centre is a quadrangular yard for horses and mules, and round three sides are flat-roofed sheds, one side of which is formed by the outer wall. The sheds are for the animals and their drivers, who all sleep together in the winter months. On the fourth side, near the gate, there are generally two or three windowless and doorless sheds, plastered inside with mud, having a hole in one corner for a fire-place, which invariably smokes. But perhaps the more common arrangement is for these places to have a hole somewhere in the roof, and then the fire can be lighted on any part of the floor. In this way the smoke is blinding; but if a Persian has not his eyes and mouth full of smoke, he seems not to think he is getting fully the worth of his fire-wood, which is always costly. A smoky chimney appears to be not at all unpopular in a country where no necessary of life is so dear as fuel. These two or three holes or hovels are used by native travelers, and it was in one of these places that our servants prepared our food.

We very rarely met with a chapar-khanah which had not a bala-khanah. The latter word would seem to have some philological connection with "balcony," because it is used to denote any apartment above the ground-floor; and the most distinctive feature of a Persian apartment thus elevated is the platform which the occupant enjoys upon the flat roof of the lower buildings. Inside the quadrangle, near the doorway, there are, as a rule, two ways to the bala-khanah; high steps in the stable wall, by which one climbs to the roof and the level of the bala-khanah. This single room, the sole erection above the flat roof of the parallelogram-shaped stables, is generally about eight feet square, built, like all the rest, of mud-bricks and covered with mud-cement. The rafters of the roof are usually festooned with cobwebs; the walls are grimy with issues from the fire-place, which is rudely constructed to smoke. Indeed, we often found the flue purposely stopped with clay and stones which had been placed there by thrifty Persians who, having lighted a fire of wood on a winter's evening, had stopped the chimney, in their desire for economy of heat. As a rule, there are two or three doorways without doors, and sometimes a hole or two intended for windows. If the wood fire smokes, one is glad to have no door until the charred wood is flung outside, and the pure wind of evening has blown the pungent odor from the place.

Upon the high table-land extending from Teheran beyond Shiraz, the nights are intensely cold from December to April, and a fire is necessary in these vile lodgings. When, as is the rule, there is no door, the traveler nails up a horse-cloth, a "nummud," as the Persians call their serviceable felts of pressed camel's hair, or, better still, the canvas door of a military tent; and when the same work has been performed at the other doors, and about the holes which serve as windows, and the breeze, to which the bala-khanah is pre-eminently exposed, is thus partially blocked out, the thermometer may possibly, in the warmest hours of a January night, creep as high as zero. In the summer and autumn, in such heat as that in which we rode from Resht to Teheran, there are worse discomforts than a freezing temperature. The bala-khanah, which in winter is free from vermin, then swarms with the most troublesome of insects.

In the caravanserais, of which there is generally one near to every chapar-khanah, the traveler has no trouble whatever about windows, because there are none. Around the large horse-yard there are a number of dark arches, opening upon a brick terrace, raised about three feet above the yard. Generally, the arches have a circular hole in the roof for the outlet of the smoke; but sometimes there is a flue. The end of the arch next the yard is filled with rough masonry, a square door-way being left, in which, if one wishes for privacy—or in winter for greater warmth than that of a north wind careering over miles of snow—there must be nailed some covering from the traveler's baggage. But whether in chaparkhanah or caravanserai, his baggage must include every thing, and for security all must be placed with him or his servants, in their respective arches of the caravanserai, upon the dusty floor of the bala-khanah, or in one of the mud caverns near the gate, which may during the previous night have been used as a stable for mules. Every morning and evening an hour is spent in packing and unpacking, in loading and unloading. On arriving, the apartment is bare, littered with the rubbish of the last occupier, and, on going out, there is little danger of forgetting any part of one's baggage. It is only necessary to see that the place is stripped of every thing; that nothing useful remains behind; there will be no risk of taking aught that does not belong to the traveler.

We left Kudem in the morning, when the grass was wet with dew, and the unrisen sun showed the outline of the mountains in a clear, gray light. When the forest was at its stillest hour, our little caravan moved on toward Rustemabad, but not noiselessly. In spite of our protests, the first horse carried a whole peal of bells; bells on his neck and bells on his hind quarters, bells which I had heard tinkling in some distant pasture during the night, and that rang in our ears all the day long. These were gentle in their tones, compared with the two "Big Bens," each nine inches high and four wide at the mouth, which I had argued against at Resht to no purpose, and which were still carried by one of our baggage-mules. At times we urged our horses onward to escape from the sonorous stroke of these dreadful bells; but Tydides, as we named the bell-mule, was ever "rushing to the war." His step was fast, and the projecting trunks with which he was loaded were terrible when he charged upon us. Subject to his load, he was, to a great extent, the master of his own actions; the course was completely open to him. At about two feet distant from each of his sides the sharp iron-bound angle of a wooden trunk projected. An ancient Briton with scythes attached to the wheels of his chariot could hardly have been a more dreadful neighbor. Whenever the clang of his bells was heard close behind, we looked to our legs with fond solicitude, and hurried away. Tydides was utterly careless of the wounds he inflicted upon us with our own trunks for his weapons of war.

In traveling "caravan," that is, at walking pace, in the long hours of the day's journey, and especially in the presence of beautiful scenery, one often becomes listless and inattentive—an attitude which certainly will bring into painful operation the too dangerous proclivities of caravan mules and horses. If the road is inclosed, these animals will probably turn every corner with an eye to saving distance, rather than of regard for the full space required for the rider's legs; and when the path is on one side precipitous, if his legs are not forced against the rocky side of the path, he will be taken to the extreme outside edge, on which a stumble or a tiny land-slip would probably prove fatal. When we emerged from the forest, our path began to be of the latter sort—a track made with no regard for level, but simply up and down the stony ledges, over the spurs of hills which had been broken by the course of the yellow river, the Safid-Rud, the windings of which we had now to follow for about fifty miles.

We were riding in the outskirts of the forest, when a Persian, whose dress and saddle-cloth proclaimed him to be a man of rank, overtook us. He wore the usual high black hat, with a peak strapped round it upon the side from which the rays of the morning sun were already hot, a coat of light cotton, the skirt thickly gathered at the waist; very loose trousers of black satin, and high riding-boots rising above the knee. He had evidently learned all that was to be known about us at Kudem, and surprised me with "Good-morning, sare." He was a handsome man, but there was something artificial in his face. The ambition in Persia to have a black or red beard is overmastering. For the former color the Persians mix indigo with khenna, and it was with this mixture that his hair and beard were dyed a blue-black. Years ago, he said, he had been attached to the Persian Legation in London, and even now he told us he liked to be "very Englishman." The ideas of the khan (I will not further identify him) on the subject of baggage appeared to be enviably simple. His servant carried saddle-bags which contained a brass samovar (the Russian kettle), a couple of small carpets, a well-stuffed pillow, two or three coats, and a few pomegranates. He was traveling "chapar," posting, upon his own horse, and could proceed at trot or gallop. I had reason to know all this in the course of a twelve days' journey, in which the khan kindly insisted on keeping company with our caravan, partly, as he said, because in Persia nobody travels alone if he can help it; partly, I think, because he wished to be well spoken of to the English-minister and the Persian Government in Teheran by an Englishman; and not a little from a kindly, genuine desire to be of service to us.

The exquisite scenery through which we were passing seemed to give him no special pleasure. The sun had risen gloriously above the mountain peaks, varying in height from ten to fifteen thousand feet. The bare sides of the Elburz chain showed almost every known tint of color. The bright reds and greens of these mountains can mean nothing less than that they are metalliferous to enormous richness. The yellow stream of the Safid-Rud, stretching sometimes over a bed a quarter of a mile in width, ran between the mountains and our path, which was for miles overhung with trees. In the woody hollows we sometimes forded rushing streams which covered the knees of our mules, then mounted a hill, to dip again into the next watery hollow, where beside the stream grass grew deliciously green; and our active muleteers, careful in nothing so much as to keep their feet moderately dry, walked, sure-footed as goats, across a prostrate tree, which in every difficult case formed the only bridge.

The sun was intensely hot when we reached Rustemabad, at two o'clock, having passed through a mud-built village which lent its name to the station. The buildings of the village were of the simplest order; the material, the river-mud mixed with chopped straw; the flat roofs of the same material laid upon what in England we should call bavin-wood, which rested on rafters placed upon the mud-walls. A round hole here and there in the mud roof served for a chimney. The huts were so close together that there was not left a roadway of more than three yards in the bazaar, where grapes, pomegranates, melons, green figs, fowls, and ropes of camel's hair were exposed for sale.

As usual, a servant had gone forward to prepare and furnish the room which we were to occupy, but the nature of the floor defied the efforts of any broom to remove the dust. The apartment had six windows and three doors. In the former, half the glass was gone, and the doors had never seen a lock. In fact, locks are not used in Persia. The Persians have not as yet advanced further than bolts and padlocks of the rudest manufacture.

We had just succeeded in getting our beds set up, our carpets spread, and tea made, when we received a visit of ceremony from the khan, who was immensely amused at my elaborately made bed, with sheets and counterpane in the good English fashion, and, on my returning his visit, contrasted his simple carpet and pillow with my complicated arrangements. He had courteously given up to us the only room which had doors. In his resting-place there had been windows, but there were now only the wide openings. However, the samovar was boiling, and we had a glass of tea in the Persian manner—that is, very weak, without milk, and with an almost sickening quantity of sugar. Next morning, on resuming our journey, we passed through groves of olives, quite unfenced, the trees growing in rich and well-watered oases by the river's side, through the mud village of Rhudbar, wealthy in splendid fruits. We bought a delicious melon for the value of twopence English, and grapes more luscious than those of Italy or Spain for less than a half-penny a pound. Near the end of the day's march, we crossed the river by a bridge and arrived at Manjil, another mud-built village. We had risen above the level of universal richness which belongs only to the provinces of Persia which border the Caspian Sea. Now our road lay through an arid country, which was only green near the river, or where artificial irrigation made an oasis.

We left Manjil on the 18th of October, about daylight, and at nine o'clock forded the river three times, which was high enough to be quite inconvenient; and as we approached Parchenar, the resting-place for the night, we anticipated bad things of that station, on seeing that there was nothing above the ground-floor level of the buildings. The inclosure was, as usual, occupied by mules, and littered with dirty straw. A tall old Persian, dressed in the blue-cotton robe and trousers common to the peasantry and working-classes of the country, showed us a hole in the wall, leading, upon the same level as the yard, into what was a stable or a dwelling room, but what in another position every one would call a dungeon: a stone-built room, with no window of any sort, dark but for a fire of wood, which was burning unconfined on the centre of the floor—a room of which the natural illumination came only from a small hole in the roof, through which some of the smoke was finding exit, and the door-way, which was as open to the mules or dogs in the yard as to ourselves. After mature deliberation, we preferred to encamp in the open air.

At the gate of this wretched chapar-khanah we met the khan, who pointed to a solitary tree, in the shade of which he had already spread his carpets. He offered us his "tree" with ceremonious courtesy, if we preferred to pass the night beneath its branches; but we chose a place under the wall of the post-house, from which we could see across the valley. We sent Ali, a lanky lad whom we had engaged upon the road, to the river to cut some of the tall green rushes, with which we strewed the ground before we laid down our carpets. The melancholy Houssein built a fire-place of stones from a ruined wall with all the skill of a Count Rumford; we had dined before the light of day departed, and presently our servants appeared bringing every article of our baggage, which they placed upon our encampment. In vain I tried to make them understand that these things would be safer with them inside the walls; they protested, for a reason I have never yet discovered, that the baggage would be more secure at our side.

We were soon left alone with the starry night, one lying in a well-made bed, and one rolled in a rug on the carpets. There were three fires burning in the valley, two marking the resting-place of long strings of camels laden with goods for Teheran, and the third that of our muleteers, one of whom disturbed our first attempt to sleep with a caution against wandering thieves. This made us regard with increased suspicion the motions of two men, who half an hour afterward glided noiselessly, as all Persians walk, round the wall of the chapar-khanah, and stood talking together near to our solitary resting-place.

The night was beautiful; not a cloud nor the slightest mist

obscured the stars, or concealed any part of the hard, jagged outline of the mountains, from behind which the moon, a little less than full, rose about nine o'clock, throwing a flood of silvery light upon the two men, whose position, one on each side of us, about thirty yards distant, gave us uneasiness, and prevented sleep. At last they lay down upon the ground, intending, as it seemed very possible, to wait until we fell asleep before they approached our baggage. We agreed to watch these disquieting visitors in spells of two hours each; but I had scarcely entered upon the second watch at half an hour after midnight, when our chief servant appeared and suggested that, as the next day's journey included the very severe work of crossing the Elburz Mountains by the Kharzan Pass, it would be well for the horses and ourselves, if we were willing, to start at once, so as to get to the top before sunrise. We were soon in our saddles, when it turned out that one of the suspected thieves, who lay like a log near us, was none other than the landlord of the miserable place in which we had refused to lodge. He had come out to guard us during the night: and, had we but known who he was, we need not have been sleepless.

"The bells!" I said, with something of the horror which Mr. Irving expresses in his painful representation of Mathias, when I heard the too well-known clangor of our baggage-mule. It was weird work, fording the river, and pushing our way through the tall rushes of the valley, in the morning moonlight; but when we saw the terrible steeps up which the mules and horses had to climb, we were very glad we had not slept till sunrise. For hours we mounted, until we had gained an elevation of about seven thousand feet. The air was keen and cold, the stony path narrow, and in places dangerous. Just at the worst part of the ascent, an hour before daybreak, we heard the sound of other bells, and in the moonlight saw the first of a long line of loaded camels coming down the pass. There were, in all, nearly a hundred divided into strings of about twenty, fastened to a rope, which passed from the nose of one to the nose of another. To have met the camels in the narrow path would be perilous, and we stood aside, on the widest ledge at hand, to let them pass. But they moved very slowly; and meanwhile mules, horses, and camels *en route* for Teheran collected behind us, and some of the more unruly mules forced their loads among us, making great confusion. Such moments would be unbearable if one thought of nothing but the possible danger of the position. But there is so much kicking and cuffing, and active work of self-protection to be done, one's legs are so exposed to injury, and form such an engrossing embarrassment, that one has no time to think of the precipice, and of the death which a sudden push from a stumbling mule or camel might, or rather must, cause.

CHAPTER X.

How Hills are Made. — Kharzan. — Mazara. — A Persian Village. — John Milton and Casbeen. — The Plain of Kasveen. — The Mirage. — Gardens of Kasveen. — Dervishes. — Decay of Kasveen. — A Persian Town. — Women of Kasveen. — Persian Costumes. — "Allahu Akbar." — Mosque of Kasveen. — Telegram from Teheran. — Visit to the Khan. — His Love Affairs. — Lost in Kasveen. — Abdulabad. — An Alarm and an Arrival. — "Gosrozink." — Native Plows. — On to Karij. — Lodged in the Shah's Palace. — The Imperial Saloon. — An Imperial Bedroom. — Approach to Teheran. — Population of the Capital. — The Kasveen Gate. — Mud Houses and Walls. — The Imperial Theatre. — Entrance to the "Arg." — Neglect of Public Works. — British Legation. — Mirza Houssein Khan. — Teheran Bazaar. — Caravanserai Ameer.

THEY say in the Herzegovina that when the Creator had made the world he passed over it strewing the smooth surface with mountains and hills, but that over that country he let fall a great part of his burden. In this way they account for its peculiarly unlevel surface. And as the rising sun glowed upon the summits of the lower mountains of the Elburz chain, upon which we looked down shortly after our encounter with the camels, the whole land seemed to be covered with hill-tops. The khan had ridden on to Kharzan to a caravanserai near the end of the pass, and was standing in the door-way when we rode up, shivering with cold. He pointed cheerfully to his servant, one Syed Ali, who was blowing the charcoal in his master's samovar to a white heat. Our servants were provided with cold fowl, boiled eggs, bread, and grapes and wine. We had a pleasant bivouac in this mountain station, and soon forgot the sleepless night at Parchenar. Two hours afterward, we had descended about fifteen hundred feet, and arrived at the village of Mazara. The post-house, like the village, was built of mud. We mounted by a ladder, with rungs terribly wide apart, on to the flat roof of the ground-floor, and there found a little room with two wooden doors, which also served as windows. Inside, there lay our bright carpets, and upon them a tray covered with pomegranates, a present from the khan, which we acknowledged with the gift of a melon. The sun was intensely hot, and the advantages of mud construction in point of coolness were very perceptible. We all slept through the middle hours of the day; and toward evening, when I came out upon the roof, activity had been resumed. I had to avoid stepping down the chimneys, which, however, were smoking remindfully and pungently. Below in the yard there were dancers keeping slow time to a monotonous tom-tom. I fancy they had an eye to the remains of our dinner, which they afterward enjoyed. The neighboring roofs were for the most part covered with a layer of horse and cow dung, spread out to dry. When dried, it is mixed with clay, and forms the fuel of the village. On some roofs the manufacture of desiccated dung and clay was being carried on. Close by the village a piece of ground had been trodden hard by use as a threshing-floor. There were two small bullocks and two large men at work in this way. The beasts were dragging round and round, over the broken straw, a wooden sledge, in which were set two circular harrows, also of wood, which revolved simply by being drawn over the straw. They had trodden and dragged until none of the straw was more than two inches in length. The oxen and the men were knee-deep in it, and beneath the broken straw lay the golden grain. The tilled land surrounding the village looked but a patch upon the vast plain stretched out before us. The cultivated soil was naturally no better than much of that which was waste, but it was watered, and irrigation brings forth rich crops of corn and fruit.

Mazara, lying under the Elburz Mountains, upon the edge of a sharp slope, is a fair specimen of a Persian village. The earth is brown, the houses are brown, and crumbling into the dust of the plain, from the mud of which they have been made. If human beings were wont to burrow in the earth, their habitations would, I suppose, look from a distance very much like the mud-built villages of Persia. There is no street, no order in the arrangement of the huts, no provision whatever for drainage. The houses are set together anyhow; sometimes with space enough between for a loaded mule to pass, but rarely more, though the plain is so vast and barren. The miserable kennel of dried mud in which we rested was the only elevation, and its raised position was the cause of one of us having a fall which might have had a very serious result. The roof outside our sleeping-place was very infirm, and my shadow concealed a hole jagged with broken sticks which lay beneath the clay. In the early morning, when we were preparing to start, my wife stepped through this hole, and to a considerable extent disappeared. It was most fortunate that she was not badly hurt.

Our path lay directly to Kasveen, or Casbeen, formerly one of the chief towns of Persia, a city which was famous in Milton's day, for the author of "Paradise Lost" wrote—

"Or Bactrian Sophi, from the horns
Of Turkish crescent, leaves all waste beyond
The realm of Aladule, in his retreat
To Tauris or Casbeen."

We rode to Casbeen, or Kasveen, over the nearly flat plain which stretches far beyond Teheran, and of which the average level is nearly four thousand feet above the sea. It is inclosed by mountains and hills, and in some places is not more than fifteen or twenty miles wide. From Mazara to Kasveen the unbroken soil appears to be naturally fertile, but it is waste for want of water, which might so easily be stored in the hills. Where water is artificially provided, the method is very curious. From a spring found by digging upon raised ground, a tunnel is made until the surface is reached, the course of the tunnel being marked by shafts ("k'nats" these holes are called), the openings of which upon the plain are embanked with the earth removed by the excavation.

The illusion of the mirage, which is nowhere more often seen than in Persia, is well known. The mist of the morning, hovering upon the plain, assumes the appearance of water. Near Kasveen, the mirage was very remarkable. The cattle in the distance seemed to be drinking upon the edge of still waters, and the posts of the Indo-European Telegraph to be standing in a shallow lagoon. The deception is as "old as the hills." It has been observed in all ages. In one of the odes of Hafiz, the great poet of Persia, who has been dead nearly five hundred years, it is said of this natural illusion,

"The fountain-head is far off in the desolate wilderness;
Beware, lest the demon deceive thee with the mirage."

For hours we seemed to be riding toward water which we knew did not exist. The mirage floated deceptively before us, and when at last it cleared off, there was another illusion. The trees in the gardens of Kasveen, which were yet a dozen miles distant, seemed to be scarcely more than three or four miles from us.

At last we reached these gardens, which are for the most part vineyards; and in the way of eating there can be few greater pleasures than to devour the grapes of Kasveen on a hot day as one would currants in England. They are the small stoneless grapes, which, when dried, are sold as "Sultana" raisins. But Kasveen is a half-ruined, famine-stricken dust-heap. During the famine of 1870-'71 the poor of Kasveen died by hundreds. As we rode through the bazaar on our way to the post-house, we saw what it might cost to have a blind horse in Persia. Every now and then there was a deep square hole, open and unguarded, in the centre of the street, for cleansing the water-course which runs beneath. Near the entrance to the mud-built chapar-khanah, there were two dervishes groveling in the dust and screaming for alms. One, a strongly built man, nearly naked, was hoarse and half stupefied with his shouts, which, though few regarded, none mocked or laughed at. The other, an old man, was more methodical. In a fanatical burst, he now and then threw out "Ali! Ali!" nothing more being needed, especially in Ramadan, to show his devotion to Ali, the great son-in-law of Mohammed. The dervishes of Persia are a privileged institution. They are not a caste, for I believe any one is free to take up the profession of religious mendicancy to which they seem devoted. The madder their actions, the more respect they appear to gain. Nobody "chaffs" a dervish, and in none do his eccentricities provoke ridicule.

When, after passing through many by-paths and crooked ways, we reached the chapar-khanah, our mules rushed to the mangers, and we mounted the roof of the stables by steps, of which some were nearly two feet high, to the bala-khanah. Kasveen is still regarded as a town of much importance, where a traveler might expect to find accommodation for man and beast; yet our servants had to build a stove of bricks on the roof for cooking our dinner, which consisted of chicken-broth, followed by the stewed chicken, with rice and sweetmeats. Kasveen suffered horribly in the recent famine, and this may account for some of the ruin which surrounded us. But the decay of Kasveen is of long standing, and will not, apparently, be arrested by the absence of famine. There are miles and miles of ruined mud-walls in and about the town. At all times, and under any circumstances, a Persian town has a desolate appearance. Even in a town as large as Kasveen, with twenty or thirty thousand inhabitants, there are not a dozen houses with a second story, and not a single private house with a window opening upon the street. In Turkey, the windows of the harem—the women's part of the house—are, it is true, jealously latticed, and the lattice has sometimes a pretty appearance from the street; but one can not see an inch into the "anderoon," or harem, of a Persian house. The streets, except in the bazaars, are bounded by mud-walls, with no opening or variation except the door, which is very rarely unfastened.

We were standing on the roof of the chapar-khanah, looking down into the dusty street, when a number of women returning from a mosque passed beneath, chattering and laughing. They lifted their heads to look at us, but not an eye was visible; and though they were probably only neighbors, and certainly belonged to different houses and families, there was as precise similarity in their coloring—the indigo chudder and trousers and the white veil—as if they had worn the uniform of one regiment. The indoor costume of Persian women of the higher class appears indelicate to Europeans. The chudder and trousers are the invariable walking costume. Indoors the dress of a Persian lady is more like that of a ballet-girl, except that the Persian lady's legs are not covered, and that her bodice makes even less pretension to be a covering than that of a danseuse of these *décolletées* days. In the anderoons of Persian royalty, my wife was received by princesses thus attired, or rather unattired, the high fashion being for the short skirts to stand out in the most approved manner of the ballet.

I have often thought it would make the canal scenes of Venice far more beautiful if the gondolas were not so invariably painted with sombre black, a survival, I believe, of the stern equality of the Republican epoch. And to see the Persian women stumbling slipshod or riding over the miserable roads, all disguised in the same dismal covering—a dress far more ugly than was ever worn by nun or Sister of Mercy—is to pity the wearers of a costume which custom and the rule of the Koran have made acceptable. In Turkey, again, the women are veiled, but their dress is of many colors; in Persia, no part of their person, not an eye, is visible, and their outdoor costume has this painful and sombre uniformity.

At sunset, as usual, the voices of the moollahs chanting the "Allahu Akbar" (God is great) sounded from all quarters of the town of Kasveen; highest of all, from a little building something like a Swiss chalet placed over the archway of the court-yard of the principal mosque. Ignorant of the fact that Europeans never visit the Persian mosques, and with no knowledge of the great danger of the excursion, we set out to see this royal mosque, the only interesting building in Kasveen. We passed through a part of the bazaar, where, as in all towns in Persia, men may be seen ginning cotton with a bow, ignorant of the European inventions, and where others were laboriously embossing writing-paper by rubbing the rough sheet with polished wood. Our visit to the mosque attracted much attention, but we met with no opposition. We were followed by a crowd; but this was not unusual, and no one made any remonstrance. The building has no architectural merit, and is curious only for the pleasing effect produced with glazed bricks of different colors. Like most of the Persian mosques, this praying-place is entirely open. The high, pointed arch of the centre, beneath which is the chief or grand pavilion, has a beading of bright blue. There are panels set with highly glazed tiles; the ground of primrose yellow, on which there are flowers in red and blue. The effect is very pleasing, and might be much more so with better workmanship and a finer style of construction.

At Kasveen, there is a station of the Indo-European Telegraph Company; and, on our return to the post-house, we found the local inspector, an Italian, with a telegram in his hand—an invitation to us from the English minister in Teheran to make the Legation our home during our stay in the capital.

I had forwarded to Mr. Thomson a letter of introduction, of which this telegram contained an acknowledgment. We should gladly have accepted the minister's very kind offer of hospitality, had we remained under the impression, which we had on leaving England, that it was a matter of necessity; that there was no other place in which we could find suitable lodging. But we had learned at Baku from Count Thun, the brother-in-law of the Austrian envoy, and at Resht from Mr. Churchill, that there was a hotel in Teheran, kept by a Frenchman who had been "chef" to the Shah; and, hearing this, we did not feel disposed to intrude upon the British minister. We at once telegraphed our thanks to Mr. Thomson from Kasveen, and expressed our intention of staying at M. Prevôt's hotel.

The khan, our faithful traveling companion, had taken up his quarters at the caravanserai, where I found him lodged after the manner of his country. About the entrance, on the brick ledges of the wide gate-way, muleteers lay sleeping in every imaginable posture; and inside, the same might be said of their mules, among which I recognized our own animals. Surrounding this yard was the usual brick parapet, about four feet high and as many broad, by which the human inhabitants of the caravanserai reached their apartments, which were simply deep niches, closed on the outside with paneled wood, in which there was a door, and a sliding shutter for a window. The khan, with his shutter raised and his door open, sat cross-legged on his traveling carpet at the mouth of his arch, of which both floor and ceiling were of plain, unconcealed brick-work. It was very curious to see a man whose manners evinced in some respects great refinement, lodged, with apparently perfect contentment, in a dark arch looking upon a stable-yard. Beside him lay three or four melons, and far in the background two live fowls, with their legs tied together: this was his larder.

The ritual or etiquette which regulates, in Persia, the making, and the exchange, and the duration of visits, as well as of presents, is very severe. The anxiety of the khan that I should pay him a visit in the caravanserai was quite touching. He was evidently fearful that his reputation would suffer in the eyes of the Kasveen people, if, after we had traveled together to the town, and had been accompanied by him to the chapar-khanah, I allowed the day of arrival to pass without making personal inquiries concerning his health and comfort. And I was glad to please him in so small a matter, for he had been untiring in his attentions to us upon the road. While I sat with the khan upon his carpet in the Kasveen caravanserai, he told me that he had a princess for a wife in Teheran. He had once, he said, hoped to have been married to an Englishwoman. At the Legation in London there was, he went on to tell me, a servant-girl, "Emily," whom he wished to marry. She was "very beauty," "very beauty," and he confessed to having made her an offer; but it appeared, from the sequel of this story of unrequited affection, that "Emily," on learning that in Persia men had more than one wife, and that women never walked in the streets with their faces exposed to view, would not listen to the khan's proposals.

The great Mohammedan fast is not the best time for traveling. Servants and muleteers can obtain priestly permission to eat while upon the journey; but not a few of them are fanatics, and prefer to keep the fast. The consequence is that they are ill-tempered and languid all day, ravenous toward evening; and the traveler may as well whistle to the wind as endeavor to obtain their attention at the moment when, at sunset, feeding is lawful. Till sunrise, their license is unchecked; they eat, drink, smoke, and, finally, are found asleep when their employer wishes to be on the road. It was so in the morning upon which we quitted Kasveen, and, leaving the baggage to be packed by the sleepy gholams and servants, we set off quite alone two hours before sunrise, thinking that the high path to Teheran would be perfectly clear. But we were soon lost among the ruins of Kasveen, with no living thing at hand except one or two howling dogs, which stalked mournfully over the ruined mud-walls and broken archways of the decayed and decaying town. Soon, however, the rising sun revealed the posts of the Teheran telegraph, and these led us to the road, where in a short time we heard the jingling bells of our baggage-train. We met with no shade whatever during the whole day's ride until we arrived at the solitary post-house of Abdulabad; and we had not been there an hour before one of our servants rushed into the room, exclaiming, "Inglees Sahib! Teheran!" He was quickly followed by an Englishman, who reminded me at once of the photograph of Mr. H. M. Stanley. And this was no wonder; he was like Mr. Stanley in face; the same bold, active expression; and his dress was identical: pith helmet, short tunic, leather belt, garnished with pistol and pouch, and high riding-boots. His "Mr. Arnold, I believe?" was not needed to suggest the resemblance. He had brought a letter from the British minister at Teheran, repeating in writing the very kind invitation which we had received the day before by telegraph at Kasveen, and cautioning us to avoid exposure to the sun, which "even at this time of year," Mr. Thomson wrote, "is dangerous."

We left Abdulabad three hours before day-break, in order to finish our journey before the great heat of the afternoon. There was no moon; it was cold, and very dark. Ali was acting as guide, with his hand upon the bridle of my wife's horse, which at every brook or water-course he abandoned, leaving the rider to splash into unknown darkness and depths, while he sought a crossing which could be accomplished dry-shod. But Ali misled us, and it was some time before the caravan was collected upon the right track. We had, however, not gone far, after discovering this error, before there was another alarm. The khan, my wife, and I were riding a quarter of a mile in advance of the servants and baggage, when we heard loud cries of "Houssein!" "Houssein!" and saw a tramp who had, for his own convenience, attached himself to our caravan, running toward us, screaming, as Persians do whenever they are excited. I turned and galloped back in the darkness, expecting at least to find Houssein in the hands of robbers. He was only bruised by a tumble from his saddle, in which he had fallen asleep.

The way from Kasveen to Teheran is very uninteresting; the road is "where you please," for the stony plain belongs almost entirely to the rider. There is little attempt at cultivation. Now and then there is a parallelogram surrounded by a mud-wall twelve feet high, the rude fortification of a village, such as we rested in the night after leaving Abdulabad. It was called by a name which sounded like Gosroziuk; and after riding through a hole in the mud fortification, and between two ranges of miserable huts, which served as a bazaar, we arrived at the place wherein it was proposed we should sleep. The khan had gone on before, and, when we arrived, he was sitting on the wide ledge of the bramble-roofed gateway, through which every mule entering the yard must pass. He was scooping a water-melon with the utmost composure and contentment, while a servant, who had arrived before us, emerged, broom in hand, from a dark hole opposite—a cave constructed of mud cement, with no other light but that from a small door opening beneath the gate-way. Houssein seemed conscious that it would be pronounced an intolerable lodging; and when I pointed, in preference, to one house in the village which had a room raised upon the roof of the ground-floor, he at once darted off, and, to my horror, I saw him flinging out the furniture, which consisted of bundles of rags and a few pots of earthenware, before, as it seemed to me, he had consulted the wishes of the proprietor. But it soon appeared that he was not wrong in taking this for granted. The lady of the house hurried up the ladder which led to the apartment I coveted, and assisted in the removal and sweeping. Then I saw that the room had no door; but this it was not difficult to supply with a rug.

The place was a fine observatory for watching the doings of Gosrozink. Across the squalor of the undrained village, over the inclosing wall, which was literally and purely built of mud, the view of the mountains was delightful; and as the moollah of the village loudly proclaimed the hour of prayer, numbers of the people knelt upon their roofs, and made their evening prostrations and prayers in the direction of Mecca. In the zigzag ways of the village were stored those wretched primeval plows which, from the Adriatic Sea to the Pacific Ocean, are the bane of agriculture. A beam of wood three or four inches in diameter, with a prong of wood (not always tipped with iron) fixed at an angle of forty-five degrees—that is the plow with which the rich lands of Greece, of Turkey, of Persia, and eastward to the ocean, are tilled. The plow of the time of Herodotus and of Constantine was in shape precisely the same as that which scratches the soil of these countries to-day. Who would venture to say what might be the increase in the production of corn, if the light iron plows of English manufacture were to pass into general use throughout Eastern Europe and in Asia?

It is terribly wearisome to ride over a plain so flat that, in the morning, one can see the goal of the evening—a ride in which nine hours of traveling bring no material change of landscape. When the sun rose, shortly after we left Gosrozink, we could see almost the lowest rock of the spur of the Elburz Mountains, under which lay a palace of the Shah, where the khan had promised us we should, through his influence, obtain good lodging for the last night of our long journey. We reached the palace early in the afternoon, scarcely less tired than our horses with the heat and dust. It is one of half a dozen palaces in the neighborhood of Teheran, and was last occupied by the Shah when his majesty returned from London.

There are palaces and palaces, and this palace of Karij is not in accord with the English notion of a palace. The gateway, placed in the mud-wall which surrounds the buildings and gardens, is in style a compound of a Swiss chalet and a Chinese pagoda. It opens into a large yard, where we dismounted. The khan assisted, and then offered his arm in English fashion, to the evident astonishment of the Shah's domestics, to lead the lady of the party to the palace. Through a side door we passed from the yard into a garden, and, beneath trellised fig-trees, walked by a shady path to the main building. This was long and narrow, crossed near each end by two staircases, a large landing on the first floor dividing the back and front stairs. The steps were painfully steep, and covered with blue-glazed tiles, which were generally broken.

Not the Shah-in-Shah,* or any other potentate, could maintain a dignified deportment while climbing up such steps as those of any one of his palaces. With few exceptions, an easy staircase seems to be one of the latest triumphs of civilization. The imperial steps in the Roman Coliseum are so

---

* This title, "Shah-in-Shah" (King of Kings), is said to have been originally assumed by the Persian monarchs in right of their suzerainty over four kings—those of Afghanistan, Georgia, Kurdistan, and Arabistan.

high that the Cæsars must have looked like bears climbing a pole or alpine travelers in difficulty, when mounting to their throne in that vast amphitheatre. We found the Shah's stairs really painful, after our tiresome ride. On the landing there were double doors on either hand, covered with a rough, red paint, and without locks or handles. We entered on one side the large saloon of the palace, the only apartment which contained a single article of furniture, and in this room the solitary provision was a carpet, or, rather, four carpets; one large carpet in the centre, and thick felts, extending for about six feet from the wall, on three sides. At both ends of the room, from the roof half-way down the wall, were paintings, each containing the portraits, or supposed portraits, of about a dozen Shahs, every monarch having a square black beard of impossible dimensions and singular uniformity. There was one thing in the saloon besides the carpets—a large, circular metal tray, about a yard in diameter, on which were three large melons, cut in halves, for our refreshment. I think every half-melon was more or less scooped before the tray was carried away; and we left the saloon to look at our bedroom, which was a large oblong, with doors opening upon the mud-cement roof of the under offices, of which our servants had taken possession, with the result of filling the place with the smoke of their cooking fire, for which they had to purchase wood.

The light of the bedroom came from the ends, according as we raised or lowered the heavy wooden shutters. There were no other windows. On the rubbishy concrete floor there was a layer of dust, which rose in small clouds as we walked across the room. It was not without hard labor that we shook off the dust of the Shah's bedroom from our carpets the next morning before starting for Teheran. This palace of Karij possesses a feature not uncommon in the residences of the Shah—a tower joined to, but easily shut against access from, the palace—a high, square building, ascended by flights of stairs, with slits for windows, just large enough to admit a glimmer of light. There is no ornament or furniture; the tower is merely a place of temporary retreat and security in case of sudden attack or attempted revolution. I have spoken of a "bedroom," but a Persian palace has, properly speaking, no apartments specially devoted to sleeping. The khan, in the true Persian fashion, passed the night on the thick Khorassan felt upon the floor of the saloon.

One looks in vain for the signs of a great city on approaching the capital of Persia. The plain is stony, nearly level, and utterly wearisome. There are strings of camels and droves of asses entering and leaving the city. Much of the daily food, all the fire-wood, and all the foreign produce consumed in Teheran must be so conveyed. A wheeled carriage for such service is never seen. No fine building presents a remarkable outline. At one or two points, the sun's rays gleam upon the vitrified tiles of the dome of a mosque or shrine; but these are miserable in elevation. Nobody knows how many people there are in Teheran: some say fifty thousand; some say eighty thousand; but in other countries and climates a town with twenty thousand inhabitants makes far more show. Were it not for the plane-trees, one might overlook Teheran as one would a sleeping crocodile on the banks of the Nile. The city is of the color and of the material of the plain. It is a city of mud, in an oasis of plane-trees. The flat roofs continue the level of the plain. As one approaches Teheran in autumn, the eye passes over the wretched dwellings, is relieved with the verdure of the trees, and delights in the high mountains, of which the tallest summits, covered with perpetual snow, chill the evening and the early morning air, even at that season.

The area within the heaps of earth which form the defenses of Teheran is much larger than the city. For the most part, there is no wall, only an irregular trench, at the side of which the excavated sand has been carelessly heaped. We approached the Kasveen gate in quite a cavalcade. The khan's brother, his two sons held by servants upon white donkeys, and three mounted servants, had ridden an hour from the city to meet him. A man seated on the extreme end of a donkey had come out from Prevôt's, the hotel of Teheran, having heard by telegraph of our probable arrival. Altogether we formed a small crowd in passing the gate, which, like all the entrances to Teheran, reminds one of Tunbridge ware. The style of building, and the mode of arranging the glazed bricks, of various colors, is like nothing so much as the surface of the boxes one buys, or does not buy, at that pleasant town in Mid-Kent.

No European could enter the gates of Teheran for the first time without a feeling of intense disappointment: the city appears so insignificant in area and elevation. One sees nothing but wide, dusty spaces, broken occasionally by a mud-wall of precisely the same color as the road. After riding within the gates across country for about a mile, through holes in the walls of dusty inclosures which looked as if somebody had at one time thought them worth a mud-wall, and on second thoughts had arrived at an opposite conclusion, we came to something that had in the uniformity of its width the aspect of a street; but, like all the other ways of Teheran, this was bounded by apparently interminable walls of mud, broken only at about every twenty or thirty yards by an iron-bound door, the single sign that this erection was the outer wall of habitations. At last we arrived in the Belgravia of the Persian capital—the place of highest fashion; and there the only difference was, that the twelve-foot wall was paneled, and the mud cement covered with finer plaster, and washed over with blue, upon which were scrolled decorations molded in the same plaster.

The uniformity and ugliness of some of our own streets—say Gower Street, for example—are bad enough, but a brick wall would be worse; and a brick is a thing of beauty, and of many colors, compared with mud. Dried mud is the prevailing material and color in Teheran. One of the principal sites in the city is occupied by the "taziah," or theatre, in which religious representations are given, after the manner of the Ober-Ammergau Passion-plays, of the sufferings and death of Houssein. The front of this building is a good specimen of modern Persian architecture, which in England we should recognize as the Rosherville or Cremorne style—the gewgaw, pretentious, vulgar, and ephemeral style, erected in those places of amusement, only to be seen at night, and to last for a season. The façade is shaped like a small transept of the Crystal Palace, and covered with florid, coarse decorations in plaster, with beadings of bits of coarse looking-glass, bright blue, red, yellow, and green being plentifully laid upon the plaster wherever there is opportunity. Behind this is the Shah's palace, which is better, in that the plaster is uncolored. The gate which leads to this central inclosure, the citadel, or *arg* (the same word probably as "ark"), of Teheran, is of the same Tunbridge-ware pattern as the town gates; but the arches are filled with extravagant representations, in tiles of the coarsest colors, of the triumphs of legendary heroes of Persia over terrible creatures which can have existed only in the fancy of the artist. The excessively grotesque in these mosaics gives them a certain curious interest. It is upon the inner side of this gate-way that one sees to what a low level Persian art has descended. The ornaments of this most important and central gate in Teheran are representations of Persian soldiers, life-size, the painting of the glazed tiles being very much such as is seen in the east end of London upon the street bills of the lowest music-halls. In drawing, each soldier is like the "men" we are accustomed to see from the pencil of children of three or four years old. The features of each man are upon one plan; they have the same leer as those of his companions; the mustache is a brick and a half long, and the black boots are hanging painfully, as if tortured in the search for some clod or cloud to stand upon. The ornamentation of the exterior of some of the mosques with these colored bricks, chiefly of light blue and yellow, is very effective; but we met with no place in which this work was not more or less disfigured by ruin; and repair does not seem to be the business of any person or department.

From one end of Persia to the other, this miserable condition of decay, dilapidation, and ruin is characteristic of all public edifices—the mosques, palaces, bridges—every thing. It is probably correct to say that this invariable condition is a consequence of the universal corruption of the Government. The work of maintenance and repair belongs to the Executive Government, and the funds which should be thus expended pass into the rapacious pockets of the governors of the country. The gross neglect of useful public works in Persia recalled to my mind a passage in which Adam Smith refers to this as one of the worst symptoms of the worst administration. He nearly describes the state of things in Persia in the following passage, which had reference to the condition of the by-roads in France about the middle of the eighteenth century; with the difference, that in Persia no one delights in expenditure of any sort for the public advantage. Expenditure is never made except with a view to private plunder. "The proud minister of an ostentatious court may frequently take pleasure in executing a work of splendor and magnificence, such as a great highway which is frequently seen by the principal nobility, whose applauses not only flatter his vanity, but even contribute to support his interest at court. But to execute a number of little works in which nothing that can be done can make any great appearance, or excite the smallest degree of admiration in any traveler, and which, in short, have nothing to recommend them but their extreme utility, is a business which appears in every respect too mean and paltry to merit the attention of so great a magistrate. Under such an administration, therefore, such works are almost entirely neglected."*

Passing from north to south, almost the first house in Teheran, and certainly the best, is that of the British Legation. John Bull must have been caught in a liberal mood, and with loose purse-strings, when the vote was taken for this array of buildings; or is it not probable that poor India helped to pay for this residence? In Persia, it is the fixed idea of all people that Russia and England are rival powers. The ascendency of the influence of one or the other at the court of the Shah varies with men and circumstances. But although the Russian Legation is not nearly so fine a place as the house of the British minister, yet it is generally understood in Teheran that at present Russian authority is predominant. Most Persian statesmen have a decided leaning toward England; and His Highness Mirza Houssein Khan, the present chief minister of the Shah, is no exception. But, of course, the Persian liking for England is a natural preference for that power which is the less suspected of designs upon the independence of the country. However, it is certainly believed that a complainant is better off when he is backed by the Russian envoy. The Sadr Azem, as the chief minister is called (though Houssein Khan was Sipar Salar—commander-in-chief—when we were in Teheran), may prefer the English envoy to the Russian; but I have no doubt whatever that he would move more quickly at the demand of the latter. From the British Legation, in a straight southward line, are the taziah, the palace, and, farther on, the most interesting part of the town, the ba-

---

* "Wealth of Nations," book v., art. 3, part i.

zaars and caravanserais. It is there one can take the truest measure of Persian civilization. Every one knows what an Oriental bazaar is like; in Teheran it is a labyrinth of narrow ways, some of which are covered with well-executed brick arching, in which customers, camels, donkeys, Persians of high degree, attended by half a dozen servants, who rudely clear a way for the great man; Persians of low degree, and in almost every stage of undress; veiled women, and once a week perhaps a European — jostle all day long, while the sellers sit mute and motionless, rarely soliciting the custom of the throng. The dark shade, flecked with patches of bright sunlight, which is perhaps not the least noticeable feature of an Oriental bazaar, is broken occasionally by the entry to a caravanserai or mosque. The commercial caravanserais are sometimes attractive, the centre of the open square being occupied by fountains, and the space itself with plane-trees. Around the square, in large boxes, closed with heavy wooden shutters when the day's work is over, sit the merchants. The name of the finest caravanserai recalls to mind the great crime of the Shah's long reign—the cruel execution, at his majesty's word, of the most honest and best of his ministers, the Ameer-el-Nizam. The "Caravanserai Ameer" of Teheran is known on all the paths of Persia.

CHAPTER XI.

Teheran.—Street of the Foreign Envoys.—The British Minister.—Lanterns of Ceremony.—The English in Teheran.—The Shah's Palace.—Mirza Houssein Khan.—The Sipar Salar.—An Oriental Minister.—Persian Corruption.—Mirza Houssein Khan's Policy.—His Retinue.—Brigandage in Persia.—Saloon of Audience.—The Jeweled Globe.—The Shah's Throne. —The Old Hall.—Persians and the Alhambra.—The Shah receiving Homage.—Rustem and the White Devil.—Reports in Teheran.—The English Courier.—Character of Persian Government.—The Green Drawing-room.—The Shah's Album.—Persians and Patriots.—The Shah's Jewels.—The "Sea of Light."

At an open door in the wall of the best street in Teheran, which I have referred to as the "Belgravia" of the city, and which might be called "the Street of the Foreign Envoys," our twelve days' march ended. We were at Prevôt's, a Persian house, kept by a Frenchman as a hotel, with Armenian servants. We found three small rooms prepared for us, looking upon a paved yard about as large as the rooms, with a door-way leading to the larger quadrangle, which forms the usual centre of a house in Teheran. From the windows we could see a plastered wall four yards distant, and that was all; a miserable, depressing prospect in a city the situation of which is highly picturesque. In an hour I called on the English minister, Mr. Taylour Thomson, whose visit to us the next morning was followed by entertainments which made us more or less acquainted with the European element in the population of Teheran.

Mr. Thomson is in some points undoubtedly well qualified for his post. But it is only just to say that his long service in countries so remote as Persia and Chili (he acted as chargé-d'affaires for fifteen years in South America) has had the natural and inevitable consequence. Mr. Thomson is far better acquainted with Persian modes of thought and with Persian politics than with the affairs, and the thoughts, and the policy of his own country, and I am inclined to doubt very much if this is desirable for one in his position. Local knowledge is unquestionably valuable—it is, indeed, indispensable; but I believe it to be far more important that the envoy of a country should be closely familiar with the mind and disposition of those whom Lord Derby has lately called his "employers," and this can not be the possession of a man whose memory has to pass over five-and-forty years before it reaches the time when he was resident in England.

Mr. Thomson is a man in whom strength of will and directness of speech, two important qualities in English dealings with Orientals, are plainly marked. His deficiencies, I should say, are due to the absence of a life-time from the polishing influence of the capitals of Europe, and in political knowledge, from the stimulating action of English opinion, which, during the years of his long and honorable diplomatic service, has undergone a change far more remarkable than was ever brought about at one stroke by the swift agency of revolution.

He has mastered, and that is no small matter, the curiosities of Persian etiquette. It baffles the simple English mind to conceive a plan by which rank can be indicated at night in a dark, unlighted city, where the streets are full of holes. But with the Persian rank is every thing; and this is denoted at night according to the size and number of lanterns by which the progress of the great is illuminated. The ceremonious lanterns of Teheran, about eighteen inches in diameter, have a metal top and bottom, the intervening and luminous space being of plain or colored linen, about a yard deep. Through a ring in the top the bearer passes his arm, and, holding it high, he can just keep the lantern from off the ground as he walks. On the occasion of a dinner at the British Legation, or any similar festival elsewhere, these lanterns are seen advancing from all quarters, followed by guests, who are invisible in the surrounding gloom.

We were received with much kindness by the English in Teheran. I can imagine nothing more wearisome than their position. Their houses, for the most part built in Persian fashion, are dull beyond description, because they have no view of the grand outlook upon the mountains, to which it is always a relief to turn from the wretchedness of Teheran. They have what they call "a drive"—a long, straight road over the plain in the direction of a suburban palace belonging to the Shah—a road which is flat, tedious, and horribly dusty, one of those dreadful promenades of which the end is seen from the commencement. They have their parties, their coursings, their balls, in all of which they are doomed to look on combinations of the same faces. "We are now," writes one of them, "looking forward to a ball next Monday, given by ——, the —— chargé-d'affaires. Fifty-eight Europeans are invited. They are all sure to come; and as the ladies do not number, all told, fifteen, the black-coat element necessarily preponderates." Narrowness is born of such circumstances, but there is an absence of scandal among the European community of Teheran which is praiseworthy.

The English minister obtained permission for us to visit the Shah's palace in Teheran, and added the honor and advantage of his company. As is usual in Teheran, Mr. Thomson's carriage was surrounded by mounted servants. It is impossible to avoid much ceremony when the English minister visits the palace. We passed through the gate of the citadel, adorned with the soldiers, to the taziah, which closes the end of the street. Then, turning between the walls of the palace gardens, which were lined with lounging guards, we alighted at the simple entrance to one of the court-yards of the palace, the buildings of which are all low, and divided by these inclosures, in which there are rows of tall plane-trees and paved rectangular walks.

The minister was received by a large cluster of officials and servants, with whom we approached the principal hall of audience, which resembles an open temple. There is a mixture of Swiss and Chinese forms in the construction of the wooden roof, the sides of which are supported by four large twisted columns richly gilded. There are hangings of stout hempen stuff, by which the whole saloon can be protected from the weather; but the intention is that it should be open, and the Shah's reception visible to all upon the lower level of the court-yards. This is the place in which his majesty (who was at the time living in one of his palaces near the Caspian shore) receives, on the occasion of a salaam or levee, the diplomatic body and other persons of distinction. This saloon is raised by six high steps from the court-yard, and is nearly sixty feet long, with a width of about twenty-five feet. From the richly carpeted floor, we overlooked the court-yards, through which ran a stream of clear water, passing beneath the saloon in a paved channel.

We were enjoying a first glance at this curious apartment, the ceiling of which is set with facets of looking-glass (these, if they had been clean, would have been gorgeous with prismatic colors), when a posse of barefooted servants entered, something after the manner of a theatrical procession, evidently preceding some very great personage. It was His Highness the Sipar Salar, acting Prime Minister of the Shah, Mirza Houssein Khan, who, when he accompanied his imperial master to London, was Sadr Azem, which is the highest official title, and is, in fact, the Persian equivalent of Prime Minister. But Mirza Houssein Khan is not a popular man, and upon his return to Persia with His Majesty the Shah, a storm of hatred had risen against him, to which the Shah inclined so far as to deprive his clever minister of the title of Sadr Azem. The life of Mirza Houssein Khan was thought to be in danger, and it is said in Teheran that an order for his execution was arrested only by reminding the Shah that one who has the Grand Cross of the Star of India must, as a member of a most illustrious English brotherhood, be regarded as a person not to be given over to the knife or the bowstring of the executioner, without consideration for the opinion of Europe.

The Sipar Salar, next to the Shah himself, the greatest personage in the country, was in undress uniform of Russian cut. His overcoat resembled precisely, excepting its ornaments, that of a Russian officer. He wore the Persian hat, black trousers, and "pumps" of polished leather, which made a considerable exposition of his white stockings. Probably his highness wore these slight shoes in order to place himself upon equality with the Europeans who were treading the imperial carpets in their walking-boots. In pumps, he was equal to the customs of either continent; these could easily be laid aside if he desired to appear in Persian fashion, in his stockings. His highness was the only Persian whose feet were shod. Of his large retinue of more than fifty persons, those who mounted with the Sipar Salar into the saloon had left their shoes upon the pavement below. Mirza Houssein Khan is a man about middle height and middle age, with, for a Persian, commonplace features, full of mobility, and expressing great cleverness. He talks French fluently, and has a quick *rusé* manner. An artificial manner is cultivated by Persians, who in public affairs and correspondence do not affect sincerity. The Sipar Salar is a man whom, even at first sight, one feels little disposed to trust; a statesman of very superior ability and intelligence, probably spoiled by the cruel difficulties of his position. If the reports current in Teheran are true, his highness has not found it easy to keep his head on his shoulders in a great position in a country governed by a wayward despot, whose mind may at any time be fatally influenced against his minister.

An Oriental minister, even so clever a man as Mirza Houssein Khan, does not seem desirous of pushing his own country into European grooves when he has traveled in the Western Continent. If such ideas ever enter into such minds, they are, at all events, soon abandoned. He has, and that in itself is no small advantage, a truer estimate than can be formed by his untraveled countrymen of the strength, power, and wealth of the nations of Europe. But it is the Palais Royal of Paris rather than the Palace of Westminster which fills the largest place in his mind. His longing, as a rule, turns rather to the former than to the latter. In his shallow, courteous conversation, Mirza Houssein Khan did not appear to me to have any other view for Persia than that of battling with the difficulties of his own position, which I have no doubt are very engrossing. As he is certainly in experience the ablest and most competent of Persian statesmen, Mirza Houssein Khan would seem to be the right man in the right place. But his is a position which would break the heart of a good man. One can imagine a good man killing himself in the effort to reform the Government of Persia. But success would seem impossible, and endurance must lead to compromise with evil and corruption of every sort. A violent death would be the likely end of a good man in such a position, and wealth that of one who would accept the place and swim in the stream of corruption.

People say that Mirza Houssein Khan has preferred the latter course. A week before we met his highness on this visit to the Shah's palace, the following was written for publication with reference to him by a resident in Teheran, who has had opportunity of forming a mature judgment upon the estimation in which this undoubtedly able minister is held in Persia:

"Since Mirza Houssein Khan has been at the head of affairs in Persia, the country, both socially and politically, has followed a visibly retrograde movement. On him at one time all hopes of progress were centred: his promises of reform were great; but events have now shown either that he never meant to keep those promises, or that he is incapable of the task. Of all the influences that act against the true interests of the State, the selfish ambition and the avarice of this powerful minister have been perhaps the most effectual. To keep in his own hands the whole power of Government, and to enrich himself by this means, are with him the sole ends of existence; and, to effect his purpose, he leads the Shah's attention as much as possible away from public affairs while his majesty is at home, which is now rarely the case, as his chief adviser contrives to persuade him to undertake repeated journeys into the provinces. Thus it happens that during the last eight months the Shah has passed barely ten days in the capital. His majesty is now on a hunting expedition near Sari, in Mazandaran; and Mirza Houssein Khan, left completely his own master, has surrounded himself with almost regal pomp. Yesterday, at the Beiram ceremony of the salaam [a levee held by the third son of the Shah], he was followed by a cortége more numerous than that which the king himself leads on great occasions. In contrast with these displays, the affairs of Government have fallen into deplorable confusion, and oppression has become so rampant that an open manifestation of popular discontent is to be expected. Never was there a more unpopular minister. Two years ago, when the Mirza was execrated as a reformer by the nobles and the priesthood, he succumbed for a time to the opposition of these conservative classes. Now that the hatred of the populace is added to that of his political rivals, his fall, when it comes, will be signal indeed. It is not to be denied that brigandage is flourishing in Persia. Caravans and travelers are plundered at the very gates of Teheran. Want and oppression have turned the most peaceful of the population into highwaymen."

It may be that Mirza Houssein Khan, who nearly lost his life on account of his reputation as a reformer on his return from London, is now content if he can keep his head on his shoulders, and himself above all his rivals on the surface of the foul pool of official life in Persia.

Close to the insignificant door-way by which we entered the saloon, there is hung upon the wall a very large picture, which, somewhere about the centre, contains a full-length portrait of the Emperor of Austria. The picture is so large, and is hung in so important a position, that, should other monarchs who are on friendly terms make the Shah a similar present, it would be quite impossible for his imperial majesty to give even to one of them an equally advantageous display. When the Shah received this portrait, he resolved to present in return a likeness of himself, and declared it should be placed in a frame of solid gold. But inquiry and calculation modified his majesty's intentions, and at last he consented to order a gilt frame in Francis Joseph's own capital city. Beneath this huge canvas were hung a landscape and a sea-piece, evidently purchased from some French gallery, the small tin plate bearing the exhibition number of each picture being still in the corner.

It is at the opposite end of this saloon that the "Shadow of God" sits on his heels, or stands to receive the envoys of Europe. But the Shah's movable throne was not occupying the central niche. There, in that place of honor, we were permitted to gaze upon one of the characteristic feats, perhaps the greatest art-work, of his majesty's long reign. This is an eighteen-inch globe, covered with jewels from the North

Pole to the extremities of the tripod in which this gemmed sphere is placed. The story goes that his majesty bought— more probably accepted, at all events was in possession of— a heap of jewels, for which he could find no immediate purpose. Nothing could add to the lustre of his crown of diamonds, which is surmounted by the largest ruby we have ever seen, including those of her majesty and the Emperors of Germany and Russia. He had the "Sea of Light," a diamond in size but little inferior to the British Koh-i-noor, the "Mountain of Light." He had coats embroidered with diamonds, with emeralds, with rubies, with pearls, and with garnets; he had jeweled swords and daggers without number; so, possibly because his imperial mind was turned toward travel, the Shah ordered this globe to be constructed, covered with gems—the overspreading sea to be of emeralds, and the kingdoms of the world distinguished by jewels of different color. The Englishman notes with pride and gratification that England flashes in diamonds; and a Frenchman may share the feeling, for France glitters illustrious as the British isles, being set out in the same most costly gems. The dominion of the Shah's great neighbor, the brand-new Empress of India, is marked with amethysts; while torrid Africa blazes against the literally emerald sea, a whole continent of rubies.

Near the globe, side by side with a French couch, worth perhaps a hundred francs, stands the Shah's throne, which is, of course, arranged for sitting after the manner of the country. It occupies a space almost as large as Mr. Spurgeon's or Mr. Ward Beecher's pulpit; for the occupants of this throne are fond of space, and occasionally have a kalian of wonderful dimensions with them upon the splendid carpet, which is fringed with thousands of pearls. The embroidered bolster upon which the Shah rests his back or arm is sewn with pearls. Behind his majesty's head is a "sun," all glittering with jewels, supported at the corners with birds in plumage of the same most expensive material.

On the other side of the niche in which the globe stands, there is a table grimy with dust and extremely incongruous, the top inlaid with the beautiful work of Florence, and a model, in Sienna marble, of the Arch of Titus, both gifts from his holiness the infallible Pope. Near these presents, in a recess, and in a very common wooden frame, is a portrait of the late Sir Henry Havelock; and, not far off, a time-piece with "running water" and a nodding peacock, a gift from the defunct East India Company in the days when Shahs received such toys as pleased them, and were not considered eligible as knights of the great orders of European courts.

At a short distance is another and a much older hall, still more exposed to public view. In this pavilion, which is built to cover and give increased dignity to the ancient throne of the Shah, the arrangements are wholly Persian. The marble floor is raised not more than three feet above the pavement of a large oblong court-yard, up the broad paths of which the sons of Iran throng to make salaam before their monarch. The Shah sits in the motionless majesty of an Oriental potentate, upon a high throne built of the alabaster-like greenish marble of Yezd, the platform which the "Shadow of God" occupies being supported upon animals, having the same queer resemblance to lions which is noticed in the supporters of the great fountain of the Alhambra at Granada. With reference to this likeness, and to other points of resemblance, both in this palace and in the decorations in some of the modern palaces of Persia, Major Murdoch Smith, R.E., the accomplished director of the Indo-Persian Telegraph, has indicated, in a report to the Council of the South Kensington Museum, the probability that the Alhambra of Granada was itself designed by Persian architects; and, with regard to this supposition, has pointed to the statement of Señor Rivadeneyra concerning the existence of official documents assigning Rioja in Spain to "Persians" as a place of residence.

The ceiling of this old reception-hall in the Shah's Palace at Teheran is fashioned in stalactites, like the ceilings in the ruins of the famous Oriental palace in Spain, and then covered with pieces of looking-glass, which, if the work were not bad, and the glass were cleaned, would have a very glittering effect. Externally the roof is suggestive of a Chinese pagoda. In this pavilion, the background of which is hung with a few pictures in frames of looking-glass, including a portrait of a singularly handsome young Englishman, formerly attached to the British Legation, the Shah reclines upon the marble platform of his throne, on those very great occasions when the hundred and fifty yards of the inclosure before it are filled with a moving crowd of his subjects, to whom he is the impersonation of law and authority. For their reverent homage, he makes no sign of gratification or acknowledgment. The "proper thing" for his majesty to do, when thus exhibiting himself in solemn state, is to regard their expression of loyalty and devotion as something far beneath his notice; and probably the imperial gaze passing over their heads is now and then fixed upon the coarse mosaic on the wall at the end of the court-yard, showing how Rustem, the "Arthur," the legendary hero, of Persia, destroyed the White Devil — an encounter, it should be remembered, of authenticity as respectable as that of St. George and the familiar Dragon which is stamped upon so many of the current coins of England.

I had scarcely ceased talking with the Sipar Salar, whom I had seen at several entertainments in London, when one of the numerous company whispered in my ear, pointing to his highness, "He had one of his wives strangled lately." I did not for a moment believe that this was any thing but a piece of idle gossip, yet it is worth recording, because it is one of many pieces of evidence which came to our notice indicating the bad state of society in Persia, owing to the uncivilized system prevailing both in the family and in the State. Perhaps the worst symptom of the body politic in Persia is that no one hesitates in ascribing horrible crimes to the most highly placed men in the State, and that the venality of such exalted persons in regard to the misappropriation of public money is regarded as a foregone conclusion.

A few days before our visit to the palace, the talk of all the soldiery in Teheran, as we heard from several of their officers, had been that the crown prince, the Governor of Tabriz, had caused his wife to be strangled in his presence. Homicide or murder is a prerogative of royalty in Persia. But what was most amazing was the ready reception given to the report, which was regarded, even by Europeans, as quite authentic. The report was untrue. It had origin in the fact that the prince's aunt had lately sent a second wife to her illustrious nephew in Tabriz, and the anger and grief of the first wife, on seeing the new arrival, had been magnified into her death. The minister of public works is said to double his estimates, and to retain the surplus for himself, after silencing those whose mouths must be stopped. The frequent robberies of the messengers of the British Legation, while carrying letters and dispatches overland from Teheran to Trebizonde, have been the subject of much talk, and Persians wag their heads and say that this happens because his highness Mirza Houssein Khan likes to read Mr. Thomson's letters to Lord Derby, and the replies of the British Foreign Office.

With reference to this curious charge, I will make the following extract from a letter written by a resident in Teheran, dated November 2d, 1875: "The English courier, on his last journey from Constantinople, was attacked and robbed on or near the frontier. The previous courier had been stopped and examined by the police at Tabriz, on suspicion of smuggling contraband goods into the country. As the English parcels alone were opened, however, the couriers of the other legations never meeting with adventures of this kind, some people affirm that the attack upon the British post was instigated by the Mushir-ul-Dowleh himself, who wished to intercept or to make himself acquainted with the contents of certain dispatches. I can not, of course, pretend to say whether or not this assertion is true, but it must be said that the Mirza's known unscrupulousness gives it some color."

It is universally believed that a little money will mitigate, and that much money will obviate, the punishment of crime. That every "hakem," or governor, may commit offenses against the property and lives of the Shah's subjects within his province with impunity, no one seems to doubt. It matters little, in forming our judgment as to the social condition of Persia, whether these reports are true or false. They are not all true—some are certainly false—they may all be false, and yet the tacit, unastonished acceptance of them as true by the populace implies that they have at least the common flavor of the ordinary fruits of Persian government.

From the great halls of state, the commander-in-chief, the minister of commerce, and other Persian grandees led our party to an orange house, through the centre of which ran the stream of clear water I have noticed before as passing beneath the saloon of the gilded columns. On the marble pavement beside this running water there were chairs and couches arranged, upon which his highness invited us to be seated. Snowy sherbet and warm tea were then served, and afterward we proceeded to a more homely saloon than those we had seen. The architecture of this room, a succession of arcades, again carried our thoughts to Spain, in its resemblance to the mosque, now the cathedral, of Cordova. It was a large oblong apartment, the walls colored green, with raised decorations in white plaster, the room containing three rows of arches. On the walls were a great many pictures very irregularly hung. Many had in the corner the exhibition number in the gallery from which the Shah had bought them during his recent tour; and in no very conspicuous place was a small portrait of her majesty, a gift presented by Mr. Thomson to the Shah on behalf of the queen. The floor was of parqueterie-work, and upon it stood several Sèvres jars of great value. Very uncomfortable chairs, evidently bought by people with little knowledge of what a chair should be, were ranged against the walls. On a table lay a photographic album containing the portraits of actresses, of whose personal charms the Shah may be supposed to have become acquainted by report, and by diligent attendance at theatres during his stay in Europe. At one end of the apartment was an object in strange contrast with the trumpery by which it was surrounded. This was an awkward, ugly chair of state studded with jewels, having a footstool, before which stood a cat-like representation of a lion, each eye a single emerald, and the body rugged with a coating of other precious stones. It was so entirely in keeping with the mixture we had everywhere observed, that the stand upon which this chair was placed should be studded with white-headed German nails worth about twopence a dozen!

None of the great rooms of the palace have covered communications, and from this green saloon we crossed another open court to a pavilion in which the Shah frequently gives audience, which is distinguished by the possession of an English carpet, and by the exhibition upon the walls of two fine pieces of Gobelins tapestry. One sees in the figures upon this tapestry, and in the portraits upon the walls of the palace, how far the Persians have departed from observing the rule which was certainly that of the architects of the Alhambra, and which is observed by the Turks and all Sunni Mohammedans, of excluding imitation or resemblance of life from the ornamentation of their public buildings.

In another room we saw the imperial jewels, which, by special command of his highness the Sipar Salar, were laid out upon tables for our inspection. I fancy that no sovereign in Europe has a regalia of equal value. The Shah is especially rich in diamonds of large, but not the very largest size. He has a great number of which the surface is as large as a silver sixpence. The imperial crown is topped with a ruby which is probably the largest in the world. The "Sea of Light," a flat, ill-cut diamond, mounted in a semi-barbaric ornament, is inferior to the great jewel worn by the Empress of India. The display of the Shah's riches in precious stones included, of necessity, the exhibition of several coats, the fronts of which are studded and embroidered with jewels. Several of these became well known during the Shah's tour, when they were shown to the admiring gaze of European cities. There, too, was the wonderful aigrette, which the Shah's brow sustained during the grandest of the London entertainments, and beside these garments lay a number of jeweled swords and daggers. From the dazzling spectacle of this display we passed again to the orange house, where coffee and pipes were served, after which we took leave of the Shah's ministers, his highness the Sipar Salar having promised Mr. Thomson that we should be provided with vizierial letters to the Governors of Koom, Kashan, Ispahan, Shiraz, and Bushire.

CHAPTER XII.

The Shah.—The Kajar Dynasty.—Boxes of Justice.—Persian Soldiers.—Their Drill and Pay.—Military Supper in Ramadan.—Jehungur Khan.—The Shah's Presents.—Zoological Garden.—View from Teheran.—Demavend.—Persian Fever.—Persian Honesty.—Europeans and Persians.—Caps and Galoches.—A Paper War.—The Ottoman Embassy.—A British Complaint.—A Turkish Atrocity.—Persian Window Law.—English in Bazaars.—The Indo-European Telegraph Stations in Persia.—The English Clergyman in Persia.

THE Shah is of the Kajar tribe—a dynasty yet young, the annals of which have been marked by great cruelties. Nazred-deen Shah, Kajar, the reigning monarch, has in this matter a better character than his predecessors, with whom it has not been uncommon to put out the eyes of those relations who stood in their way to the throne, or who might be rivals when they had attained that position. The Shah himself is not unpopular, and is believed to have at heart the welfare of his subjects. Persians frequently speak of him as in personal character the best among the governing men of the country, and they are never shy in talking of their rulers. If there is any tempering in the Persian despotism, it is that of abuse of all who surround the despot. His majesty recently issued an order that a "Box of Justice" should be fixed in a prominent place in all the large towns for the reception of petitions, which were to be forwarded direct to himself. But the oppressors found means to thwart this innocent plan by setting a watch over the boxes and upon those who wished to forward petitions.

Thrice the amount of the British Prime Minister's salary, or twice that of the President of the United States, does not satisfy men of the first official rank in Persia. And while the prince governors in the provinces and all the high functionaries of State plunge their greedy hands thus deep into the miserable revenue, forced—often at the bayonet's point—from the poorest of peasants, the soldiery are not seldom marauders, with the excuse that they can not obtain their pay from the Government. The creditors of the peasants and small traders are generally in the uniform of the Shah. In Persia the trade of small money-lenders is usually carried on by soldiers, for these only feel sure of the requisite power to recover their loans. The defaulter well knows that if he does not repay the soldier, his house or his store in the bazaar will be plundered of all that is worth taking by a gang of military money-lenders.

There is a parade every morning in Teheran. It takes place in a dusty inclosure near the meidan, or principal square. We were present on several occasions at these parades, where European drill-instructors vainly labored. The Persian soldiers are fine in physique, though they look more awkward, I fancy, even than Japanese in European hats, tunics, and trousers. In England one is apt to think that militia-men display every possible awkwardness in wearing an infantry hat and scarlet tunic, but the Persian soldiers beat the rawest of our militia-men. Some wear the hat on the back of their heads like a fez, others at the side; with some it falls over their eyes. Their drill is wretched. Their officers are probably the worst part of the force. This is the special weakness and inferiority of all Oriental armies. I saw a Persian officer box the ears of a private on the parade-ground, rushing into the ranks to execute this summary punishment.

There is a reason for the deficiency of the rank and file in drill. No soldier comes to parade who can obtain work in the city. The consequence is that the personnel of each skeleton regiment is changed every morning, and the unhappy drill-instructor has never before him the same body of men. But this immunity from service must of course be paid for, and the absent privates devote a portion of their earnings to their officers, who, from their colonel to the corporal, divide the fund contributed in respect of this temporary desertion. From the officers and middle class of State officials, a somewhat intricate method of plunder is adopted. Their pay, although appropriated from the revenue, is withheld, and after repeated applications they are told that the minister will advance the sum with a deduction to cover his personal risk. The offer is generally accepted from pressing necessity, and the gains of the higher functionaries from this line of conduct are said to be not inconsiderable. I was assured by an officer that he himself suffered this treatment, and that he knew it to be common in the civil and military service of the Shah.

Every evening in Ramadan, of which there remained some days after our arrival in Teheran, the Sipar Salar entertained a regiment at dinner. The repast was served by candle-light in the straight street between the gate of the citadel and the taziah. Two lines of thick felt (*nummud*) were laid equidistant from the centre of the street, leaving about a yard of the bare road between them. Shortly before the gun-fire, his highness's guests were seated in long files upon the felt. After the gun had boomed permission, huge dishes, one to every four soldiers, each piled high with rice and stewed meat, were placed in the centre of the road, and were at once hidden from view by the overhanging heads of the hungry men, every one hard at work with his fingers. Under such circumstances, the nearer the mouth can be brought to the dish, the larger is the share which can be pushed into it. Close over every dish four heads were laid together, and not a word was uttered till the platters were empty.

For the officers there was spread a white cloth between the

carpets, and a little adornment was attempted in the way of bouquets placed between the lighted candles, which were protected by Russian bell-glasses, and shone like glow-worms down the long street. In company with a member of the British Legation, I was looking on, when Jehangur Khan, the adjutant-general of the Persian army, one of the stoutest and most courteous men in the country, asked us to join the soldiers in the fruit and tea which followed the pillau. We sat down, doing all we could to get rid of our legs, which had an awkward, natural tendency to cross the dining-table. My immediate neighbors were officers of the Shah's irregular cavalry, gentlemen wearing turbans almost as broad as their shoulders, and with a very Bashi-bazoukish look.

At that time a story was in circulation with reference to this Jehungur Khan, which is very possibly untrue, but, being accepted by many as correct, is curiously illustrative of Persian government. It was said that one of the courtiers who owed him a grudge had told the Shah that he (the adjutant-general) had saved eight thousand tomans out of a work in hand, and that he wished to present them to his majesty. The King of Kings is much addicted to presents, and, as usual, graciously signified his willingness to accept, and Jehungur Khan had to produce the money, which he had *not* saved. The Shah does not appear to be very scrupulous in regard to presents. There is at least one tradesman in London from whom articles were purchased by order of his majesty for presents to some of his ladies, which have not yet been paid for, and probably this is not the only city of Europe in which the Shah obtained articles of value in this way without paying for them.

In the quarter of the town near the Legations there are several walled gardens, and one of these is devoted to zoology. We were about to apply for admission, when an Englishman recommended us to remain outside. The caging of the few beasts was, he said, quite uncertain. The lion was sometimes observed taking an airing, roaming where he pleased within the walls, and the bear had been seen from outside climbing a plane-tree. One is named the Shah's "English" garden, and from this his majesty lately received, with great effusion, a bunch of radishes as a present from his English gardener. If it were not for these gardens, the appearance of Teheran would indeed be miserable. We mounted upon one of the highest houses, from which we could overlook the city. Parallelograms of mud varied with cupolas of mud, representing the roofs of the houses, are the general features, the long succession of mud roofs being now and then broken by the taller plane-trees and the cypresses of a garden. But the landscape is charming, and even the Himalayas do not present grander elevations than may be seen from Teheran; the loftiest peak of the Elburz Mountains in sight being that of Demavend, an extinct volcano, the top of which is not less than eighteen thousand five hundred feet above the sea-level. The conical summit of this high mountain is covered with perpetual snow, and some of the peaks near Demavend are not of much inferior altitude.

At the latter end of October I was prostrated with fever. I remember that, in the witless condition in which I lay, the pains appeared to my disordered imagination as if I were suffering from the effects of a terrible beating, and, with every muscle sore and painful, were condemned to be rolled about upon sheets of heated copper. When I became convalescent, the closeness of the apartments at Prevôt's seemed intolerable, and, through the kindness of a Danish officer, Mr. Læssoë, resident in Teheran, we removed to a suite of rooms in his house, which had been the residence of the French Legation. There we had a large garden, and an open view of the plain and mountains. Mr. Læssoë holds the position of chief instructor of artillery in the army of the Shah. His wife, from whom also we received much kindness, is a daughter of the distinguished painter, Madame Jerichau.

At the house of every European of position in Teheran there is a permanent guard of soldiers, who hurriedly forsake their pipe, or game of cards upon the dust, to present arms upon the arrival of any visitor. The doors of these houses are generally open throughout the day; and as Persians regard an open door as an invitation to enter, and the rooms are never locked, and rarely closed with any thing more obstructive than a cotton curtain, it is necessary there should be some guard in the door-way. Europeans talk much of the dishonesty of Persians, but our experience did not confirm the bad opinion. Our suite of rooms in this mud-built house, which had formerly belonged to the French envoy, opened upon a large square garden inclosed by a mud-wall, ruined and broken down in three or four places, by which any one might enter. Our doors and windows had no fastenings, and by either it was never difficult to enter the rooms from the garden. On the other side was a court-yard, with a fountain and a few trees in the centre; and this, except for the soldiers and servants who lay about in the passages connecting it with the crowded street, was quite open. Yet we never suffered any loss from theft.

The manner in which Europeans meet Persian habits half-way, in their intercourse with the highest class of natives, always appears to me ridiculous and humiliating. It is a cleanly habit, that of Mohammedans, not to enter their carpeted apartments in the shoes they have worn in the mud of the filthy ways and streets of Oriental towns. No doubt, if we could choose, many of us in London would prefer that our visitors should carry their boots in their hands and their hats on their heads, rather than the reverse, especially upon a muddy day. But the English in Persia confound both practices in a most unseemly way. They wear their hats in the presence of Persians of high rank as a compromise with native prejudice, which from habit dislikes to see the head uncovered, and embarrass their feet with galoches in order that they may leave these overshoes at the door of the great man's apartment. In the course of our own travels in Persia, I noticed this on the part of Europeans; but even after such experience, I was rather surprised to find it elevated to a duty in the recently published volumes edited by Sir Frederic G. Goldsmid, and entitled "Eastern Persia." By officers of the Boundary Commission galoches for ceremonious receptions were provided as indispensable, and the members of the Commission always sat on these occasions in their undress caps. I should fancy that, to a quick-witted people like the Persians, this appears very absurd. For my own part, in any intercourse with men of the highest rank and of the imperial family in Persia, I never adopted these fashions. One need not soil carpets in a country where riding is universal, nor encourage premature baldness by wearing one's hat when there is no need of shelter from the sun or the outer air.

During our stay in Teheran, a fierce paper war was raging with reference to a dispute which, in continuation of the above remarks, shows what a tendency Englishmen have to take local coloring in their domestic habits. The peculiar construction of Persian houses has an object, that of securing most complete privacy for the inmates. It is true that there is no part of a Persian house which can not be looked into by any of the inhabitants; but this does not offend Mussulman ideas, of which the first is that the male head of the household is lord of all, and that none can have rights separate from his supreme authority. Persians much dislike rooms raised above the ground-floor, because these erections may enable neighbors to observe their domestic arrangements. Many tales are told of the fierce opposition which the intention to raise a second story has aroused in the hearts of neighbors, and, as a rule, it is not permitted by the authorities to any one to build so as to overlook another house.

War had broken out upon this domestic question between the representatives of Great Britain and of the Ottoman Empire. The mediation of Persia had been called in, and Mirza Houssein Khan was engaged in arranging a treaty of peace and future amity. The British envoy's object was to circumvent the wicked and abominable design of the Ottoman embassador (the politicians of the Porte have, as a rule, no Mussulman prejudices), who had dared to build an embassy-house in sight of that of Great Britain, and to add a second story, from which it was possible to see something of the ladies of the British Legation (the subsequent tale about the archives is too ridiculous to be true) if they happened to be walking in the extensive grounds in which are the houses of the secretaries and attachés, as well as the residence of the minister.

The Bulgarian atrocities had not then been heard of, and one might have thought that no subject of Great Britain need object to be exposed to the eye of a Turk with an interval of not less than five hundred yards. But this was not the view of the British Legation. That the British establishment should command a view of the Ottoman quarters was quite unobjectionable; but that the Turk should be able to cast an eye upon the Englishman's garden was intolerable. I do not know how this great international difficulty has been arranged; but, since our return to England, I have met with a published letter written about the time of our visit by a gentleman who lives in Teheran, which is probably, at least on some points, well informed. This correspondent says: "A short time ago the Turkish Government hired a building for fifteen years, to serve as a residence for its representative. The edifice stands within a few hundred yards of the British Legation, which is surrounded by a garden inclosed by a high wall. The wall is, however, not high enough to conceal the upper part of the Legation. The Turks wished to add a story to their Legation; but the English minister, on hearing of their intention, opposed it, on the ground that, if carried out, it would afford to the denizens of the Turkish 'palace' a view into the apartments occupied by the secretaries of the English mission, and, to give greater weight to his assertion, said that the archives of the Legation would be exposed to prying eyes. The Mushir-ul-Dowleh received a complaint to this effect in due form from Mr. Thomson, and, instead of declining to interfere in a matter which did not concern him, promised to arrange matters to the satisfaction of the English minister. By his order, a commission was appointed to examine the relative positions of the two edifices; but the result of their inspection was far from satisfactory for Mr. Thomson. They stated not only that the distance between the two Legations was too considerable to allow of any person in the Turkish Legation becoming acquainted from that vantage-ground with the contents of any documents exposed to view in the archive office of the English Legation, the latter being situated at least a third of a mile from its Turkish neighbor, but that none of the windows of the English archive office faced the new building. They observed, moreover, that if Mr. Thomson desired absolutely to conceal the roof of his habitation, he had only to add a foot or two to the height of his garden walls." The letter (which appeared in the *Levant Herald*) goes on to state that, undaunted by this adverse decision, "Mr. Thomson raised the precedent of one Melcom, an English subject at Bushire, who, in the course of certain building operations, was sued at law by some neighbors jealous of their privacy, and forced to abandon or modify his undertaking. The dispute has thus been placed in a new light. Either it is not lawful in Persia to have windows commanding a prospect of another man's house, even at a distance of five hundred yards, or it is lawful to have windows possessing that not uncommon peculiarity. In the former case, the Turkish Legation has no course left but to close up all its windows permanently and alter its façade; in the latter case, the judgment pronounced against Mr. Melcom of Bushire is illegal, and the Persian Government owes him heavy damages." Let us hope that this storm about mud-walls and windows has now been arranged to the satisfaction of all parties.

To my mind, the most interesting part of Teheran is to be found in the bazaars, which the Europeans of the legations very rarely enter, and their ladies never. The men appear to regard the shoving-about to which one must more or less submit in the narrow ways of the bazaars as a serious infringement upon the dignity of their position, and the ladies consider a visit to the bazaars as simply impossible. The sight of an unveiled woman has no doubt a tendency to make Persians use language which can not but be taken as insulting; and if Englishmen in their company are acquainted with Persian slang, they are likely enough to have a quarrel or two on hand in passing through a bazaar. Ignorance of the vernacular has unquestionably some advantages in Persia.

A long inclosure separates the buildings of the palace from the bazaar. There are in this open space two large tanks, at which camels, horses, mules, and men are always drinking. Upon a high stand a very long, huge cannon is placed, which is said to have been captured in India, and brought as a trophy from Delhi; but this is probably untrue.

Second only to the British Legation in importance is the establishment of the Indo-European Telegraph in Teheran. From the Persian capital to London the telegraph is a private enterprise; from Teheran through Central and Southern Persia to Bushire and by the Persian Gulf, to Kurrachee and the chief centres of India, the wires belong to the Indian Government. There is an arrangement by which the Shah's

Government has the use of a wire in Persia. The maintenance of this telegraph engages a considerable staff, of which the local director is Major Murdoch Smith, R.E., who, with much advantage to the British public, has bestowed some of his leisure hours in collecting specimens of the ancient artwork of Persia, with funds provided by the Council of the South Kensington Museum. Many of the articles which are now in the Museum were kindly shown to us by Major Smith in the neighborhood of Teheran. In the work of the Persian telegraph, he is assisted by a staff of superintendents, inspectors, and clerks, whose health is cared for by three medical men, the chief of whom, Dr. Baker, is resident in Teheran, his two colleagues being placed, one in Ispahan, the other in Shiraz. The testing-stations, most of which we visited in passing through Persia, are generally placed about a hundred miles apart, and the chief duty of the clerks at these stations is to correspond at stated hours in morning, afternoon, and evening with the men on duty at the stations on either side, in order to see that no break has occurred in the line, and that all is in good working order. If the connection is broken, the native horsemen attached to each station are at once sent out to ride along the course of the wires till they reach the fracture. As the break must be known to two stations, the horsemen are sometimes sent out from both, and meet where the repair is needed. The fracture of the wires by design or malice is of very rare occurrence; but they are broken now and then by bullets. Persians are ambitious of skill in rifle-shooting; and in the plains, where natural targets are scarce, they find in the earthenware insulators of the telegraph a most inviting object. Sometimes the poles are overthrown by storms of wind, and sometimes the wires are broken and the poles borne down to the ground by the weight of frozen snow which collects in thick, icy bands from pole to pole. We were much indebted—as every English traveler by the same path must be—to the Government officers of the Indo-Persian Telegraph.

One of the most interesting persons whom we met with in Teheran was the Rev. Robert Bruce, the only English missionary—in fact, the only English clergyman in Persia. He is stationed at Ispahan, and we accepted an invitation to stay in his house during our visit to that central city of Persia. When we met with Mr. Bruce in Teheran, he was returning from England to his duties in connection with the Church Missionary Society. In the Persian capital he was in great request for the baptism of the babies born during the long time which had elapsed since the visit of an English clergyman. An exception to the rule of other legations, religion is not represented in that of Great Britain.

CHAPTER XIII.

Teheran.—Snow in November.—Our Servant, Kazem.—Getting a Takht-i-rawan.—Abd-ullah, the Carpenter.—Preparing for the Road.—A Charvodar's "Beard."—Black Monday.—Trying the Takht-i-rawan.—Loading the Caravan.—Servant's Merchandise.—"*Zood! Zood!*"—Leaving Teheran.—The Road to Ispahan.—Seeing the Khanoum.—Shah Abd-ul-Azim.—Moollahs on the Road.—On to Kinaragird.—The Great Salt Desert.—Pul-i-delak.—A Salt River.—A Negro Dervish.—Salt-water Soup.—A Windy Lodging.

I WAS slowly recovering from a fever—taking quinine, as every one does at some time or other in Persia—when we determined to set out for Ispahan. Already the snow was creeping down the mountains, and seemed, in spite of the noonday sun, to be firmly established for the winter within about two thousand feet of the plain of Teheran. Though the days were hot, the nights were becoming cold.

The first thing was the construction of a takht-i-rawan. Servants brought in reports of takht-i-rawans for sale. A khan had one to dispose of, in which two of his ladies had just arrived from the sacred city of Meshed. I went to look at it. Through the narrow streets, between brown walls of mud, I followed two of the khan's servants to the outskirts of Teheran. In a small yard, surrounded by walls, half of which lay in a dusty heap under the takht-i-rawan, I examined the conveyance. It was coarsely decorated with somewhat indecent figures; it had no windows, was simply a box, like an elongated Saratoga trunk, built on two long poles, and had seen so much service that it was none too strong for a journey of six hundred and fifty miles to Shiraz. The French Secretary of Legation heard of our want. His wife had just arrived from Astrabad in a takht-i-rawan, but the poles of his conveyance were decidedly rotten. It was better to have one made, even though we must leave it, after thirty days' journey, in Shiraz. To travel in a takht-i-rawan from Shiraz to Bushire is well known throughout Persia to be impossible.

Among the servants in the household of Mr. Læssoë was one Kazem, who urged us to engage him for the journey to Bushire, and presented a written character from the Hon. Evelyn Ellis, whom he had accompanied in the same journey two or three years before. Mr. Læssoë very kindly consented, and we at once placed this bright-eyed, active, intelligent little Persian at the head of our arrangements. In all things Kazem did his part well. His first business was to introduce a carpenter, to be instructed in the most improved plan of a takht-i-rawan. Abd-ullah was the carpenter introduced by Kazem. We were told that Kazem was sure to have made an arrangement, after the manner of Persian servants, with Abd-ullah, by which the latter was to give him ten per cent. upon the price. This is no doubt the way in which Persian servants increase their gains; but it does not come to much. The method is well known, and it is probable Europeans would not obtain articles at a lower price if they purchased for themselves. The carpenter, though the picture of abject humility, as he stood at the edge of our carpet with meekly folded hands, was a well-dressed man: his turban was of spotless white, his robe of red, his trousers blue. Together we set out to see the takht-i-rawan at the British Legation, which was better than the native carriages in that between the seats it had a well, like that of a European carriage, for the feet, drawers beneath the seats for stores, and glass windows. Abd-ullah looked it carefully over, notched its measurements on a piece of stick, and entered into an agreement to make one like it for a specified sum, money to buy wood being paid at once.

This is quite usual in all transactions. When he came to the iron-work, he wanted money to buy the iron. No tradesman seems to have any capital, but every one has a seal, which, after most careful scrutiny of every letter, he will affix to agreements and notes of advances. Persians are fond of written agreements, and these seem more common than in England, where no one would think of having an agreement for so trifling a piece of work. I drew up an agreement in English for the building of the takht-i-rawan; it was read to Abd-ullah by an interpreter of the Legation, and the carpenter, with many bows, almost prostrations, sealed it, and received part of the sum agreed to be paid for the carriage. He had bound himself to complete the takht-i-rawan in nine days. During this time, we ransacked the bazaars for stores and equipment of all sorts. "You are neither of you strong enough for such a journey," said the good medicine-man of the British in the Persian capital. "The cold, snowy blasts are such as you can not conceive from English experience; and your lodging will be the most wretched, and exposed to the same temperature, to say nothing of the dangers of the road, especially for you, who have no English-speaking servants, and who can not talk Persian." We laughed at his fears, and told him we had made some progress in Persian; could ask for horses, and for any sort of food; that we had tracings of the route enlarged, and marked with the name and distance of every station. At his suggestion, our iron stirrups were covered with thick felt of camel's hair, to prevent the risk of frost in the feet; and we bought felts, nearly half an inch thick, to nail up in the door-ways of the unprotected hovels in which we must sleep. Among a score of other things, Kazem strongly recommended a bag of picked and broken walnuts mixed with green raisins. We had double counterpanes, thickly lined with cotton wool. Our kind friends, Mr. and Mrs. Læssoë, ordered the baking of half a dozen large loaves of bread in English fashion; and when the takht-i-rawan was built, we sent to the bazaar for a muleteer. Up came a man seated on a leggy little chestnut horse —a "yaboo," as these much-enduring and sure-footed animals are called. This is the special name for the horse of a charvodar. Sometimes it carries a traveler, sometimes the muleteer himself, and at other times it bears a load of goods, and, with jingling bells attached to every part of its harness, gayly leads the caravan. This charvodar was a short, old man, with sunken eyes and gloomy, fanatical aspect. His beard, his hands, and his feet were dyed deep-red with khenna. He hitched his waist-belt of camel's hair rope, straightened his long, loose robe of blue cotton, and salaamed when he saw us standing in the door-way. He sat on his "yaboo" inside the door while we discussed the proposed journey. "The sahib wants to go to Ispahan?" said our friend. "Inshallah" ("By the will of Allah!") was the reply of the charvodar. "He wants horses and mules."—"I have horses and twelve mules, but I can load any the sahib does not want with merchandise."

At last the price was settled—so many krans for each animal, the two in the takht-i-rawan to be paid for as four; and then came the question of advance and security. "My beard is in your hands," said the charvodar, meaning that if we advanced money after he had sealed an agreement, we could punish him if he did not go. "No," urged our friend, in the Persian phrase; "the sahib's beard will be in your hands, and you may go off to Ispahan: leave saddle-bags and cloths as security, and then we shall have your beard in our hands." He was sitting on saddle-bags, which he at once threw down as a pledge of service to Kazem. Then as to the time of departure, we declared that we must set out on Monday; but the charvodar said "No," he would not go on Monday. He was quite ready, but it was not a lucky day. He would go on the afternoon of Monday, and put up for the night at Shah Abd-ul-Azim, whose shrine is held sacred by all Persian travelers. But "it was not good," he said, to begin a journey on the morning of Monday, and as we determined to reach Kinaragird—a distance of eight-and-twenty miles—on the first evening of our journey, we sent him away. Another came—a tall, dark man, with bare, hairy legs showing beneath a short green tunic. He had a skull flattened like that of a wild animal, and a step like a camel, so long, and noiseless, and untiring. Equally inexorable as to Monday, we agreed with this man to start on Tuesday, the 23d of November.

The next work was to try the mules in the takht-i-rawan, which was declared, on handling it, to be a very heavy one. We had already purchased harness, which for a takht-i-rawan is of peculiar construction, provided with very strong saddle straps and stout hooks of iron, which are passed through rings upon the extremities of the shafts of the carriage. The Persians never lift all together, as European laborers are taught to do, and the consequence is that half a dozen men are required to do the work of two. All called loudly on "Allah" as they lifted the points of the front shafts to the back of a mule. The hooking was accomplished with difficulty, while the carriage rested on the iron-shod points of the rear shafts; the second mule was then placed between them, they were lifted and hooked, and the takht-i-rawan was then fairly arranged. But the motion was violent, for the hinder mule resented the position of his face against the back boards of the carriage, and kicked out until I feared the harness would give way. Yet he was compelled to move on, for as his hoofs plunged wildly in the air, he was dragged awkwardly forward by the front mule, who of course knew and could see nothing of his colleague's objection, and soon there were concert and progress. Of course the experiment interested half Tcheran; and when the charvodar expressed, in the

Persian equivalent, that the mules "went beautiful," which was the declared opinion of Mr. Thomson's servant, who was passing, there was a highly enthusiastic and gratified crowd to witness the performance.

Where are all the things to go? I look with dismay at the baggage while we are waiting for the mules at sunrise. The back seat of the takht-i-rawan, to be occupied by my wife, is padded with a wool mattress, which covers the back and sides, and is held in position by straps at the corners; pillows and a rug are used for cushions, and on the opposite seat the rest of the bedding is secured in cotton bags. But there are bedsteads and boxes, tables and camp-stools, matting and carpets, and a heap of pots and pans. Kazem has been marketing, and has bought half a sheep, a quantity of potatoes (such as in England would be given to pigs), some large onions, huge turnips, coarse carrots, and enormous cabbages. There are, besides, some mysterious packages, which he confesses are merchandise. He is going to do a little trading on his own account by the way, at our expense as regards his time, and as regards the carriage upon the backs of our mules. The extra weight is not great, and his excuses are so well made that we readily forgive him. The practice is very common with Persian servants, and has this advantage: that when it is known to their master they can never grumble about the trouble of loading, nor complain if their seat is not quite comfortable, though to make it uncomfortable would appear difficult; for if they are raised by saddle-bags and bundles to an awkward height above the mule's back, they seem to be just as happy. The load is well secured, the softest things placed on the top, where the rider sits, his legs swinging on either side with all the regularity of a pendulum.

It is, as I have said, eight-and-twenty miles from Teheran to Kinaragird, and, traveling as fast as possible—that is, three and a half miles an hour—we could hardly get there before sunset. "*Zood! zood!*" ("Quick! quick!") we called to the chattering servants and muleteers. At last the takht-i-rawan has received the English lady, who from north to south in Persia is always an object of the deepest interest to the population; and the charvodar, with his abominable whip of iron chain girded round his waist, leads out the first mule by a halter. We straggle after the takht-i-rawan, a string of loaded mules and riders, surrounded with servants, some mounted and others on foot, the servants of the house attending us, in Persian fashion, not only to the door, but for some distance toward the gate of the city. After going with us a few hundred yards, they kiss our hands, accept a present, and depart, salaaming most impressively.

In Persia, travelers by caravan rarely or never set out alone. It is the established rule for some of their friends to accompany them, if only for a little way. It is well at such times to avoid sneezing, or falling, or any other thing which the most superstitious of muleteers can interpret into a bad omen. Sometimes these men will take days to recover from the saddening effects of a maladroit sneeze. On our path to the Ispahan gate of Teheran, we met a coffin in a way which, I believe, was not exactly as it should have been. I do not allude to the arrangement of the dead body, which seemed indifferent almost to carelessness. It was inclosed in a long, light box very much like those in which French eggs are shipped for England, and the whole, covered with white cotton, was slung across the back of a mule, and swung, sometimes high, sometimes low, with the motion of the animal. In some parts of Persia caravans are met with, conveying dead bodies to the sacred soil of holy cities for interment. Before the Turkish Government declined to receive such imports, the road from Teheran through Bagdad to Kerbela was much frequented by these mortuary caravans, and the work of embalmment was either imperfect or unattempted, for the smell of these funeral processions is described as having been most horrible.

The gates of Teheran are a reality, and the belated traveler may knock in vain; but the walls in the direction of Ispahan, as well as in that of Kasveen, are, for the most part, not walls —nothing but heaps of earth thrown from a trench. The Ispahan gate, like most others, is faced with glazed bricks, colored blue and yellow, the main structure being surmounted with quaint pinnacles of no particular shape, which have, after the manner of all high buildings in Persia, short, thick poles standing out at right angles, the ends built into the brick-work so as to support a ladder. Looking back at Teheran, as we pass through the gate, we can see nothing but dried mud, and all is of the color of dried mud. The plane-trees, still green with lingering leaves, rise over houses of which nothing is seen but the bare, blank walls. If the Persians were African savages, the general aspect of their chief town could hardly be more barbarous and wretched.

There is, of course, no road outside the gate; there are tracks leading over the plain in every direction. Like most of the Persian plains, that in which Teheran is situated is stony; and, in the direction of Ispahan, mules and camels have trodden clear of stones eight or ten, and in some places fifteen or twenty, parallel paths. Into these we turn, on leaving the gate, the charvodar leading the front mule of the takht-i-rawan, and one of his assistant gholams bringing up the rear, his chief business being to see that no part of the load of any of the baggage mules falls off and is left in the desert.

Now and then one of the mules bearing the takht-i-rawan stumbles, and the carriage is shot forward, to the very great discomfort of the occupier. It is common, when caravans meet on the plains, to indicate, by holding up the hand, to which side the indicator will direct his troop; and those whom we met appeared, when they reached us, to be happy or unsuccessful, according as they passed upon the open or closed side of the takht-i-rawan. The desire to see a "feranghi" lady is, however, always mingled with an evident feeling that prying is both impertinent and improper. An Englishman may do much as he pleases in Persia. He must be very faithless before people will hesitate to take his word as the best security—as much better surety than any fellow-countryman can offer. An Englishman is obeyed and honored in the same way, but the English lady is a puzzle. The Persian can not quite comprehend the union of what he acknowledges to be severe propriety with exposure of the charms of face, and with a manner kindly and gracious toward men of all nations.

At noon we are three farsakhs * from Teheran. We have been rising gently, and can still make out one or two colored domes amidst the green trees, an oasis in the desert-like plain we are traversing. Behind the city rise the Elburz Mountains, with snowy summits all along the ridge, from the perpetual white of lofty Demavend to the point where the hills slope to the Karij Palace. All around, indeed, are mountains and hills, glistening with snow or brown with arid surface beneath the glaring sun. The hills are lowest of all before us in the distance, which we must surmount before sunset. On our left, the groves of Teheran seem extended to include the shrine of Shah Abd-ul-Azim, the gilded cupola of which shines brightest of all objects in the landscape. There is a ruined hovel on the plain, which casts a sharp shadow. In this Ka-

---

* I have spelled this word as it is pronounced. It is sometimes spelled "parasangs"—the Persian measure of distance, varying in our experience from three miles to four. A farsakh is, by some who are well acquainted with Persia, held to mean an hour's journey for a loaded mule, which would account for the farsakhs being shorter in a difficult country than upon the plains.

zem has already arranged a seat and spread a carpet. The takht-i-rawan is unhooked and lowered, a work which engages every hand, and the mules drink at a stream, which is the justification of this point in the plain as a stopping-place. The muleteers have a luncheon of bread and a poor sort of cream-cheese. Kazem produces a bottle of good wine and a cold fowl, which looks as if it had been carried round the world since it was cooked, after a life of semi-starvation. Our horses and mules wander where they will, which is not far; and at the end of half an hour, at a sign from us, the caravan is made up.

Miles before us, when we resume our journey, near the foot of the hills we are approaching, there are black specks like flies on the plain, some twenty or thirty, which are evidently loaded mules. We overtake them at a ruined building, a crumbling caravanserai, in which they are going to rest for the night. The mules are carrying two moollahs, their wives, and households; the animals belong to our charvodar, who wishes us to stay under this ruined mud-wall, over which lizards are coursing in scores. The accommodation is perhaps as good as we shall meet with at Kinaragird. If this had been our first excursion in Persia, we should have been astonished at the suggestion of such a lodging as this, which was only better than the open plain, inasmuch as there was a ruined wall which, if it had been provided with gates, would have been an inclosure. We had, however, been advised to stay nowhere but in the chapar-khanahs marked upon the chart which Mr. Preece, of the Telegraph Service, had kindly made out for us in Teheran, and therefore determined to push on across the hills to Kinaragird. It was certainly an advantage that we could not fully understand the language in which the charvodar and all our train vigorously expressed their objections. We, however, refused to give way, and drove the caravan onward over the brown hills, which were without a sign of vegetation. But afterward we had reason to believe that the distance was farther than that marked upon our guide map; and when we looked down from the summit of the hills upon the Salt Desert in which the station at Kinaragird appeared a distant dot, it was gilded with the rays of the setting sun; and in Persia there is no twilight. Just at this moment my horse refused to move, which the charvodar explained was owing to the discomfort of the English saddle, to the pressure of which he was unused. I had therefore to walk nearly two farsakhs into Kinaragird, which we did not reach until the moonlight was our only guide upon the border of that immense desert, which extends for hundreds of miles to the confines of Afghanistan. We had entered upon the Great Salt Desert of Persia, which occupies part of the centre and a great portion of the north-east of the country, in which there is no vegetation or good water. We had to cross a corner of this very desolate region, in which we should not see a tree or a blade of grass for days. The surface of this desert is in many places so thickly incrusted with salt that it looks as if there had been a slight fall of snow in these spots; the streams are brackish and unwholesome, neither good for man nor beast. There is no fire-wood. Our mules carry sufficient for our *pot au feu* until we shall have reached the place where in the desert there are a few dried camel-thorns, of which some Persian boy will collect a donkey-load for half a kran. At Kinaragird the water was barely drinkable; the next day it would be worse.

No imaginary picture can exceed the desolation of the scene on any part of the road between Kinaragird and Haus Sultan, our next stopping-place. Not a drop of water for our animals from morning till night; not a shadow in which to escape from the glaring light. In the morning the mirage played before us, dividing the mountains from us by the semblance of a lake. To watch the changing forms of this illusion was our only pastime. On the third evening we reached Pul-i-delak, a station like the others, where there was nothing but the chapar-khanah and a caravanserai. At Kinaragird, our bala-khanah had doors, though in these there were holes large enough to put one's hand through; but at Pul-i-delak there were no doors, and, when we entered it, every corner of our apartment was visible from the plain. We had to close it up with our hangings of thick felt, but the openings were so numerous that we were forced to borrow empty sacks from the charvodar. From the chapar-khanah the ground sloped to a stream, of which the waters were yellow as those of the Tiber after a heavy flood, and nauseous with a flavor of sulphur and Epsom salts. The river had once been crossed with a substantial bridge, but now four of the brick arches were broken and ruined, and the roadway severed. Nobody minds. The consequence is that in winter, and whenever there is much water, every caravan has to go about a mile out of the way, in leaving or approaching Pul-i-delak, up or down the stream to a suitable ford.

At the river I met one of our gholams bearing a pitcher of this fluid for our consumption, and had no pleasant anticipations of the soup or tea to be made with it. The moollahs and their party, with one or two other caravans, had arrived at the caravanserai, the door of which I passed in returning to the chapar-khanah. There was a group of Persians lounging about after the day's journey; they were eating pomegranates, walnuts, and raisins. Two of them advanced toward me, both with the palms of their hands held together before them as people would do who were trying to carry water without a vessel. One held in this way a small pomegranate, and the other about two dozen raisins, which they presented to me. We entered the caravanserai together. In the door-way sat a dervish, a negro, ugly and fierce, who at this hour of sunset was proclaiming continually in loud, harsh tones, the greatness and the unity of Allah, the all-powerful, the merciful. He spit, and cleared himself visibly, and most impolitely, from the contamination of my presence; and when I smiled and bowed, pretending to receive his curses as blessings, his expressions of disgust were violently renewed. Inside, there were the usual scenes and noises; in two or three arches, a clatter and chatter of women and children, hardly concealed by suspended carpets; in another, half a dozen muleteers sat around the precious blaze of a single log, which warmed their evening mess of bread and sour goat's milk. In the centre, the donkeys brayed, the mules rolled, and occasionally fought, all of course carrying their heavy pack-saddles, and some noisy with the discordant music of suspended bells. In the caravanserai I heard Kazem's cry, "*Sham, sahib!*" ("Dinner, sir!") and, wondering how soup made with the water of the Pul-i-delak River would taste, mounted to the bala-khanah.

At night-fall the cold was so great, the wind so piercing, that I had to make excursions in search of big stones to place upon the ends of our doors of camel's-hair cloth. But the wind drives in all directions through our little chamber. If any poor were so lodged in such a night in England, the "boasted civilization" of our country would be upheld to scorn in journals of "largest" and "world-wide" circulation. But in bed, if one is neither cold nor hungry, the freest ventilation is not often hurtful, and we were encouraged with the prospect of reaching Koom next evening—one of the two holy cities of Persia, to which the shrine of Fatima, sister of the eighth Imām Réza, attracts thousands of faithful Shi'ahs.

CHAPTER XIV.

Koom.—Approach to the Holy City.—The Golden Dome.—Koom Bazaar.—The Governor's Procession.—The Itizad-el-Dowleh.—Mirza Teki Khan.—Disgraced by the Shah.—Order for his Assassination.—The Shah's Contrition.—A Visit to the Governor.—A Coat of Honor.—Pipes of Ceremony.—Mesjid-i-Juma.—Tomb of Feth-Ali-Shah.—The Shrine of Fatima.—A Pretended Pilgrim.—Reception at the Mosque.—Not allowed to Enter.—A Temperance City.—Takht-i-rawan in Bazaar.—The Road to Sin-sin.—View from the Chapar-khanah.

SOMETIMES in Western lands one is reminded of Oriental scenes. "This is like a bit of India," the retired proconsul is heard to say in Kent or Surrey. But just as there are some richly verdured scenes, purely English, which can not be matched, so there are others, always more or less arid, which are purely and entirely Oriental. One never can forget, one will never be reminded in any part of England, of the approach to Koom. The writings of Orientals tell us that the aim of their architecture is harmony with nature; that their swelling domes and cupolas represent the mountains, their minarets the trees, their roofs the level of the plain. Perhaps in such a comparison of Oriental architecture with nature, the highest buildings are most especially useful in the landscape, because they assist the eye to some measure of the vast space which is a chief element of the undoubted beauty of such a scene.

For days we had traversed a plain of unvarying brown; and even the muleteers, to whose untiring tread all ground seems alike, broke into songs as they approached the holy city. "*Manzil, manz-i-i-i-l*" (rest, rest), they chanted, rolling the word in the dirge-like monotone of Persian song from one to the other, from end to end of the caravan. The mules quicken their pace at sight of the green trees, where even they seem to know that the thirst of days may be quenched in sweet waters.

The golden dome which covers the remains of the Imām's sister, shines the central point of the scene. The town lies flat on the plain, but it is set like a gem in a wide surrounding of hills. To the right, as we approach, the hills appear red, not with passing sunlight, but with natural color; and behind the town, high above its domes and gardens, are mountains, literally of all colors—snowy at their highest, red and green at their lowest ranges. Nearer, the scene is still more interesting. In the outskirts of the town there is a pyramid fifty feet high, the outer surface resplendent with blue-glazed bricks. This is the tomb of Feth-Ali-Shah, and it is only one of many curious monuments in Koom. Nearer still, and much of the beauty has suddenly vanished. We are amidst the realities of ruined walls of mud-brick; we are enveloped in dust; the miserable bala-khanah, with blackened walls and broken doors, is before our eyes, and we are on the edge of the river—the cloaca of Koom.

We were prepared to stay two nights in the holy city, and it is worth while to nail towels over the holes in the doors, and to "glaze" the windows with linen, so that within we may have a little light and less wind. While this is being done, we have sent a servant to the governor with a letter from the Sipar Salar, or Grand Vizier, as Mirza Houssein Khan is sometimes styled.

As usual, I perform my evening toilet upon the open roof of the stables, protected from observation from without by the mud parapet. From this elevation I can look down into the shallow river and across the bridge, where the road passes at once into the shade of the bazaar. This is the main thoroughfare, connecting the two capitals of Persia; and to pass with a horse or a camel through the bazaar of Koom in the busiest hours of the day is no easy matter. But it has to be done, and in the doing of it, without doubt or question, the weakest will go to the wall. That is the way in Persia. An unprotected woman, or a peasant driving a bargain, or his donkey, such are pushed away by the servants of some great man, tumbled over on to the fruit or cotton stalls bordering the narrow path which, in front of many of the shops, especially those in which cotton prints are sold, is further contracted by one or two high stools, on which purchasers may sit through the slow process of settling the price of their bargains. As a rule, the shop-keepers are silent, but the place is full of noise. A dervish clad in white, his face encircled with long black hair, screams eulogies of Houssein, supposed to be peculiarly acceptable when the Mohurrem is drawing near. A half-naked peasant rattles his scales, and shouts aloud the praises of his grapes; a water-seller clashes brass cups together, the noisy exhibition of his vocation; and beggars clamor for relief in the hoarse voices of age and the treble of childhood.

I have sent word to the governor that I will follow the grand vizier's letter immediately. The bazaar is intricate, but our servants are very intelligent, and I am soon at the entrance to his residence. It is a small brick arch, through which two men could not easily walk abreast; the way is cumbered with dust and ruin; at about fifty feet from the outer door there is a rectangular turning into a small yard, which is heaped with broken mud-bricks, over which the path mounts and falls. I was making my way through these miserable precincts of the governor's palace, when a man entered on the scene, evidently the herald of a procession. He was silver stick in waiting, and bore a large staff topped with heavy ornaments of silver. I stood aside in the ruined yard. The superior servants and secretaries followed him, two and two, after the manner of our stage in Shakspearean revivals. At last appeared the governor himself, dressed in a gold-braided robe of cashmere. He was a young man, with an appearance of great refinement and of feeble health. We exchanged salaams, and I gathered from his highness's Persian that he had just sent servants to the chapar-khanah with orders to present his salaam, and to say that he would be happy to receive me the next morning "two hours after the sun."

In Persia, all time has reference to sunrise. Caravans start two, three, or four hours "before the sun," and visits of ceremony are frequently paid, as the Governor of Koom proposed in my case, two or three hours after sunrise. I joined his highness in the procession, and walked beside him to the gate, where, as is usual before the houses of the great, there sat a dervish, a man of wildest aspect, with long, black hair falling upon his shoulders. He was dressed in white, from turban to his bare feet. He shouted "Allah-hu!" while the governor's procession was passing, and scowled at me with most obvious disgust, appearing extremely offended at the civility with which the prince governor shook hands and expressed his hope of seeing me in the morning.

The Governor of Koom is a great personage, to whom the Shah has given the title of Itizad-el-Dowleh (the Grandeur of the State). He is married to the eldest daughter of his majesty, the Princess Fekhrul Mulook. Her highness has also a title from her imperial father; she is addressed as "the Pomp of the State." It is easy to see that the Itizad-el-Dowleh has neither vigor, energy, nor ability, and that the advantages of his natural good-breeding are wasted by excesses, such as Persian *viveurs* most delight in. He owes his position, his title, and his wife to the contrition of the present Shah for having consented to the murderous execution of his father, the Mirza Teki Khan, the great Ameer-el-Nizam, whose conduct as commander-in-chief of the army and acting grand vizier, in the early part of his majesty's reign, is referred to by Persians with unbounded pride and satisfaction. They speak of Teki Khan as having been honest, as having had no itching palm for public money or for private bribes—a political phenomenon, therefore, in their eyes. The handsomest and largest caravanserai in Teheran is, as I have said, named after him; and over the Ameer's tomb in that city the repentant Shah has built a structure, the blue dome of which is one of the most prominent features in the general aspect of Teheran.

In his high station, he was of course the object of jealousy and hatred; enemies intrigued against him, and represented to the young Shah that Teki Khan not only held himself to be greatest in the empire, but that the Ameer-el-Nizam boasted of his personal security as guaranteed by the Tsar of all the Russias. The Shah listened unwillingly, for Teki Khan was high in favor and repute, and was his majesty's brother-in-law, having been recently married to a sister of the King of Kings. But Nazr-ed-deen was versed in the traditions of his house. All men say he is a true Kajar, and his dynasty won and has retained power by killing, or rendering impotent, by blinding or maiming, any who are suspected of rivalry.

Teki Khan was disgraced, and sent away from the sight of "the Shadow of God;" but it was long before the Shah would consent to his being put to death. Day after day his enemies urged that he should be disposed of, and suggested the sending of assassins to the country palace near Kashan, in which he and the princess, his wife, were living, with orders to kill him in his own apartments. The Shah hesitated; he had some affection for his sister, who was devotedly attached to her distinguished husband. The princess believed that Teki Khan's life was in danger, and never quitted his side, knowing that her presence was his chief security. At last his enemies spread a report that the Tsar intended to interfere, and to obtain from the Shah an assurance of the safety of the Ameer. The plot was now successful. The Shah was told that the Russian envoy was about to demand that the person of Teki Khan should be inviolable, and it was artfully represented that this would render the Shah contemptible in the eyes of his subjects, who, in their anger, would probably depose or murder himself. He was persuaded to give his consent to the immediate assassination of Teki Khan, in order that his death might be accomplished before the Russian envoy applied for audience.

The Shah gave way, and the murderers set out with glee to take the life of the ex-minister, who had been so great a benefactor to his country. Their only remaining difficulty was in detaching the princess from Teki Khan, and this they accomplished by stratagem, representing themselves as bearers of returning favor from the Shah. Teki Khan received them alone, expecting to hear that his imperial master was once more his friend. But he was quickly undeceived. Yet these emissaries of "the Shadow of God" were no hireling assassins, anxious to finish their job with fatal dagger in the quickest possible manner; they were men who had come, with true Persian cruelty, to enjoy personal and political revenge in watching the long-drawn agonies of their victim. They seized and stripped Teki Khan, cut the arteries of his arms, and then stood by and beheld, with gloating, his encounter with death.

Time quickly brought the truth to light, and the Shah felt guilty of the murder of the noblest of his subjects. His majesty had two daughters; his sister, the widow of the Ameer, had two sons. The four children were betrothed in marriage, and the penitent sovereign pledged himself to regard the welfare of the boys he had made fatherless. So it happened that the elder had become his majesty's son-in-law and Governor of Koom, with power to keep for himself the surplus of the results of taxation, after paying into the imperial treasury the sum at which the province of Koom is assessed to the revenues of the State.

On the morning after I had seen his highness, at "one hour after the sun," which at that season was eight o'clock, I heard a noise of arrival, and stepped out from the mud hovel, which was our only apartment, on to the wide roof of the stables of the chapar-khanah. Four of the governor's servants, splendid in costume and armory, had arrived, to be my escort to the palace. Our way led through the crowded bazaar, and the servants, who marched before me, did all possible honor to the occasion by the most offensive rudeness to the people. I threatened to lead the way myself if they did not cease from pushing the women and men alike aside, sometimes knocking them down upon the traders' stalls, in their zeal to exhibit the importance of their master and of his visitor.

No one complained, and in no case was there apparent even a disposition to return their blows; for the violent manner in which they pushed and drove the people with their sticks frequently amounted to assault. "Away, sons of a burned father!" "Away, sons of dogs!" they cried, belaboring the camels and asses, which were slow to perceive the necessity of clearing the centre of the path for our passage. There may be some alleys in the East End of London with entries as mean and dirty as that of the palace of the Itizad-el-Dowleh; but, then, in London the path is not choked, as it was at Koom, with bits of sun-baked clay, and with heaps of dust, contributed in part from the breaking-up of the mud cement with which the walls are plastered.

The white-clad dervish spit, with unconcealed disdain, as I entered; and on emerging from the passage into a court-yard, in which were placed a square tank and a few shrubs, there was a crowd of about thirty servants and hangers-on, who bowed with that air of grave devotion which is a charm of

Persian manner, and followed toward the mud-built house, a single story high, which bounded the court-yard on the farther side. The rooms of Persian houses very rarely have doors, and a curtain of Manchester cotton, printed in imitation of a Cashmere pattern, was hung over the door-way of the Itizad-el-Dowleh's reception-room, which was not more than fifteen feet square.

His highness looked very uncomfortable in his coat of honor, which, I believe, was a present from his imperial father-in-law. It is common in Persia for the sovereign to send a coat when he wishes to bestow a mark of favor; and, of course, if the garment has been worn by "the Shadow of God," the value of the present is greatly enhanced. The State coat of the Itizad-el-Dowleh was made from a Cashmere shawl, of which the ground was white. The shape was something like a frock-coat, except that it had no collar, and the waist was bunched up in gathers, which gives, even to well-made men, an awkward and clumsy appearance. It was lined throughout with gray fur, resembling chinchilla. Upon his head he wore the usual high black hat of Astrakhan fur. His black trousers were wide and short, after the Persian manner, allowing an ample display of his coarse white socks and shoes. He rose from an arm-chair, which had probably formed part of the camp equipage of a Russian officer, and on his left hand there were ranged three similar chairs—folding-chairs, with seats of Russian leather. The walls and ceiling were whitewashed, and the floor, as is usual, covered with the beautiful carpets of the country. The governor's chair and mine were placed on a small Austrian rug, which was probably valued for its glaring stripes of green and white; the farther corners of it were held down by glass weights, on the under side of which were photographic portraits of the Emperor Napoleon III. and of the Empress Eugénie.

The Itizad-el-Dowleh could speak a few words of French,

and understand simple phrases in that language; but he had never been in Europe. While we were exchanging civilities in French, two servants were brewing tea upon the floor with a steaming samovar. The infusion was sweetened in the pot, for Persians are of one mind in the matter of sugar, and invariably like as much as the water will hold without ceasing to be fluid — that which chemists call a saturated solution. The tea was served on metal trays of Persian design, in pretty cups of French porcelain, with lemons cut in halves; and afterward pipes were brought in, the live charcoal which was laid upon the damp tobacco being blown occasionally by the servants until the tube reached the mouth of the smoker. I refused, and the jeweled mouth-piece of the flexible tube was then presented to the governor, the water-bowl of the kalian being held by a slave, while his highness languidly inhaled the smoke.

I am sure that my dislike for tobacco was not unwelcome to any one of the grandees of Persia. To a true Mussulman, it is very disagreeable to place in his mouth the tube which has just quitted the lips of an infidel; and I have heard of Persians of rank being provided with a double mouth-piece, so that, after fulfilling the hospitable duty of presenting the pipe to a Christian guest, they could unobserved slip off the piece from which he had drawn the smoke, and enjoy the second without defilement. The feeling which leads English people to wipe the brim of the loving-cup before passing the goblet to a neighbor has no place in the Persian mind. The governor knows perfectly well that the pipe from which he draws a few puffs of smoke will be finished by his servants; and indeed a kalian is always tried after it is lighted by the pipe-bearer, who, if necessary, keeps it alight by smoking until his master is ready for it. The pipe is always followed by black coffee, thick, strong, and sweet, the quantity served to each person never exceeding the medical dose of "two table-spoonfuls," in china cups without handles, which, in the houses of the great, are usually secured in metal egg-cups of gold or silver, studded with turquoises and garnets. After the coffee one looks for leave to go—to obtain permission to retire; a word which, in Persia, is always supposed to be given by the greater person, whether the visitor or the visited.

In Persian fashion, the governor placed himself and all his power at my disposal; but I found it impossible to make him understand that at the suggestion of Mr. Ronald Thomson, the very able secretary of the British Legation in Teheran, I wished to see as much as could be permitted of the sacred buildings of Koom. We sent for the clerk of the Indian Government Telegraph, which has a testing station in Koom; and with his help it was arranged that the Itizad-el-Dowleh's servants should take me to the Mesjid-i-Juma, the oldest mosque in Koom, to the tomb of Feth-Ali-Shah, and that I should enter the door-way of the golden-domed mosque of Fatima, and look upon—for it could not be expected that an infidel should approach—the shrine of that sacred sister of the most holy Imām Réza.

The two servants who were appointed to lead this excursion looked as if they had been chosen for their strength; they were two of the largest, most powerful men I had seen in Persia. The Mesjid, or mosque, of Juma was very like the mosque of Kasveen, but rather more decayed and dilapidated; and from this we passed quickly to the tomb of Feth-Ali-Shah, which was in the outskirts of the town. The tomb is a parallelogram, in shape like many which were erected in English church-yards a hundred years ago. It is a simple structure of brick, covered with very beautiful tiles, with brown letters raised in high-relief on a ground of blue, not much unlike the samples of this work which have been procured for the South Kensington Museum by Major Smith. Over the tomb there is a small building or mosque.

From the resting-place of Feth-Ali-Shah, I returned through the centre of the town toward the grand mosque containing the shrine of Fatima. I expected difficulty there. Koom is renowned throughout Persia for devotion to Islam and for hatred of infidels. Not long ago, an Armenian doctor was in imminent danger, from the fact that he, a Christian, had entered this mosque in disguise. It appears that he had in this way been successful in seeing the Caaba at Mecca; and this success had, no doubt, made him contemptuous as to danger from the fanaticism of Persia. Clothed as a pilgrim, he had entered the mosque we were approaching; and having seen the shrine of Fatima, was leaving the building. He met with a moollah in the door-way, and could not refrain from boasting of his success. "There is not much to see here," he said, and compared it with Mecca. The priest's suspicions were aroused; he told the by-standers that he believed the sanctuary had been violated by a Christian, who had committed the graver offense at Mecca. The anger of the people grew hot and hotter by talking together; and at last a crowd rushed down to the chapar-khanah, where the pretended Moslem was staying, in the mud hovel which we occupied during our stay in Koom. He was warned just in time to save his life by flight over the back wall of the post-house.

My appearance in the court-yard of the mosque caused great excitement. Along the sides of the inclosure, which is nearly half an acre in extent, there are seats, upon which idlers of the "Softa" class, and beggars, with no pretensions to learning, but with abundant fanaticism, were sitting. Most of them rose at the sight of my procession, which was making directly for the main door of the mosque. In the centre was the usual tank, around which were ranged a few shrubs in wooden boxes; the golden dome of the mosque rose, glittering and grand, in the foreground. In the door-way hung a heavy chain, festooned in such a manner that none could enter without a lowly bending of the head; and behind this stood a black-bearded moollah, wearing a huge turban of green—the sacred color—and next him I recognized, with a sense of coming defeat, the wild-looking dervish who had cursed and frowned at me from the door-way of the governor's palace. His face now wore an expression really terrible.

The two gigantic servants of the Itizad-el-Dowleh, who led the way, mounted the steps, and, standing outside the chain, informed the priest that it was the governor's wish that I should be allowed to enter so far as to be able to see the shrine and the surrounding tombs. The moollah replied with an angry negative, and the dervish supported him with wild gesticulations. The servants pushed forward, evidently thinking that I should demand the fulfillment of their master's order. But to force a passage appeared to me not only very dangerous, but unjustifiable; and, from all that we had seen of Persian mosques and shrines, I doubted if the contents of this mosque were sufficiently interesting to warrant the slightest risk or disturbance. Clearly, too, the moollahs were stronger in this matter than the governor. Already a crowd watched the altercation, and every man in it could be relied on to support the moollahs, while in the crowded bazaar close at hand they had a reserve of force willing and eager to do the work of fanaticism—a force which could destroy any other power in Koom. I ordered a retreat; and, lest the servants should not understand my words, beckoned them to quit the door-way. Fortunately I had learned to beckon in the Persian manner. I had noticed that when I held up my hand and waved it toward my face in the European way, our servants did not understand this direction. The hand must be turned downward, and the waving done with the wrist uppermost. This was the sign I made in the court-yard of the mosque at Koom. Our position in recrossing the long court-yard was not very enviable; in Persia the vanquished are always contemptible; but there were no unpleasant manifestations.

In Koom we found it impossible to refill our empty wine-bottles. Something stronger than the Maine Liquor Law prevails in this sacred city and in that of Meshed, where the brother of Fatima is buried. Intoxicating liquors appear to be absolutely unattainable, and intoxication is accomplished by those who desire that condition with bhang, or opium. That which can be purchased anywhere in Koom, cheaper and of better quality and manufacture than elsewhere in Persia, is pottery, for which the town is famous. The water-bottles of Koom are seen all over Persia. The clay, when baked, is fine, hard, and nearly white, and the potters have a specialty in the way of decoration. They stud the outside of their bottles with spots of vitrified blue, like turquoises, in patterns varied with yellow spots of the same character. The effect is very pleasing. In the bazaar of Koom we bought three delicious melons, each about a foot in diameter, for a kran, the value of tenpence in English money.

The muezzin was shouting "Allahu akbar," and the call to the day-break prayer, when our caravan set out for Pasangan, the next station south of Koom. There is difficulty, as we afterward found, in the passage of a ship of three thousand tons burden through the Suez Canal; but there is much greater difficulty in passing a takht-i-rawan through the bazaar at Koom at about seven o'clock in the morning. What with the opposing stream of traffic and the anxiety of all to see the English *khanoum*, the operation was most difficult. After enduring many collisions with loaded camels and mules and donkeys, we escaped from the crowd of black hats and brown hats, green turbans and white turbans, and were once more in the open plain, where the only variety occurred in the fording of water-courses which crossed the path between artificial banks raised for the purpose of irrigation.

We thought we had never beheld a more lovely sunrise than that in the faint light of which we left the chapar-khanah of Pasangan. Above, yet near to the horizon, having a clear space beneath it, there hung a dense dark cloud. In a moment this was infused with rose-color; then it became a floating mass of gold, increasing in splendor until the arisen sun passed behind it, and over all was gloom. Through the day we rode across the dusty plain to Sin-sin, a mud-built chapar-khanah and caravanserai, so entirely the color of the plain that it was difficult, when there was no shadow, to see the buildings before we were close to the walls. When the usual operations of sweeping out the bala-khanah and covering the doors and windows with hangings had been performed, the carpets laid, our beds set up and made, the table spread for dinner, I sat, as usual, on the roof, avoiding the smoke-holes. Through the clouds rising in one of these holes I could see Kazem tending his stew-pots in an atmosphere dense with smoke, and unendurable to any but those who are accustomed to sit on the ground. Outside, the scene was, as always, charming; as always of magnificent extent, and as invariably bounded on every side by mountains. In the plain, toward the town of Kashan, a few patches of softest green, the wheat crop of next year, were the only vegetation. Before us, distant two days' march, lay the snowy outline of the highest mountain pass in Central Persia. Cold and clear in the fading sunlight, it seemed very near; and the black, serrated outline of the lower ranges against the silver sky gave that aspect to the landscape which, while it fills the mind with melancholy, is accepted as most beautiful.

CHAPTER XV.

Kashan.—Visit to the Governor.—Kashan Bazaar.—The Governor's House.
—The Governor on Railways.—Tea, Pipes, and Sherbet.—A Ride round
Kashan.—A House pulled down.—Present from the Governor.—Presents
from Servants.—Manna.—Leaving Kashan.—Gabrabad.—Up the Mountains.—A Robber Haunt.—Kuhrud.—In the Snow.—A Persian Interior.
—A Welcome Visitor.—Kazem as a Cook.—The Takht-i-rawan Frozen.
—Pass of Kuhrud.—Soh.—"The Blue Man."—Beauties of the Road.—
Province of Ispahan.—Moot-i-Khoor.—Ispahan Melons.—Village of Gez.

EARLY in the morning of the last day in November we left Sin-sin, and rode toward Kashan, which lies beneath high mountains. About two in the afternoon we arrived in the court-yard of the telegraph-office, where Mr. Nicolai, an Armenian, gave us hospitable welcome. His house, extraordinary as a building having a second story, though the upper floor was so ruined that no part was habitable, stands at the commencement of the town, beside a broad road, horribly rough as to pavement, within a hundred yards of the entrance to the bazaar. No picture could give an adequate conception of the appearance of such a town as Kashan. There are hovels in the County Meath hardly more comfortable, though far less roomy, than the flat, square boxes, plastered with mud and broken straw, in which the Persians dwell. But in Western countries the roofs of the houses give variety of outline and of tint; in a town like Kashan, all is of the dusty color of the road.

Immediately upon our arrival, we sent a servant at once to the *hakem*, or governor, with a letter of recommendation from the grand vizier; and very soon an answer was returned that the governor was waiting to receive me. Two led horses and five servants followed the governor's letter, and, mounting one, I gave the other to Mr. Nicolai, who was kindly willing to act as interpreter in my interview with the governor of Kashan.

The town is famous for saucepans and scorpions. A hundred wooden hammers were ringing upon as many copper pots and pans when we entered the bazaar, the governor's five servants clearing the way in the usual unceremonious fashion. The brass and copper work of Kashan is useful rather than ornamental. Some of the pans and kettles are engraved with rude ornament; but although this is the Birmingham of Persia, there is no lavish bestowal of labor on any of the productions of Kashan—no elegances in metal-work such as may be purchased in Ispahan or Benares. The bazaar of Kashan has a vaulted roof of stone, from which the noise of the saucepan-makers resounded so loudly that conversation was impossible. Other alleys were devoted to more quiet industries. In the East the carpenters and turners make no small use of their toes. Being always barefooted when at work, and seated either on the ground or upon the level platform of a stall or shop in the bazaar, they from childhood accustom their toes to such motions and functions as European fingers are wont to undertake; and in bowing or ginning cotton, in turning or in carpentry, the toes often do the work of a third hand.

The life of Eastern tradesmen, especially of those engaged in the comparatively inert occupations of selling groceries or manufactured cottons, must be very unwholesome. They spend their days, for the most part, seated in the perpetual gloom of the sunless bazaars, which are icy-cold in winter, and through which draughts of chilling air are always blowing. Their only fire is a pan of charcoal, upon which they sometimes sit, when it is covered with a perforated box. At other times two or three may be seen crowding together to warm their hands over this lifeless fire. Very many sleep in their shops, and never see the sunlight except in the morning, or midday, or evening walk to the mosque, the court-yard of which is usually entered from the bazaar. Bread and fruit are their ordinary food; the kalian, their solace and diversion. They dread none so much as the servants of the governor, who are the instruments of extortion and oppression in the name and with the authority of the State.

One could see all this in the swaggering, bullying manner of those who were leading me to the governor's house, which was of the usual character. Near the mud-plastered entrance I saw two black slaves running, each with a chair held high above his head, and knew immediately that these were being "requisitioned" for the interview. About twenty servants received me at the door, and made a sort of procession through the customary covered way into the customary court-yard, with the regulation tank and shrubs; and as many as could get there, including our own servants, crowded into the little room, about twelve feet square, in which sat the ruler of the province of Kashan, a man of very high and rare repute for justice and public honesty—a sickly, ascetic-looking person, dressed in a long robe of dark Cashmere, who rose from his chair, laid his hand upon the front of his high black hat, and bowed with grave dignity in reply to my salaam. At his feet on the floor, with hospitable intent, was placed a tray with cups and saucers, and a steaming samovar, the fire of which was occasionally blown by a squatting attendant.

In opening a conversation at a formal interview of this sort in Persia, it is always expected, not merely by the great officer himself, but by all, who with open ears stand around, that some compliment—the more high-flown the better—will be given and repaid. To any traveling Englishman who is well recommended, the governor will be likely to say that he is proud to entertain one of the most noble and exalted men of the English nation, the friend of his master the Shah; and the Englishman, mindful that with this man formality is every thing, must do his best to combine truth with flattery in his reply. Reminded, probably by the appearance of an Englishman, of Baron Reuter and his proposed railways, the governor proceeded to remark, very languidly, that a railway would be a good thing, and would make traveling more pleasant for persons like myself. I do not think he had the faintest idea what a railway was like, or he would probably have regarded it in relation to the country and to the Persians. He seemed to think that a railway was something in which Englishmen liked to travel — something which peculiarly belonged to them. No doubt in his heart he looked upon a railway as a machinery for bringing Englishmen into countries where they were not wanted, and which they would not leave if once introduced by this mysterious and mechanical steam caravan.

Mr. Nicolai remarked that there had been a band of robbers on the mountains between Kashan and Ispahan, and suggested that the governor should furnish us with a guard of soldiers. He said that he believed the road was safe now, but that he should wish to give us a guard; that he should order some soldiers to accompany our caravan across the mountains to the next telegraph station at Soh. Meanwhile, the ordinary entertainment was proceeding; the sweet tea had been duly served; then pipes; then sherbet, with ice and sweetmeats; lastly, coffee. The governor, according to the strict etiquette of Mohammedan countries, made no inquiry for my companion: to allude directly to a visitor's wife would be an excess of impropriety. His excellency was sorry, so he said, that I intended to leave Kashan the next morning. He had hoped that he might himself have shown me some of the interesting sights (there were none) of the town; but he thought that at least I should do well to ride through the streets of Kashan, and he would send mounted servants as a guard of honor.

In a Persian town few of the streets have a greater width than ten or twelve feet, and the way is generally encumbered with a dirty water-course (worn more or less deep, according to the elevation of the ground), and with stray bricks and stones from the ruins of houses. There is no town in Persia in which there are not probably as many houses in this condition as there are houses which are inhabited. But at the corner of two streets I saw, in my ride through Kashan, a house which looked as if it had been suddenly tumbled by earthquake into ruin; and this, I was informed, had recently been thrown down by order of the governor. It had been a house of ill-fame, and had in this way been punished for its sins.

After a ride round the town, I arrived at the telegraph office, and dismissed, with *pishkish* (the equivalent for backshish), the large retinue with which the governor's courtesy had provided me. In half an hour, another procession approached from the governor's palace. His major-domo led the way—a tall Persian, whose beard, dyed blue-black with indigo, descended near the scarlet girdle of his waist. This man was followed by two black slaves, in white tunics and turbans, each of whom carried on his head a circular metal tray, about a yard in diameter, on one of which there were six plates piled high with fruit, apples, pears, pomegranates, dried apricots, figs, and oranges, and on the other sweetmeats in an equal number of plates. This was the governor's present, and by far the best part of it was the picturesque appearance of the bearers, a complete realization of a scene in "The Arabian Nights' Entertainments." The slaves laid the huge trays at my feet, and, according to custom, all held out their hands for money. Whenever a governor makes a present, which is regarded as doing great honor to the receiver, nothing less than ten kraus will satisfy the servants.

About eighteen months ago, an Englishman, who had an appointment in Persia, arrived in one of the principal towns, and received a present of this sort from the governor. He gave liberal *pishkish*, and two days afterward there arrived another present; he gave more largess; again, another present came, and another, until his suspicions were awakened, and he discovered that none but the first had come from the governor; that the servants of his highness had purchased and presented the succeeding presents for the sake of obtaining his more valuable gifts. It is very probable it is quite in keeping with the general conduct of affairs in Persia that the governor should obtain his servants at a cheaper rate than others, upon the implied, if not expressed, understanding that they are to make what they can by oppression of the people, and by looking for presents in every direction. Of the dozen earthenware plates on the two trays, we noticed that most were of the familiar "willow pattern." In each there was a red paper, with edges cut ornamentally, and on this was placed the fruit or sweetmeat. Of the latter, one plate was filled with small circular cakes of manna. We met with this very nice sweetmeat in other towns, but nowhere so good as that we received from the Governor of Kashan. The manna is found, in appearance like dew, upon the leaves of the tamarisk (*gez*, Persian; *athl*, Arabic) plant, and is collected in the morning with the utmost care. The ground beneath the bushes is swept clean, and a cotton cloth spread under the branches. These are then shaken, and the manna collected, and made, with sugar or honey and flour, into circular cakes about two inches in diameter and half an inch thick. Split almonds are sometimes set in the sweetmeat before it is baked.

It was warm in Kashan, except during the night, at the

end of November. In summer this is one of the hottest places in Persia. Scorpions gambol in the dust. The telegraph clerk said that in summer he had burned his hand by merely touching a bottle which had for some time been exposed to the sun. When our caravan left Kashan in the morning before sunrise, we had the prospect of passing in our day's ride from this climate, by an elevation of nearly five thousand feet, into the snows of Kuhrud, a village which gives its name to the highest pass, and to the highest chaparkhanah, in Persia. In the gray dawn we rode through the quiet town. As in no Persian house, except in the exceedingly rare case of a second story, is there a window visible from outside, no house gives light or sign of life, and the way was very dark and crooked beyond description. After passing about half a dozen corners, I saw some horsemen standing in the road-way. There was only just light enough to see them, in the obscurity of the walled street. Their "Salaam, sahib!" as I approached, suggested the fact that they were the escort promised by the governor. They proved the best guard we had in Persia — handy, docile men, strong and quick, ready to lift the takht-i-rawan to the mules' backs, or to dart away over the plains if there were a chance of scouring a partridge, a wild duck, or an antelope.

Outside Kashan, we at once entered upon a brown, pebbly slope, which extended in a gentle gradient for fourteen miles to where the mountains rose abruptly to the snow, which lay white and deep upon the summit of the pass. For hours we toiled up this bare and barren slope, and, before we entered the mountains, turned to enjoy the extensive interesting view over the plain of Kashan, in which the brown flats of the town would have been hardly visible but for the trees, and the few domes and minarets marking the position of a community which is regarded by Persians as immensely busy and prosperous, on account of the trade in hand-made pots and pans. About noon we arrived at Gabrabad, a ruined caravanserai, a notorious hiding-place for robbers. It was then so cold that we were glad to find a sunny spot among the ruins on which to sit and eat our luncheon—a fried cutlet of kid, which was a failure, and an omelet, in the manufacture of which Kazem was an expert.

From Gabrabad, for six or seven miles, we mounted the course of a rapidly descending stream. The lady of the takht-i-rawan had in this part of the journey a most uneasy ride, for we crossed the purling stream more than twenty times, and the front mule slid down and scrambled up the banks, dragging the hind mule after him, with no regard for the level of the takht-i-rawan, the shafts of which were sometimes nearly in the ground at one end or the other. In such a country it is not easy, with baggage mules, to make three miles an hour, and our pace hardly equaled that.

The mountains rose darkly on either side up to the line of snow which we were approaching. No robber band could desire a more eligible field for operations. The stream of melted snow was a zigzag among hills any one of which would have concealed a large force; and Kazem made the way more agreeable by riding up to me and saying, half in Persian (the words "good" and "bad" in Persian have very much the same sound as in English), half in English, "*Bad, bad*, robbers;" meaning, as he swept his hand around the landscape from east to west, that the country had a most evil reputation in this particular place for insecurity. But we were fortunate, and the cold season was all in our favor. From November to April, on the highlands of Persia, caravans are rarely attacked.

As we drew near the top of the mountain, the country became more open; and when our horses were treading through patches of snow, we were close to one of the best-cultivated village lands in Persia. There were well-tilled gardens terraced up the side of the mountain, reminding us of the toilsome industry of Switzerland, and the neatness of the work was not less suggestive of the comparison. The road—for there was now a road between the fenced patches of tilled land—passed beneath overhanging boughs of walnut-trees, which in the time of leaf must afford most delicious shade. There were groves of poplar and hazel, giving promise of abundant fire-wood in this snowy region. The mud-huts seemed stronger and cleaner than those of the plains, and the people more active. One could well understand that these swarthy mountaineers could furnish terrible bands of robbers. In their work, they sprung about from crag to crag, and the mountains echoed with their calls to each other, or to their flocks of small, wiry-haired goats. This village of Kuhrud is said to be peopled by members of the Bakhtieri tribe, an unsubjugated people, feared throughout Persia for their wild and lawless character, and possessed of energy, as displayed in their agriculture at Kuhrud, which is not found among the people who may more truly be called Persians.

I was so charmed with the appearance of the lonely village, so elevated and remote, that in passing the mosque, at the door of which stood the chief moollah of Kuhrud, I ventured to offer congratulations upon the industry of his flock. But his reverence received my advances in a very surly manner, and we passed on to the chapar-khanah, which was placed in a grove of fruit-trees. There was only just room between the door-way and a stream descending from the higher mountains to place the takht-i-rawan for the night. We were often obliged to display this much of confidence in the honesty of the people, and we never suffered for it. The doors of the chapar-khanahs were rarely wide or high enough to admit the takht-i-rawan, which was therefore of necessity left outside, in a country where it is by no means uncommon to rob doors and window-frames for fire-wood. The tired mules rolled off to a caravanserai which was close at hand, and we entered the post-house, the yard and roof of which were covered with snow and ice. Just inside the strong gates of wood there was the usual small, dark, cavernous chamber, mud-plastered within and without, lighted only by the narrow door-way, in which of course there was no door, and by a nine-inch circular smoke-hole in the roof. Into this our servants and soldiers carried, as usual, the saddles, bridles, luggage, stores, and cooking utensils. There was the ordinary furniture—that is, a pile of wood ashes in the centre, and a few large stones from the bed of the stream outside, to be fashioned, at the pleasure of the occupiers, into a grate.

All chapar-khanahs are more or less alike, and the only peculiarity in this was that the bala-khanah, the room above the gate-way, was smaller than usual. The high steps, with an average rise of eighteen inches, leading from the horse-yard to the flat roof of the stables, on the level of which the bala-khanah is placed, were broken, and fearfully slippery. Our servant had swept the snow away, and this had perhaps increased the difficulty of ascent. On the roof we had to walk through snow to the wretched eyrie in which we were to pass the night. But we thought ourselves in great luck on finding that the fire-place did not smoke very much, and that it was possible to have a fire. The room was so small that when our beds were set up, and our two-feet-six table extended, we found it necessary that one, at least, should sit on a bed. Wherever on the smoke-stained wall there was a trace of the original whitewash, we could see the scribbling of Persians. Those Persians who can write are very much given to composition upon the walls of the bala-khanah; and in a country where the renewal of whitewash is rarely, if ever, thought of, they thus secure for their scribbling the notice of at least a generation.

Comfort, after all, is comparative; and, spite of the snow,

which lay deep and white up to our door-ways, and the cloths of pressed camel's hair, which were all that stood in these wide apertures between us and the inclement night, we began to think ourselves not in very bad circumstances when the blaze of the logs roared up the narrow chimney, and glowed on the colors of our carpets and our coverlets, which appeared of startling magnificence in a mud hovel so mean and earthy, with walls and floor like the surface of a country road. The beams of the flat roof were rough, unshapen poles, cut from the Kuhrud wood, and laid from wall to wall, the grass and brush-wood, upon which the outside roofing of mud was laid, showing between them, with a plentiful hanging of cobwebs; the whole being nearly black with smoke from the fires of past occupants, who had not cared to clear the chimney before setting light to their wood. This is very necessary; for, as I have said, in Persia it is a common practice to block the flue with bricks or stones after the fire has been lighted for some time, and a body of red ashes has been collected.

We were looking for the early arrival of Kazem with the "*soufe*"—which appears to be Persian for soup—when we heard the trot of a horse outside, and a servant announced the arrival of Mr. Bruce, the English missionary, whom we had met in Teheran, and whose guests we were to be in Ispahan. Mr. Bruce has the first and most indispensable qualification for successful life in Persia—he is a good and a bold rider. When he lifted our camel's-hair door, we were sorry to see that his arm was in a sling, and his face badly wounded. His horse had fallen on a stony slope, and he was much bruised. The missionary was dressed as Europeans generally dress on the road: he wore high riding-boots with spurs, and breeches, a strong short coat with a leather waist-belt, and a wide-awake with a "puggree," or turban, of white muslin. We were delighted to see him. Kazem soon produced a saucepan—our only tureen—half full of nearly boiling soup.

Any other mode of bringing it to the table would have involved failure, in the icy atmosphere through which he had to pass. A chicken and rice came next; and Kazem, to my surprise, declared that he had cutlets of mutton "quite ready," and an omelet "to follow." He had accomplished all this, including potatoes, with nothing but three big stones for his fire-place. His dark eyes glowed with pride as he produced the unlooked-for cutlets and the omelet. Like all Persian servants, he felt it a matter of honor, when a guest arrived, to have plenty of dinner, and would have thought nothing of "requisitioning" mutton or eggs in the village or caravanserai.

Mr. Bruce was "chaparing down," in Anglo-Persian phrase, to Ispahan, riding fifty to seventy miles a day. People traveling "caravan," as we were, would take more than three times as long as he on the road between Teheran and Ispahan. He had no luggage except a small bundle, wrapped in a water-proof sheet, and carried on his saddle: this included a bag which, when he stopped for the night at a chaparkhanah, was stuffed with straw, and formed the usual bed of Europeans, who wish to "chapar" quickly through the country. The chapar horse he had ridden from the last post-house, and that of the attendant, were put up at Kuhrud for the night, and would return in the morning. How merry we were, laughing at the dessert served in dishes of paper, at the service of cups for wine, and at the missionary's amusing stories of his life in Afghanistan and Persia!

It was bitterly cold an hour before sunrise, when we, in our warm beds, heard Mr. Bruce setting off for Ispahan, his horse's hoofs clattering on the hard frozen ground. The morning light showed the imperfections of our door; and from my pillow I had an uninterrupted view of the snowy exterior through the spaces in which our hangings did not touch the door-way. Outside, the takht-i-rawan was frozen to the ground, and needed the united efforts of the escort to detach it. The mules slipped and slid; the cold wind was piercing, as we rode from the village up toward the summit of the pass, the horses cracking at every footstep through the thin ice which had been formed in the night from the melted snow of the previous day. Up the shallow valley we rode for an hour between the ridges of the mountains; no part of the soil was visible; all was snow and ice. My riding-boots of stout leather seemed, in presence of the wind, as if they were made of the thinnest kid, or even muslin. The top of the pass is eight thousand seven hundred and fifty feet, and near us were the peaks of Derman, or Girghish, of Kisteh, and of other high mountains, the lowest of which rises to more than eleven thousand feet above the sea-level. Near the summit there was not even a track. The way to Ispahan lay over a rocky hill, at sight of which every body dismounted, and all began to scramble anyhow over the stones, the horses being left to their own unassisted judgment as to the way.

At nine o'clock the sun was very hot, the path sloppy, and the glare upon the snow painful. Among the tops of the mountains we rode for some hours, making at last a very small descent to the telegraph-office at Soh, where we were to pass the night. This was, as usual, a walled inclosure, with a single opening, a door on the south side, near which stood the clerk, an Italian, and the inspector, a Scotch sergeant of Engineers. Both Signor Castaldi and Sergeant MacGowan spoke English — one with the accent of Tuscany, the other with that of an Aberdonian. They gave us a large room, which had a door, and clean matting on the floor, on which our servants quickly arranged our beds and carpets. With the thermometer twenty degrees below freezing-point, it was a drawback from the comfort of this house that, to dine with the kind and hospitable Mrs. MacGowan, we had to walk through the snowy yard.

In the morning it was too cold to ride, and we began our journey to Moot-i-Khoor on foot. The view down the slope, and over the vast plain toward Ispahan, was splendid. Far in the distance, beyond the yet invisible city, there was another chain of mountains; and through a gap in these we could see a hill, which Sergeant MacGowan told us (and afterward we proved the fact for ourselves) was not less than a hundred and ten miles from where we then stood.

Of our soldier attendants, we named two, who were favorites, " the Blue Man " and " the Green Man," from the color of their dress; the former was particularly agile and handsome. He could run up a very steep hill almost as quickly as an antelope, though loaded with his rifle, his pistol, and short sword, to say nothing of powder-flask and ramrods, which, in the most primitive fashion, were carried separately. Soon after leaving Soh, we saw him upon the craggy slope above our heads, and heard the report of his rifle. Down he came with what he called "*arduk*," a wild duck, in his hand, which he offered to the lady in the takht-i-rawan, and looked somewhat astonished at her unwillingness to handle a dying and bleeding bird. It is not uncommon for European travelers to forbid their guards to fire *en route* except at an enemy, and for this we heard at least three good reasons. The report of a gun may be a signal, prearranged between soldiers of the guard and robbers; at all events, it informs any robbers who may be near of the arrival of a caravan, and so attracts attention; and again, by emptying the gun, it for a time deprives the soldier of the use of his weapon, and in case of sudden attack leaves him unarmed. But I never interfered with the sporting tendencies of " the Blue Man." Nor could we always be thinking of the dangers of the road. Its beauties were far more apparent; the rich coloring of morning and evening light; the boundless space which, while he is passing, is all the traveler's own, in which he may ride where he will. It is very rarely that a patch is fenced, and the oases in the neighborhood of villages are few and far between.

The sun was high when we reached the plain. On the bare, brown wilderness there rose, about four miles off, a broken wall, the ruin of a chapar-khanah, and a small shrine, the tomb of some departed sheik. Beside these buildings we were to make the usual midday halt, and Kazem's mule exhibited his common obstinacy and performed his customary *pas seul*, when required to hasten on in front of the caravan. The mule kicked, turned round and round, but nothing could dislodge the merry little Persian. At last a soldier undertook to drive it before him, and Kazem was soon trotting on to light a fire. Having brought us through the mountains from Kashan, and into the territory of his Royal Highness the Prince Governor of Ispahan, the soldiers were now to leave us. We gave them a present of money, with which they were evidently delighted, and a note to the Governor of Kashan stating that they had left us in safety on the road to Moot-i-Khoor. This I wrote at their especial request, which, in its urgency, reminded me of that of a Hindoo ayah, who, in traveling toward England, from Alexandria to Naples, was overwhelmed with astonishment at the sight of Vesuvius. When it was explained to her that the mountain was smoking from natural causes, she exclaimed, "Mem sahib, do give me a 'chit' [a note] to say that I've seen it." She evidently felt sure that none of her own people would believe in her account of a volcano if she could not produce a "chit" from her mistress.

The village of Moot-i-Khoor is closely surrounded by a high wall, above which nothing was visible but the green dome of a small mosque. The chapar-khanah and caravanserai were the only buildings outside the walls. I deplored the cold chiefly because the temperature was unfavorable for the enjoyment of Ispahan melons, the perfection, the *ne plus ul-*

tra, of fruit. It seems an error on the part of nature that this golden fruit, so luscious and refreshing, ripening late in the autumn, should be for sale when to eat a melon makes one's teeth chatter. But at Moot-i-Khoor, before a large fire, I did manage to enjoy the larger part of a melon, and carried the outside to my horse, who seemed to think he had not met with any thing so good for many a day. Upon leaving Moot-i-Khoor, we had but one more station before reaching Ispahan; and after riding about one farsakh, on the way to Gez, we passed a caravanserai three hundred feet square, which, though, for a Persian building, in excellent repair, was quite deserted. We had met with an official at Tcheran, upon whose caravan a band of robbers rushed out from this caravanserai. We therefore eyed it with some anxiety; but when we arrived there was not a living creature to be seen, and nobody could explain the cause. One supposed it was left thus desolate because it was so near Moot-i-Khoor, and therefore obtained no custom; another said something about evil spirits; but to the charvodar it appeared possible—and his was the wisest opinion—that it had been built without thought of water supply, and had been abandoned because no water could be had at a less distance than four miles; and, moreover, nothing would grow in the neighborhood. Much of the ground round about was covered with white salt, which in the morning looked like hoar-frost, and had the unpleasant flavor of saltpetre. There was nothing remarkable or unusual at Gez, which is only sixteen miles from the city of Ispahan.

CHAPTER XVI.

Ispahan.—Approach by Road.—Suburbs of Ispahan.—A Ragged Bazaar.—Departed Greatness.—The Grand Avenue.—The Great Madrassee.—River Zayinderud.—Pipes on the Bridge.—Djulfa-by-Ispahan.—Russia and the Armenians.—Gate of Djulfa.—The English Missionary.—Mr. Bruce's House.—Armenian Women.—The British Agent.—Church Missionary School.—Armenian Priests.—Enemies of the School.—Visit to the Governor.—The Prince's Carriage.—"The Forty Columns."—The Prince's Anderoon.—The Shah's Eldest Son.—His Estimate of the Army.—Zil-i-Sultan.—His Hope and Fears.—His Court at Ispahan.—His Carte-de-Visite.—The Princess's Costume.

THE Persians rave about Ispahan as Spaniards do of Seville, or Italians of Naples. "*Isfahán nisf jahán*". ("Ispahan is half the world"), says one writer; and Hakim Shefâ'ee, a poet of Ispahan, has taken even a higher flight. He has sung:

"The moving heaven of heavens is the father, and the towers of the earth the mother;
But Ispahan, their famous child, surpasses both the one and other."

When we were about three miles from the city, we overtook a party of priests. Several of them were mounted on white donkeys, and some were persevering in their desire to see the occupant of the takht-i-rawan. While we were riding beside them, an incident occurred which shows in a very striking manner how little intercourse there is between the chief towns of Persia, or, rather, how ill-adapted the paths (there are no roads) are for much traffic. A muleteer coming from Ispahan reported that, for purposes of irrigation, a new water-way had been banked up across the track, and at once we all turned into wheat-fields, and made our way round by circuitous courses. On the main track there were many bridges. But there are bridges and bridges: these were Persian bridges, of which the most common form is a long stone thrown from bank to bank, over which only one animal could pass. The larger bridges of brick were in such a state of dilapidation that, with less careful animals, or at night-time, it would be highly dangerous to cross them. The mules seem to know that these are traps well calculated to break their legs, and avoid the holes in these crazy bridges with wonderful care.

We had heard much of Ispahan, and were dismayed at the wretchedness and ruin in the outskirts of the town, in the general view of which from the level of the plain there was nothing to be seen that was not of mud, except the few domes and towers, which rose but little above the low houses. The environs of Ispahan are dotted with a cordon of round towers. These are not high, or in any way extraordinary; and one would pass them with the notion that, like the village defenses throughout Persia, they were suitable fortifications against enemies who had no artillery. But these are pigeon towers, maintained, in the interests of the melon-gardens, for the guano, which, after a season of occupation by hundreds of pigeons, is found inside the doors at the base. Like every thing else in Persia, these towers are falling into decay; and there are but few pigeons. Time was when there were many, and when the melon-growers of Ispahan paid a considerable rent for each tower.

A stranger to Persian ways and means seeing us fording water-courses, winding round ruined walls, passing between miserable sheds scarcely eight feet apart, would hardly suppose that, by the most frequented route, we were entering the chief city of the Persian Empire. The main street of Coomassie was, according to the sketches of correspondents, hardly more barbarous than the ragged bazaar through which we rode in the suburbs of Ispahan; in fact, we were reminded by it of the picture we had seen in the *Illustrated London News* of Coomassie. Not a few of the people were of the color, and almost as naked, as the Ashantees. The ragged roof of boughs and straw, which was intended to cover the way, but the result of which was to checker the path with patches of sunlight, was supported by saplings just as they were brought from plantations by the river-side, and the road was such as it had pleased the population to make it. Some used it as a sewer; others had thrown earth from the foundations of their stalls upon it. In some places there were pools of filthy water, with a bed of mud, into which our horses' feet sunk deep; then hillocks which jerked the unwary rider in his saddle. There was improvement, not in the road-way, but in the buildings of the bazaars, as we approached the centre of the town. We avoided the principal bazaars, owing to the difficulty of passing through with the takht-i-rawan. At last we entered by a narrow gate-way upon the grand avenue, which, though itself a ruin, and in a city which is for the most part in ruins, remains the glory of Ispahan.

From near the centre of the town for half a mile this avenue slopes in straight lines to the river. Six rows of large plane-trees, many with signs of great age and of approaching dissolution, overshadow as many roads. I was about to write that at the sides, along the walls, are footpaths; but in Persia there are no footpaths, or, rather, all ways are footpaths. The raised paths at the side may have been specially designed for foot-passengers; but in a country where there is no wheeled traffic, and where no one who is of the higher classes is ever seen far from home on foot, there are, properly speaking, no footpaths, no place in which a horse, or mule, or camel is not free to walk. The greater part of the avenue is paved; but nearly a century must have elapsed since any thing has been done to repair or replace the huge stones which, in their present disarrangement, make the road far worse than it would be if there was no paving whatever. The central road of the avenue is interrupted at three places by tanks, the masonry of which is now in ruins. These tanks hold no water except the stagnant rain or melted snow; and where the tanks occur, the long straight line of wall at the sides of the avenue is broken with buildings, imarets, large summer-houses, with two or three apartments elevated above the wall, covered with a timber roof with large projecting eaves. In this roof, as well as in the highly colored decoration, there is fresh evidence of the relationship between the architecture of Persia and that of the Alhambra of Granada.

About half-way down, on the left hand, as we approached the river, we came to the *Madrassee*, or great mosque-school of Ispahan, which has the most notable dome in the city. The building itself is unimportant, constructed, as usual, of sun-baked bricks, and plastered with mud. There is some decoration, composed of colored bricks and tiles; but the dome, seen far and wide upon the plain, is perhaps the finest example of tile-work, and the most lamentably striking picture of ruin, in Persia. Originally it was covered with tiles, on which the prevailing colors are blue and yellow. The scroll-pattern is so large that it extends over two yards of the tiling, occupying a great number of tiles for its complete exhibition. About two-thirds of the tiling are in excellent condition; the colors bright, the pattern regular, and the effect charming; but from the remaining third, on the south side, the tiles have completely disappeared, and the bare bedding of brown cement is exposed. For generations it has been so; and there is no prospect of repair. No Persian seems to give a thought to the preservation of the buildings of the country.

At the end of the avenue — in which the foot-fall of our horses and mules had that peculiar hollow sound, so melancholy and so suggestive of departed greatness—a sound singular and solemn, which is always the reverberating accompaniment of the horseman in a scene of mingled grandeur and decay—the roads converge to the bridge, a long, straight viaduct upon high, semicircular arches of brick, by which we crossed the river. This stream, the Zayinderud—a beautiful feature in the view of Ispahan — is a river with no outfall. Prodigal of its waters from the beginning, flowing hither and thither upon the plain in half a dozen courses, wastefully filling shallow basins from which the sun carries off its waters, and in winter claiming a bed wide enough for ten times the flow, tapped at every turn, and its waters led away to irrigate fields and gardens, the gay Zayinderud dies in the plains to the east of Ispahan.

The sides of the flat bridge are inclosed with walls about twelve feet high, which would shut out one of the most enchanting views in Persia, if they were not pierced with small openings so frequent that these boundaries are arcades rather than walls. There are no paths or pavement — nothing but a level way upon the bridge. At either end, from day to day and year to year, there are two Persians seated on the ground, whom at first we supposed were placed there to receive toll from passengers. They rose at our approach, and from one of the arches brought forward a lighted kalian, all ready for indulgence in the favorite form of smoking. They make this advance to any mounted passenger, and, indeed, to every one willing to pay a copper. The traveler, if he pleases, takes the pipe, and after smoking from one end of the bridge to the other, leaves it with the second pair of pipe-bearers. It is a curious way of getting a living, and reminded me of that poorest of all trades in Naples, in which one member of the family passes the day picking up the chewed ends of cigars in the Via de Toledo, now del Corso, and another offers this choice commodity for sale at ten for a half-penny in the Marina.

At the farther side of the bridge the avenue is continued, with the plane-trees and pavement as before, gently sloping upward to its termination at the ruin of an imperial summer-house. But in the December afternoon we turned sharply to the right, among the green patches of young wheat, to where the suburb of Djulfa borders on the river. This is the Christian quarter of Ispahan—the home of about two thousand Armenians, the largest Christian community in Persia, who named it Djulfa, in fond remembrance of that other Djulfa upon the borders of the Caucasus, in Georgia, from whence came the ancestors of the present population. Perhaps there is not in the world any more extraordinary manifestation of the sentiment of patriotism than that which is seen among Georgians and Armenians, the very names of whose countries have been wiped out by Imperial Russia from the map, and whose nationality is scornfully regarded by the dominant power. As a mark of the insolence of conquest, I have mentioned the monument in the Saski Place of Warsaw; but probably there is nothing in the history of Poland to equal the terms of the proclamation in which the Emperor Alexander I. of Russia announced to the Georgians, in 1801, the loss of their independence. "Ce n'est pas pour accroître nos forces, ce n'est pas dans des vues d'intérêt, ou pour étendre les limites d'un Empire déjà si vaste, que nous acceptons le fardeau du trône de Géorgie;" and the Tsar, in diplomatic phraseology, proceeds to add that it is in order to extend to them the blessing of Russian Government that he has conquered the people who are, without dispute, the handsomest in the world.

It was easy to see that the Armenians of Djulfa-by-Ispahan are miserably poor, and that wine-shops—very rare in the Mussulman city—are frequent in the Christian settlement. One of the gates of Djulfa, the wooden frame of which was about seven feet six inches in height by five feet in width, would not admit the takht-i-rawan, the top of which came in violent collision with the structure. We were obliged to unharness the first mule, and slope the takht-i-rawan to the ground. By this movement we were just able to get inside the town of Djulfa, of which the narrow ways are utterly unkept, as indeed is usual throughout Persia—quagmires of mud in the wet season, irregular blocks of frozen filth in the winter, and noisome dust-heaps in the summer. Through a small maze of mud-walls, past the Armenian cathedral, with its brown dome, built of sun-baked bricks, surmounted by a gilt cross, we approached the house of Mr. Bruce, the missionary—the only Englishman resident in this part of Persia, where the British Government is represented by an Armenian agent, subordinate to the envoy in Teheran. The missionary's house is thoroughly Persian; and from the street in which we set down the takht-i-rawan there was nothing visible except the line of mud-wall common to this and the adjoining houses. But unlike most Persian houses, the strong doors, studded with iron bolts, were, as is usual with Mr. Bruce's doors, standing wide open. In Persian eyes, the construction would indeed be faulty if any thing of the interior could be seen through this one opening of communication with the outer world. There is always a turn in the dark, covered entry. We had been met outside the town by one of Mr. Bruce's servants, Kalifat by name, an intelligent youth, mounted on a white pony, who could speak English with some readiness, and was himself inclined to walk in the ways of the Anglican Church. Before the door of the house stood the missionary—the centre of a small crowd of his Armenian neighbors—no longer booted and spurred, but all in clerical black, with orthodox white tie, a man who deserves as much as any one in Persia a brief description of the character and personal influence which he brings to bear upon so wide and desolate a field of action. Tall and spare, with the keen eye and the strong hand of one accustomed to rural life from childhood, frank in face, and with winning, well-bred manner, Mr. Bruce is quite an exceptional missionary. One sees at a glance that the man is by nature a theological soldier with a particular taste for religious warfare in the remotest places of the earth. Capable of enduring immense fatigue, accustomed in boyhood to more or less reckless riding in an Irish county, gentle in temper, firm and broadly liberal in argument, with gustatory tastes so simple that the worst of Afghan or Persian fare is always sufficient, a laborious scholar, already better acquainted with Persian dialects than any other of our countrymen in Persia, the one missionary in that empire is, in his way, a remarkable man.

On passing through the covered entry, we came upon the quadrangle of his house, in the centre of which there were bunches of the pretty little flower which at home we call "Michaelmas daisy," and the invariable tank. A paved terrace surrounded the square patch of garden, on the side of which next the street were three rooms of the house. The first, a vaulted, whitewashed chamber, about five-and-thirty feet long, had two doors opening upon the narrow terrace. This answered to what in English farm-houses is called the "keeping" room — at once drawing-room, dining-room, and library. The missionary's books, all of them more or less relating to his calling, were ranged in those recesses which are always constructed in the walls of Persian rooms. The only decoration was a native painting of queer animals, with some likeness to birds, over the fire-place, upon the floor of which there was a cheerful fire of logs. Between this and a similar apartment, occupied by ourselves, there was an intermediate and smaller room, which, like the others, opened upon the terrace, and in front of which we had always to pass under the sky in going from our apartment to the "keeping" room. On the right of the quadrangle, which was perhaps a hundred and twenty feet square, there were the kitchen offices, and a small staircase, leading first to an anteroom, and through that to the grand room of the house, which was used as a chapel.

The Christian subjects of Mohammedan powers always adopt, to some extent, the customs of their masters. The Armenian women at Djulfa veil their chins, and expose their painted cheeks and dyed eyebrows. Every morning at eight there was a procession of these women, draped from head to foot in coverings of spotless white, into the missionary's room. The few boys and men made a louder clatter, and all left their shoes on the terrace outside the door before they entered to hear the missionary recite prayers and read the Bible in Persian; and on Sunday many of these people came to an early service in the same language. They were men and boys exclusively who attended the afternoon service, when the missionary read the familiar liturgy in English, and preached with pleasant simplicity and engaging earnestness, usually, however, choosing some dogma or miracle, the truth of which he declared in detail with much of the minuteness and determination of the school of Calvin. To hear and to appreciate the labors of Mr. Bruce expounding to converted Armenians the indispensable connection between "the covenant of circumcision made with Abraham" and the crucifixion of Jesus Christ, was very instructive as to the strength and the weakness of the teaching of dogmatic Christianity.

The British agent, an Armenian, named Agenoor, was the first person to call upon us. I gave him a letter addressed to himself by his official chief in Teheran, and another from the grand vizier addressed to the Prince-governor of Ispahan, which I requested him to forward to his royal highness, who is the eldest son of the Shah. Mr. Agenoor is a respectable but timid little man, who seems to gain all the strength he has from his connection with the British Government. A walk through London, or a sight of the British fleet in Turkish waters, would strengthen his nerves. England is to him, and to many such who are placed in positions of much importance, powerful only by report, while the Mohammedan authority surrounds them as an existing reality, and the misery of their fellow-Christians is before them as an ever-present warning. There are many disadvantages in the representation of Great Britain by members of the subject Christian races of the East.

We visited the missionary's school, in which we were soon afterward to take an unexpected interest. We were much pleased with the excellence of the teaching and its admirable results. The class-rooms were in a house adjoining that of Mr. Bruce, and very similar in construction. The schoolmaster, Kalifat Johannes, was a native of Djulfa, who had for years enjoyed the position, to gain which is the chief motive power in all self-improvement among these Armenians. He had been in India, and had there learned the art of tuition. In the Djulfa school there were, at the time of our visit, a hundred and thirty-one pupils, of whom all but three Mussulman children were Armenians. The poor people of Djulfa warmly appreciated the benefits of this school for their boys as a means of enabling their children to emigrate from poverty-stricken Persia to India, from whence there flowed back rills of pecuniary aid to embarrassed parents in Djulfa. Religious conformity with the tenets of the Church Missionary Society of Great Britain, by which the school was entirely maintained, was not enforced as a test of admission. As a matter of fact, many of the children so educated did find their way on Sunday to join with their school-master in Mr. Bruce's services, but not all; and there were even children of Armenian priests among the pupils.

The satisfaction of the people with the school was not, however, shared by the priests of the Armenian population, nor by the Roman Catholic priest, who rules a dwindling community in Djulfa. There are no fewer than sixteen priests, including a bishop of the Armenian Church, in this wretched suburb; and all these, with their families, have to obtain a living, as unproductive creatures, from the piety of a population little above beggary. Naturally they are more than dubious as to the advantage of training the boys of Djulfa in schools established by members of the Church of England, with the probable result of making them Anglicans in religion, and the likelihood that the flower of them, the most promising of the future wealth-makers of Djulfa, will leave the valley of the Zayinderud and emigrate to British India. There could be no more obvious menace to their means of living; and to these poor priests it is the more aggravating, because there is nothing that each one of them so much desires for himself as to be sent to minister to some Armenian flock in the land of rupees. They say that the Armenian bishop never sends a priest to India who does not first lay at his episcopal feet an offering of fifty tomans; and if any kind person were to give an Armenian priest of Djulfa the sum of twenty pounds, it is not at all unlikely it would find its way to the bishop, so that the giver might obtain translation to India.

For some time past, Mr. Bruce told us, the school had been regarded as an offense by the priests of Djulfa, who, conscious of their own political insignificance, had not scrupled to arouse Mohammedan feeling by denouncing the school to the moollahs as an English engine for the destruction of Islam. In this evil work, I have no doubt that the Roman Catholic priest lent a willing hand; and perhaps it was not unnatural he should do so when he compared his miserable school with the comparatively bountiful appliances of that ruled by the English missionary.

We had forwarded our letters of recommendation to the

prince-governor, who immediately sent ferashes to the missionary's house to be my personal attendants during our stay in Ispahan. It was quite in accordance with Persian custom that I should give them a present and send them back, as I did. On the day upon which the prince was to receive us, more servants arrived, and brought news that the prince's carriage was on the way in order to convey my wife to visit the princess. We knew that the gate of Djulfa, which had stopped the takht-i-rawan, would not admit a carriage; we therefore hired mules and set out, a large party, including the British agent and the missionary, our servants and those of the prince, all on horseback, surrounding the takht-i-rawan. When we arrived in the open fields by the river, there stood the prince's carriage, drawn by two white horses, the manes and tails of which were dyed a lively red. They had spots of the same color upon the forehead, which, if they had been men, would have given them the look of a clown at a circus. As for the carriage itself, in hardly any sale-yard in London could such a wretched rattle-trap be found. The lining was torn, and hung in large rectangular rents, and this was only the most striking "note" of the general condition of the vehicle. It was not inviting; but the anxious British agent thought the prince would be offended if "the lady" did not make use of the carriage. So the change was made, and my wife had an opportunity of learning, by painful experience, why it is that wheeled carriages are not used in Persia. The postilion set off delighted. The barb-like horses switched their red tails and dashed down a steep place into the river, the carriage banging about over the bowlders in the bed of the Zayinderud, to the satisfaction of no one but the postilion. No doubt it was as good as any other road, and perhaps he rarely got an opportunity of displaying his powers as a charioteer. We, however, caught him, and compelled him to walk his horses for the rest of the way; but even this pace over the stones of the avenue was described by the unfortunate occupant of the carriage as being almost unendurable.

We stopped at a mud-wall in which there was a gate, not large enough to admit the carriage, and all dismounted because my wife was obliged to do so. Above the gate-way a patch of the mud was smooth and whitened. On this was painted a large heraldic lion, with his head in the rays of a gilded sun, the sign of Persian royalty. We had some distance to walk to the palace through ill-kept grounds, in which there were many plane-trees. The low buildings of the palace, in the distance, were in no way attractive. They presented a long, straight wall toward the garden, divided in panels, covered with fine white plaster, and decorated in fantastic patterns, colored red, blue, and yellow. About the centre of the grounds, there was a building which is regarded as one of the sights of Ispahan. It is a pavilion, the roof supported at a height of about fifty feet by twenty columns of wood, the octagonal surfaces of these columns being covered with mirrors. The floor was of various colored marbles, and the roof, which was fast falling into decay, was highly colored in kaleidoscopic patterns. The building is known as "The Forty Columns," and was probably constructed to be used as an outdoor throne-room for "the Shadow of God." There is in it an admixture of the barbaric and the tawdry, which, together with the unsubstantial character of the building, are the usual characteristics of Persian architecture. At a distance the effect is very pleasing, and one sees that "The Forty Columns" would play a grand part in Persian pageantry; but, nearer, the illusion vanishes. The floor is unwashed, the mirrors are grimy, the tall, slender columns are awry, and the roof is falling to pieces.

During the short time we staid at "The Forty Columns," a number of people, only some of whom were of the prince's household, gathered round us, and not a few followed toward the palace. In a theocratic government, which is the real nature of authority in all Mohammedan countries, one notes the mixture of democracy with absolute authority. There are two powers—that of Allah and that of the Shah, ruling in the name of Allah, and in strict accordance with his will as revealed in the Koran. In the sight of Allah, all men are equal; and among men, none are great save those who wield his power. Servants, peasants, beggars, all went with us toward the presence of the prince. Not one of these people would understand exclusion, except as an arbitrary exercise of power; not one would resent it, because he who has power may do what he pleases; and if the prince had singled out any one, and ordered the ferashes to give him a "hundred sticks," there would have been no outcry of injustice. But until repelled, they feel they have as much right to be in the governor's room as the flies which buzz about his head.

We separated in the first court of the palace, my wife being led to the "anderoon," or harem, the women's quarter, while I passed to the rooms of the prince. He was not there, and I was received by members of his household, including his *hakim*, or doctor, an agreeable young man, who spoke some French. The prince was, in fact, taking an unfair advantage of me, and availing himself of the customs of the East and West. While it would have been in the highest degree improper for me to propose a visit on my own part to the anderoon, the prince, with laudable curiosity, received my wife there, and himself presented her to his wife, the only one whom he had then married. A pipe was passed round while we waited for his highness, and those of the population who could not crowd into the corners of the little room watched us through the open door-way. It was presently announced that the prince was ready; and we passed through another court, the doors of which were covered with cotton hangings, and up two high steps into a narrow passage, in which stood a servant supporting the hangings before the door-way of the room in which the Governor of Ispahan was seated. There was a clatter of shoes, which were left in a heap on the threshold, and the prince, a youthful likeness of his father, rose from his arm-chair to shake hands with me, and to place me in the chair next to himself. He has exactly the bold, dark eye of the Shah, which I am told is the family feature of the Kajar tribe; and his face, though hardly so pleasing, has the same look of good-nature, with evidence of an unexhausted appetite for enjoyment and consciousness of arbitrary power. The breast of his frock-coat was covered with jewels, his waist-belt blazed with rubies and diamonds, and, when he resumed his seat, he laid across his knees a richly jeweled sword. He had plainly placed himself for the occasion in full dress, and was anxious to escape from his load of jewels.

Our conversation proceeded in the usual way. I said that, having had the honor of meeting his majesty the Shah at several entertainments in London, I felt very happy in being thus kindly received in Persia by his eldest son, who so much resembled his majesty. The prince replied with an unmeaning flourish of compliments, and then expressed his fear that we found traveling in Persia very difficult. "There is no railway," he said, in a tone which seemed to repeat the apparent belief of the Governor of Kashan that Englishmen and railways were inseparable. He never said a word to indicate that he had seen my wife, and that he had just left her in the anderoon; that would have been a breach in the code of Persian manners. "Here we have every thing as from nature," he observed, when I told him that we had enjoyed our journey the more because there were no railways. I spoke of the physique of the Shah's soldiers. "Yes," he said, "Allah be praised, the army is very good; my father has five crores [a Persian crore is 500,000] of soldiers." He uttered this monstrous exaggeration so quietly that one could see he was utterly ignorant of the real meaning of numbers. He attributed every thing to Allah. It was Allah's will that Persia should be afflicted with famine, therefore it was useless to take means against it; but his father had given two or three millions of tomans (another tremendous exaggeration) in relief, and "now, mashallah! there was no famine."

The dialogue was interrupted by the appearance of a richly jeweled kalian, from which, after I had refused it, the prince drew a few puffs of smoke. It then passed away, and in the corridor I could see that the attendants were handing about this royal pipe among themselves with a freedom which is certainly Oriental. The prince was much inclined to talk; but, with one exception, I had always to start the subject of conversation. That exception was Don Carlos, in whose contest for the crown of Spain the prince evidently took intense interest. He asked me how many men Don Carlos had, and expressed an earnest hope that this pretender would soon be in Madrid. I fancy there was something of a personal character in the feeling he had for Don Carlos, and that he was thinking of himself, and of the imperial throne of Persia, while he followed with such curious ardor the fortunes of the civil war in Spain.

This eldest son of the Shah, who is now about twenty-seven years of age, is known, and is always spoken of, by the title "Zil-i-Sultan" (Shadow of the King), a title of honor given him by his father, "the Shadow of God." But though first-born, he is not crown-prince. In Persia, the Shah names whom he pleases as his successor; and his majesty has long since designated his son by his second wife to that position, and has confirmed the heirship by informing the powers of his selection, and by making this second son Governor of Tabriz, a position always held by the heir to the throne. The reason given for passing over the natural claims of the Zil-i-

Sultan is one usually accepted in Persia as quite sufficient—he is not, and his brother is, the son of a princess. But the Zil-i-Sultan is a vigorous, violent, headstrong young man, accustomed from his earliest manhood to hold in his hands virtually irresponsible power of life and death—a being, in his own opinion, and in the eyes of his followers, superior to all laws; a bold sportsman, with the ambition to be a warrior; a man with abundant capacity for matching the cruelties with which the pages of Persian history are red; and yet the bad rearing, the indulgence of untaught self-will, which has developed his very strong natural impulses into tyrannical ferocity, has not bereft him of genial good-humor, the natural accompaniment of high health, so evident as to win for him some devoted followers, and to please all to whom he wishes to be gracious.

He is supposed not to acquiesce in the devolution of the crown upon his brother's head, and is said to have expressed his determination to fight for it upon his father's death. But his vagaries, which have been many and serious, are held to have destroyed any chance of success which his undoubtedly superior vigor might have given him. No man better understands that which failure involves, even upon suspicion of an attempt in this line. Blindness, with perhaps some other mutilation, or death, is the lot of rivals of the Kajar tribe when the successful one attains supreme power; and in Persia it is not as in Europe—flight is unthought of. Outside Persia there is no world for fugitives of royal blood.

While we were taking coffee, I had leisure to observe the surroundings of the Zil-i-Sultan. At his feet sat an old moollah, one of the great religious authorities of Ispahan, who seemed to consider that any attention on his part to what was going on would be an improper subtraction from his duty to Islam. His bright eyes were overshadowed with a huge white turban; he sat on his heels, and, I am sure, lamented, as a sign of decadence, the elevation of the prince and that of his visitor in chairs. Beside the prince stood his vizier, or *vakeel*, a man dressed as one of high authority, and with a face full of intelligence and power. My servant, Kazem, in right of his position, had squeezed himself into the little room, and squatted in a corner: there were a few others, including the British agent, who acted as interpreter, and Mr. Bruce. When I rose to leave, the prince called for pen and ink, and wrote his name and mine on the back of a photographic likeness of himself, which he presented to me as a souvenir; and then, after shaking hands, turned to the missionary, and desired him to remain. Intelligence was conveyed to the anderoon, and my wife returned to me, attended by two negroes, the peculiar guardians of that place, men of horrible ugliness. She had been received very kindly by the princess, who, with bare legs, was seated upon cold pavement, which had but a thin covering of cloth. Her highness's face was painted with red and black, not in tints, but in large patches; and though a young woman, she had that greatest of beauties in a Persian lady—excessive obesity. Her two black-eyed children were introduced, and the usual refreshments were provided.

CHAPTER XVII.

The Zil-i-Sultan.—Order about the School.—Not Responsible for Murder.—Telegraph to Teheran.—Reports and Rumors.—Excitement in Djulfa.—Closing the British School.—Relapse of Fever.—Letter from the Prince.—Persian Compliments.—Prescriptions by Telegraphs.—A Persian Doctor.—Persian Medical Treatment.—Persian Leeches.—The Prince's Hakim.—His Letter of Introduction.—His Newspaper and Autobiography.—The Prince and the Province.—A Son of a Moollah.—"The Sticks."—How Punishment is Given.—A Snow Torture.—A Persian Dinner-party.—Before Dinner.—An Englishman's Legs.—A Great Khan.—The First Course.—Les Pièces de Résistance.—Going Home.

Mrs. Arnold had such painful experience of the Zil-i-Sultan's carriage, that we hoped she would not return in it, and had sent a servant to bring up the takht-i-rawan; but, as we afterward learned, the mules were not easily found, and we had to leave as we arrived, with my wife in the carriage. Mr. Bruce joined us in about twenty minutes. I was anxious to know the cause of the missionary's detention. He was evidently very much disturbed. He told us that, after I had left the room, the Zil-i-Sultan had said to him, in presence of the moollah and the vakeel, and indeed of all who remained, that his school had caused much complaint, and that it must be closed at once. Mr. Bruce asked the reason for this sudden order. Then the prince began a rambling statement made up of the accusations he had heard from all sides: the missionary had boasted of having converted a Mussulman; there were Mussulman children in the school; the teachers were not good men; he or they had said that the Virgin Mary was just like other women; the Armenian priests had said the school was doing harm in Djulfa; in short, the Zil-i-Sultan would not have it; the school must be closed. His highness concluded by turning to the officer who had charge of his relations with aliens in religion and allegiance, and saying, "You see that this is done, or I'll cut your ears off." This officer, whose place is an established one in the imperial system of Persia, bowed, and Mr. Bruce endeavored to excuse his school. "It is quite free," he said; "no one is constrained to attend, and to the people of Djulfa it is a very great benefit." "Free!" shouted the Zil-i-Sultan, with a show of the native Kajar tiger—"free! No one is free except my father and me. If I please that the people shall not go to school, and grow up barbarians, that is my affair." He would hear no more. But Mr. Bruce is a persevering man, and still he argued that his school ought not to be closed, and intimated that he could not obey the order. "If you are murdered," replied the prince—with cruelly thoughtless exposure of this good man's life to the fanaticism of all who heard him, and all to whom his words were to be reported—"I shall not be responsible."

And so the interview ended; the fanaticism of Ispahan encouraged to attack and murder the British missionary, and his school to be closed. It was a dangerous position, not only for Mr. Bruce, but in a less degree for ourselves. The American mission schools in Teheran and Tabriz have never been molested by the Shah's Government, and the missionary naturally felt most unwilling to close this, the only British school in Persia. We agreed that it would be best not to close the school until there was further pressure, amounting to force, from the prince; and Mr. Bruce determined that the pupils should be received next day as usual. We had just settled this when the takht-i-rawan came in sight, and on the Zayinderud bridge, after enduring the pavement of the avenue, we dismissed the carriage, having first satisfied the clamor of its five attendants for "pishkish."

On arriving at Mr. Bruce's house, we immediately arranged

a long telegram to the British minister in Teheran, informing Mr. Thomson of the prince's order and of his invitation to murder, requesting that immediate steps might be taken to secure Mr. Bruce's personal safety and to enable him to continue the useful work of his school. We had not long to wait for evidence that the Zil-i-Sultan's rash speech was known throughout all Ispahan. Next morning an Armenian came in, full of the news. A report—and a very accurate report—of the prince's words was circulating in Djulfa, with embellishments of Persian flavor. This man said he had heard that the Roman Catholic "padre," the Armenian bishop, and the chief sheik of Ispahan, had given the prince two hundred tomans as the price of the order for the closing of the school, and that Mr. Bruce, who is popularly regarded as a rich man because he aided very largely in obtaining and distributing the Persian Famine Relief Fund, had since capped their bribe by the larger one of six hundred tomans, for which sum the Zil-i-Sultan had agreed to put three of the missionary's enemies to death.

Throughout the day, many of the pupils were absent from the school, and by evening the order of the prince and his threat of "the sticks" to the parents of those who disobeyed were known to all. The school was nearly deserted, and the Christian people of Djulfa very fearful of outrage by the Mussulmans. The excitement was intense; and in the circumstances Mr. Bruce thought it his duty, for the preservation of peace and order, to close the school. In the ordinary course of events, the Christmas holidays would have commenced in ten days; and on closing the school, he affixed a notice upon the doors announcing that the vacation would begin ten days earlier than usual.

Unfortunately, I was at this time in bed suffering a serious relapse of fever, accompanied with the most agonizing rheumatic pains. For a fortnight I could not put my feet to the ground. I fell ill within a few hours after leaving the palace. The Zil-i-Sultan had quitted Ispahan for his favorite hunting-grounds at Marg, a chapar-khanah in the mountains, about twelve miles distant. On the day after our interview, the controller of his palace arrived at Mr. Bruce's house, followed by two slaves, who carried a large antelope tied to a pole, the ends of which rested on their shoulders. It was the first-fruit of the prince's sporting expedition, very kindly sent to me as a present. With the venison the prince-governor sent a letter, in Persian, which is a very interesting specimen of polite letter-writing in a country where it is a breach of good manners not to employ compliments, and of good sense to take them for more than mere words. I am quite sure his royal highness would not object to see his letter in English print:

"EXALTED IN DIGNITY, COMPANION OF HONOR, MR. ARNOLD!—In the first place, I write to inquire after your health, and am extremely desirous that your time should be spent happily, and that you should enjoy good health and peace, especially during your sojourn in Ispahan. You should, without fail, visit the ancient buildings of this place, which are the memorials of mighty kings who had their wars, their cares, and pleasures in this world, and against their wills left this earth and have passed away. Now, here are we remaining behind, and what Allah may decree concerning us—

"It would have given me much pleasure to have remained in the city, that I might fully enjoy your society, for you appeared to me to be a perfect man and well-informed. I shall return on Saturday.

"I should be delighted if you could come to these hunting-grounds, and see with what difficulty and courage Persian horsemen strike this kind of game, for without doubt it is a sight well worth seeing. The chase in Persia is attended with much hardship, and is not as it is in Europe.

"I send you by my servant an antelope which I have shot with my own hand. I hope you will eat it in company of friends.

"Sultan Mazūd Mirza, Kajar, Zil-i-Sultan."

The least acquaintance with Persian habits of speech reduces such extravagant expressions as are met with in the above letter to their proper meaning, which is simply that of a mere flourish of the pen. To say in Persian that Mr. So-and-so is "exalted" and "perfect," means nothing more than, or nothing very different from, the words in which any Englishman, refusing the prayer of a humble correspondent, assures that suppliant for favor that he (the great man) remains the "faithful servant," or the "most obedient humble servant" of the disappointed place-hunter.

In thanking the prince for his letter and present, I did not feel able to allude to his arbitrary decree concerning the school, and soon I became much too ill to leave my bed. There was no English doctor nearer than Teheran on one side and Shiraz on the other, a ride of a week for any one who "chapared" hard either way. We sent an account of my condition by telegraph to Dr. Baker, the medical superintendent of the Indo-Persian Telegraph, and with prompt kindness he prescribed by "wire." As for medicine, there was fortunately a small supply of that he recommended, at the telegraph-office in Ispahan, but he also ordered immediate application of leeches, and accordingly we dispatched Kazem in search of those live lancets which seem common to all countries. There had been a heavy fall of snow in the night, which lay white and deep about the doors and windows of my bedroom. Kazem returned with tidings of a man renowned for the application of leeches, who was to follow him. Presently the hakim himself arrived with his box of leeches, an old man with a long beard dyed a most fiery red, his eyes deeply sunken, his head covered with the drab skull-cap of the country; his outer garment of sheep-skin, fitting loosely over a long tunic of blue cotton; the lower part of his legs was bare, and almost as dark in color as the woven socks which covered his feet. His shoes were, of course, left outside the door, and his tread was noiseless as that of a cat.

The ideas of a Persian doctor are few. He relies most conspicuously upon the aid of Allah, whom he invokes every minute, and at every step in his proceedings. He has a decided tendency to blood-letting, and a delight in strong medicines. In a morning's walk through the streets of Ispahan, we have often seen the snow blood-stained, as if slaughter had been done in these public places. Sometimes we saw, in passing, the actual operation, a patient extending his bare arm in the street for the barber's lancet. We inquired of several why they were thus bled? One replied that he had a cold; another that he had a pain in his stomach; a third that his head ached, and so on. Perhaps it may be said without error, that such drastic treatment, whether purgative or phlebotomic, will remove, in ninety-nine cases out of a hundred, the particular sensation which led the patient to the doctor. It is not for us to assess the amount of subsequent injury or physical deterioration. The probability is of itself alone sufficient to account for the high esteem in which ignorant people hold strong treatment, a regard always exhibited with inverse ratio to the education and enlightenment of people. In a country like Persia, every Englishman is tempted to play the doctor; to Persians the mere sight of a European seems to suggest a cry of "*Dvor! dvor!*" (medicine! medicine!). We have met with sufferers from ophthalmia who shouted the word as they laid fingers on their eyes, and who turned away with disgust when we recommended a plentiful application of water, the neglect of which is half the cause of that terrible and disabling disease.

My Persian had something of the manner of an English medical man, though with a gravity which does not belong to Europe. "He had seen worse cases," and "inshallah!" (God willing!) he would make me better. I felt interested in seeing what there would be of novelty in his simple work. He prescribed a hot bran mash to be used as a vapor-bath, and, before applying the leeches, provided himself with a quantity of the tinder of burned linen, in which he placed the utmost faith for stopping undue bleeding from the leech bites. He did his work well; came on three consecutive days to see how it was progressing; and when asked to name his own remuneration, mentioned three krans, about two shillings and sixpence, with evident doubt as to whether he was not making an exorbitant demand.

But we were to receive a far greater medicine-man. The news of my illness reached the ears of the Zil-i-Sultan, who sent the following letter, in Persian, by the hands of his own hakim, a man of great renown in Southern Persia, not only for medical skill, but for literary acquirements. There was commotion at his arrival with a train of royal servants. He was a bright-eyed, pleasant-looking man, about six-and-thirty years of age, dressed in military uniform, of European cut, with the high black hat of the Persians. He had a sword at his side and a cigarette in his mouth. Throwing off his shoes at the door, he approached my couch with a low bow, and presented the prince's letter, which, upon translation into English, ran thus:

"EXALTED IN DIGNITY, COMPANION OF HONOR, MR. ARNOLD!—God knows that on hearing continually of your illness I have been greatly distressed for two reasons. First, because I saw you were a good and perfect man; and it is a sad thing that such a man as you should be ill without any apparent cause.

"Secondly, I could not in any wise be happy that you should not pass your time pleasantly while you are in my province; and with all lowliness of mind do I pray and beseech the blessed and most high God, and those near his presence, to give you complete restoration to health, that you may leave my Government in great happiness.

"I send my chief doctor, Mirza Tagi Khan, colonel, a man who has traveled, and who is skilled in home and foreign sciences, to look to your health. If you will consult him, he will have much pleasure in prescribing for you. This is that distinguished individual who cured my hand when it was so bad that I had no hopes that any one in the Empire of Persia could heal it. He made that perfect cure which you have seen, and, inshallah! he will work as wonderfully in future. It was with that very hand I shot the deer I sent you.

"I long to hear of your recovery and to enjoy your society. As soon as you are well, I hope I shall have the pleasure of a talk with you.

"SULTAN MAZŪD MIRZA, KAJAR, ZIL-I-SULTAN."

Tagi Khan could talk more French than any Persian we had met with, and we made no objection to his very simple prescription of quassia, which he subsequently sent in a queer-shaped bottle "corked" with cotton-wool. The Persians are badly off for bottles, and have no corks. The bottles they make of very brittle glass, have small mouths, and the cotton-wool used for stopping is, when necessary, secured with sealing-wax.

Tagi Khan willingly turned the conversation from my illness to his own accomplishments. While attending the Zil-i-Sultan, when the prince was Governor of Shiraz, he had edited a newspaper, of which twelve copies had been published. These he had bound into a volume, of which he kindly proposed to send us a copy. He had also written an autobiography, of which he would send us a copy containing his photograph. Both arrived in the evening. The newspaper is a curiosity, in size equal to two pages of the *Echo* in its first and most prosperous days. Its pages contain, together with a few telegrams and extracts from foreign letters translated from European journals, nothing but accounts of the movements of the Shah and of the imperial family. It is, however, much better than nothing at all; and when Tagi Khan came again to see us, we pressed him to continue in Ispahan the work he had begun in Shiraz. The copy of his autobiography is a beautiful manuscript, a mode of publication which, having passed away from Europe, survives in the more ancient countries of Asia.

The Zil-i-Sultan is worth looking at again if only because he is a fair type of a Persian ruler. It is impossible to be insensible to his good qualities or blind to his faults. Perhaps it may be said that while the former are natural, the latter result from defective education and from the unbridled exercise of despotic authority. With the tastes of a hunter, with no idea of government but that of force, with no shadow of doubt as to the absolute right of his father and himself to dispose, at their pleasure, of the liberties and lives, the property and relationships, of every one in Ispahan; controlled only by fear of exciting a fanaticism which would rise in a body stronger than his authority, and taught from infancy to regard the people as existing only to make wealth for the monarch and his officers—why should we look for good results from the absolute rule of such a man? To me the prince seemed a wayward, passionate youth, moved by strong impulses, alternately good and very bad. Disliking, yet fearing, the priests of Islam, utterly untaught as to the higher principles of morality, such a man's standard of right is never erect. I can quite believe that the writer of those gracious, kindly letters I have quoted is at other moments the ferocious tyrant he is said to be by the people of Ispahan.

Shortly before our arrival, the Zil-i-Sultan had displayed some energy in opposing the domination of the priesthood, had sent soldiers to force a criminal from sanctuary, and had banished a sheik-priest who, in his capacity of judge in the Court of the Imām-Juma, had been guilty of horrible oppression. When we were riding into Ispahan, we met this ecclesiastic on his way into exile, seated upon a white donkey, and attended by three moollahs. But before he reached the first stage out from Ispahan, he had been fetched back, and reinstated by the prince, who had thus quickly given way to ecclesiastical influence, and perhaps menace. There lived in Ispahan a man, the son of a moollah, well known for the liberality, as we should say, of his religious opinions—one who had been treated in a friendly manner by the Zil-i-Sultan, who is known to share his theological views. To the horror of the sheik-priest, this man wore clothes which did not indicate that his parents belonged to the sacred order, and frequent complaint of this impropriety was lodged at the palace. It was during my illness that the prince sent for this man, and bid him change his clothing, which his highness said was offensive upon one of his descent to the Sheik-ul-Islam. The man, eager to obey the wish of his illustrious friend, departed, and quickly re-appeared in orthodox costume. "Go," said the gratified prince, "to the sheik, and show him how quickly you have, at my request, conformed to his desire." The man went; but immediately upon reaching the presence of the religious authority, he was seized and ordered to be beaten with "one hundred sticks." We were told of this in a street of Ispahan, and at once made close inquiry into the truth of the story. We found that no exaggeration had been made, and that the sufferer had been so cruelly punished that for weeks he would be unable to put his feet to the ground.

In Persia, death or "the sticks" is the commonest punishment. The man, in the latter case, is laid on the ground, and, after his shoes and stockings are removed, his ankles are passed through leather loops fastened to a beam, which is held by two men at nearly the length of his legs from the ground, and by them is turned until his ankles are so tightly secured that no writhing of his back can unplace them. Near him are laid the precise number of sticks to which he is sentenced. These are lithe switches, five or six feet long and rather more than half an inch thick in the centre. Two experts — who usually wear scarlet coats bound with black, which is the uniform of the Shah's executioners — then take their places near the beam, each armed with a stick, with which they in turn belabor the soles of the feet until the stick is broken too short for use. In the case above referred to, the beating was continued until the hundred sticks were reduced to this condition. The prince was annoyed at the severe punishment of his friend, but his highness had to bear it; for in Persia, unless stirred to unwonted effort, the Shah's Government is far less powerful than the chief priests of Islam.

A European doctor, to his shame be it said, talking one day with the Zil-i-Sultan upon the interesting topic of torture, suggested an ancient method which, we were told, at once struck the prince as applicable in the snowy region of Ispahan. To draw the teeth of Jews who refused gifts to the Government was the practice in days when the civilization of England was no more advanced than that of Persia; but I never heard before of stuffing a man's trousers with snow and ice as an efficient way of combating his refusal to pay a large demand in the season when the thermometer stands— as it does in Central Persia — for months below zero. We were told that one day when the prince was returning from hunting, he met two dervishes on the road, who did not recognize or make way for him. The Zil-i-Sultan at once snatched his gun from a servant, and wounded the unhappy dervishes—a story to which it would be easy to add many others of similar import.

I was invited to a dinner which was to be thoroughly Persian. It was a bitterly cold evening, and the guests arrived mostly on mules, and all wrapped from head to foot in furs. At first, it does strike one as odd to be received, upon an occasion of ceremony, in a room without chairs or table—indeed, with nothing but a carpet. The room was high, the ceiling domed and painted, and upon it there was a good deal of gilding and stalactite ornament such as is seen in the Crystal Palace revival of the coloring of the Alhambra. There were hung on the walls several pictures of women such as are exhibited for view in the Palais Royal, and there were also one or two familiar prints from the *Illustrated London News*. At a lower level, there were some pictures painted in Persian style, that is, crowded with figures, no regard being had to perspective or to gradation of color. One represented the miraculous procession of birds and beasts into Noah's ark, the rear brought up by Noah himself, whose beard, colossal and black as a raven's wing, drew attention to the far background.

The shoes of all the guests who were not European were outside the door; their overcoats thrown in a corner of the apartment, which was at once reception and dining room. In a rectangular recess, three musicians, sitting on the floor, discoursed strange song and music. One had a wiry instrument, resembling a small guitar; another produced short screams from a sort of flageolet; and the third, who also contributed the chief part of the vocal entertainment, had a small drum. In the centre of the room there was a Persian carpet of many and beautiful colors: round the sides were felts, nearly half an inch thick, and five feet wide, upon which most of the guests sat or reclined.

It is not considered good manners in the East to display much of one's legs upon the carpet. Mohammed, the founder of Islam, has been praised by his biographer because he never projected his legs or his feet before company; and we are told that the prophet showed his humility of spirit in never suffering his knees to stand out beyond those of the person with whom he was conversing. But an Englishman at a Persian dinner wishes in vain for the power of fulfilling the rigorous demands of etiquette. To sit on one's heels, as camels and Persians do, requires the training of a life-time. No one can assume the fashion for the first time in manhood. I found my legs appearing so awkward that I was glad to hide the exhibition with a shawl. The imposing dignity with which my neighbor, a man of splendid apparel and appearance, managed his naked extremities, fondling now and then his toes with his hands, made my legs and booted feet so very obvious a nuisance. This man wore a robe of honor, of cashmere, which had been given him by the Shah, and underneath this garment, upon the junction of his green tunic and loose trousers of black satin, his waist was bound with a magnificent scarf. He seemed a man of immense strength; his face, full of power, was bounded on the top by his black hat, and beneath by a dense beard, dyed with the same color. He had but one tone of voice, and that the loudest in the room. He had, it was said, amassed great wealth from farming the customs in all the south of Persia. I had already heard of this person, and had met with some account of his transactions in official reports. For the privilege of collecting as much as he could obtain under the name of customs in the port of Bushire, the principal port of Persia, in the year 1873, this khan paid thirty-two thousand tomans, or about twelve thousand eight hundred pounds. None but his dependents are employed in obtaining the revenue; there is no interference of any sort by employés of the Government, and no returns or reports are required of any of his transactions. In these circumstances, surely it was mild language which the British resident at Bushire used in reference to this monstrous abuse of fiscal authority, when he wrote to the Indian Government that "the system is felt to be inconvenient by traders."

Having disposed of my intrusive limbs, I asked my neighbor on the other side something more about this man, and he told me it was notorious he had begun life as a robber, and that his greatest success in that line had been in connection with a royal caravan. "But," said he, "the khan has bad times. I met him the other day coming from Teheran, and he looked so miserable that I at once believed I had heard a correct account of his visit to the capital. He is obliged to pay so much every year to the imperial revenue, but occasional contributions are forced at Teheran by threats of loss of office, or of the sticks."

The khan was roaring, the singers twanging, piping, drumming, and shouting monotonous love-songs, when the first "dish" was served. A servant walked round the room carrying a large bottle of arrack in one hand and wine in the other. The khan took half a tumbler of the fiery spirit, and drank it off without winking; most of the guests preferred arrack. Another servant followed with a plate, in which was laid about half of a sheet of Persian bread, thin, tough, and flabby. Upon the bread was a heap of kababs—pieces of meat about an inch square, well cooked, and covered with the remainder of the bread, which was turned over them. Each guest raised the bread flap, took a kabab with his fingers, added a piece of the flap, or wiped his fingers upon it, as he pleased. For three hours this was the form of the entertainment; the talk and the music went on while the kababs, the arrack, and the wine circulated. About ten o'clock the real dinner began. A table was brought in, a cloth spread; bowls of sherbet, piles of boiled rice, other piles of pillau, a mixture of rice and stewed fowls, were introduced. In one huge dish was placed a lamb roasted whole, presenting a horribly sacrificial appearance. I watched the khan, curious to see if it was possible that appetite for boiled rice remained after he had drunk about a pint of raw alcohol, intermixed with kababs. His attendants—the servants of every guest share in the work on these occasions — drew a couch toward the table, upon which the khan lifted himself; then he pointed with a loud laugh to the soup-tureen, from which the British agent, an Armenian, was helping himself. "That's what makes you such a little fellow," he said. "I like pillau." He bared his huge arm to the elbow to vindicate his preference, and for the better handling of the rice. Plunging his fingers into a pile, he kneaded a huge bolus of the greasy rice at a single pinch, and pressed it into his mouth; another and another followed, until he had made a great hole in the heap of pillau. For nearly an hour there was little talk, much eating and drinking; then some coffee; and after that the guests were hoisted on to the high saddles of their steady, patient mules, and jogged homeward through the narrow streets, lighted only by the lanterns of their attendants.

CHAPTER XVIII.

Ispahan.—Zil-i-Sultan and the British School.—Church Missionary Society. —The "Crown of Islam."—A Ride through Ispahan.—The Meidan.— Runaway Horses in Bazaar.—"Embassador Lilies."—New-year's-eve.— Severe Cold.—Sufferings of the Poor.—A Supper in Ispahan.—Kerbela and Nedjif.—Houssein and Ali.—Imām Juma's Court.—Confiscation of Christians' Property.—Bāb and Bābis.—Execution of Bāb.—Attempted Assassination of the Shah.—Punishment of the Conspirators.—Revenge of the Koran.—Bāb and Behar.—The Followers of Behar.

As soon as I was able to leave my bed, I desired the British agent to ask the Zil-i-Sultan for an audience, that I might offer some remarks upon the closing of the British school. The prince appeared glad to see me, and at once cleared his room, that we might talk more freely. I suggested that possibly he was not aware of the character of the school, which I explained was not, as many Persians supposed, maintained by the missionary, but by a great society (the Church Missionary Society), to which hundreds of thousands of English men and women, including the queen, subscribed. The English people would not, I said, contend that they had a right to establish schools in Persia; I could not question the authority of his royal highness to close the school; but I ventured to add that this arbitrary proceeding would be regarded by England as a very unkindly act, and would do much, when it became generally known, to destroy all the good feeling which the liberal professions of the Shah during his stay in England had caused to prevail toward the Government of Persia; that the English people were not ambitious of changing the established religion of Persia was, I urged, evident from the fact that the Church Missionary Society, with an income of about one hundred and seventy-five thousand pounds a year, expended no more than a few hundreds in the Persian Empire, and confined all that expenditure to Ispahan.

I did not refrain from adding that his highness's order appeared the more unjust because the Armenian Orthodox and the Roman Catholic schools in Djulfa were not molested; and because in Teheran and in Tabriz the schools of American missionaries had been long established, and were prospering under the immediate government of the Shah and of the crown-prince.

The Zil-i-Sultan appeared somewhat moved by these arguments, and said he was very anxious to explain the circumstances under which he had felt bound to issue the order for closing Mr. Bruce's school. "The Shah, my father, and I," he said, "are friends of education. You must do us the justice to admit that. I am no fanatic. I mean to ask my father to allow my children to be educated in Europe. That will show you I am not a bigot. But Ispahan is Ispahan. They call it the 'Crown of Islam,' and the moollahs are very strong here. I closed the school to preserve the peace of the town. The Armenian bishop came to me; the Roman Catholic priest came to me; the moollahs complained; they came here and cried; tears ran down their faces. What could I do? They said that Mr. Bruce had converted a moollah; that he had spoken in the streets of the Virgin Mary as being not different from other women; they stirred up the people, and I was obliged to close the school. But, I give you my word, it shall be opened again — at the proper time. I will see Mr. Bruce. He thinks I am not a friend to him, but I am his friend. I will show him how to act so as not to excite the moollahs."

After taking leave of the prince, I rode for some hours about the streets and bazaars of Ispahan. There are literally miles of ruins in and about the city, and of ruins that are never picturesque nor in any way attractive. Along the side of the river there is nothing but ruin. Thick walls of mudbricks which have not lost their original color by exposure to the sun (the only baking that Persian bricks ever get), are broken into heaps of dusty ruin, and have remained untouched, the home of birds and lizards. Some of the bazaars are well built, with lofty, vaulted roofs of stone, but of these not a few are deserted. I rode through these sombre, cold, deserted places, the way incumbered by stones fallen from the overhanging roof, in momentary danger of another fall. Decay, dilapidation, and ruin are never out of sight. In the largest open place, the meidan, which is about five hundred yards in length and two hundred broad, there is the best view of the life of the city. Caravans of camels or mules, carrying travelers, pilgrims, merchandise, or supplies of fuel and vegetables, are always there. At one end is the Mesjid-i-Juma, the great mosque of Ispahan, the dome and minarets adorned with colored bricks and tiles. In the centre of the meidan is a small, circular mound, built of brick, about as big as half a dozen wagon-wheels piled together; and where the axle would be is reared a ragged pole. This is the execution ground, and the pole at times bears the head of a criminal.

Some of the bazaars which we entered from the meidan are full of life and interest, crowded the whole day long. It is perhaps as difficult to ride as to walk through the bazaars. A passing donkey with a load of wood is a dangerous neighbor for the knee on horseback, and on foot the jagged sticks may strike one in some tender and vital place. And, then, a horse may be frightened, and run into a hundred dangers of this sort. On one occasion, I dismounted in a bazaar of Ispahan to buy a fur coat; and while I was trying it on, with the assistance of a crowd of idlers, attracted by the sight of a foreigner, my horse broke away from my servant, and, with a loud neigh, flung up his heels, rushed at the servant's horse, threw himself upon it, bit it in the neck till it screamed with pain, and, breaking loose, started away down the narrow bazaar, my horse in furious pursuit. I was in great fear as to the result. Such a rout I never saw. Steady-going camels roared and groaned with fright; purchasers bounded on to the stalls for safety; several people were knocked down. Fortunately, no damage was done, and nobody much hurt. The runaways were caught before they got outside the bazaars, but they would not be held, and it was only by remounting that we could control them.

Ispahan would look its best in April or May, when the dark violet lilies—called "*eelchee soosun*," or "embassador lilies," because they are the first to blossom—appear, and when the mud color of the town is relieved by the tender green of the young leaves of the plane-trees. Then, as at all times, the charm is not in the buildings of the city, but in its exquisite situation, with immensely expanded views of plain begirt with mountains. The view of Ispahan from the Djulfa side of the river is not easily effaced from the memory. No doubt the great name of the city has something to do with the impression which the prospect plants upon the mind. But the real glory of the scene is the ever-varying color of the many-shaped mountains, and the indescribable, yet not less real, sense of freedom which is imparted by the aspect of the plain.

It is difficult to enter any Mohammedan city without treading on the graves of departed citizens. Main roads in the East often cross burial-grounds. Indeed, no place of sepulture is more desired than that in which there are most travelers. Fences there are none, and the tombs afford the only sign of burial. As with us, the grave is sometimes marked with a horizontal stone, and sometimes with a perpendicular slab. A translation of an epitaph not uncommon in the grave-yards about Ispahan runs thus:

"The Lord of earth and sky is our helper.
The eyes of all are fixed on the Prophet.
We need not fear the light of the searching sun of the resurrection,
While the protection of Murteza Ali surrounds and covers us."

On the last day of 1875 we rode out of Djulfa to the great cemeteries on the edge of the plain. An icy wind blew over the frozen snow, in which most of the grave-stones were buried; only on the slopes which lay exposed to the southern sun could the brown earth be seen. One or two peasants, miserably clad in cotton, covered with a ragged sheep-skin, were trying to get a handful of fuel by uprooting the camel-thorns from the desert. In the far distance some black dots upon the snow indicated a caravan of mules approaching the city. The sun was dimmed with clouds, and where its rays did not shine there all remained hard bound with frost.

Anywhere in the world, for those who have money in a city full of people, cold is more endurable than heat. One is not prostrated by cold as by heat, and one recovers more quickly from its effects. Frost-bite is better than sun-stroke, and to be chilled to the bone less painful than fever. For my part, I would rather endure an attack by robbers than be perpetually the prey of vermin; but in the extreme cold of the Persian winter there is less danger of either pest. Both hibernate in the season of frost and snow. And do not the warmth and the pleasant blaze of a wood fire make amends for the cold? while for the heat which has fevered one's brain into sleepless misery there is sometimes no relief.

But as we turn homeward from our ride on New-year's-eve, and pass through the walled, and narrow, and deadly cold streets, the deep mud frozen into hard rocks, over which our horses roll and stumble, we are forced to remember how little the poor of Persia are armed against cold more intense than is ever felt in London. In Persia the poor have no firing, few clothes, and little food. Of a group comprising half a dozen huddled round a handful of live ashes in an earthenware dish, not one had any covering on the legs between the ankle and the knee. Among the poorest of Persia, frost-bite is not uncommon. They walk barefooted, or in miserable shoes, in the snow; then ride, perhaps for hours, their feet covered with half-melted snow: upon these the frost fixes with fatal grip, and the poor wretches, ignorantly seeking relief from their tortures at the first fire they approach, lose sometimes their toes and sometimes their feet.

Happy are those who are not forced to endure extremes of climate: theirs is the most pitiable condition who sustain both severe heat and extreme cold, as do the Persians. "*Tres meses invierno; nueve meses infierno*" ("Three months winter and nine months hell") is the saying of Spaniards concerning the climate of Madrid. But the poor of Persia suffer in a magnified degree the miseries of poverty in Madrid.

For me there was organized a supper, to which every person in Ispahan who could speak even a few words of any European language was invited; and the Roman Catholic priest had lent a bell, which, being suspended upon a temporary stand of poles, was to be made to resound the witching hour of midnight by the servants of our entertainer. In the motley company assembled in his rooms, Armenian was perhaps the predominating element, and the Armenians are not a jovial people. The entertainment was a failure, by reason of the cold. Only one room had a fire-place, and in that a few damp logs fizzled, but refused to burn continuously, and warmth could not be obtained by drinking cold thin wine of Shiraz, or by egg-cups of lukewarm coffee. Hot punch would have relieved the iciness of the supper, but warmth was conspicuously absent from the feast. And there was a mechanical failure. When we were trying to make merry with cold meats and colder wine, news was brought that the bell had fallen from its perch, and we were therefore left to form our own ideas as to the moment of midnight. When no doubt remained as to that having passed, we lighted our lanterns, and began the work of the new year, by groping our way home through the unlighted streets of Djulfa-Ispahan, disturbing no one but the wolfish dogs which prowled, in piteous hunger, upon the snow.

While we were in Ispahan, a report was spread that Kerbela, where Houssein was buried, and Nedjif, where rest the remains of his father Ali, were to be ceded to the Shah. This, which would naturally delight the hearts of all true Shi'ahs, was reported in two ways. First it was said that the Sultan would give up these sacred towns to Persia as the price of an alliance, offensive and defensive, against Russia; and, again, it was said that Kerbela and Nedjif were to be purchased by the Shah from the Porte for a million of tomans. One day I showed a sketch of Kerbela to our servants and to a knot of by-standers, telling them what it represented. Immediately the picture was in danger. All wished to kiss it, to press it to their foreheads, and cried "Ah, Houssein!" with an expression of deep regret, more true and tender, in the ardor of sincerity, than one expects to find uttered over a grave which has been closed for twelve centuries.

There is but little expression of dissent in Persia, and in Ispahan orthodoxy is practically enforced by the court of the Imām Juma. Armenians in Djulfa have actually been robbed of their property by authority of this court, upon the representation of a renegade member of their family who had joined the community of Islam. Mr. Bruce assured us that, after he had purchased a piece of ground from an Armenian, he was cited to appear in the Imām Juma's court, to answer the complaint of a Mohammedan, who alleged that the property did not belong to the vender, but had passed to him, a member of the family, who had adopted the faith of Islam. The English missionary declined to acknowledge the authority of the court. But this defiance, which was not dangerous in the case of a well-known British subject, is quite beyond the power of his poorer Christian neighbors, who are naturally fearful of the courts of law, which are strictly governed by the language of the Koran, and presided over by priests as fanatical and cruel as any inquisitor of that European period which is well described as the Dark Ages.

The measure of injustice and oppression which these courts of the Koran inflict upon the Christians may seem mild in comparison with the treatment by which they suppress non-conformity within the pale of their own community. We have seen an example in the sentence of "a hundred sticks," which the incautious expression of liberal views brought upon the friend of the Zil-i-Sultan, who added to free speech the wickedness of wearing trousers of European cut. There is, however, in Ispahan a surviving heresy, the most notable in Persia, which, when proved against a man, is almost a death-warrant.

Early in the present century a boy was born at Shiraz, the son of a grocer, whose name has not been preserved. Arrived at manhood, this grocer's son expounded his idea of a religion even more indulgent than that of Mohammed. He is known by the name of Bāb (the gate), and his followers are called Bābis. In 1850, Bāb had established some reputation as a prophet, and was surrounded by followers as ready to shed their blood in his defense as any who formed the body-guard of Mohammed in those early days at Medina, when he had gained no fame in battle, and had not conceived the plan of the Koran. Bāb was attacked as an enemy of God and man, and at last taken prisoner by the Persian Government, and sentenced to death. He was to be shot. Tied to a stake in Tabriz, he confronted the firing-party, and awaited death. The report of the muskets was heard, and Bāb felt himself wounded, but at liberty. He was not seriously hurt, and the bullets had cut the cord which bound him. Clouds of smoke hung about the spot where he stood, and probably he felt a gleam of hope that he might escape when he rushed from the stake into a neighboring guard-house. He had a great reputation, and very little was necessary to make soldiers and people believe that his life had been spared by a genuine miracle. Half the population of Persia would perhaps have become Bābis, had that guard-house contained the entrance to a safe hiding-place. But there was nothing of the sort. The poor wretch was only a man, and the soldiers saw he had no supernatural powers whatever. He was dragged again to the firing-place and killed. But dissent is not to be suppressed by punishment, and of course Bābism did not die with him. Two years afterward, when the present Shah was enjoying his favorite sport, and was somewhat in advance of his followers, three men rushed upon his majesty and wounded him, in an attempted assassination. The life of Nazr-ed-deen Shah, Kajar, was saved by his own quickness, and by the arrival of his followers, who made prisoners of the assassins. They declared themselves Bābis, and gloried in their attempt to avenge the death of their leader, and to propagate their doctrines, by the murder of the Shah. The baffled criminals were put to death with the cruelty which the offenses of this sect always meet with. Lighted candles were inserted in slits cut in their living bodies, and, after lingering long in agony, their tortured frames were hewed in pieces with hatchets.

In most countries the theory of punishment is, that the State, on behalf of the community, must take vengeance upon the offender; but in Persia it is otherwise. There, in accordance with the teaching of the Koran, the theory and basis of punishment is that the relations of the victim must take revenge upon the actual or would-be murderers. In conformity with this idea, the Shah's chamberlain executed, on his majesty's behalf, and with his own hand, one of the conspirators. Yet the Bábis remain the terror and trouble of the Government of Ispahan, where the sect is reputed to number more followers than anywhere else in Persia. But many of them have, in the present day, transferred their allegiance from Báb to Behar, a man who was lately, and may be at present, imprisoned at Acca, in Arabia, by the Turkish Government. Behar represents himself as God the Father in human form, and declares that Báb occupies the same position, in regard to himself, that John the Baptist held to Jesus Christ. We were assured that there are respectable families in Ispahan who worship this imprisoned fanatic, who endanger their property and their lives by a secret devotion, which, if known, would bring them to destitution, and probably to a cruel death.

CHAPTER XIX.

Getting out of Persia.—Northern and Southern Roads.—Advantage of Russia.—Russian Goods in Persia.—English Interests in Persia.—Mr. Mackenzie's Plan.—Navigation of the Karun River.—From Ispahan to Shuster.—A Subsidy required.—Price of Wheat.—East India Company's Survey.—Letter to Lord Derby.—Baron Reuter's Concession.—Traffic in Persia.—Mules and Railways.—Difficulties of Construction.—Intercourse between Towns.—Estimates of Population.—Traveling in Persia.—Mountain Scenery.—Plains covered with Snow.—Persia and "The Arabian Nights."—No Old Men.—The Lady and the House.—The Greatest Power in Persia.

The ways and means of getting out of Persia are especially forced upon the mind of the traveler from Europe when he is in Ispahan, the central city of the empire. If he is fatigued, or not in good health, one fact will weigh upon his mind—he must ride, or be carried in a takht-i-rawan, for five hundred miles before he can be clear of the dominions of the Shah, or obtain any more easy conveyance.

It is far less difficult to ride northward to the Caspian Sea than southward to the Persian Gulf. And as it is with travelers, so it is with goods. Nothing in the way of merchandise can arrive in Ispahan except on the backs of mules, or horses, or camels. The consequence is, owing to the easier access from the north and to the proximity of Russia, that Russian imports are pressing southward to the exclusion of English manufactures from the markets of Persia.

The entry of English goods to Persia, and the export of corn, cattle, wool, and other products of that country, have been rendered much more easy by the construction of the

Suez Canal; but as regards the market for our manufactures, we shall be beaten back to the coast by Russia, unless some better road be opened for the conveyance of goods to Ispahan. Russia has a great advantage over us, in this respect, from the north, and the bazaars of Teheran are chiefly supplied with Russian manufactures. The proposal—which was noised as being the first large work to be undertaken upon the concession to Baron Reuter—to construct a railway from Resht to Teheran, would, if carried out, have facilitated most obviously the entry of Russian goods, and have enabled Russia to command the trade, not of Teheran only, but of Ispahan, and probably of Shiraz.

Of all the powers, Russia is the most ungenerous and unenlightened in her tariffs. She forces her wretched hardware and inferior cottons upon her subjects, and her near neighbors of the semi-barbarous sort, to the complete exclusion of the superior goods which England could furnish; the north gate of Persia is absolutely in her keeping; and the proposal to carry her commerce to the chief towns of Persia by a railway, to be constructed with English gold, implied either great ignorance of the nature and consequences of the work, or an astounding confidence in the unselfish disposition of British capitalists. Moreover, we have never been able, in passing over the ground, to see what security could be obtained for expenditure in this direction. There can be no doubt that Russia would be grateful to any foreign capitalists who would make a railway from the Caspian Sea to Teheran and Ispahan; but this would hardly diminish any desire she may have to possess the rich northern provinces of Persia; and it is undeniable that she may take them at any moment she pleases to put forth her hand. There is nothing but the Persian army to withstand her; and the railway, besides promoting her commerce, would render the military occupation of Northern Persia less costly, and much more secure.

For English interests it is very necessary to improve the means of communication in the south; and the best scheme I have met with, is that which was pressed in January last, though without any success, upon the Shah's Government by Mr. George Mackenzie, a British merchant, of the firm of Gray, Mackenzie, & Co., resident at Bagdad. The united waters of the Tigris and the Euphrates flow past the Turkish town of Bussorah into the Persian Gulf. This confluence of the two rivers is called the Shat-el-Arab. At right angles to this great stream, and nearly opposite the town of Bussorah, the Persian river Karun contributes its flow, the junction being at the town of Mohammerah, the taking of which was the only considerable achievement of the British expedition under the command of Sir James Outram in 1856. At Shuster, nearly half-way between Mohammerah and Ispahan, the Karun is navigable by steamboats drawing four feet of water; and Mr. Mackenzie, who has lately been over the whole route, has reported that the passage of mules from Ispahan to Shuster would be far more easy than upon the difficult path between Shiraz and Bushire. The path by which English manufactures must be carried on mules, camels, or donkeys from Bushire to Ispahan is very little less than five hundred miles in length; whereas from Shuster to the central city of Persia the distance would be not more than two hundred and seventy miles.

Mr. Mackenzie, probably the first Englishman who has passed over this little-known region of Persia, found the Bakhtiari tribes, by whom it is inhabited, better than their reputation, which is that of marauding gypsies. He states that they are hospitable, obliging, and free from caste prejudices. Mr. Mackenzie says of the tribes between Ispahan and Shuster, "They evinced no objection to eat out of the same dish with me, smoking the kalian, too, at all times after me." He found the Bakhtiari people "ignorant of the division of time or of distances." "Generally," he says, "they know of two other nations only; the Farangi [a term equivalent to "Gentiles," but generally employed in describing the English] and the Russ. To the latter they appear to give precedence, as I was at more than one place asked whether the Emperor of Russia was not the Shah-in-Shah. They are a happy and contented people, entirely under the control of one chief, the Eelkhanie, whose authority alone they acknowledge." Mr. Mackenzie's proposal was that the Shah's Government should concede to his firm—which is in close relations with that of Messrs. Gray, Dawes, & Co., of London—permission to put steam-vessels on the Karun; and these gentlemen have informed Lord Derby that if the British Government would give them a subsidy of four thousand pounds a year, they would undertake to run a steamer monthly from Shuster to Mohammerah and back. From the latter town, the vessels of the British India Steam Navigation Company, of which the firm above mentioned are agents, run to Bushire and Bombay, and, by the Suez Canal, to London.

I have no means of judging whether the subsidy is justly calculated; but I know that the Russian Government gives a large subsidy, nominally for carrying the mails, to the line of steamers belonging to the Caucasus and Mercury Company—a purely Russian undertaking—which call at all the Persian landing-places on the Caspian; that the British Government adopts a similar policy with regard to the British India Company; and it is obvious that in both cases this is done with a view of promoting influence and trade in Persia. But English trade is being beaten out of Persia for want of a better entry than by the terrible road from Bushire to Shiraz, and Persia would benefit immensely by having a more ready outlet for her surplus produce. In villages not distant from the Karun, a quarter of wheat may be bought for about four shillings; so that Persia might hope, if this river were made available, to reduce the adverse balance of trade, which, in its constant augmentation, threatens the country with ruin. I am not acquainted with the precise language in which the refusal of the concession was conveyed; but I have no doubt that the negotiation failed because some Persians in high official position wanted to be paid, and largely paid, for allowing Englishmen to confer gratuitous benefit upon their country.

In 1842, when Lieutenant Selby ascended the Karun River by direction of the East India Company, he concluded his report with the words, "I feel sure the day is not far distant when these rivers will be as well known and traversed as the Indus and the Ganges." As to the present condition of British in competition with Russian trade, Messrs. Gray, Dawes, & Co., than whom probably no persons are more competent to form a trustworthy opinion, have written to Lord Derby as follows:

"Ispahan, the centre of the Persian trade, may fairly be taken to be the common ground where Russian and British commerce meet; and until recently the expense of transporting goods to and produce from that point, by the northern and southern routes, was nearly the same. Of late years, however, the Russian Government has so far improved the northern facilities, that, by degrees, various articles of commerce (for instance, copper, iron, refined sugar, manufactured hardware, candles, etc.) have been closed to us, and their trade is extending farther south; and, in some instances, we are beaten even at the coast ports. The facilities provided are—frequent, cheap, and direct communication to the Caspian; abolition of the transit duties through the Caucasus on goods *via* Poti and Tiflis; and a resolute insisting upon a prompt settlement of the claims which their traders have against the Persian authorities.

"To compensate for these growing disadvantages, we would respectfully urge upon your lordship's consideration the necessity of adopting some protective measures for our trade in the south; and we would suggest, first, that a British consul should be placed at Ispahan; and, secondly, that the Shah's Government should concede to us the privilege of placing steamers on the river Karun, to run from Mohammerah and Shuster, in connection with the steamers from Bombay and London.

"About fifteen years ago, in the interests of trade, the Government subsidized river steamers to ply between Bussorah and Bagdad. This has resulted in a very large and still increasing trade: the subsidy, we believe, was four thousand pounds per annum. For the same subsidy, we would be prepared to place a steamer on the Karun, and maintain a monthly service between Shuster and Mohammerah, connecting at Mohammerah with the mail steamers from Bombay, Kurrachee, and London."

Baron Reuter has not yet abandoned Persia, and is still engaged, I believe, in projecting railways, having turned his attention from north to south. If it were possible to obtain money for the construction of a railway in Persia, there can be no doubt that British interests would benefit most by a line from Yezd, through Ispahan, to Shuster, to run in connection with steamboats on the Karun. But I can not believe that a railway would be profitable in any part of Persia. The passengers would be but very few, and it would be extremely difficult to take the goods traffic from the backs of mules at profitable rates. We have sometimes ridden for eight hours between Teheran and Ispahan without meeting a traveler of whom it might reasonably be supposed that he would have paid to go by rail. For the ten or twelve mules and horses we required, we paid little more than the value of a shilling a day for each—a sum which included the attendance of muleteers as well as the feeding and stabling of the animals. In his report to Baron Reuter upon improved communications in Persia, Captain St. John, R.E., made the following statement of the cost per ton per mile:

	Miles a day.	Maximum.	Minimum.	Average.
By mules, average speed..............	22	15*d.*	3*d.*	3*d.*
By camels or asses, average speed..	12	9*d.*	2*d.*	4*d.*

These are low rates, and the muleteers' trade in Persia is one that would die hard. The charvodars, and all of their men, are accustomed to enormous fatigues, and the class is certainly one of the most honest and worthy in Persia. In the towns, many of the wealthiest people have invested money in mules; and these, too, would look with unfriendly eyes upon the new mode of traveling.

But such interested objections, of course, wear out. The real question is, whether the concession of power to construct and work a railway would be respected, and whether the traffic is, or is likely to become, sufficient to render the undertaking profitable. From all that we have seen during five months in Persia, I am inclined to think that no sufficient security could be given to justify confidence that the concession would be respected, especially if the railway were successful; and that there is nowhere in Persia—one of the most sparsely inhabited countries of the world—sufficient traffic to render a railway profitable. As to the cost of construction, although in the plains the work would be very inexpensive, yet it must be remembered that no two towns can be connected without overcoming great engineering difficulties. Between the chief towns of Persia there are mountains which must be crossed at a height of six thousand or eight thousand feet, and which are, without exception, rocky, some of them composed of the hardest stone. These, however, are only such obstacles as English engineers delight in surmounting. The real difficulty is in the want of security, and in the unsatisfying prospect of remunerative returns.

There is very little intercourse between the chief towns of Persia. Those doorless hovels of mud-brick, covered with a rude cement of mud and straw, which are placed at distances of twenty to thirty miles apart on the way from Resht, through Teheran and Ispahan to Shiraz, have but the one room, the bala-khanah, elevated above the noisome yard in which horses and mules are inclosed for the night. In a ride of about four-and-twenty days to Ispahan, we had never found, on arriving at a station, this one room already occupied, which is perhaps the strongest evidence that could be afforded of the scarcity of native or foreign travelers. Perchance some bold speculator will in the next budget of bubbles be prepared to "float" a company for working the Teheran or Ispahan Steam Tram-ways, Limited, regardless of the fact that it is more than doubtful if a carriage of any sort could make its way through any town in Persia. It is certainly a fact that no carriage can be obtained for hire in either of those places.

As to the population of the towns and of the country generally, there exist no trustworthy figures. The number of the inhabitants of Ispahan is stated to be more than ninety thousand; but after passing five weeks in the city, and becoming well acquainted with nearly every part of it, I am not inclined to believe that more than half that number of people can ever at any one time be found in the "Crown of Islam." The Persians do not seem to retain their senses, or their calculating faculties, when the numbers rise over one thousand. I have said that the Zil-i-Sultan told me that the Shah had five Persian crores of soldiers (two million five hundred thousand men); but after seeing much more of his father's dominions than he has himself beheld, it would not surprise me to learn that the whole number of men, women, children, and slaves in Persia does not exceed his royal highness's estimate of the Persian army. We have never traveled in a country so thinly populated, and in this respect the contrast with India is very striking. Even on the most frequented track in Persia, the mule-path from Teheran to Ispahan, we have ridden eight-and-twenty miles in daylight without seeing a human habitation, or, except the foot-marks upon the road, a trace of man.

But the charm of traveling in Persia is utterly lost when one weighs all that is met with in the scale of progress. In Persia, passing from the swift and, on the whole, steady career of Western Europe in the ways of civilization, there appears to be not only an absence of progress, but rather retrogression. That which is truly interesting in Persia is the extended scenery, and the outdoor life—for no European sees much of the indoor existence—of the people. Persia is, *par excellence*, the land of magnificent distances. In summer the mountains, always in sight, and in many places strongly colored with the metallic ores which they contain, glow with wondrous beauty in the rose-light of the morning sun, and harden into masses of deep purple and black when the clear and pleasant starlight is substituted for the glare of the blazing sun of Persia. In another season, when looking from the snow-covered mountains, we have seen the plains resembling an arctic sea, the apparently perfect level covered with a dazzling expanse of untrodden snow; and, again, when the white hills loomed through the blinding storm like icebergs of polar regions.

Wherever the people are seen, their presence adds to the charm of the landscape. The men are handsome and picturesque, in their costumes of blue or white cotton, with here and there one in red or yellow. In the towns the traveler recognizes in the people the characters of the tales in " The Arabian Nights." There is the handsome, stalwart porter, the *hamal*, with panting breast exposed and darkly sunburned skin, scratching his shaved head, ready for any new summons, including that of the mysterious lady, the mistress of the equally mysterious house, wherein he may be murdered or enriched, killed and buried like a dog, or clad in splendid robes, and served by lovely maidens bearing dishes of gold and silver, according to the good pleasure of the genii. There, in the streets or bazaars of Ispahan, is the merchant from Bagdad, wearing the respectable marks of a pilgrim, and saluted, in virtue of his journey to Mecca, by all men as "Hadji." His green or white turban is spotless and ample; a cloak of fine cloth, gold-braided, hangs from his shoulders, and his tunic of purple or green is bound with a costly sash, in which probably the case containing his materials for writing is thrust like a dagger. Everywhere is seen the priest or moollah, riding, with nothing of meekness in his face, a white donkey, his dress proclaiming him to be a member of the caste which is strongest in Persia. There are no old men; for those whose beards are naturally white with age have been transformed into unnatural youth by dying the hair bright red with khenna. The hands and feet of such are often colored with the same preparation, and they sit smoking a kalian, or reading the Koran, upon the front planks of their stall in the cool bazaar, without any more apparent interest in their business than if it were a mere cloak for the supernatural concerns of their active life in such another sphere as that in which moved the genii of those wonderful tales.

Even without aid from the genii, there are always present in Persia two mysteries, which no doubt will serve to transmit, as long as they exist, the ideas of "The Arabian Nights." These are the veiled lady and the walled-up house, into which no outside eye can penetrate. No giaour can see even the eyes of a Persian woman of the middle and superior classes. She moves through the streets and bazaars on her white donkey, or on foot, in complete disguise. Even her husband would not recognize her. She is covered—as I described the women of Resht—from head to foot in the loose chudder of indigo, or black-dyed cotton or silk. Over her face there is the long white veil tied across the chudder, where that envelop covers all but the visage. The legs are hidden in loose trousers of cotton or silk of the same color as the chudder, which are not worn in the house. In all her outdoor life she is a moving mystery. She may be young or old, white or black, fair or ugly, on a mission of sin, or upon an errand of charity; no one knows who she is, as she shuffles along upon shoes which are difficult to keep upon her feet, as the upper leather ends far before the heel. She raises, at some mud-walled house, an iron knocker upon a door like that of a fortification; is admitted; the door is closed; and what goes on within that house, what is the fate of the women, the children, and the slaves, no one outside can know. There is no window from which they can communicate with the outer world: it is a despotism within a despotism. Each one of these walled houses is the seat of a despotic sovereignty, established and confirmed by the greatest power in Persia—that of the Koran.

CHAPTER XX.

Leaving Ispahan.—"The Farewell" Hill.—Opium Manufacture.—The Telegraph Superintendent.—Punishing a Servant.—Khadji Josef's Tea-party.—Marg.—Kum-i-Shah.—The Baggage lost.—Neither Ispahan nor Shiraz.—Ahminabad.—English Doctor robbed.—Doubt and Danger.—Yezdikhast.—A Vaulted Chamber.—A Black Vault.—Telegram from Shiraz.—The Abadeh Istikbal.—A Traveling Pipe.—Display of Horsemanship.—Abadeh.—The Governor's Present.—Bread from Teheran.—Letter from Abadeh.—An Ill-looking Escort.—Khanikora.—Miserable Lodging.—Soldiers refuse to March.—Up the Mountains.—Houssein Khan.—Dehbid.—Shooting Foxes.—Khanikergan.—Meshed-i-Murghaub.—Robbers about.—Persian Justice.—Tofanghees.

OVERLOOKING the rich and extensive "Vega," or Plain of Granada, there is a hill called "El Último Sospiro del Moro" ("The Last Sigh of the Moor"). It is supposed, or assumed, that the last of the Mohammedans, on quitting the Alhambra and its glorious neighborhood, cast from this hill "a longing, lingering look behind" at the Spanish city, the name of which is forever associated with their rule. Near Ispahan, on the way to Shiraz, there is a hill commanding a view as extensive, and it is called "The Farewell," or "The Good-bye."

It is not every day that travelers set out from Ispahan for Shiraz, and on the day of our departure all Djulfa was astir. A superintendent of the Persian Telegraph, who was about to make his annual inspection of the line, which ran at all times in the neighborhood of our path, very kindly arranged his journey so that he and his five servants might join our caravan. We had engaged mules and horses on the recommendation of an Armenian merchant, one Khadji Josef, in whose service our mules had carried opium to Bushire. During our stay, there were always men engaged in the manufacture of opium at Khadji Josef's house. In the process, the opium looked exactly like Menier's chocolate. Each man had a large tin tray before him, under which was a small fire of charcoal. On the tray was a quantity of crude opium, which with sticks the workmen always kept in motion, until, after much stirring and kneading, it was poured into molds, and came out in the shape of small two-pound cakes ready for export to England. Most of the Persian opium, it is said, is sent to this country, to be used here, and exported from England to other countries for medicinal purposes, for which it is especially suitable, owing to the large quantity of morphia it contains. Khadji Josef, the opium merchant, had hospitably resolved that, as the thermometer was not below zero—it was very little above freezing-point even in the sun—he would give an *al fresco* entertainment at "The Good-bye." In Persia, where it is common to take one's food upon the desert, the notion of sending out into the wilderness half a dozen servants to make tea, and to get pipes ready and in good smoking order, does not appear strange.

Of course hours passed before we were prepared to start. It is always so; the loading of each mule for the first time is a tedious work of art, in which charvodars show great skill. Weights, as nearly as may be equal, must be suspended on each side of the animal. If a trunk is put on one side, and another trunk upon the other side is not so heavy, then in the same slings an iron bedstead, or something else to make up the weight, must be placed upon the lighter trunk; then on the top of some bulky goods the small things must be stacked, so that they will not be upset by the motion of the animal, nor injured by collision. While all this was being arranged, the cavalcade grew larger: Khadji Josef and his pretty wife, an Armenian girl, with no other enjoyment but that of riding high-spirited horses over the plains of Ispahan, were there;

the British agent; our good friend the missionary, and every body we had known in the Persian city, all mounted, and attended by mounted servants. The Telegraph superintendent had ten baggage-mules, besides the five servants, who were mounted on his own horses.

Kazem told me he was glad this superintendent was going with us; he would be a good protection against robbers; and certainly it seemed, from his armament, that robbers we must expect to meet. Every man of his following carried a carbine; one or two had sword and pistol; he himself had a revolver stuck in his belt. But Kazem had another reason; he said that one of the superintendent's servants was his "brother." I understood him literally, and wondered to see no personal resemblance. It was explained that there was no relationship between them other than that they had vowed affection, and called each other by the name of "brother," after a fashion not uncommon in Persia. We were talking of this man when we heard a cry something like a yell, and saw the superintendent, a strong, thick-set man, standing in his stirrups, and with a heavy horsewhip beating the very person. Kazem's "brother" had come up to join the caravan, the worse for wine; and his master, waving the terrible thong of his whip over his head, was executing summary punishment in a land where there is no justice. The servant was a good-looking man, with dark and sombre face, over which his high black Persian hat was perched like the shako of a guardsman. He wore a plum-colored tunic of stuff made of goat's hair, and black trousers. His feet were firmly set in the huge, sledge-like stirrups, and though his face was pale with fright, he took his beating as if there were no possibility of resistance or escape. The poor wretch howled like a dog; and when the superintendent refolded the thong of his whip, the man seemed to be perfectly sober, but without power of steadying himself in the saddle. He paused a minute as if writhing with pain; then touched his horse, which sprung at once into a gallop. The man rocked fearfully in his saddle as he rode off; but he was soon too far from us to appear any thing but a vanishing spot upon the plain. We could see, however, that he knew where he was going, and that he had merely preceded upon the road we must follow. It turned out that we had ascribed this sudden gallop to the right cause—to his desire to escape from the sight of those who had witnessed his disgraceful punishment.

At last we set off—a band of very irregular cavalry—my wife's takht-i-rawan being the rallying-point of the caravan. My horse had those qualities most advantageous for a nineteen days' ride—steadiness and endurance, which, however, are not showy. Our Persian friends were prancing over the plain, dashing from right to left in true Oriental fashion, while we plodded on up the gentle ascent from Djulfa to "The Good-bye." After riding about four miles, we reached a small plateau, where Khadji Josef's servants were already expecting us with boiling samovars, and a white cloth spread upon the desert, on which were laid cakes of Persian bread, manna, sweetmeats of many kinds, boxes of sardines, and pots of jam imported from Europe. There were bottles of wine, for which the servants had dug holes in the desert, and arrack for those who preferred that fiery liquor. A heavy spirit duty would not be an evil in Persia. The best quality of this pure alcohol may be bought in Tcheran or Ispahan at fifteen shihees (seven and a half pence) a bottle.

We all dismounted, and enjoyed not only the tea, but also the view over Djulfa and Ispahan, divided by the silver streak of the Zayinderud. It was a perfectly barren place where we stood, and we had passed not a sign of cultivation in the four miles we had ridden. The air was not very cold, though upon the plain there were large patches of snow, and the mountains all around were white and glistening. We were sorry to part company from all who had ridden out with us from Ispahan; but more than all with Mr. Bruce, the missionary. Our way lay toward the mountains, which, when they obscured the sunlight, looked very cold and desolate. The sky too, which had been clear, was gathering in clouds. But we were soon at Marg, and hard at work in the endeavor to make the bala-khanah somewhat wind-proof for the night, which after sunset was bitterly cold.

Next day about noon, having collected some withered thorns, which are the only vegetation of the desert, the servants made a fire, and gave us a hot luncheon of stewed meat and rice, by the side of a stream, the water of which produced in the food something of that chalybeate flavor which Sam Weller identified with the taste of "warm flat-irons."

We rested at the chapar-khanah of Mayar on the second night after leaving Ispahan. From Mayar to Kum-i-Shah, the third day's march, is a distance of about twenty miles. Kum-i-Shah is the place of a shrine—in ruins, of course. We had just come in sight of the green dome, which marked the sacred place, when two men, evidently Europeans, wearing the pith helmets so common in India, appeared on the scene. They were the Telegraph clerk and the inspector resident at Kum-i-Shah, both Scotchmen; and, after kindly attending us to our wretched lodging, a mud hovel in a town of still inferior mud hovels, they appeared again in the morning to ride with us part of the way to Mux-al-beg, the next station. The temperature had been falling every day since we left Ispahan. The cold on the plain from Mayar to Mux-al-beg was the most severe we had experienced. For hours we crawled over the plain, for the most part covered with snow, at the rate of three miles an hour, exposed to a wind so keen that my mustache was painfully weighted with pendants of ice, which were renewed as often as I melted them by pressing my hand upon my face. I was clad from head to foot in a fur coat I had bought in the bazaars of Ispahan, a quite invaluable purchase. Externally the coat was of yellow leather, so long that the skirt touched the toes of my boots, and in circumference ample enough to lap over a foot in front. It was secured at the neck with strings of Persian silk, and at the waist with a leather strap. The outside was beautifully worked in patterns with amber silk; inside was the warm long wool of the Cabul sheep. The sleeves, which reached nearly to the ground, and were at the elbow ample as a bishop's lawn, were almost tight at the wrist—an excellent arrangement for excluding the icy wind of the Persian plains.

The gholams who had charge of our baggage mules were always lagging behind, so much so that I was afraid they might get cut off by robbers, for whom they would have been an easy prey, and our baggage a rich booty. I called them forward, and made them understand that they were to push on before us and get to Mux-al-beg as soon as possible. But they missed the way, and we experienced perhaps the acme of misery as travelers, in waiting for a couple of hours in the cold bala-khanah, without seats or furniture of any description. Just as we arrived, snow began to fall heavily, and this added to our anxiety, for the sea does not look more pathless than an Asiatic plain in a snow-storm.

After snow has fallen, the weather is always less cold. But the landscape the next morning, when we straggled out about sunrise into the deep snow, was one of the most cheerless I have ever beheld. The sky and the ground were of one whiteness, and there was no sign of the position of the sun. For some time our mules and horses blundered into holes and out of holes, until we found the track. Through the white gloom, we rode on, and on, over the snow for three hours. Then we reached a ruined caravanserai. From this we could just see, in the farthest distance, another building, which the Telegraph superintendent told me was a second caravanserai, and "the ground between the two is," he said, "no man's land." This disowned territory lies between the governments of Ispahan and Shiraz; and although offenses have occurred upon it, the two governments have never decided which is responsible. "At this caravanserai," continued the superintendent, pointing to the ruined and deserted building, "I was robbed. We were passing, as we are passing now, and a lot of fellows rushed out, armed; they surrounded us, and robbed us of every thing." But we passed safely over the neutral ground; and though I was so stiff with cold and rheumatism, on arriving at the second caravanserai, that it took me some five minutes to get off my horse, I was able to enjoy a stew of kidneys and rice, which Kazem, with the assistance of about fifty ragamuffins who stood round his fire, and interfered on every possible occasion, had prepared. Where those people came from, what they were, what they subsisted upon, I can not tell. But perhaps a Persian would feel equally puzzled with regard to the hangers-on about the public-houses of England—men whose business in life seems to be that of secreting an appetite for gin by standing outside the licensed doors with their hands in their pockets.

With some difficulty, I hoisted my painful bones into one of the deep arches in the wall of the caravanserai, and the bystanders watched every mouthful, with an eager eye to the remainder, which I took care should be as large as possible. My wife was taking luncheon in her takht-i-rawan. But her mules would not stand still; and at last she was obliged to set off in advance of the caravan, with no one in attendance but her mule-driver and one servant. When I mounted again and rode out of the caravanserai, which was called Ahminabad, I could see that my *yaboo* was tired with trudging through the deep snow. We had yet twelve miles to go before reaching the end of our day's journey at Yezdikhast. Snow began to fall, and I had no indication of the path except the half-covered foot-marks of my wife's mules. I urged my horse forward to reach the takht-i-rawan, but could do no more than keep it in sight. I was glad to hear the cheery voice of the Telegraph superintendent as he galloped up behind me. The ground was for the most part level; but now and then there were gentle undulations which hid the takht-i-rawan—"ups and downs," which, he said, were "famous places for robbers." "It was about here," he continued, "that Dr. W——, one of our medical staff, was attacked. A band of men sprung out upon him from behind that turn in the road. There they stripped him literally naked, and tied him to one of those scrubby trees." "How was he released?" I asked. "Oh," replied the superintendent, "it was in this way: a foot-passenger, a Persian, arrived at the chapar-khanah from which the doctor had hired a horse, which he was to leave at the next station, and the keeper of the post-house naturally asked him if he had met the doctor on the road; and when the traveler said 'No,' then they all suspected the truth, and several of the villagers took up their guns, and set out to look for the doctor, whom they found in a most miserable condition."

The superintendent was full of anecdotes concerning the perils of Englishmen in Persia, and I, interested, took little note of the way. We had found by experience that nothing faster than a walk could be obtained from my horse, and had resigned ourselves too completely to the slow rate of progress. The superintendent appeared to be suddenly alarmed, on looking at his watch. The falling snow and mist hid all but the plain from our view, and I could well understand that to lose our way, or to fail in reaching the village before nightfall, might mean death. There could be no possibility of keeping in the track after dark, and there was much room to doubt whether we should be alive in the morning, after passing the cold hours of the night, without food, upon the plain.

We pushed forward, and tried to keep the takht-i-rawan in sight. Our baggage-mules and all our servants were far in advance; the greater number had not staid with us at Ahminabad. The difficulty was, that as we were unable to see the mountains, even those who knew, or believed they knew, the road had no indication of our whereabouts. At last, when we were becoming extremely anxious, there loomed in front of us the vague outline of a mountain, which dissolved all doubts and alarms.

Soon afterward, almost suddenly, we came upon a ravine in which the village of Yezdikhast is most singularly situated, upon an isolated rock, the surface of which is level with the plain. The village seems from a distance to be seated on the level; from the edge of the ravine the sight appears extraordinary and picturesque. Nearly a hundred feet from the ground, some of the inhabitants peered at us from the village walls on our arrival. We descended, cold and covered with snow, to the bottom of the ravine, where the caravanserai stood outside the village. The recollection of our apartment at Yezdikhast is almost enough to induce catarrh. To clear away the snow from the steps which led to the roof was no easy matter. Upon the roof snow lay thick, and the only room on that elevation was as big as a small chapel, with a vaulted roof five-and-twenty feet from the floor, which was like a chalky road with heaps of ashes here and there, the remains of past fires, lighted, in the Persian manner, in any part of the room. The open door-way was wide; over that we suspended rugs. High over the door was a square hole, almost as large and quite out of reach. The idea of warming such a place was, of course, absurd. We lighted some logs, had a hasty dinner, and got into our beds. Next morning the snow was so deep, and my wife so unwell, that we determined to stay where we were, but not in the bala-khanah. Kazem and I selected the best of the gloomy arches which surrounded the yard, had it swept out, lighted a fire, hung a mat in the door-way, had our furniture moved, and my wife carried down into this brick vault, which, when the door-way was screened, was utterly without light. After the manner common throughout Persia in such places, the domed roof was covered with a black coating of bitumen, and one of our difficulties was in dealing with the impenetrable darkness. The glow of the fire seemed pressed back into the grate, and the light of our candles to extend no farther than the table on which they were placed. All day long we lived in this Cimmerian gloom, with our traveling thermometer too near zero. Our strenuous efforts to warm the bricks of this black vault involved a most unusual consumption of fire-wood, which was regarded by the people as reckless extravagance; but with us it was really a question of life or death, for my wife had symptoms of inflammation of the lungs, and I could not get the temperature up to 40°. I have seen a more comfortable room at the bottom of a coal-pit than that in which we passed the 13th of January at Yezdikhast. The rough curtain over the door did not exclude the freezing wind, nor the brayings and the shouts from the mules and their drivers, who thronged in the yard, from which this curtain was our only separation. All day long snow fell fast and thick. We became anxious as to the possibility of crossing the mountains, which we should reach after four days' march from Yezdikhast.

When we set out on the morning of the 14th for Shulgistan, the snow was inconveniently deep—so deep that a bivouac at midday, except in the saddle, was out of the question. For eight hours we toiled through it, meeting no living creature all day, except one small caravan of donkeys from Shiraz. At Abadeh, the next station after Shulgistan, we expected to find an escort, provided by the Governor of Shiraz. At Kum-i-Shah I had received a telegram from his excellency, forwarded in translation by the English clerk at Shiraz, saying that he had heard of our approach, and that he wished to place a residence at our disposal during our stay at Shiraz, to which I replied that we had already accepted an invitation from Mr. Odling, the resident medical officer of the Indo-European Telegraph at Shiraz, but that I would be obliged if his highness would send us a suitable escort of soldiers, to accompany our caravan from Abadeh to Shiraz.

At Abadeh we were to lose the company of the superintendent and his servants. I noticed that all of them were humanely provided with blue spectacles, which are indeed the only means of escaping the torture of inflamed eyes in crossing these snow-covered plains. The all-penetrating dust of summer, and the painful glare of snow in winter, are sufficient to account for the prevalence of sore eyes among the muleteers. Along the way to Abadeh, the superintendent gave fresh illustrations of brigandage in Persia, and soon after midday he and his troop galloped off. I sent on our baggage at a quicker pace than was possible for our takht-i-rawan, and soon afterward I told our own servants to get in and prepare an early dinner. We were left alone on the plain with two muleteers. It was about three o'clock in the afternoon, as we were approaching a ruined village which lay half a mile to the left of the path, that I saw a number of wild horsemen straggling out from these ruins. They galloped hard toward Kazem, who was perhaps a mile in front of us. I had no doubt that they were robbers. Their place of hiding and mode of attack were precisely such as had been described. To fight forty armed horsemen was impossible, and of escape there was no chance. I saw them gallop up to Kazem, surround him, and bring him back in our direction. Kazem, seated between his saddle-bags, looked about as the prisoner of these Persian bashi-bazouks. I could see them gesticulating fiercely around him. The appearance of the band was the wildest imaginable. Hair, and clothes, and horses, they were alike only in this quality of wildness. I placed my horse close beside the takht-i-rawan as we advanced to meet them. I had not a doubt we were about to be robbed, and perhaps ill-treated; and when half a dozen sprung forward, I was intensely surprised, though I am sure I exhibited no astonishment, when, instead of pointing their carbines and lances, they bowed to their saddles, and the leader, touching himself, said, "Hakem." Then I saw in a moment that this wild troop had been sent out to meet us, as a guard of honor, by the "Hakem" or Governor of Abadeh, and that they had been waiting, probably for hours, in the ruined village.*

They had ridden to Kazem to inquire if we were the expected Ferangis, and, this point being settled, they surrounded us. The leader called for the kalian, which is never absent on these occasions of ceremony. Two of the wild horsemen were concerned in producing the ceremonious pipe. One, who was pipe-bearer, carried, dangling at his saddle, far below the belly of his horse, a perforated pot of charcoal, which swung and jangled as he rode, and on the other side was suspended the water-bowl of the kalian, the stem and fittings of which were carried by the second man. No one stopped while the pipe was being prepared; and when I refused it, and the machine was passed on to the leader of the wild horsemen, he supported it on his saddle, while he laboriously inhaled the smoke in which Persians so much delight. Meanwhile the horsemen commenced a display on their own

---

* The troop formed an *istikbal*, which is the Persian word for a welcoming party. The number of men composing the *istikbal* is a matter of great importance with ceremonious Persians. The native princes of India are extremely ambitious in the matter of gunpowder salutes: the number of guns with which they are welcomed is an indication of rank which they regard with jealous attention; and so it is in Persia with the numbers composing the *istikbal*. Terrible has been the wrath of great men when they were received outside Persian towns with a meagre *istikbal*.

account. They rode round and round us, shouting and leveling their lances or their guns. These soon dashed away over the snow, in pretended encounter; others dropped their lances, and then, galloping at full speed, picked up the weapon without dismounting. In some form or other, these exhibitions were kept up until we reached Abadeh, where the whole population seemed to have turned out in the miserable streets. The superintendent had kindly promised, as the chapar-khanah had a very bad reputation, to engage for us the best room he could find in the town. But the streets were so narrow, and so incumbered with frozen snow, that it was impossible for the takht-i-rawan to approach the town. To the great delight of the crowd, it was lowered from the mules at some distance; but their curiosity was disappointed when the lady preferred to be locked in her carriage until the room was ready for her reception. The "room" would be called a "shed," and a very insecure shed, in any part of Western Europe. Nothing would induce the door to close within about two inches, and there was a greater defect of the same sort about the other doors which served as windows; the floor was of beaten clay, the walls plastered with mud, and the smoke-dyed beams of the roof were well hung with cobwebs. Upon the beams dried grass had been piled, and hung in dusty festoons.

Kazem and his helpers had hardly completed all the necessary arrangements when a train of soldiers and slaves arrived from the governor, a petty potentate, subject to his highness who rules at Shiraz, bearing a present, which consisted of two plates of sweetmeats, two pots of sweet cream, a large tray covered with cakes of the thin bread of the country, and three live fowls. The governor's servants said he was very anxious that I should pay him a visit. They were extremely frank about their master's feelings on the subject. They urged that it would be such a humiliation if I did not see him, and that this was the reason why he was so anxious. I had been riding all day, I was very tired, and we were to leave the next morning early; but, however, I promised to pay his excellency a visit, and took with me, as a present from Mrs. Arnold to the governor's wife, a pretty little pocket-book, which he accepted with great enthusiasm. He had received orders, he said, from the Firman Firma (the title given by the Shah to Yahia Khan, the Governor of Shiraz), that we were to be attended from Abadeh to Shiraz by the captain of the road-guard and six of his men; and after the usual set-out of coffee, pipes, and tea, I returned to our dinner of soup and pillau. But on the way I was stopped by our charvodar, from whose loud lamentations I gathered that one of his gholams had deserted, taking with him a few krans belonging to the charvodar. There could be no doubt that the gholam had engaged to go to Shiraz, and immediately I took steps to have him found, which did not appear to be a work of great difficulty. When the missing gholam had been found by the governor's officers, I took him apart and asked if he was willing to go the whole journey. He said "Yes," and that he had run away only because of some dispute, which the charvodar was willing to settle. I warned him that, on leaving Abadeh to cross the mountains, no desertions would be permitted, and that our guard would have orders to look after him. He seemed quite intent to give no further trouble.

With three soldiers for escort, we set out again over the snow for Zurmak, a short march of sixteen miles upon a nearly level plain. We had just gone to bed in the customary discomfort of the bala-khanah, when there was noise of tremendous knocking at the outer door of the chapar-khanah, which is always exactly under the bala-khanah. This, we soon learned, was the arrival of the embassy messenger, on his monthly journey from Teheran to Shiraz, with letters for the Indian mail. To us he brought a most welcome present —six loaves of good bread from Madame Læssoë. A soldier who traveled with him, and who had orders to add himself to our escort, brought us a letter from the Governor of Abadeh, of which the following is a translation:

"At the service of the exalted, excellent gentleman, the munificent—I forward abundance of well-wishing and congratulation.

"God willing, I trust you have arrived in safety at the stage of Zurmak, and that your time will pass pleasantly. I am exceedingly sorry that I have not been of service to you during your stay here. Because fortune did not assist me the day you left, and proper service was not done by me to you, and because I was not ennobled by being able to help you, I am indeed sad and grieved. I feel certain that the services which should have been done for you have not been accomplished. Forgive me. God is witness, I hoped to be some days in your company, and to show my devotion to you.

"I trust you will let me know of your arrival at Shiraz, that I may be assured of the safety of your noble person. I have no more to say.

      "(Seal of)   Mohammed Reza."

In Persia very few persons sign their name—very few, perhaps, have the power of doing so—but many who can write prefer to give their letters the greater dignity of their seal. And as we found at Teheran, so throughout all Persia, every body who has, or is likely to have, a financial transaction carries a seal. The raggedest charvodar, with the sorriest troop of mules, produces the engraved stone or brass, which is his seal, and stamps an agreement for a journey. The letter of Mohammed Reza is a fair specimen of the flowery and complimentary style common to all Persian letters of ceremony. His excellency had provided four soldiers; their captain and the rest of the troop were to join us on the top of the pass at Dehbid. We were approaching the most dangerous part of our travels, and the most famous haunts of robbers in the mountains between Ispahan and Shiraz. In the world it would hardly be possible to find four more ill-looking fellows than our escort. Appearing upon any stage as the villains of a play, they would have had an immense success; and, for my own part, I felt very little confidence in their protection. A better friend was the cold, which was every day becoming more intense as we ascended toward the pass of Dehbid. To ride at a walking pace for nine hours through a freezing wind involves suffering of which even the recollection is painful; and on the way from Zurmak to Khanikora I was not able to walk part of the way, because I found that if I took to the saddle again after my boots were covered with snow, there was danger of frost-bites from the boot being incrusted with ice. Seeing a brown, bare patch about midday, I got off to take luncheon; but this was worse than any other place, for it was not, as I supposed, cleared of snow by wind, but by the salts in the earth, which melted the snow as it fell into a freezing mixture. Standing in this terribly cold slush, I took from the takht-i-rawan the remainder of a piece of brawn, which had been made for us in Ispahan. But it was frozen into crystals of ice, and had no taste but that of extreme cold.

We have an abiding recollection of the bala-khanah at Khanikora; the cold was the most severe we had experienced, and this was one of the most wretched. From the yard, filled high with frozen snow, the mules, their drivers, and the soldiers crept quickly into the hovels at the side, where all lay down together. The bala-khanah was about eight feet square and seven feet high, black with smoke, and with a hole for door-way or window on every side. We lighted a fire, and the place was at once filled with stifling smoke. We saw that though the thermometer was many degrees below zero, and a frosty wind blowing through the wretched place, it would not be possible to have a fire. Having stuffed up the windows and door-ways with rugs and stones and sticks and planks, we got through the night, and learned, the first thing in the morning, that the soldiers refused, on account of the extreme severity of the cold, to proceed up the defile to Dehbid, which is seven thousand five hundred feet above the sea.

There were two good reasons for pushing onward: our miserable position at Khanikora, and our firm belief that the intense cold preceded another fall of snow, which would block the pass, and detain us not one, but possibly many, days in this wretched chapar-khanah without fire or food. I sent word to the soldiers by Kazem that we intended to start immediately, and that they could go, or remain behind, as they pleased. I knew we should have no more of their objections; which, however, when we got well out upon the frozen snow, and in the full grip of the wind, had, I was compelled to admit, a really terrible foundation. Up the slope we passed in Indian file for hours, the snow lying in drifts ten, fifteen, and in some places twenty feet deep. One caravan had passed before, and in the footsteps of these pioneers we found security. If a horse or mule missed the track, which zigzagged from side to side, it was at once half buried in the snow. There could be little reason to feel fear of robbers, even in this favorite place of attack, in such weather. My face was skinned and burned a reddish black in a few hours by the wind and sun. The snow drifted into my hair, and froze in lumps and icicles about my face. Not a word was heard; none were in the humor for talking. Two of the soldiers and Kazem lay down in their large saddles, and covered themselves over with their goat's-hair cloaks, so that no part of their faces or bodies was visible, to hide themselves from the biting wind. At twenty yards' distance no one could have supposed that their horses carried men.

At last, in the teeth of this wind, we reached the summit, from which the view was such as I can fancy would much resemble the lookout in polar regions from the top of some huge iceberg. The apparently limitless, snow-covered plain looked flat as the frozen ocean, and the hills rising from it like the ice-mountains. There was not a tree, nor a house, nor a bare patch, to vary the white monotony of the scene; and overhead the dull sky seemed loaded with snow, which was just beginning to fall. We were still ten miles from Dehbid, when the path began to descend gently. Presently we saw a party of horsemen approaching, whom, from my experience at Abadeh, I presumed to be friends. It was Houssein Khan, the captain of the road-guard, who was to conduct us to Shiraz, and a troop of his followers. He was a thin, roguish-looking man, his saddle a perfect armory of handsomely inlaid weapons. He made his salaam, in spite of the freezing temperature and the falling snow; his pipe-bearer produced the traveling kalian. But the ceremonies of greeting, which in Persia can not be disregarded, were scarcely ended when the storm broke. The wind hissed, and the snow fell in blinding clouds. Houssein Khan was vanquished by the weather. He had for a little while adopted our walking pace, and placed himself behind me, his men being divided about equally into a front and rear guard. But the snowstorm and the freezing wind made him think only of himself. He had come out with the wind at his back, and had not suffered much. It was now unendurable, and he trotted past me, then gained a corner of the road, and there set off at a gallop for the shelter of Dehbid. One by one, the rear-guard stole past, and soon we were left alone with our muleteers.

We could not see more than a hundred yards before us, and the track was getting covered up. The wind seemed to pierce my riding-boots as if they had been made of cotton. At last, after nearly two hours of this difficult and solitary progress, we met Mr. Markar, the Armenian clerk of the telegraph at Dehbid, who had kindly ridden out to look for us. It was at his house we were to pass the night. I was delighted to see him, and he, the inhabitant of one of the most desolate and lonely stations in the world, was evidently glad. But in such a wind and storm it was impossible to talk. We were soon at his fireside, recovering warmth from cups of hot tea. We were rejoiced that we had made the journey and pushed through to Dehbid. Had we given way to our escort and staid at Khanikora, we should have been imprisoned. It would have been quite impossible to leave that most wretched chapar-khanah for days, perhaps for weeks, after such a storm, which must have filled the defile in many places with impassable depths of snow.

Mr. Markar's house was of the usual kind. A quadrangle of mud-bricks, mud-cemented, with no external opening but through the strongly barred door; the buildings having a uniform height, that of all the rooms placed round the central court. Our apartment had a door, and over that a curtain of Manchester cotton; but when I got out of bed in the morning I found the snow lying in a white drift across the room, having been blown in the night through door and curtain. Mr. Markar was a sportsman, and had outside his wall what he called a fox-trap. This was the remains of a dead mule, near which he posted himself at night, and sometimes shot one or two foxes, which are valuable for their handsome gray fur. No one in Persia seems to understand the proper preparation of fur. The Persians have a means of temporary preservation sufficient for the skins until they reach a European market. In Ispahan and Shiraz there is a considerable traffic in these skins, which are bought by the merchants at about two krans apiece. They are then sent to England or Russia, to be dressed and made up. Although among the higher classes much fur is worn in Persia, none is made up in the country.

Houssein Khan and his men were glad to leave the mountain-tops. They looked blue with cold when we were getting the caravan together to proceed toward Shiraz. We could take the warmest part of the day for leaving Dehbid, as the distance to Khanikergan, the next station, was only twelve miles. For the whole of the way the ground was covered deep with snow. One caravan had set out before us and marked a track, but we met no one. We were prepared by evil report to find none but most wretched lodging at Khanikergan, but had not placed our expectations low enough. The caravanserai was an old stone building, and the surrounding arches were not, as usual, raised above the yard, but were on the same level. We had the best, but it was disagreeably evident that it had been recently occupied by mules; and from the smoke-holes in the centre of the roof the melting snow dripped slowly into the hole which served as a stove when this place had been occupied by animals who cook their food. We could only have a fire at the cost of being stifled with smoke, so we preferred to lay a stone over the hole in the roof—an undertaking which brought down the snow in heaps into the room. Until sunset, the stone walls of this noisome place trickled with cold moisture, which then froze hard in icicles and stalactites. We had no security that some curious mule would not push his head through the flimsy covering of the door-way. But, however, we slept; and when Kazem brought the usual kettle of hot coffee with the first dawn of the morning, we were rejoiced to think that Khanikergan was to be a place of the past.

At Meshed-i-Murghaub, which we reached on the evening

of the 21st of January, the chapar-khanah was outside the village, which was surrounded with a mud-wall. This is one of the most dangerous centres in Persia; and as we rode up, a number of the villagers armed with guns, and accompanied by others who had no weapons, came out to meet us, making a great noise, in which I could hear the Persian word for "robbers" frequently mentioned. It appeared that a band of robbers had been seen in the neighborhood, and these poor people had taken up arms to defend themselves and their property in case of attack. We were looked upon as a valuable re-enforcement, and as a possible source of danger; for, according to Persian laws, the districts in which robbery occurs have to make good the losses sustained by travelers; and this, though inoperative when Persians are the subject of attack, is, the people well know, not likely to be disregarded when Europeans have been plundered. Not that they believe the proceeds will be conveyed to the plundered party: they have not sufficient conviction of the honesty of their Government for that; but they are shrewd enough to know that the robbery would afford excellent ground for the extortion of money by the officers of the governor.

A Persian argues with himself that when there is trouble in the country, some people will have to pay, with life or property, or both; and it is most likely this will fall upon those in the neighborhood. The circumstances of his country have never led him to think of justice as an abstract matter, or of justice as pursuing criminality with discrimination or discretion. He knows by experience that the victims of justice are more accidental than those of crime; and when that authority which stands for justice in Persia is abroad, his first thought is to fly away, or to hide every thing which he possesses. When a European traveler has been robbed or murdered, it has happened that large encampments of Iliats, and even villages, have been deserted, owing to the universal fear among these people of being selected to suffer punishment for the criminals. On such occasions somebody must be hanged or tortured to death; and if the criminals are not taken redhanded, Persian justice sees none so likely to be guilty as those nearest to the scene of crime.

In every village there were a certain number of men accustomed to carry arms, tofanghees (gun-carriers) they are called. More or less, these men are under the orders of the governor. He can require their attendance in any part of the district surrounding their village, either as an escort for travelers or merchandise, or for the destruction of robber bands. But no one seems to place much confidence in a tofanghee. Generally he is "a man with a gun," and nothing more. In the South of Persia, the attentions of the tofanghees to the traveler are frequent and embarrassing. Sometimes they march out with him in the morning, whether he will or no; and when they are tired, when they approach the boundary of the next village, or especially when they think there is a band of robbers at hand, they ask for money and for leave to make their salaam. Surrounded by a dozen wild-looking men well armed, and asking for money in this attitude, a doubt has crossed my mind whether they are so very different from the robbers against whom they pretend to be a protection.

CHAPTER XXI.

Classic Persia.—The Tomb of Cyrus.—Date of the Ruins.—Passargardæ.—Columns of Cyrus's Tomb.—Color of Ruins.—Neglected by Persians.—Kawamabad.—Takht-i-rawan in Danger.—Houssein Khan and the Sheep.—Village of Sidoon.—Ruins of Istakr.—Situation of Persepolis.—Araxes or Bendemeer.—Staircase at Persepolis.—Darius and Xerxes.—Cuneiform Inscriptions.—Study of Cuneiform.—Chronology of Assyria.—Great Hall of Xerxes.—The Persepolitan Lion.—Hall of a Hundred Columns.—Professor Rawlinson on the Ruins.—Tomb of Darius.—"The Great God Ormazd."—The Bringer of Evil.—Dios and Devils.—Errors in Religion and Art.—Pedigree of Architecture.—Persians, Medes, and Greeks.—Origin of Ionic Architecture.—Leaving Persepolis.—Plain of Merodasht.

At Murghaub, we approach the grandest relics of the time when Persia was the great empire of Cyrus, of Darius, and of Xerxes. At three hours' ride from the village the plain is fringed with low hills, among which stands, close by the path from Ispahan to Shiraz, the tomb of Cyrus. Near this, we had seen rising from the snow all that remains of his city of Passargardæ, where the inscription "I am Cyrus, the King, the Achæmenian," may be read more than once upon the ruins. It is partly from the proximity of these unquestionably genuine ruins, and also from the dignity and obviously funereal character of this massive mausoleum, that it has become accepted as the original resting-place of the body of the great king.

The period which these highly interesting ruins illustrate is concurrent with the Achæmenian dynasty, or, to put it in another form, it is the period extending from the accession of Cyrus, in 560 B.C., to the death of Alexander, in 323 B.C. The reigns specially illustrated are those of Cyrus, of Darius, of Xerxes, and Artaxerxes. We shall fix the time more clearly still in the mind if we remember that the buildings of Persepolis are of about the same date as those of the Acropolis of Athens. We may find many points of curious and interesting comparison between the work of Darius and that of Pericles; and regarding both, we see at once how great a disadvantage the Persians suffered in not having at hand such marble as that of Pentelicus.

It was on this plain of Murghaub that Cyrus won Persia. I think it is Professor Rawlinson who tells us, in his "Five Ancient Monarchies," how King Darius was bound, whenever he visited this ancient city of Passargardæ, to present to each Persian woman who appeared before him a sum equal to twenty Attic drachmas, or about sixteen shillings of English money, according to a custom established in commemoration of the services rendered by the sex in the battle wherein Cyrus first repulsed the forces of Astyages.

We dismounted at the tomb of Cyrus, and walked about in the snow, while Kazem made a fire, preparatory to the manufacture of an omelet. As a rule, Oriental monuments owe much to the grandeur of their situation; and this is no exception. They are set in solitude; they have a surrounding of space, which is all their own. When the thought of the traveler is arrested by so vast a retrospect, he becomes more impressed with the natural grandeur of the desert; and there seems to be a hush, a natural silence in the air, which moves around these most ancient monuments as if Nature herself were paying homage at these shrines of departed greatness. For more than two thousand four hundred years this tomb has defied the leveling hand of Time; and another period of not less duration may apparently be sustained without further injury.

The tomb was originally surrounded by columns, set probably in a double row, with a covered space between. But none are left standing. Most of the columns have disappeared entirely; some are prostrate; and of only a few is there a broken fragment remaining in position. These columns were not colossal, probably not more than eighteen feet high; and the space inclosed is hardly more than a hundred and fifty feet across. In the centre of this space stands the tomb, approached by a pyramid of steps, about forty-five feet square at the base. These steps, the rise of each being two feet, are composed of large blocks of marble, the color of which has darkened to a yellowish brown. Upon a platform about eighteen feet from the ground, and twenty feet square, stands the tomb—a small, solid, unadorned building, composed of a few blocks and huge slabs of marble; the whole being scarcely more than fifteen feet high from the platform to the peak of the marble roof. In shape it exactly resembles a child's "Noah's ark," with the boat arrangement cut off. At one end there is a low, massive door-way, through which, if the remains of Cyrus really rested there, they were carried, to be deposited upon the floor of this little temple. By all writers, including our own Professor Rawlinson, this is accepted as the resting-place of the great king; and it is believed that his body was placed here in a golden coffin.

That it is a tomb, or that it is the tomb of some very exalted personage, or that it was constructed about the same date as the neighboring ruins of Passargardæ, which are unquestionably erections made in the reign of Cyrus, there can be no doubt. Some travelers appear to have thought that the marble has not sufficient aspect of antiquity to warrant this conclusion. But what, then, would they say of the Parthenon? The marble masonry upon the Acropolis of Athens is similar to this upon the plain of Murghaub, in massiveness, in coloring, and in the absence of mortar or cement, of which none was used by the builders in either place. But the tomb of Cyrus has a less fresh appearance than the walls of the Parthenon. Alas that no Historic Monuments Bill can apply to the plains of Murghaub! There is nothing to attract the acquisitive powers of an Elgin, for the marbles are utterly without inscription or adornment, and there is nothing to hinder ravage by the Persians. I have never seen in any Mohammedan people an exhibition of the slightest desire for the protection of the great historic monuments of which they have been or are possessed. The pashas of Stamboul looked on unconcerned while the marbles of ancient Greece were burned to make lime for building cattle-sheds. Were it in ruins, they would as soon burn the stones of Santa Sophia as the timbers of an old man-of-war; and for the Persians, these great ruins, which should be the pride and most sacred treasure of their country, are nothing more than useless heaps of tumbled stone. If any man needed lime in the neighborhood, or stone to build a caravanserai, he would probably use the stones of Cyrus's tomb, or the columns of the Hall of Darius; and these invaluable records and memorials of a period concerning which very much more than our present knowledge might be gathered by excavation and research upon the spot, are regarded with no more concern or attention than the bones of a dead camel.

From Cyrus's tomb we rode through a narrow plain for several hours to the village of Kawamabad, a collection of mud-huts lying near the mountains. There was no chaparkhanah at Kawamabad, and we were obliged to hire a room in the village, to get at which we had to pass through two cow-sheds and into a walled straw yard, from which our apartment, upon nearly the same level, was entered. The takht-i-rawan could not enter the door-way of this range of buildings, and was, as usual, left outside. But immediately upon its being lowered to the ground, the villagers who stood looking on said that would never do. "Robbers! robbers!" they cried, and pointed to the hills. They were in a state of great excitement. A band of robbers had visited Kawamabad that day; it was feared they would return, and the poor villagers did not want to be responsible for the rifling of our takht-i-rawan. It was impossible for the mules to carry it within the building, so the villagers took the work upon themselves; and with many invocations of "Allah," of "Ali," and "Houssein," and with an amount of force of which a third, if disciplined, would have been more than sufficient, they lugged the takht-i-rawan into greater safety.

If the band which had visited Kawamabad were disposed to attack our caravan, I expected we should meet them next day during our ride to Sidoon. In addition to Houssein Khan and his soldiers, half a dozen villagers, with guns in their hands, set out with us in the morning, and by their advice we kept the baggage-mules close up, and allowed no straggling on the part of those animals. But Houssein Khan did not seem apprehensive; and when the villagers were tired and returned, he was quite ready to do a little highway robbery, or, rather, sheep-stealing, on his own account. We were in a region of moderate fertility; there were a few flocks of sheep and goats upon the plains, each flock tended by one or two herdsmen. Whenever we approached a flock of sheep, Houssein Khan galloped off, as I at first supposed, to consult the herdsman as to the security of the road, and the position of the rabble musketeers who were supposed to guard the path under his command. Gradually I perceived that these rides had a more strictly personal object. From every one of these visits he returned with a sheep across his saddle, or upon that of one of his men, which was soon afterward set upon its legs, until there was a small flock of half a dozen following him, under the care of one of our own Persian bashi-bazouks. At first I thought Houssein Khan was buying the animals for food; but we were within two days' march of Shiraz, and it was evident that one would have been enough for the whole caravan. I had not sufficient Persian at command to obtain a thorough explanation. But I called Kazem, and made him understand that I thought the herdsmen were being robbed, and told him to let Houssein Khan know at once of my suspicions, to watch what was done with the sheep, and to report to me every thing. Kazem smiled, as if he thought such concern was extremely prudish, and said something, in which a word sounding like "wedocle" occurred. This, I knew, is the Persian mode of expressing forced and illicit contributions; and in Sidoon I learned that the sheep were sold by Houssein Khan at about two-and-sixpence each. The chapar-khanah at Sidoon lay in a terribly cold situation, in the shade of a range of mountains; but we bore the discomforts of the place, with the recollection that on the morrow we should see Persepolis, and in two days end our journey in Shiraz.

The natural formation of the country in the neighborhood of these illustrious ruins is very suggestive and imposing. Journeying from Ispahan, the plain, at one end of which stand the remains of Persepolis, is approached through a vast natural gate-way, in which run the road and the river Pulvar, and of which the pillars are strangely shaped and the many-colored mountains of the hardest limestone. The table-rock, or mountain, on the right is very remarkable; and in this entrance, which is too wide to be called a gorge, are found the massive ruins of the city of Istakr, which one has not patience to examine carefully when so near to the far more interesting remains of Persepolis. At Istakr the road winds to the left round the bold spur of the mountains which forms the background of Persepolis.

On approaching the ruins of the halls and temples and tombs of Darius and his descendants, the traveler, recalling perhaps to mind all that he has seen at Baalbec, at Pæstum, and upon the Athenian Acropolis, will surely be struck with a sense of disappointment, because there is here no outline of ancient hall or temple, no realizable structure in which he can place the form of Darius or Xerxes. There is nothing more than remains of the temples of Jupiter in Athens and in Rome—a few solitary or connected columns, and the massive stones of some part of an ancient hall or propylæum. The distant aspect of the ruins of Persepolis will fall below anticipation as much as the results of their examination in detail will exceed expectation. In fact, the most interesting ruins in the world, because they are covered and adorned with eloquent records of the past, these stones are not arranged for a *coup d'œil*.

The mule-path passes close to the side of the mountain from which the platform of Persepolis is projected into the plain of Merodasht. Through this plain runs the river, which in classic times was called Araxes, afterward known as Bundamir, or Bendemeer, as Moore has called it in "Lalla Rookh." Standing upon the platform of Persepolis, the view across the river is uninterrupted for more than twenty miles. The extreme height of this platform where it faces the plain is about forty-five feet, its length from north to south about fifteen hundred feet, and the meagre depth from east to west about eight hundred feet.

The grandest work at Persepolis is in connection with this platform. The masonry of the supporting walls of the platform is irregular, the blocks, mostly of huge size, presenting angles of every degree. The surface of this immense work is true and sound as it was two thousand years ago. But it is not in this that the glory of this platform rests. At its greatest height, the platform is ascended from the plain by a staircase which, for the magnificence of its proportions and the beauty of construction, deserves to have been regarded as one of the wonders of the world. The staircase at Persepolis has had no equal in ancient or modern times. Compared with this, a work probably of the time of Darius, the marble stairs which lead to the Parthenon are insignificant, and the imperial steps in the Roman Coliseum barbarous. A regiment of cavalry, ten abreast, could ride easily up the double flights of the Persepolitan staircase. The steps, which appear to be composed of the hardest syenite, are twenty-two feet wide; each step rises only three and a half inches, and has a tread of fifteen inches. In some places the blocks of the masonry in the staircase are so large that three or four steps have been hewed out of the same piece of stone.

We little thought when, in spite of the timid counsels of Mr. Erskine, then British minister at Athens, we passed a day upon the Plain of Marathon, that a few years afterward we should stand among the ruins of the Hall of Darius, the place to which he probably returned after that unsuccessful expedition against the Greek; or that when we stood in sight of that splendid landscape, near where

> "A king stood on the rocky brow
> That looks o'er sea-girt Salamis,"

we should afterward enter the magnificent ruin of the Propylæum of this King of Xerxes at Persepolis. It is this building which stood at the top of the grand staircase, and the most massive of the ruins upon the platform of Persepolis are those of this edifice. Upon the piers there are inscriptions in cuneiform letters, which as clearly as the winged bulls above these writings testify the relationship between the Assyrians of Nineveh and the Medes of Persepolis. The inscription is the same on each pier, and is written in three languages. It has been translated by Sir Henry Rawlinson into the following:

"The great god, Ahura-mazda (Ormazd); he it is who has given (made) this world, who has given mankind, who has made Xerxes king, both king of the people and lawgiver of the people. I am Xerxes the king, the great king, the king of kings, the king of the many peopled countries, the supporter also of the great world, the son of King Darius the Achæmenian. Says Xerxes the king, by the grace of Ormazd I have made this gate of entrance (or this public portal); there is many another nobler work besides (or in) this Persepolis which I have executed, and which my father has executed. Whatsoever noble works are to be seen, we have executed all of them by the grace of Ormazd. Says Xerxes the king, may Ormazd protect me and my empire. Both that which has been executed by me and that which has been executed by my father, may Ormazd protect it."

This is repeated twelve times in all; and, looking upon the original with Sir Henry's translation in one's mind, it is surprising how so much can be conveyed in so few letters. Not much more than a fourth of the space which could be required for this inscription in English is occupied by the cuneiform letters.

It would be interesting to trace in detail the process by which scholars have acquired the art of deciphering these and similar inscriptions; of forcing the secret of their long-concealed meaning from these strange characters, which no more resemble the Arabic or Persian letters of our day than do the forms of the English alphabet. It is, however, perseverance and acuteness, rather than scholarship, which are required for this discovery. The study begins by observing, from obvious similarity of letters, when the same word occurs in the same or in different inscriptions. The importance of the word, if a long one, or its unimportance, if short and frequently recurring, will be observed. At last, by considering many, if not all, possible combinations of the supposed meaning of one word, some light will dawn with regard to three or four words, perhaps a large part, or even the whole, of an inscription. This is undoubtedly the method in which the meaning of these inscriptions has been mastered. It is generally admitted, I believe, that no one has done more in this work than Professor Grotefend, of Göttingen, of whom Mr. Fergusson says, in his "Nineveh and Persepolis," that we owe to him "the key which has led to all we know in this matter." Professor Grotefend made laborious analysis of two inscriptions among those which are met with at Persepolis. The first is that which may be seen upon the ruins of the Hall of Darius, and which has been translated: "Darius, the great king, the king of kings, the king of nations, the son of Hystaspes the Achæmenian. It is he who has executed this sculpture." The second is upon the Hall of Xerxes, and in English is as follows: "Xerxes, the great king, the king of kings, the son of Darius the Achæmenian." These inscriptions obviously afforded hopeful matter for analysis. The frequent recurrence of the word translated "king" suggested that it was a title of ceremonious honor; the position of the word "Darius" at the head of the first, and its place in the second inscription, suggested that it was a proper name; while its occurrence in the second inscription immediately before the words "the Achæmenian," which appear in the first, led naturally to the supposition that "Hystaspes" was in like manner a proper name. But while the briefest consideration of this mode of acquisition may increase our respect for the actual labor of scholars who devote their energies to this work, it also suggests how many imperfections there may be in any knowledge so acquired — discrepancies of signification which in some cases it may be forever impossible to repair.

While we are dwelling for a moment upon this order of research and discovery, it will be interesting to note the account given by Professor Rawlinson of the finding of collateral evidence in support of the generally accepted chronology of the Assyrian history, upon which is based that of the Achæmenian dynasty. Among the records of Assyrian history was discovered the mention of phenomena obviously a description of the effects of a total solar eclipse. This was stated to have taken place in the month Sivan (or June), in the ninth year of King Asshur-damin-il II. Sufficient was known of the annals of the kings of Assyria to identify with some degree of certainty the century in which this particular monarch lived; and the time of his reign appeared to be fixed with unquestionable accuracy when the calculations of astronomers showed that the only total eclipse of the sun falling about the middle of the year, visible in Assyria between B.C. 847 and B.C. 647, within which time the reign of Asshur-damin-il II. must certainly have fallen, was the one which, according to these figures, must have taken place on June 15th, B.C. 763.

With regard to the Propylæum of Xerxes, of the two readings given by Sir Henry Rawlinson, "this public portal" is probably better than "this gate of entrance," because these gates were in all Oriental countries, from the earliest dawn of Christian times, places of business as much as of passage. Upon the inner sides of the massive stones of this "public portal" are sculptured in low-relief the massive forms of winged bulls, some with human, others with bovine, heads. The largest of these quadrupeds have the human head, covered with a tiara, and on the shoulders wings, similar in all points to those which Mr. Layard introduced to the world from Nineveh.

Upon the vast platform at Persepolis there are remains of at least five important buildings—four lying to the right of the Propylæum of Xerxes, and no two of them being precisely upon the same level. The first of these important buildings is the Propylæum; and near that a staircase (as elegant in construction, though much smaller than the grand flights of stairs rising from the plain to the platform) leads to the level of the building known as the Great Hall of Xerxes. This name "Hall" is given in ignorance of its real object or designation. Mr. Fergusson, the distinguished architect, to whose work* I have before alluded, has written upon these ancient stones, and has, in fancy, reconstructed them with remarkable insight, though, like most who have written about them, he has never beheld the ruins of Persepolis. But, had he seen these remains, he could not have described with greater truth and accuracy the real difficulty in forming any supposition apart from the actual evidence afforded by inscriptions and ruins, than he has in the true remark: "At Persepolis we have pillars, door-ways, and windows, but not one vestige of the walls that clothed them, or of the roofs they supported." That the Great Hall and other buildings of Persepolis were roofed, is pretty obvious, both from the shape of the capitals of the columns and from the number of the columns, which are not placed, as in Greek buildings, merely at the sides of the structure, but at equal distances over all the floor. We can see that the columns which supported the portico of the Great Hall of Xerxes were of marble. Those which remain are crowned with capitals composed of two bulls' heads, placed neck to neck, forming an excellent rest for the entablature. These columns are fluted, and have upon their pedestals that ornamentation which was so long considered as a Greek invention—the honeysuckle, with the bud of the lotus; in fact, the decoration known everywhere as "the Greek honeysuckle." In the north portico of this Great Hall there is yet more striking evidence of the debt which the perfection of architecture in Greece owes to Persia, to Assyria, and possibly to Egypt. In the capitals of these columns there is an elongated or double volute, al-

---

* Fergusson's "Nineveh and Persepolis."

most identical in figure with that which is seen upon the later buildings of Greece; while upon the walls of door-ways there are sculptures, truly Oriental, of kings on thrones or on foot, attended by slaves holding the parasol of state, or the fly-chaser, equally an emblem of royal dignity. By the Persians this hall is called "Chehil Minar," or "Forty Columns," which is, in fact, a common name for any columned buildings of grand dimensions in Persia. The shabby old pavilion at Ispahan, with twenty tall columns of wood, set with grimy mirrors, is called "Chehil Minar."

I do not feel at all sure that the columns of the interior of some, if not all, of the great buildings of Persepolis were not of wood. There can be no doubt that, in those remote days, the lion had the characteristics of strength and supremacy which are still attributed to the "king of beasts." At Persepolis, the angular sides of the staircase leading to the Great Hall of Xerxes are filled in with very powerful sculptures in low-relief, in which an animal of enormous strength, with much resemblance to a lion, has fixed its teeth and claws into the hind-quarters of a bull, which fills the higher angle of the space by rearing and turning its uplifted head in helpless anguish from its devourer. From that time to this there have been lions in the mountainous region round Shiraz; and, apropos of Persian lions, I shall never forget the tone of plaintive envy in which the formidable Zil-i-Sultan spoke of his father, the Shah, "having killed a lion." In this feat, he seemed to consider, lay the real superiority of the Shah over himself.

It is noticeable in the buildings of Persepolis, as compared with the Parthenon, that there is nothing resembling the continuous action displayed in the processions upon the frieze of the Greek building. At Persepolis, upon the sides of the staircases and in other places, there are processions; but, as a rule, one figure is exactly like the next; there is no connected action. The modern ornamentation of Teheran is like that of Persepolis in this respect: a soldier occupies a panel, another soldier of the same pattern is seen in the next, and so on.

The grandest of the buildings of Persepolis, the ruins of which are known as those of "the Hall of a Hundred Columns," stood behind the Great Hall of Xerxes. The bases of the columns and parts of the outer walls remain. We can trace the regular position of the columns, but can not decide whether, being of wood, they have perished; or, being of stone, have been carried off for the adornment of some mosque or palace. They were certainly not very large. The area covered by this building was considerable; but neither this nor any of the buildings of Persepolis could have had any thing like the grand proportions of the Temple of Jupiter at Athens. In reading Professor Rawlinson's careful work, "The History of the Five Ancient Monarchies," one is often reminded of the disadvantage under which an author labors, be he ever so learned and acute, who writes of buildings and of countries he has never beheld. Had Professor Rawlinson seen the buildings of Italy, of Greece, of Egypt, and of Asia, he never would have written of these ruins of Persepolis, and in particular of this Hall of a Hundred Columns, as "the great pillared halls which constitute the glory of Arian architecture, and which, even in their ruins, provoke the wonder and admiration of modern Europeans, familiar with all the triumphs of Western art, with Grecian temples, Roman baths and amphitheatres, Moorish palaces, Turkish mosques, and Christian cathedrals." This is just the point in which the buildings of Persepolis fail. They are deeply interesting as records of the Achæmenian dynasty; they are illustrated books of priceless value in their inscriptions and sculpture; but for grandeur, and even solidity, they never were comparable to some of the buildings of Athens, nor, among modern and Christian buildings, to the Church of St. Isaac in St. Petersburg.

The floor of the Hall of a Hundred Columns is, for the most part, buried deep under rubbish, the washings of ages from the neighboring mountains. Against the stoutest blocks of the richly sculptured walls this detritus lies undisturbed, concealing sometimes the legs of a winged bull, at others the lower garments of a king, and how much besides which the passing traveler can not see nor guess. What new lights for history, what treasures of antiquity, may be lying within two or three feet of the surface in these neglected ruins! In the walls of this hall there are deep recesses or niches, the likeness of which is invariably met with in every modern Persian house.

That portion of the platform farthest from the great staircase and the Propylæum of Xerxes is occupied, first, with the Palace of Darius, and, last, with the Palace of Xerxes; and in the far background, in the side of the mountain, originally approached by steps, is the tomb of Darius. Above the small door-way, which lets into a cave hewed from the solid rock, the face of the mountain is smoothed and sculptured. In the foreground of this work of ancient art is the crowned figure of the king, and at the opposite end, on the same level, an altar with fire burning upon it. Above this altar is the round full orb of the sun; and hovering in mid-air, between the sun and the monarch, is what Mr. Fergusson calls "his *ferouher*, or disembodied spirit." But this is unintelligible. Professor Rawlinson suggests, with greater show of reason, that this figure is the emblematic resemblance of Ahura-mazda, the "good" god of the Medes, the Ormazd of the inscriptions of Xerxes. The figure is that of a man crowned and robed like King Darius, his feet unsupported, his body passed through a ring, which connects a pair of vast wings; and of this Professor Rawlinson says, "The winged circle, with or without the addition of the human figure, which was in Assyria the emblem of the chief Assyrian deity, Asshur, became with the Persians the ordinary representation of the Supreme God, Ormazd."

The language of the inscriptions of the time of Darius has been described as an old form of Persian; closely allied to the Vedic Sanskrit of India, on the one hand, and to the more modern Zend of Persia, on the other; and the religion seems to have been the ancient representative of the faith of the Parsees of to-day. In this tomb of Darius, the greatest place in the heavens is given to the sun, and on earth to the altar of fire, the terrestrial emblem of the sun. Then in the heavens, again, Ahura-mazda, or Ormazd, is the god of all good things, prayed to, and revered by humanity below. We know that, according to the belief of the time, Ormazd was not all-powerful. Whatsoever things were good came from him, and to him all the hopes and fears of mankind under the sun were addressed. But there was another besides Ormazd, the spirit of evil, Angro-mainyus, who, for obvious reasons, does not appear in this sculpture. He, the bringer of all trouble and pain, was helped by "divs," bad spirits, whose delight was to thwart the work of Ormazd. Is it possible that these were the forerunners of our own familiar devil, the belief in whose existence and obnoxious activity is passing away from this generation like a bad dream? In time to come, when the orthodox devil has followed the "divs" of the time of Darius into the tomb of the past, there will remain none the less a true and inexpugnable devil in the world, a sum of evil made up by individual ignorance and excess, of disregard of duty toward one's self and one's neighbors, a devil within ourselves, which, however, will be the more easily attacked, and the more probably vanquished, when we shall have recognized that it is no supernatural force which opposes our appreciation of the enduring pleasures which follow in the train of those lines of human conduct which we rightly call virtues.

In religion, the people of Western Europe, proud of their civilization and enlightenment, have been, however, the victims of an error now grown inveterate. In daily contemplation of the doctrines of Christ as the oracles of God, they have been surprised to learn that the germs at least of that which is most ennobling and sublime in these doctrines had been long present in the world before the birth of Christ. And instead of feeling strengthened in their faith, and in acceptance of these doctrines, by this larger and fuller evidence of their truth, and their title to the allegiance of mankind, they have been prone, not to abandon these doctrines, for that is beyond their power, but to feel, as it were, disappointed, in learning that ideas which they cherished as supernatural revelation are not less honored as the transmitted experience of humanity.

A like error has been made in the lesser sphere of art. To many generations past, the Greeks have been in art a people endowed with capacity for leaping at once into the highest realms of knowledge, gifted with genius unapproachable by later peoples; the men who from nothing, and with no previous light, gave to Athens her gorgeous temples, and to Rome all that she has known of art. But now a truer conception is passing into the mind of the world. Such supernatural ability as has been in past times ascribed to the Greeks is seen not to be the monopoly, much less the sole invention, of any people. The roots of the tree of knowledge, it is now perceived, may be hidden, but must exist; and it is understood that the magnificence of Ionic and Corinthian architecture could not spring fully clothed even from the rich soil of Greece, but that, like every good thing in the possession of mankind, these must be the results of long and laborious growth, of transmission or transplantation from one scene to another in the life of the universe.

Highest in the records of history stands the foundation of

the Egyptian monarchy; and it is probable that the oldest buildings upon the soil of the earth—the Pyramids of Ghizeh—were erected about seven centuries after that date, in 3200 B.C. We know that Assyria was a country of renown two thousand years before that birth occurred at Bethlehem, in the lower lands of those wonderful valleys of the Tigris and Euphrates, from which all Europe, except Turkey, reckons the beginning of time. We can trace in the sculptures of Nineveh and in those of Persepolis a substantial resemblance. We know from the names inscribed, and from other evidence, that the latter is the descendant of the former, though probably with an interval of a thousand or fifteen hundred years. The winged bull of Nineveh has its ancestors in Egypt, and its successors in the same image and likeness at Persepolis. The bulbous columns of Egypt and of Nineveh have, in the later work of Persepolis, given birth to columns containing features which had not then appeared in Greece, but which were soon to be seen there, improved and refashioned, if not reproduced, by the most artistic people of the world. The historical connection is, link by link, in the mind of many a school-boy.

The most illustrious epoch in the history of the country we have been treading shows us, first, the victorious Cyrus; then the victor of the Nile, Cambyses, the master of Egypt; then, of the same dynasty, the great Darius, who carried his legions to Greece, and met defeat upon the Plain of Marathon. Again, another association of the Greeks with the Medes and Persians occurs through the ambition of Xerxes, whose name stands imperishably upon the roll of fame—not for his successes, not for his works at Persepolis and elsewhere, but for his defeats at Thermopylæ and Salamis. Of that period, Persepolis is the illustration in stone; and, looking upon the ruins, I am quite disposed to concur in the opinion so confidently expressed by Mr. Fergusson, that "all that is Ionic in the arts of Greece is derived from the valleys of the Tigris and the Euphrates." The volute, that distinctive feature of Ionic architecture, suggested perhaps by the use of bulls' heads or rams' heads in couples for the capitals of columns, was in use at Persepolis before it passed to Greece; while in Greece there was as yet only to be seen the massive simplicity of Doric architecture.

At Persepolis we have witnessed not only the origin of the volute, but also the "Greek honeysuckle," before that decoration had passed into Greece; and there, too, upon the Palace of Darius, are those well-known rosettes, so often repeated upon Ionic door-ways; the same which may be seen upon the Erechtheum of Athens, and which are faithfully copied upon a thousand edifices, including the well-known church in the Euston Road of modern London. Greek art brought out in stronger and more perfect form the members of Eastern architecture. The sculptors of Persepolis did not attempt to carve their columns in human form, and to lay the burdens of architecture upon the heads of slaves. The Caryatides are essentially a Greek production; but is it possible to concede to them all the merit of perfect originality when one sees vast stones piled upon the human heads of these winged bulls, which in part present to us a form very like that of man?

It was only in obedience to the setting sun, the god of the builders of Persepolis, that we reluctantly turned our backs upon the tomb of Darius, and descended by the grand staircase to the plain. May the sun shine upon that, the noblest work of Persepolis, in all its present completeness, until it shall be in the East as it is in the West, and there shall be no more fear of ignorance accomplishing the ruin of the finest ascent ever made by human hands! It is recorded in the Second Book of Chronicles, of the Queen of Sheba, that when her majesty went into Solomon's house, and saw "the ascent by which he went up into the house of the Lord, there was no more spirit in her;" she could contain her admiration of his works no longer, and her heart poured over with delight in the words, "It *was* a true report which I heard in mine own land of thine acts." It is hardly possible to doubt that, had she been received by King Xerxes at Persepolis, her amazement and rapture would have been far greater. It is probable, too, that then the plain across which we rode toward the stream of the river Araxes, or Bendemeer, was not treeless, arid, and waste as at present. We have, indeed, good evidence that there, as in so many other places, Persia has gone backward in production. Chardin, the French traveler, to whom the world has been so much indebted for its knowledge of Persia, says of this plain of Merodasht, that it is "fertile, riche, abondante, belle et délicieuse." When we passed over it in the present year, it produced nothing but a few scrubby thorns, nibbled by the goats of the village of Kinara, to which our steps were directed.

CHAPTER XXII.

Kinara.—A Family House.—A Troublesome Cat.—Houssein Khan and the Sheep.—Soldiers and their Debtors.—Zergan.—Persian Scenery.—A Persian Funeral.—Zergan to Shiraz.—Pass of Allahu Akbar.—Snow-storm at Shiraz.—The English Doctor.—Gate of Shiraz.—A Good Persian House.—A Present from Firman Firma.—Letter from His Excellency.—A Dervish at the Gate.—Meidan of Shiraz.—Visit to Firman Firma.—Widow of Teki Khan.—Firman Firma's Character.—Poverty of Persia.—Passion-play in Mohurrem. — Bazaar of Shiraz. — Tomb of Hafiz. — Odes inscribed on Tomb.—Translation of Hafiz.—The New Garden.—Tea in an Imaret.

OUTSIDE the village of Kinara there was a hole in the mud-wall through which we might have passed the takht-i-rawan; but had we done so, the narrowness of the streets would have prevented its approach to the house in which a room had been secured for us. We halted, therefore, in a field of young wheat, at a place where rubbish had been flung out from the houses of the village and over the wall in such quantity, that, now it was frozen hard and innoxious as rock, we could walk up the slope and over the wall into the village.

The mode of access prepared us for the characteristics of Kinara. The family in whose house we were to lodge was much disturbed by our sudden arrival. We had struggled through the dirty snow in the narrow street, and entered the low door in the mud-wall of the house. In the yard, deep in filth, much of which was happily frozen, were two mules and a donkey, and about their legs a legion of fowls, of which one lay headless at the requisition of Kazem, whose imperious airs in a Persian village were sometimes very amusing. Up a narrow passage, past a stable in which two donkeys were eating straw, there were some mud-plastered steps leading to the roof of the buildings surrounding the yard. Upon this roof was the shed which it was the delight of the family to let to us for the night, with the prospect of some payment in the morning.

Like the roof, our apartment was of mud. In the hole which was the door, there was a shutter of wood, which could not be made to close by half a dozen inches; and in the hole at the farther end, which served as a window, there was nothing to keep out the frosty wind until we stuffed a saddle-bag into the refrigerating aperture. The roof was extensive; and in another place there was a second shed, in which the family hay and melons were preserved, and into which the contents of our apartment, previous to our occupation, were hurriedly thrust by the retreating inhabitants, some of whom sat on the roof, while some stood among the other animals in the yard, contemplating with avid interest every one of our movements. Upon any pretense, and sometimes without pretext, one of them would appear upon that portion of the roof which was in front of our place of refuge; and at last I was obliged to draw a line upon the dried mud, and intimate that I should deal in a summary manner with any who overstepped that boundary. Whatever they had to bring must be laid down at this line, and none but Kazem might pass over it. The precision of this arrangement met with the entire satisfaction of the family. But there was one member—a black cat— whom I could not instruct, and through the evening and night this green-eyed monster sought, often with success, to violate the sanctity of our mud-cabin. To secure greater privacy and higher temperature, I had nailed a camel's-hair rug inside the imperfect door, and, as a fortification against the cat, had weighted the lower end with heavy stones. As for the wooden door, that, like nine doors out of ten in Persia, presented no hinderance; and with time on his side, the tomcat was always more successful than I with the rug. Twice in the bitter cold of the night I expelled the enemy, and renewed our defenses. But the cat was always victorious, and in the morning I found he had been successful in carrying off the greater part of a tongue which had been placed in a position, as I believed, of absolute security. On the whole, we were not sorry to leave Kinara. But, forgetting the squalor of the village and the lodging, looking across the five miles of level plain to the still visible ruins of Persepolis, with their high background of mountains varied in color as in shape, we were ready to admit that it would be difficult indeed to name a scene of greater natural beauty or of higher antiquarian interest.

Our way to Zergan, the next station, wound through low hills at nearly a continuous level. About midday we came to a bridge crossing a river which was swollen and foaming with melted snow. There was a wretched hovel at hand, from which half a dozen of Houssein Khan's ragged tofanghees emerged, and hovered round us while we sat in the only patch of shade, to make a luncheon of lamb and eggs. During the morning their chief had possessed himself of two more sheep from flocks which were feeding near our path; and we felt so indignant at the continuance of this system of robbery, carried on under our eyes, and probably, in the opinion of the victims, with our connivance, that we resolved to be silent no longer, and desired Kazem to ask Houssein Khan for an explanation of what we wished him to tell the khan appeared to us nothing better than robbery. The captain of the guard sat on a stone close by, with his ivory-hilted sword laid across his knees, a dagger and two pistols in his belt, when Kazem delivered my demand for an explanation of his conduct. I could see he was very much disturbed by the inquiry. He came himself to explain that he had done no wrong in taking the sheep; he declared that they represented a payment on account of loans he had made to the peasants, and that this was the only way he could obtain consideration for his advances. Although Kazem smiled incredulity as he assisted me in comprehending Houssein Khan's explanation, I was obliged to accept it, and to admit that possibly it might be correct, although I do not believe there was a word of truth in his statement. It is, however, unquestionable, that in Persia money-lenders are most often soldiers—the only class which feels strong enough to secure payment. This is so general, that a defaulting debtor is looked upon as in a particular degree obnoxious to the military class, who, if they get an opportunity, subject him to severe ill-treatment *pour encourager les autres* in the payment of their borrowings. I have met with people who have seen the dead body of a debtor, stripped naked and dragged by the heels with a rope, in the midst of a party of soldiers, through the bazaars of one of the chief towns in Persia, by way of warning to those who owe money not to fail in discharging their obligations to the usurious military before they pay the debt of nature.

Houssein Khan was in a very black humor when we resumed our journey, toward the end of which there lay between us and Zergan a vast morass, extending for miles from mountain to mountain. The charvodar and he had had a quarrelsome difference of opinion as to which was the best path, and I decided, much to the disgust of the soldier, that the muleteer should select the way for the caravan. He had the greater property at stake. He and his mules were inhabitants—natives, in fact—of the village we were approaching, and the result justified my decision.

We met a string of dromedaries coming out of Zergan. Their swarthy riders were seated between the humps of the animals, enduring the swaying motion, and passing us with imperturbable gravity. "English reserve" is a common subject of joke, but it is certainly not greater than Oriental reserve. It is more true, perhaps, that the reserve practiced on some occasions by Englishmen appears inconsistent with the absence of reserve upon other occasions. But in the deserts of Persia and Arabia it is common experience to meet but one or two persons in a whole day's journey, and not by any means uncommon to pass these without uttering a word. Sometimes the ejaculation "Salāām!" is exchanged between one or two of the members of a caravan, but a prolonged greeting is of very rare occurrence.

I was about to say that the situation of the chapar-khanah at Zergan is very remarkable; but I am conscious that in all Persian scenery there is a sameness in certain features, though these have invariably a peculiar beauty of form and coloring. The mountains are never out of sight, and in January there is always snow in the landscape. When the plains and hillsides are visible, there are always the browns peculiar to Oriental scenery; and when there is a village, the flat roofs of mud, and straight walls of the same color and material, give an unmistakable character. At Zergan the plain was so narrow that all these features were brought in unusually close contact. At sunset, when the moollah of the village, too poor to have a minaret, was standing on the roof of his mosque, and crying, "Allah-ah-ah-ah-u akbar-ar-ar-ar" in the tones to which we had become accustomed at night and morning, I walked for a long time on the roof of the stables (which is, as it were, the terrace of the bala-khanah) enjoying the scene, watching how the silence of the plain seemed to deepen with the lengthening shadows, and the rose-color of the distant snow turned first to a pale gilding, and then to iron-gray, and the bell of a mule coming to rest for the night resounded for miles in the still, clear air, given over by the parting sun to the dominion of frost, which immediately sealed all until the morning.

I was awaked by a direful wailing of many voices, and, hastily turning out upon the roof, saw a funeral passing from the village to the grave-yard upon the plain. In Persia, as in Turkey, great haste is generally made in burial; the bearers hurry along, unwilling to keep the soul from rest in earth. In this case, the body was wrapped or swathed in white linen, and laid on a bier, the mummy-like form of the corpse being entirely exposed. In front, the wailers, professionals probably, trotted at a pace a little faster than would be possible had they walked at their utmost speed; the bearers, of whom a relay followed the body, did their best to keep up, and the succeeding crowd of mourners and sympathizers straggled onward as they could.

This was the 26th of January, and we were happy in the thought that we were about to rest in Shiraz after the fatigue of traveling. For eighteen nights, from Ispahan, we had endured the miseries of chapar-khanahs and caravanserais. With the exception of one day's painful rest at Yezdikhast, we had ridden, on an average, for eight hours every day; and as we rode up and down the snowy hills toward Shiraz, we longed for a sight of the famous city in which we were to be for some time the guests of an Englishman. The snow was deep, and the road almost the worst we had met with. Underneath the soft snow there were hidden bowlders of every shape, upon which our horses and mules stumbled and slipped. In places where the sun had power, the hoofs of the animals were covered with slush at every footstep. We had not gone half-way from Zergan to Shiraz, when the sun disappeared behind thick clouds, and the magnificent panorama was closed by a heavy fall of snow.

In the mountains, slouching through the snow, we met two rather large parties of armed men, who would possibly have shown themselves to be robbers had we been less strong; and at length, in a hollow, we dismounted at a ruined caravanserai, and awaited Kazem's preparation of a stew. The good little man was bringing it toward where I sat, almost shivering, upon the frame-work of a well, near to my wife, who did not leave the shelter of her takht-i-rawan, when his foot slipped, and the savory mess fell into a hopeless quagmire of mud and snow. We had to put up with less comforting provision. But what did that matter. In three hours we should be in Shiraz. We mounted again, and rode up and down over hills of which we could not see the end. Progress became very difficult on account of the snow, which every hour fell fast and faster. I saw it was the intention of our guard to creep away and leave us to walk through the storm. Houssein Khan himself set the example. When a projecting rock hid him from my sight, he pressed his horse onward, and was soon out of sight. My contempt for the whole troop was too great to permit of entreating the soldiers to remain and trudge slowly through the snow with the baggage mules and the takht-i-rawan. Every man of them soon trotted off, and we, attended only by our muleteers and servants, moved slowly along, the whole caravan white with the falling snow, the takht-i-rawan and the baggage fringed with icicles. We had passed the last summit, and were descending from the path of Allahu Akbar in a gorge, the grandeur of which was perhaps enhanced by the severity of the weather, when we met the English doctor, Mr. Odling, who had kindly invited us to stay at his house in Shiraz, attended by a stalwart Persian groom. Both were mounted on splendid horses, and well armed. The doctor wore a long coat of English frieze, and riding-boots; a young man with the strong, quiet manner characteristic of Yorkshiremen — a man of whom, at first sight, one would say that he was well chosen for the service in which he had engaged. He had some difficulty in reining his fiery horse to our caravan pace. Worse traveling I had never known. Snow and stones, and mud beneath, and above a cold, blinding drift and fall, which froze where the lingering warmth of the body did not melt it into greater discomfort.

From the high hills by which Shiraz is approached by way of Ispahan, a broad path leads down to the city. In other places it would be called a road; but where wheels are never seen, such a word might be misleading. Had the day been clear, we should have enjoyed from these hills one of the finest views in Persia. Close beside the path, as it slopes into Shiraz, is a grave-yard, with a garden attached—an inclosure in which dark-green cypress-trees rise high above the walls. In this place rest the remains of the poet Hafiz; and about a mile farther to the left, in another inclosure of the same character, Sa'di was buried. Upon the right of the road is a garden, also set with cypress-trees, with a pavilion or palace at the higher end — a very favorite resort of the Shirazees, who carry their tea-pots there, and, sitting on their heels upon the open floor of the pavilion, enjoy the view over the flat roofs, the blue domes, the minarets, and the green "chenar," or plane-trees, of the city, bounded by the opposite mountains rising high above Shiraz, and inclosing that which they fondly believe to be "the hub" of the universe. This quotation is the more permissible, because there is some parallelism between the reputation of Boston in the United States and that of Shiraz among the Persians. Shiraz is pre-eminently the literary city of Persia.

But in the snow-storm we had no disposition to turn to right or left, even to do homage at the grave of Hafiz. Straight on we pushed, until, at a council including the doctor and the charvodar, it was decided that the takht-i-rawan, three feet wide, seven feet high, and in length perhaps not more than that of three mules, could not pass through the town, and that it would be necessary to ford the river, and enter the walls as near as possible to Mr. Odling's house.

I shall never forget the mud inside the gate of Shiraz. It was about a foot deep, and spread from wall to wall. A labyrinth of walls and narrow ways rendered the farther progress of the takht-i-rawan impossible. We had, at the entry of this famous city, to place my wife on a led horse, and to have the takht-i-rawan carried in the hands of men, because, with the more extended length of harnessed mules, it could not follow the windings of the miserable streets of Shiraz. That operation of "swapping horses while crossing a stream," which Abraham Lincoln condemned as the height of impolicy, is as nothing compared with the manœuvre we were forced to effect in this sea of mud. At last we arrived at a brick wall, in which was the door of Mr. Odling's house. For the kindness and ability with which he conducted, under the double oppression of a snow-storm and of a Shiraz crowd, the difficult arrival of ourselves and our train, I have an unfading recollection of esteem and obligation.

There is no one of the Englishmen resident in Persia—and we became acquainted with all—of whom we retain a higher opinion than of Mr. Odling, partly because no one is more careful to vindicate the superior characteristics of his country, by the continued observance of them in a land where, as a rule, right appears to have no significance but that of might. His home in Shiraz is a good Persian house of the usual style; mud-built, of course, with no view from within of the external world, and with rooms arranged upon paved terraces around two small quadrangles, in which there are the usual tank and bit of garden — the latter, in his case, set with orange-trees. The walls of the rooms in a house of this sort are finished with fine plaster, whitened, and paneled with recesses in which pictures, books, or china may be placed. The fire-place is always the same—a hole in the wall beneath a flue; and the floors, of course, are more or less covered with carpets, those best productions of Persian industry, with their unrivaled blending of soft colors. When we arrived, and indeed during the few days of our stay in Shiraz, the quadrangles of Mr. Odling's house were heaped high with snow, including a large quantity thrown from the roofs. It is obviously unwise to allow a great weight of snow to melt on the mud-roof of a Persian house. Careful housekeepers always remove it quickly; and upon the roof of every Persian house in which there is pretension to good management, a cylinder of stone is always kept, to solidify the roof by rolling after wet weather, and upon the occasional application of a new layer of wet clay.

Houssein Khan had orders to report our safe arrival to the Firman Firma (the Decreer of Decrees), and I sent at the same time by a servant a letter of thanks to his excellency, together with a vizierial letter from his brother, Mirza Houssein Khan, the Sipar Salar. Early the next morning the inevitable present arrived. This time it was much bigger, more imposing in its arrival, and more useless, in fact, than before. Preceded by the Firman Firma's major-domo, whose every stride was marked with a movement of his silver-mounted wand, walked several servants, followed by negroes bearing the present on their heads in huge trays of metal each a yard in diameter. Three were piled with oranges, and in others there were arranged ten large china plates full of sweetmeats. Shortly after all this was delivered, a handsome young Persian, the governor's aid-de-camp, the "nazir" of his excellency's household, arrived with the following letter from the Firman Firma, which is not only in the French language, but is without the slightest touch of Persian manner:

"Monsieur,—J'ai eu le plaisir de recevoir la lettre de S. A., et je m'empresse de vous réitérer mes sincères félicitations pour votre arrivée dans cette ville.

"Demain, vendredi à midi, je vous attends avec le plus

grand plaisir. En attendant je vous prie de vouloir bien présenter mes respectueux hommages à Madame Arnold. Je m'imagine des fatigues qu'elles a dû endurer pendant un voyage en ces froids.

"Je vous prie d'agréer l'assurance de ma parfaite considération. YAHIA."

One may live for months in a Persian house without acquiring any knowledge whatever of that which is to be seen outside the door. Upon our arrival in Shiraz, I had been so confused by the falling snow and the mingled noise of porters, muleteers, soldiers, and servants, that I had taken no notice of the surroundings. In the bustle of arrival, I had not even observed the mud-hut in which a dervish lived close by Mr. Odling's door. On coming out, this holy man took care there should be no such omission, lifting his voice with ever-increasing loudness until he attained his object. It is a common circumstance in Persian towns for one of these religious mendicants to plant himself near the gate of any house of unusual importance. Of course, the residence of a giaour was not the cause of this particular dervish's presence. A Moslem house joined the residence of the Christian doctor, and one of the city gates lay close at hand. The situation was therefore a good one for a religious beggar; and a dervish, though upon one occasion he will not be sparing of his curses, which are always the only words fit in his mouth for Christians, has, as a rule, no objection whatever to money from the hands of unbelievers. The dervish at the door is regarded by Persians as a nuisance which must not be rudely expelled; much as an English squire or farmer of the olden fashion looks upon the summer birds which build their muddy nests in the angles of his porch, with a lingering belief in his mind that, after all, there is perhaps something in the old doggerel, which says,

"Martens and swallows are God's best fellows."

For my own part, I would far rather hear the twitter of the swallow, as a morning call, than the "Allahu akbar" of a self-imposed dervish at my gate. But, then, there is no accounting for taste; and the dervishes find that a lazy life, with a noisy devotion to religion, insures an easy livelihood.

Twenty steps past the dervish over the frozen slush, we arrived in the smaller "place," or meidan, of Shiraz. On one side stands the governor's palace; the other three sides are occupied with the blank walls of houses and yards. Paving has never been attempted in Shiraz, and the meidan is in hills and holes, according as the traffic and the exigencies of the people, in the disposition of rubbish, have made it. There are two or three miserable trees before the governor's palace, which was apparently at one time fenced from the open space by a wall of mud-bricks, with stone piers. But the stones have long since been cast down; they lie broken on the ground, with much débris from the wall. The front of the palace has no architectural pretensions: under a heavy chalet roof there are windows, one story above the ground-floor; but the windows and frames are broken, the mud plaster has fallen off in large patches from the wall, and on every side of this meidan the walls are in the same condition. Over all there is the usual aspect of ruin and poverty, so general throughout Persia.

Under the gate-way lounged some of the Firman Firma's servants and soldiers. On seeing us, they led the way to a brick staircase, with steps inconveniently high, to a part of the palace at some distance from the meidan, pulled aside the hangings of Manchester cotton, stamped with Oriental pattern, from a door-way, and we were in the presence of His Excellency Yahia Khan, brother of the prime minister, and husband of a sister of His Majesty the Shah. Yahia, commonly known as "the Firman Firma," is also Motemid-el-

15*

Mulk; and the title of the princess, his wife, is Izzet-ud-Dowleh. Her highness was the widow of the murdered Ameer-el-Nizam. The Shah's repentance for the crime of consenting to the death of the Ameer led his majesty, as we have seen, to betroth his two young daughters to the sons of the Ameer; and the same feeling induced him to bestow the princess, whom he had made a widow, upon the Motemid-el-Mulk, whom he afterward styled "Firman Firma."

Yahia Khan is the most accomplished and Europeanized man in Persia. His manners are charming, and there can be but very few Asiatics who have such easy command of the French language. If he were a man of firmness, vigor, of strong and lofty ambition, Yahia Khan might do great things for his country. But one sees at a glance that, though superior to his brother in culture, and probably in moral worth, he has not the energy, the boldness, or the power of intrigue of Mirza Houssein Khan. He wore a military undress of European cut—the only governor who had not received me with all the jewels and ornaments at command. In this and many other points, the superior civilization of Yahia Khan was evident. His apartment was not unlike a barrack-room in officer's quarters: the walls white and bare, the floor covered with matting, with two carpets laid upon it. Chairs are always scarce in Persia; there were only three in the Firman Firma's room—two (for Mr. Odling and myself) besides the arm-chair of the governor, which he compelled me to accept. The British agent, a native of rank, the Mirza Hassan Ali Khan, a man of very agreeable manners and of much cultivation, arrived as soon as we were seated; and, gracefully accepting Yahia Khan's apology for the absence of a fourth chair, took his seat, in probably greater comfort, upon the floor. All the weakness of the Firman Firma's amiable character appeared in his conversation. Of the ills in the condition of Persia he was in no way ignorant; of amendment he had nothing to say. I did not expect much in that direction from a man who, while drawing a splendid income from the province, was content to leave the front of his house a heap of ruins. It is this supine submission to the process of decay which is the bane of Persia. From highest to lowest, every thing is administered as if the only object of those in power were to seek their own momentary advantage; as if, in fact, the Persians held the country as yearly tenants, and nothing more. When Sir Lewis Pelly was (in his capacity as political resident at Bushire) in official communication with the Government of Shiraz, he showed his true appreciation of the political system of Persia in a report to the Bombay Government: "A——," he wrote, "gives to his subfarmers permission to collect the revenue by force: this is done. Next year some of the peasants are fled; some of the land is lying waste. The country, in brief, is revenued as if the Government were to end with the expiry of the governor's lease."

The Firman Firma had but one word of explanation concerning the condition of Persia: the country, he said, was "very, very poor." There had been a few robberies lately in his province, but he believed it was generally quiet (he has since been recalled, owing to his inability to control the turbulent people of Shiraz); he should provide us with an armed escort from Shiraz to Bushire, which he had intended should be ten men and an officer; but as I preferred to have only two sowars, he would give orders that but two, and those the most trustworthy, should accompany our caravan. He provided the customary entertainment of tobacco, tea, and coffee, and was most polite in desiring to do any thing which could conduce to the comfort and pleasure of our stay in Shiraz.

I had one favor to ask—a very small one—but I thought it would be more proper not to put it to him personally; and on leaving I directed the attention of his "nazir," or controller, the same agreeable young man who had brought the Firman Firma's letter soon after our arrival to the large tent adjoining the palace, in which during the first days of the Mohurrem, then just commenced, there was acted the representation of the closing period of the life of Houssein, the grandson of Mohammed. I was aware that this taziah, or theatre, was visited daily by the Firman Firma and the ladies of his anderoon, as well as by hundreds of the people of Shiraz; and I requested, if his excellency thought my visit would not be displeasing to the people, and therefore a possible embarrassment to himself, that he would kindly make provision for our admittance to witness the performance.

For days this strange "passion-play" of the last days of Houssein had been going on, and for days it would continue. On the tenth day, the tearful tragedy of his death at Kerbela, with that of seventy of his followers, would be represented. The canvas of the large tent had, I should think, been purchased in England or in India. On three sides the theatre was closed in by the walls of the precinct of the palace. Upon the top of these, and covering the fourth side, the canvas was arranged. The whole of the centre of the tent appeared to be the stage. It seemed that no scenery was introduced, but the events were made life-like by the employment of soldiers, camels, horses, and mules, of which there were generally some standing outside the theatre. These were, for the most part, splendidly equipped, and lent for this sacred occasion by the governor and great people of Shiraz.

The young nazir called at Mr. Odling's the next evening, and, expressing the great regret of his excellency, said that the Firman Firma thought it better we should not visit the theatre. The moollahs would certainly object, and he feared there might be a disturbance. We therefore failed in this respect in Shiraz, as we had failed in Teheran.

The Persians are so strict in excluding Christians from their religious places that we had some doubt if we should be able to enter the cemetery in which is placed the tomb of Hafiz. We rode in single file through the crowded bazaars, and soon gained the broad way by which we had entered Shiraz. Leaving our horses outside the gate, we entered the mud-built gate and walked among the dark cypresses. An open mosque stood at the higher end of the grave-yard, which was full of tombs, and at the other end there were charming views, through the cypress groves, of the blue sky and the snow-covered mountains which lay on the farther side of the valley in which is placed the city of Shiraz. There were two moollahs near the mosque, wearing white turbans and long robes of green. One of these ran toward us, but not with the intention of objecting to our entry. Mr. Odling's dog had, unobserved, left the grooms, and followed us into the cemetery. It was against the presence of the Christian "dog" that the demonstration of the moollahs was made; and, though we aided in expelling our dog, we thought it an affectation of religious zeal on the part of the guardian priest, inasmuch as all the while there stood near the quiescent moollah a Persian, and, by hypothesis, a Moslem dog, which appeared quite at home, and welcome, in this pleasant and most picturesque retreat.

Our offending dog having been thrust outside, we were at liberty to look at the grave of Hafiz, which is placed about the middle of the square inclosure. The ground is thickly beset with tombs, mostly flat, like that of Hafiz, but none so exquisitely carved, nor, like his, of marble. Hafiz's tomb is covered with a single block of the beautiful marble of Yezd, of which about eighteen inches appear above the ground. The upper surface of this fine slab is nine feet long by two feet nine inches in width. In the centre there is an ode, written by Hafiz himself, of which the following is a translation, founded upon that made by Mr. Binning:

"Proclaim the good tidings of oneness with thee, that

above this transitory life I may be lifted immortal. A bird of Paradise am I; my heart's desire is to fly to thee, away from the traps and temptations of this world. If thou shouldst deign, in thy great mercy, to call me thy faithful servant, how joyously would I take leave of the mean concerns and miserable vanities of this transitory existence!

"O Allah! from the bright vapors which surround thy throne, pour out upon me a flood of the graces of thy goodness, before I am borne away like dust before the wind.

"Come hither, O my loved ones, to my tomb, with wine and music; and possibly, at the sound of your cheerful voices and the music of your melody, I may cease from slumber, and rise from among the dead.

"Though I am aged and weak, do thou, if it be but for one night, fold me in thine embrace, so that on the morrow I shall arise from thy side re-endowed with the bloom and the vigor of youth.

"Come forth and show thyself, O type of all good; manifest thyself, so that Hafiz may bid adieu to this life and to this lower world."

Raised in low-relief, this ode, in the beautiful letters of the Persian alphabet, occupies the centre only of the slab. Round the edges, in a band about four inches deep, appears another ode, which has been rendered into the following words of English:

"O my soul, be thou the servant of Allah, the king of the universe, and be thyself a king. Seek to abide forever under the care and protection of Allah.

"The enemies of the true faith may be many; but a thousand of them shall count as naught, and they shall be as nothing, even though hosts of such unbelievers should cover the hills.

"To-day, O Ali, we live by thy power. By the souls of the holy Imāms, be thou a witness on our behalf in the world to come.

"He who bears not true love toward Ali is no better than an infidel, even though he be most devoted in his prayers and the most learned in the mosque.

"Go, kiss the sepulchre of the eighth Imām, the prince of the faith, Réza, and stand expectant on that sacred threshold.

"O Hafiz! choose thou the service of Allah, the all-powerful, and go forward boldly in the right path."

The tomb is probably not yet two hundred years old. From this interesting place we passed to the "New Garden," which is not far distant, and commands the same charming views of the valley and mountains of Shiraz. There we met with a party of "softas," theological students, who had brought a samovar and charcoal, cups and saucers, sugar and tea, from the town. They invited us to join them in a cup of tea, which we all enjoyed upon the ruined floor of an "imaret," a palatial pavilion which had been gay and grand in the days of Shah Abbas.

CHAPTER XXIII.

Literature of Persia.—Hafiz and Sa'di.—Contemporary of Dante.—Mr. Bicknell's Translation of Hafiz.—Consulting Hafiz as an Oracle.—Nadir Shah and Hafiz.—Hafiz's Fragments.—"Tetrastichs" of Hafiz.—Sa'di's "Bustan."—Sa'di's "Gulistan."—Extracts from "Gulistan."—Sa'di's Wit and Wisdom.—Gardens of Shiraz.—Slaves and Slave-brokers.—English Surgeons and Persian Patients.—Influence of Russia.—Mr. Thomson and Mr. Bruce.—Indo-Persian Telegraph.—Major Champain's Reports.—A View of the Neighbors.—Persian Homes.—Government of Shiraz.—Eeliats in Fars.—Attack on a Caravan.—A Vengeful Government.—Cruel Execution of Robbers.—Firman Firma superseded.—Taxation in Persia.—The Shah and Shiraz.

THE literature of Persia is not extensive, and that which exists is little known outside the empire. But in any survey of Persia, however hasty, some notice must be taken of the works of the two great poets, Hafiz and Sa'di, both natives of Shiraz. There is, no doubt, immense difficulty in translating their writings. Hafiz, the later of the two, has been dead nearly five hundred years. Imagine a Persian with a smattering of English (Europeans very rarely acquire a thoroughly competent knowledge of the Persian language) as it is spoken to-day set to translate Chaucer into Persian! Dante was contemporary with Hafiz. Fancy the difficulties which the writings of Dante would present to a Persian who had but an imperfect acquaintance with the colloquial Italian of the nineteenth century!

For my own part, I have no confidence that in such translations as have been made we obtain a thorough understanding of the poet's meaning. But we should not therefore reject them. Mr. Herman Bicknell has made a very praiseworthy attempt to render the poetry of Hafiz into English verse.* This is not the place to express my opinion of his success. I have read the greater part of his work, and I am not sure if the difficulty inseparable from the undertaking is not injuriously, and needlessly, increased by fitting the translation into rhymes. Mr. Bicknell had undoubtedly a rare acquaintance with the manners and customs, the thoughts and fancies, of the East; and it may be justly said that any comparison of the difficulty of translating Hafiz truly into English with that of rendering Chaucer and Dante into Persian is not strictly fair, because the East is not as the West. The changes which have taken place in Persian and in Persia since the time of Sa'di and of Hafiz would seem as nothing when placed beside those which divide England and Italy of the fourteenth century from those same countries in the nineteenth century.

There can be no question of the high repute in which Hafiz has been, and is still, held by his countrymen. He died at Shiraz in 1388. Mr. Bicknell, in the introduction to his work, alludes to a custom of which I have often heard in Persia, and which, I believe, is still practiced in Shiraz. He says: "The admiration for the Odes had increased to so great an extent before the death of Hafiz in the year of the Hijrah 791 (A.D. 1388), that it became customary to consult them to discover future events; and this practice is still continued in the East in various ways. One method, after breathing over the volume, is to utter an invocation such as the following:

"'O Hafiz of Shiraz, impart
Foreknowledge to my anxious heart!'

The book is then opened at hazard, and the first couplet which

---

* "Hafiz of Shiraz: Selections from his Poems." Translated from the Persian by Herman Bicknell. London: Trübner & Co.

meets the eye is taken as an answer to the question of him who consults the oracle.

"When Nádir Sháh was engaged in hostile operations against the Afghans, it is related that he performed a 'ziyárat,' or pious visit, to the tomb of the poet, and had recourse to the Díván to know whether it would be expedient to continue the war. The couplet lighted on was the following:

" 'O Hafiz, by thy dulcet song, Irák and Fárs are raptured ;
Now haste, that Baghdad and Tabríz may in their turn be captured!'

Such an omen was, of course, hailed as auspicious. Baghdad and Tabríz were accordingly attacked, and rescued from the Turks. On account of the supposed heterodoxy of certain passages in the Díván, difficulties were raised as to the interment of Hafiz with the rites of religion. The poetic oracle, however, being consulted, all doubts were set at rest by the following couplet:

" 'Wish not to turn thy foot away from Hafiz on his bier:
He shall ascend to Paradise, though steeped in sin while here.' "

The following is Mr. Bicknell's translation of one of the Odes of Hafiz:

"Thou whose features, clearly beaming, make the moon of Beauty bright,
Thou whose chin contains a well-pit which to Loveliness gives light.

"When, O Lord! shall kindly Fortune, sating my ambition, pair
This, my heart of tranquil nature, and thy wild and ruffled hair?

"Pining for thy sight, my spirit, trembling on my lip, doth wait,
Forth to speed it, back to lead it, speak the sentence of its fate.

"Pass me, with thy skirt uplifted, from the dusty, bloody ground:
Many who have been thy victims, dead upon this path are found.

"How this heart is anguish-wasted, let my heart's possessor know :
Friends, your souls and mine contemplate, equal by their common woe.

"Aught of good accrues to no one witched by thy narcissus eye:
Ne'er let braggarts vaunt their virtue, if thy drunken orbs are nigh.

"Soon my Fortune, sunk in slumber, shall her limbs with vigor brace;
Dashed upon her eyes is water sprinkled by thy shining face.

"Gather from thy cheek a posy; speed it by the flying East;
Sent be perfume to refresh me, from thy garden's dust at least.

"Hafiz offers a petition: listen, and 'Amen' reply;
On thy sugar-dropping rubies let me for life's food rely.

"Many a year live on and prosper, Sakis of the court of Jam,
E'en though I, to fill my wine-cup, never to your circle come.

"East wind, when to Yazd thou wingest, say thou to its sons from me,
May the head of every ingrate, ball-like 'neath your mall-bat be!

"What though from your daïs distant, near it by my wish I seem;
Homage to your king I render, and I make your praise my theme.

"Shah of shahs, of lofty planet,
Grant for God what I implore;
Let me, as the sky above thee,
Kiss the dust which strews thy floor."

From among the "Fragments" which Mr. Bicknell's volume contains I have taken this:

"Oh Shah, an envoy came from Heaven, of húri aspect fair,
Rizvan-like in his majesty, of Salsabíl-like hair,

"Of language sound in sense, and sweet, symmetrical, refined,
Both fair and slight, of virgin mien, and unto jest inclined.

"I said: 'To this retreat of mine what cause has made thee wing?'
He answered: 'For the Shah I come, that angel-minded king.'

"Of me, O Shah, for poor am I, that youth has weary grown:
To gratify his heart's desire, accept him for thine own."

The key to this poem is contained in a note which informs us that the "envoy" is the genius of Hafiz, who, in the last couplet, is soliciting the imperial patronage. I will make one more extract from the same work, that of the following lines, which are placed with the " Tetrastichs " of Hafiz:

"Pure wine beside a brook   'Tis good to have
 Release from sorrow's nook   'Tis good to have
 Life lasts ten days, as doth the rose's time;
 A smiling, beaming look   'Tis good to have."

Without in the least disparaging Mr. Bicknell's work, which I am not competent to criticise fully, I must say he has not led me to abandon the opinion that there is a needless loss of Persian aroma in forcing the interpretation into rhymes.

The full name of Hafiz was "Mohammed Shams-ud-deen Hafiz." Probably the first of these three names was all that he possessed in his childhood. Shams-ud-deen, which means "Sun of the Faith," and Hafiz, which implies "One who knows the Koran," are appellations of honor, which were probably conferred upon him in the zenith of his fame.

A greater than Hafiz, in the opinion of many of the most learned Persians, is that older poet, the Sheik Sa'di, also of Shiraz. In view of Shiraz, yet farther in the mountains, we found the reputed tomb of Sa'di. Sa'di is supposed to have been born in 1194 A.D.

In the preface to his translation of Sa'di's "Gulistan" (Rose Garden), Mr. Eastwick says: "It appears that his [Sa'di's] father's name was Abdu'llāh, and that he was descended from Ali, the son-in-law of Mohammed; but that, nevertheless, his father held no higher office than some petty situation under the Dīwān. From 'Bustan,' ii., 2, it appears that he lost his father when but a child; while from the sixth story of the sixth chapter of the 'Gulistan' we learn that his mother survived to a later period. He was educated at the Nizāmich college at Baghdad, where he held an idrár, or fellowship ('Bustan,' vii., 14), and was instructed in science by the learned Abū-'l-farj-bin-Janzi ('Gulistan,' ii., 20), and in theology by Abdu'l Kādir Gilāni, with whom he made his first pilgrimage to Makkah. This pilgrimage he repeated no less than fourteen times.

"Sa'di was twice married. Of his first nuptials, at Aleppo, we have a most amusing account in the thirty-first story of the second chapter of the 'Gulistan.'"

The following is Mr. Eastwick's translation of this marriage story:

"Having become weary of the society of my friends at Damascus, I set out for the wilderness at Jerusalem, and associated with the brutes, until I was made prisoner by the Franks, who set me to work along with Jews at digging in the fosse of Tripolis, till one of the principal men of Aleppo, between whom and myself a former intimacy had subsisted, passed that way, and recognized me, and said, 'What state is this? and how are you living?' I replied,

[STANZA.]

"'From men to mountain and to wild I fled,
  Myself to heavenly converse to betake;
Conjecture now my state, that in a shed
  Of savages I must my dwelling make.'

[COUPLET.]

"'Better to live in chains with those we love,
 Than with the strange, 'mid flow'rets gay, to move.'

"He took compassion on my state, and with ten dinārs redeemed me from the bondage of the Franks. He had a daughter, whom he united to me in the marriage-knot, with a fortune of a hundred dinārs. As time went on, the girl turned out of a bad temper, quarrelsome and unruly. She began to give loose to her tongue, and to disturb my happiness, as they have said.

[DISTICHS.]

" 'In a good man's house an evil wife
  Is his hell above, in this present life.
  From a vixen wife protect us well:
  Save us, O God! from the pains of hell.'

"At length she gave vent to reproaches, and said, 'Art thou not he whom my father purchased from the Franks' prison for ten dinārs?' I replied, 'Yes; he redeemed me with ten dinārs, and sold me into thy hands for a hundred.'

[DISTICHS.]

"I've heard that once a man of high degree
  From a wolf's teeth and claws a lamb set free;
  That night its throat he severed with a knife;
  When thus complained the lamb's departing life:
  'Thou from the wolf didst save me then, but now
  Too plainly I perceive the wolf art thou.'"

It is well, in reading the translations of Sa'di, to remember the Eastern saying, that "each word of Sa'di has seventy-two meanings."

In the "Gulistan" (Mr. Gladwin's translation), Sa'di speaks of a man "stringing himself upon the cord of our acquaintance;" and, adopting his metaphor, I will endeavor to string this illustrious Persian more thoroughly upon the cord of our acquaintance by a few additional quotations from the "Gulistan."

He was evidently anxious, above all things, to obtain the favor of the king for himself and his work, though there is no reason to doubt that the following loyal effusion contains the expression of his genuine convictions: "A king," he writes, "is the shadow of God, and a shadow should be the image of its substance; the disposition of the subject is not capable of good unless it be restrained by the sword of the sovereign; any peaceable demeanor which is observed in the world originates in the justice of princes; but that sovereign's judgment can never be just whose rule is founded in wickedness." This last sentence being, as Sa'di evidently supposed, of a most venturesome character, he adds that it "met Abaca-an's fullest concurrence;" and then with regard to the work in hand, the "Gulistan" itself, he writes, "It will be really complete when it shall have met a favorable reception at court, and obtained the indulgent perusal of that prince, the asylum of the world, shadow of omnipotence, ray of gracious providence, treasury of the age, refuge of the faith, fortified from above, victorious over his foes, arm of triumphant fortune, luminary of resplendent piety, most illustrious of mankind, glory of orthodoxy, Sa'ad, the son of the mighty Atabak, all-powerful emperor, ruler over the necks of the people, lord-paramount of Arabia and Persia, monarch of the sea and land, successor of the throne of Solomon, Mozuffar-u'd-deen," etc.

In a less servile mood, Sa'di avows, "I swear it were equal to the torments of hell to enter into paradise through the intervention of a neighbor;" and in a higher tone he says, "Be undefiled, O brother, in thine integrity; washer-men beat none but dirty clothes against a stone."

The ways of kings and of their followers have not, it seems, changed in Persia during seven hundred years. Sa'di lays it down as proverbial that "from the plunder of five eggs, made with the sanction of the king, his troops will stick a thousand fowls on their spits." But subjects must not complain of kings; for "to maintain an opinion contrary to the judgment of the king were to steep our hands in our own blood; verily, were the king to say, 'This day is night,' it would behoove us to reply, 'Lo, there are the moon and the seven stars!'"

"Draw the foot of contentment within the mantle of safety" is an expression of rare wisdom, one which may well have made any one of Sa'di's readers "drop his head on the bosom of reflection."

"Do not sprinkle his sore with the salt of harsh words,"

and "Withdraw the hand of reproach from the skirt of my fatality" (or destiny), are among the sayings of this work.

Sudden death, in the flowing Persian of Sa'di, is rendered, "All at once the foot of his existence stumbled at the grave of being, and the sigh of separation burst from the dwelling of his family."

Sa'di could say pretty things of a lady as of a king. An Irish peasant once said to an English peer, "May every hair of your head be a mold-candle to light yer to glory!" But Sa'di was even more extravagant: "Wert thou," he wrote, "to seat thyself upon the pupil of mine eye, I would court thee to remain, for thou art lovely."

The following sentences must conclude my extracts from this very remarkable work:

"While the body of a fat man is getting lean, a lean man must fall victim of hardship."

"If in place of a loaf of bread, the orb of the sun had been in his [a stingy merchant's] wallet, nobody would have seen daylight in this world until the day of judgment."

"Whenever thy hand can reach it, pluck out thy foe's heart; for such an opportunity washes anger from thy brain."

"Whoever sees gold lowers his head, even though, like the scales of Justice, he has iron-bound shoulders."

"Were they to take the ass of Jesus to Mecca, on its return from that pilgrimage it would still be an ass."

"The money of the miser comes out of the earth when he himself enters into it."

The works of these great writers will not pass away; they are safely enshrined in letters which are frequently reproduced. We should be glad if we had the same confidence that the remains of the tombs, and halls, and palaces of Cyrus, of Darius, and of Xerxes, which adorn the road from Ispahan to Shiraz, were equally assured against neglect and injury.

Shiraz is famous for its "gardens," which, however, are not gardens in the English acceptation of the word, but rather shrubberies; groves of orange and cypress trees, delicious in their checkered sunlight and shade, in the views from between the trees; containing lovely vistas of grove ending only at the far-off mountains; inclosures, melancholy with ruined marble tanks and imarets (as the pavilions are called), falling slowly to decay.

Inside a Persian city there is nothing picturesque, except in association with the many-colored dresses of the people. In the larger meidan, or open space, of Shiraz, I saw one man kill an ox and another a sheep, and begin to dress them in the place where they fell, which seemed a "note" of great barbarism, as if it were no matter at all where the slaughtering of butchers' meat was carried on. Slaves are very numerous in Shiraz; and there are persons who act as brokers for the sale of this "property," not by public auction, but by transfer from one family to another. In this way the children of the slaves of one household are sold into another. A young boy was pointed out to us who had been lately purchased for thirty-five tomans. The English doctors in Persia, and also the French doctor who attends the Shah, are in great request among the higher class of natives, especially in cases where surgical skill is required. But the European doctors never undertake a very serious case without a bond, sealed by the patient and his nearest relatives. By this document it is arranged that half the sum to be paid for the operation is to be delivered beforehand, and the other half if the sick man recovers. It is always further agreed that under no circumstances is the doctor to be held liable for the results of his operation, which, as is natural in the very grave cases to which alone their attention is summoned, are not rarely followed by death. The operation most commonly undertaken in this way is lithotomy; and I have heard it said of the French surgeon who resides in Teheran that he has been successful in a greater number of cases than even Sir Henry Thompson himself.

"Morning calls" form a recognized part of Persian etiquette; and among those who honored us with this sort of attention during our stay in Shiraz was the priest of the small Armenian community, a man most pitifully poor, and apparently without hope of improving his miserable condition. If he could send a sufficient present to his bishop, then he might get nominated as priest to some position in India or Java, where he would obtain a good income. But he sighed hopelessly at the impossibility of acquiring the amount of silver which was requisite to move his spiritual father. The ritual of the Armenian Church is very severe; and the priests are enjoined, before administering the sacrament of bread and wine, to spend half the previous day in the "hamām," or bath, and then to fast all night without sleep. Such Christians, in a place like Shiraz, lead a fearful life, under every disadvantage that bigotry, injustice, and the absence of any possible publication of their wrongs, or official representative of a foreign power to whom they may appeal, can bring upon them. If a case of flagrant oppression and cruelty occurred as far north as Tabriz or Teheran, it is probable that, if his attention were called to it, the Russian minister or consul would interfere; and there is no doubt that the Russian Legation at Teheran can command the action of the Shah's Government.

I have not observed an equal readiness to move on the part of the English minister even in those affairs in which his influence would be greatest. When Mr. Bruce had telegraphed a message informing Mr. Thomson of the dangerous invitation to murder which the Zil-i-Sultan had rashly and thoughtlessly uttered in Ispahan, Mr. Thomson neglected the common obligation of courtesy, and of proper consideration for the dangerous circumstances of the missionary. He sent no acknowledgment whatever of the receipt of this urgent message. Mr. Bruce thought it his duty, in a matter of such great consequence, to support this message with a full statement of his case, and to send by special messenger to the British minister in Teheran an elaborate report of the past and present circumstances of his school. I was favored with an opportunity of reading this paper, a copy of which was, I believe, addressed at the same time to the Church Missionary Society in London, and I was much impressed with the tone of fairness, moderation, and respect in which it was composed. There could be no doubt that the school had done, and was doing, a great and good work, affording a valuable education to the impoverished Christians of the districts of Ispahan, and thus enabling them to improve their condition by emigration to British India. It was plain to any one that the missionary was isolated, and in great need of the friendly and personal support of the minister. When, in these circumstances, he had sent at his own cost a messenger upon an eight days' journey across the snows of Kuhrud to Teheran, I should not have thought it possible that Mr. Thomson, or any one in his position, on receiving this statement, would have sent the messenger back upon his long journey without a word of acknowledgment.

On hearing of the return of his servant, the missionary hurried from his room to meet the messenger. There was a congregation of people to witness the man's return after a twenty days' absence, and all heard Mr. Bruce's anxious and impulsive question, "You have a letter from Thomson Sahib?" "Nothing, sahib," was the reply; "I was told there was no answer." I shall never forget the blank disappointment of the missionary. He knew how grievously this reply and his chagrin, obvious to all the by-standers, would augment the dangers and difficulties of his position. We were not at all surprised to hear the next morning that in the bazaars of Ispahan and Djulfa the common talk was that "Thomson Sahib" cared nothing for what the Ispahanees might do to Mr. Bruce; and it was said that when "Thomson Sahib" got the missionary's letter he tore it in pieces and threw the bits at the messenger. This and much more of the same purport Mr. Bruce heard from his neighbors in Djulfa. I feel sure Mr. Thomson was not inactive in making representations to the Persian Government, but he was wrong in leaving Mr. Bruce without a word of support in a position of very unusual difficulty.

For the measures which followed, and for the re-opening of the school, I hardly think Mr. Thomson can claim credit. Immediately upon hearing of the prince's decree, I wrote from my bed, in which I was suffering from fever, to several friends possessing much influence at home, begging them to move in the matter; and I think it more than probable that Mr. Thomson was impelled, by consequent instructions from England in any measures he took, to obtain a reversal of the Zil-i-Sultan's arbitrary decree.

If any one were to ask me, What is there to be seen in Shiraz? I should answer, Nothing of interest besides that which I have mentioned. No great building, no historic ruin, claims attention. One of the best houses in the place is the office of the Indo-Persian Telegraph. It is entered from the larger meidan. Inside, in the spacious court-yard or garden, there were usually some piles of telegraph stores, iron poles, and earthenware insulators. The inspectors report that about Shiraz a large number of these earthenware appliances are destroyed by bullets. Proficiency in placing a bullet in the head of an enemy or in that of an antelope is an object of desire; and what mark is so good, or, when hit, so telling, as the white insulators suspended on telegraph-poles, over all the lonely plains and the desolate hills from north to south of Persia? Besides, there is in these a prize, an iron hook, which falls to the ground like a bird when the mark is well hit, and is valued more highly than a dead snipe or a partridge.

In the report for 1875–'76 by Major Champain, the Government Director of the entire service of the Indo-Persian Telegraph, the following occurs under the head of "Interruptions:" "The total interruptions were fewer than in any previous year, and amounted in the aggregate to only fifty-nine hours fifteen minutes. One break in May, 1875, which lasted thirty-one and a half hours, was caused in a rather curious way. The line crossed a village not very far from Bushire, and this village having been attacked and burned to the ground by robbers, the wires were severed by heat, and could not be immediately restored. The remaining twenty-seven hours of interruption were caused by excessive cold on the high ground in the interior of the country.

"Willful damage has, I am happy to say, somewhat decreased within the past year, although the South of Persia is probably in a more lawless condition than ever, and robberies and outrages of the worst kind continue. In fact, the road from Bushire to Ispahan, and some parts between Ispahan and the capital, are so infested with robber tribes, that traveling is out of the question except for strong and well-armed parties. The marauders, however, display no special hostility to the telegraph, and rarely touch it except between Bushire and Kazeroon. In that district every man and boy carries a gun, and the temptation to try the effect of their bullets on the iron poles seems to be irresistible."

In Major Champain's report for 1874–'75, he quotes a statement on this subject made to himself by the local director, Major Smith, who reported: "The line between Shiraz and Bushire has suffered greatly from willful damage of the most purely wanton nature. In that part of Persia every man is armed, and it would appear that, in default of more tempting objects, the people amuse themselves by trying their guns on the cast-iron sockets of the telegraph-poles. Many insulators have also been destroyed in the same part of the country for the sake of their iron hooks. An effectual remedy for these unfortunate propensities of the natives is provided by the twelfth article of the Telegraph Convention of the 2d of December, 1872, to which the Persian Government has hitherto refused to give any effect, on the frivolous pretext, as I understand, that the article refers only to the wire, and not to the mere adjuncts of posts and insulators. There is no doubt that if the provisions of the article were duly enforced, the willful damage would entirely cease. As it is, the new iron poles are shot down faster than we can put them up. The bills for the repair of willful damage already amount to upward of seven thousand tomans, of which not a penny has yet been paid."

At the telegraph-office in Shiraz, the garden of fifty yards square has three broad pavements leading from the meidan to the house—one in the centre, the others at the side-walls. Between these there are plane-trees, and at the end there is a low terrace of brick, upon which is the ground-floor of the house. In this, the large room to the left is the Persian office, while in that to the right the Indian and European business is conducted. From the roof of this house, which is of unusual height, trouble has been made. It commands a view of the interior quadrangle of several Persian houses, and many complaints were consequently made when it was first occupied by giaours. It is understood that the Persian neighbors have now grown used to the possibility of this observation, and that some are not even displeased when it occurs. When we ascended in order to obtain one of the most comprehensive views over Shiraz, I observed that our appearance excited considerable interest, and certainly no ·displeasure. And if one can withdraw one's eyes from the eternal beauty of the mountains and streams round about Shiraz, from the general aspect of the flat mud-roofs, above which rise the white stems of plane-trees, the dark-green spires of the cypresses, with here and there a brown minaret, or a dome covered with a glazing of greenish blue; if in sight of all this one does feel interested in the details of Persian housekeeping, these are well exposed to view. The ladies may be seen lolling upon the floor of their apartments, the anderoon, the front of the rooms all open to the welcome warmth of the wintry sun. There is nothing on their horizon but the narrow walls of home, and it is not surprising if the apparition of persons in strange garb upon a neighboring height is to them the most exciting event of the day. Their slaves cross and recross the quadrangle from room to room in the performance of household duties. The black-eyed children roll and play in the same open space. The father, who is patriarch, master, ruler of all, rarely appears. He is hunting, or in the bazaar, or smoking, or sleeping, or at the palace or the mosque. One can not be surprised that as the despotic ruler of his domestic realm, in which there can be no interference from without, he hates the vantage-ground of this roof from which people of a monogamous race presume now and then to look in upon his polygamous household.

The district of Shiraz, which is, I believe, identical with the ancient province of Fars, has, and probably deserves, a bad name for disorder. Crimes of robbery and violence are much more frequent in this than in the northern part of Persia. To some extent the crime of Fars may be attributed to the mountainous nature of the country, which affords shelter from observation, and probable security in case of pursuit, for bands of robbers; but it is also owing to the fact that there is a large nomad population, wandering tribes of Eeliats and others, which, according to the season, pass from north to south, or from south to north, in this province, and live a gypsy life, with the assistance of flocks and herds, and, if they are not belied, of much robbery. From Ispahan to Shiraz, there are few plains lower than five thousand feet above the sea-level. At four days' march south of Shiraz, on the road to Bushire, the path rises to above seven thousand feet. Soon afterward it falls to near the sea-level, and the climate changes in a march of thirty miles from the rigor of winter to the genial warmth of verdant spring. To these lower lands, the thousands of Eeliats and the other nomads of Persia wend their way in autumn, blocking the mountain passes with their cattle; and back again they come to the highlands when the summer sun has clothed the hills with green, and burned up the vegetation of the lowlands upon which they have passed the winter. The unsettled habits of these people are supposed to conduce to a lawless life. Certain it is that, by some people or other, the province is kept in perpetual terror; anywhere in Fars the talk of the road is of robbers and of robbery. The traveler who passes safely through the realm of the Governor of Shiraz is universally held to be fit subject for congratulation. Travelers gather together for mutual protection; and Europeans complain, when they are victims, that the English Government does not exact retribution and indemnity with sufficient vigor and determination. Perhaps, if this charge is well founded, it may find some excuse in the unwillingness of the agents of any civilized power to rouse the Persian Government to such indiscriminate and wholesale vengeance as it is ever ready, upon the motion of the minister of a European power, to wreak upon its miserable subjects. Shortly before we traveled through this ill-reputed province, the eldest son of Lord Napier, of Magdala, passed through Shiraz, on his way from India to Teheran, charged with a special mission of observation in the Persian capital. He was accompanied for some distance by Dr. Waters, who was attached to the Residency at Bushire, and from whose narrative of the incidents of their journey I gather the particulars of the attack upon their caravan. Fortunately for themselves, these gentlemen were not with their baggage when it was stopped and rifled by a band of about fifty robbers, who killed one of the mounted guards with a bullet, and with an iron-headed mace—the common walking-stick of the Persian peasantry in Fars — smashed the jaw of an Armenian who, for the better security of money upon his person, had joined the caravan of the Englishman.

Major Napier was, of course, in no way responsible for the manner in which the Persian Government pursued and punished the men who were guilty, or were assumed to be guilty, of this crime. I have been told that the prisoners were taken somewhat at hazard, the main evidence being that they were near the spot; but there is no doubt that three-and-twenty men had their throats cut by the public executioners in Shiraz on account of this robbery and murder; nor that this is a humane punishment compared with that by which the Firman Firma's predecessor, the Hissam-us-Sultan, endeavored to repress crimes of this sort in the province of Fars. He tried throat-cutting, and left the bleeding bodies exposed to the view of all comers in the meidan of Shiraz. He tried crucifixion, nailing the wretches by the hands and feet to the walls of the town, and leaving them, under a guard of soldiers, to die of exhaustion and starvation. Finally, he tried burial alive in pits, or cylinders of brick-work, of depth such as to allow the criminal's head to appear above the top. Pinioned and naked, the robbers were placed in these short open columns of brick-work, and a white plaster, not unlike plaster of Paris, was then poured, neck-deep, over their bodies, around which it set into the hardness of stone. I questioned several persons living far apart as to the particulars of this horrible punishment; and their substantial agreement left no doubt on my mind that it had been inflicted, or that the miserable men who were subject to this most cruel death were in their dying hours barbarously ill-treated, on their exposed and defenseless heads, by the rabble and the soldiery of Shiraz. On finding the Firman Firma too weak for the place, the Shah's Government have lately endeavored to persuade the Hissam-us-Sultan to return to Shiraz. But he has successfully pleaded age and increasing infirmity, and another has been appointed.

Such ruthless punishment, always uncertain in its vengeance, has never been successful in exterminating crime. The sins of the executive of Shiraz are visited upon the people, and upon all who travel among them. The Government of Shiraz, in degree worse probably than that of any other province of Persia, is a system of oppression, made, with all the power and authority and force of the State, for private advantage. The taxes are farmed, and, as a rule, the amount demanded is limited only by ability of payment; soldiers are taught robbery by being officially engaged in making demands for money, which they know to be unjust, from the all-enduring peasants; the customs are farmed, and collected by the armed servants of the contractor, who is subject to no surveillance, and who renders no accounts. Those are exempt from direct taxation who, possessing the means to render them independent of exaction, are the most able to pay. Direct taxation in Persia is levied solely upon those engaged in production, and the merchant or tradesman pays only in respect of his store in the bazaar. In the summer of 1875, the dismayed population of Shiraz heard that their sovereign, the Shah, intended to make a royal progress to the south of his dominions. An order was published that no corn was to leave the province, because all might be required for the use of the Shah and his retinue. The great people of Shiraz, who, of course, could evade this or any other edict, took advantage of the circumstances, and made money. The poor suffered most cruelly. Some say the Shah was bought off; that in consideration of receiving so many thousand tomans, his majesty agreed not to quit Teheran; and this, which sounds so scandalous, is never spoken of by Persians as a very extraordinary or even uncommon way of dealing with the intentions of the sovereign, his visits being always regarded as involving extortion and loss, owing to the rapacity of his followers, and as an evil which, like capital punishment in Persia, may by gift of gold be averted.

CHAPTER XXIV.

The Road to Bushire.—Yahia Khan's Portrait.—To Cinerada.—Last View of Shiraz.—Difficult Traveling.—Khan-i-Zonoon.—A Caravan in Trouble.—A Cold Caravanserai.—Murder of Sergeant Collins.—Death of Sergeant M'Leod.—Advantage of an Escort.—Dashtiarjan.—"Eaten a Bullet."—Plain of Dashtiarjan.—Ghooloo-Kojeh Pass.—A Lion in the Path.—Mr. Blanford's "Interview."—Up a Tree.—A Wounded Horse.—Kaleh-Mushír.—Mount Perizan.—Kotul Perizan.—A Solitary Rock.—View of Mian-kotul.

OPINION was unanimous that it was impossible to march with a takht-i-rawan from Shiraz to Bushire. For three days it was agreed that a conveyance of that length might proceed, but farther than three days' march the paths in the mountains were too narrow and dangerous to admit of this mode of traveling. We therefore left the takht-i-rawan in Shiraz, and my wife had to face the prospect of riding for twelve days through a country certainly not less dangerous than any other, and reported by those who have traversed the Himalayas and the Rocky Mountains to be the most difficult road in the world. When we were packing up, another incident occurred, displaying the habitual cruelty of the Persian muleteers to their animals. One of the string of mules which had been brought to Mr. Odling's door for the conveyance of our baggage had terrible sores upon its legs and back, caused by badly fitting harness; and it was proposed to load this suffering animal for the long journey to Bushire. We refused to have it in our caravan, and the muleteer, to whom the notion of the animal's pain seemed as strange as it would be to others to learn that a flint suffered from the presence of quartz in its side, departed to exchange the injured mule for one in a sounder condition.

On the first day we had only two farsakhs to ride to the caravanserai at Cinerada. Early in the morning, before we set out, the Firman Firma sent by his agreeable nazir a large photographic portrait of himself, "pour souvenir de Shiraz." The nazir also brought with him two sowars, who had been specially selected as our escort to Bushire. Their horses were very much better than ours to look at. Somebody suggested to Mr. Odling, who rode out of Shiraz with us, that we looked rather like prisoners of war compelled to ride our sorry nags into captivity. But in a few days, when we came to the rolling stones of the mountains, our "yaboos" covered their shabby appearance with glory.

Shiraz is not a large place; it does not occupy more than half the ground upon which Ispahan stands, and we were soon upon the plain, on a westerly course to Cinerada. The snow had melted away in many places, but there was sufficient to give a very wintry appearance to the scene, and the weather was cold enough to make my Persian coat of sheep's wool and leather a very agreeable companion. Shiraz stands at the junction of three wide valleys. One slopes from the north, the way from Ispahan; another to the west, in the centre of which lies the path toward Bushire; the largest valley falls away toward the north-east.

We took leave of Mr. Odling about four miles from Shiraz at the gate of one of the gardens in the neighborhood of the city, and staid a few minutes for a last look at Shiraz. Persian towns seen from that distance leave no vivid impression, and this is as true of Ispahan and Tcheran as of Shiraz. If they were grandly built, if they contained monuments of real value and of permanent interest, these would probably look unimportant in the wide plains and beneath the mountains of Persia. But their buildings are so insignificant, so impermanent, such rubbishing masses of mud-brick, with no beauty of form or ornament, that even large cities have no appearance of dignity, and are indeed overlooked in the contemplation of the grander features of the landscape.

My wife was mounted on a stout gray pony, which had very decided ideas of its own as to the proper mode of going to Bushire. By no persuasion could it be induced for more than a moment to alter its pace from a steady, plodding walk, and my chestnut was very much of the same opinion. The snow became more wide-spread, and the wintry afternoon darkened as our path wound through the valley. We could see far before us up the snowy steep, and were beginning to think it possible we had misunderstood the distance to Cinerada, when suddenly, behind a spur of rock, we came upon the caravanserai.

We had no more troublesome march in the whole journey than that from Cinerada to Khan-i-Zonoon. Several caravans had gone before us since the last great fall of snow, and the mules, treading always in the same track, had worn the snow in high ridges, higher than those of a deeply plowed field. When the sun shone out, the bottoms of these furrows became filled with water, which froze in the night, and sometimes the ice between the ridges would bear the weight of our horses, and sometimes not. When it bore, the animals often slipped; when it was thin, their feet crashed through with a jerk distressing to the horse and to the rider. There was but one track, and the whole caravan passed up the mountain in Indian file. Soon after noon, we had ascended about two thousand feet from Cinerada to a height of nearly seven thousand feet above the sea-level. But we found it impossible to keep the caravan together. Kazem had fallen at least half a dozen times in the deep snow, and his black mule, his saddle-bags, and himself bore many traces of these tumbles. The baggage mules had similar disasters, and after four hours' toilsome ride we had lost sight of servants and baggage—a circumstance which the sight of one or two ugly-looking parties of armed men who had met us in the narrow track rendered more disquieting. There was no place in which we could dismount, and nothing to eat if we had done so, for Kazem, our store-keeper, was far behind—we knew not where; and we were in a wilderness of drifted snow, crossing ridge after ridge, always hoping that each would be the last, and always disappointed.

Our two soldiers, Abd-ullah and Hassan, had kept up with us. I sent the latter back to bring up and protect the baggage, and, with Abd-ullah and my wife's gholam, we resolved to push on and, hungry as we were, to get to the caravanserai as quickly as we could. On the way we met a large caravan bringing merchandise from Bushire, some of the loads upon the mules extending six feet from side to side. This involved our plunging out of the track into the deep snow, and occasional sad knocks of the knees and shins against the passing packages. Far behind we could see Hassan, with his carbine erect upon his knee, standing on the summit of the mountain waiting for the stragglers, whom we assumed, from his contented attitude, were in sight from the point on which he stood. Presently the caravanserai of Khan-i-Zonoon was seen like a speck upon the far-extending desert. A rill began to trickle down the mountain, which widened to a stream, and, lower, became a river, of which the surface, frozen from side to side, remained unaffected by the midday sun. Upon the narrow plain, at the end of which lay the caravanserai, there was a scrubby forest, through which we passed upon a slippery and dangerous path. Some donkeys loaded with bags of wheat were being driven by two miserable-looking Persians through the wood; and of the number more than half had fallen, and lay helpless on our path beneath their heavy loads. In a hollow, the sides of which were a mass of ice, there was one of the loads, with no animal beneath it; the donkey, in its struggles after falling, had probably succeeded in extricating itself from sacks and saddle-bags. Abd-ullah and our muleteer were in advance of us, and we saw them seize the saddle-bags as a prize, and turn out from them a quantity of bread, which they began to stuff into their pockets. We had been nearly eight hours on the road, with nothing to eat, and they seemed to regard this as a godsend, taking no thought that this bread was probably the only food of the donkey-drivers during the same journey, in a much colder time of day. We rode up to them and forced them to put back the bread, which, although the caravanserai was now close at hand, they did most unwillingly. It seemed to us that this readiness to rob on the part of two men, really superior to the lowest class of Persians, was very indicative of the predatory instincts of this uncivilized and ill-governed people. We made a fire in one of the smoke-dried brick arches of the caravanserai; and, as there was nothing with which to construct a seat, had to stand about or sit upon the earthen floor for two hours until the baggage mules arrived. Then a covering was nailed over the door-hole, matting and carpets laid down, our iron bedsteads set up, one on either side of the chimney-hole, in which some logs were burning cheerfully, a cloth spread upon our camp-table, and we sat upon our folding-stools until Kazem appeared with a hot stew of rice and meat, and a bottle of very good Shiraz wine. Our fire had been burning for hours when we took to our beds at ten o'clock, and placed a cup of milk in the recess close by the chimney. The fire continued burning till nearly midnight; and at half-past five in the morning the frost was so intense that, although the ashes in the fire-place were still red, the milk was frozen in a solid block, and some soapy water which I had left in a large brass hand-basin on going to bed was in the same condition.

Yet we were in 29° of latitude, and very little more than six thousand feet above the sea-level.

Our ride to Dashtiarjan was hardly less difficult, on account of the ridgy snow, than that of the previous day. We found it impossible to do more than two miles an hour. The road was in such a bad state, we could not walk, and in the early hours of the ride we were blue with cold. The path was unlevel, and would have seemed varied and picturesque if it had not been for the unchanging glaring white of the deep snow. In a basin between two hills, a pole standing erect by the side of the path marked the place of the most recent murder of an Englishman by Persian robbers. We had already heard the particulars of this fatal attack. The victim, Sergeant Collins, of the Royal Engineers, engaged in the Telegraph Service, was riding with his wife and servants from Shiraz to the next station, which is at Dashtiarjan. He was challenged, surrounded, and fired at from the woods; he returned the fire, and killed one man. But he was soon afterward shot down, a bullet entering the back of his head; his body was mutilated, and his wife carried off to the mountains, where she remained for some days in captivity. I believe the murderers were never found, and that no one suffered punishment for the crime. Another sergeant died not long ago in a similar way; but the circumstances of his death were homicidal rather than murderous. The attack upon his comrade preyed upon his mind, already disordered by illness and drink, until he fancied that every man he met with on the road was a robber; and in this delirious humor shot an unoffending Armenian. Then he entirely lost self-command, and, flourishing his revolver, rode about vowing he would shoot the first Persian robber he met with. It was at a caravanserai in which we had passed a night that this mad assassin made his next attempt, regardless of the fact that there were several men with guns in the caravanserai, which, as almost every body in Persia carries fire-arms, is usually the case. The wretched sergeant was flourishing about, threatening every body he saw with his pistol. It was then that some of the by-standers, having placed a wall between him and themselves, shot him down, really in self-defense; and thus the second Englishman died the death of a mad dog.

In traveling in Persia, it is undoubtedly safer not to be too "ready with the pistol." For our own parts, we felt no very confident assurance that we should get safely through the country. All the English we met with in Persia told us it was highly probable we should be robbed, and that it was quite certain our escort would not be very energetic in defense. In these circumstances, we had deliberately framed our plans of action, or, rather, of inaction. We had a letter of credit from merchants trading in Persia, upon which we could obtain money in Ispahan, Shiraz, and Bushire; so that the silver we carried was only sufficient for the expenses of the road between any two of these places. We knew that the resistance of robbery by incautious firing involves the maximum of danger, and were quite prepared to say "Inshallah" to any band against which successful resistance would be impossible, and submit to be robbed. We believed that nothing less than a band of forty or fifty determined robbers would venture to stop a caravan belonging to Europeans; and, without the least desiring or expecting that one, two, or half a score of soldiers could or would drive off such a force, we always preferred to have an escort, because they never failed to communicate to the people we met with, and by this means to all the neighborhood, that we were specially under the protection of the governor of the province; and because attack is not improbably prevented by the fear of subsequent recognition by the soldiers of an escort.

The view from the hills over the plain of Dashtiarjan was very remarkable. A plain looks small in Persia when, like that of Dashtiarjan, it is about four miles broad and twelve miles long. Near the higher and northern end lay the buildings of the telegraph-office, and not far distant the mud hovels of the village. About the centre, a large brownish patch three miles long, in the unblemished white of the all-surrounding snow, indicated a deep morass, which is perhaps the cause of the ill reputation of this plain for the deadliest fever. Dashtiarjan is well known, too, as a hunting-ground for lions; and upon the edges of this morass there are said to be a great number of wild hogs. At the foot of the hills an armed guard of the Telegraph Service met us. They had been sent out by the clerk and inspector, Mr. Anderson, who stood on the steps of his bungalow to receive us. His house looked like an island in a polar sea, and the face of this intelligent young Scotchman, who lived alone in this wild place, beamed with the pleasantest welcome.

"I've been expecting you for two months, and longing for you for a fortnight!" were almost his first words.

Mr. Anderson gave us a large empty room; and partly from his larder, and partly from our own stores, a good dinner was provided, of the cooking of which Kazem took charge. Whether this habit is universal, or affects only traveling servants, I can not say; but we always found that no servant, even in his master's house, regarded the cooking-place, or indeed any function, as particularly and exclusively his own. When we were guests in a strange house, even for one night, our servants seemed to fall into the work as if they were quite accustomed to it. At Dashtiarjan, Kazem appeared as cook and butler, as hopeful about his dishes, his soup, and his stews as he was when we had no one else to look to upon the road.

Mr. Anderson often had to trust to his rifle for supplying his dinner, and, to judge from the noise made at night, wild beasts of all sorts seemed to be suffering hunger in the snow.

A Persian who came in, using an idiom I had not heard before, said that one of these beasts had "eaten a bullet," which Mr. Anderson explained is the common mode of saying that any person or animal has been shot. The loneliness of such a life as that of this young man is greater, and in some respects more trying, than I think the Indian Government should call upon any one to endure. For months he has no opportunity of hearing his own language spoken. In winter, the road may be closed at any time for weeks by snow. He lives surrounded by wild beasts, with the semi-savage population of Dashtiarjan for his only neighbors. Mr. Anderson seemed to be fighting bravely and resolutely, with the aid of a small library of good books, against the difficulties of his situation; but we thought that the real trials of such an existence are not sufficiently estimated by his superiors, who would do well so to arrange their stations that not less than two European officers should inhabit the same place.

Mr. Anderson and one of his tofanghees rode out with us in the morning along the plain of Dashtiarjan, when the drifts of snow were in some places ten or fifteen feet deep. The work of finding and following the shallowest depths made our path very circuitous. We skirted the morass, and in about two hours arrived at the foot of the Ghooloo-Kojeh Pass, a hill covered with scrubby trees, the trunks of which were deep in snow. From among the trees, and from the overtowering height, we heard the shouts of muleteers urging their caravans through the snow. Mr. Anderson left us when we began the ascent. He had no opportunity for the use of his rifle, though there were foot-marks of wild beasts in every direction. No one seemed to fear or to anticipate the presence of a lion, though the district we were passing through is a famous haunt, and it does now and then happen that a villager of Dashtiarjan falls the prey of a hunted or hungry lion.

It was exactly at this point that Mr. Blanford, F.R.S., the distinguished naturalist attached to the Persian Boundary Commission, met with a lioness, in March, 1867. His own account of the adventure is very spirited and interesting :*
"It was not till sunset that I entered the oak forest south of Dashtiarjan, with five miles of steep mountain road before me. Contrary to my usual habit, I carried no gun, being unarmed, with the exception of a Colt's revolver of the smallest size. I was mounted, I may say, on a bay Arab, fifteen hands high. I had crossed a tiny rivulet, said to be a favorite drinking-place of lions, and where, indeed, I had often seen their foot-prints, and had just begun the ascent of the hill by a path covered with loose bowlders, when a tawny shape moved noiselessly out of the trees some thirty yards in front. Whether my horse stopped, or I pulled him up, I do not know, but there we stood; the lioness, for it was evidently a lady, gazing at us, motionless, but for a gentle waving of the tail, and the horse and I looking straight at her. I mentally execrated my folly at not having brought a gun, for a fairer shot it was impossible to imagine. After the lapse of a few seconds, thinking it time to end the interview, I cracked my hunting-whip and gave a loud shout, to intimate to her ladyship that she had better clear out, never dreaming for a moment that lion or tiger would have the courage to attack a man on horseback.

"To my astonishment, instead of sneaking back into the forest, as I expected, she deliberately charged us down hill, and sprung at the horse's throat. Whether from miscalculation of the distance through the unevenness of the ground, or from my jerking the horse's head up with the curb, I can not say, but she missed her spring, and came down under my right stirrup. With a good-sized pistol I could have broken

---

* "Eastern Persia," vol. ii., p. 31.

her spine, as she stood bewildered for a moment; but to fire a bullet hardly bigger than a pea, with only a few grains of powder behind it, into the loose skin of a lioness, would have been folly; so I stuck in the spurs, with the intention of making tracks as fast as the nature of the ground would allow. But the poor horse was paralyzed with fear; not an inch would he budge, till the lioness, recovering from her surprise, made a swift half-circle, and attacked us from behind; not leaping on the horse's back with all fore legs, as is so often represented in pictures of Persian sporting, but rearing on her hind legs and embracing the horse's stern with her fore paws, while trying to lay hold of his flesh with her teeth. As may be supposed, I lost no time in jumping off, with no other damage than a tear in my strong cord breeches, and a slight scratch in the thighs. Directly the horse felt himself relieved of my weight, he reared and plunged violently, sending me head over heels among the stones in one direction, and the lioness in the other. Expecting the brute to be on me at once, I pulled out my miserable little pistol, and picking myself up as soon as possible, looked about me. There stood the lioness, not five yards off, sublimely indifferent to me and my proceedings, waving her tail and gazing intently at the horse, which had trotted twenty yards down the road. She made a few swift steps after him, when I fired a couple of shots over her head, hoping to drive her off. The only effect was to start the horse off again, when the lioness again charged him from behind, and, clinging to his quarters, both disappeared among the trees.

"So far I had had no time to feel much fear, but as soon as the source of danger was no longer visible my nerves began to get somewhat shaky. Perhaps I ought to be ashamed to say that I did not lose much time in ensconcing myself in the branches of a convenient oak some twenty feet from the ground. A few minutes at that secure altitude sufficed to restore my nerves somewhat, and I reflected that there were the regulation three courses open to me: to stay where I was, to go forward, or to go back. The first involved spending a March night on the top of a tree, the bottom of which was seven thousand feet above the sea; and I hate cold. The second presented the not more agreeable prospect of a five-mile walk over a villainous road through the forest, with the chance of meeting more lions without a horse to take off their attention; moreover, my holster and saddle-bags contained valuables; and even if the steed were killed, I might recover these by prompt action. I therefore made up my mind to follow the horse and his enemy, and, as the shades of night were fast gathering around me, lost no time about it. Half a mile down the road I found my unfortunate steed, bleeding fast from a wound in his quarter, and still in such a state of terror that he declined to let me approach him.

"There was nothing to be done but to drive him out of the forest into the plain, which was not many hundred yards off, and to walk on to the nearest village for assistance. This was the little walled hamlet of Kaleh-Mushír, a mile or so off, which I reached without mishap, save an alarm from a herd of pigs, which charged past me toward the lake as if a lion were after them.

"A single family tenanted Kaleh-Mushír during the winter. From them I got a little acorn-bread and dates. No bribe would induce the man to come out with me that night with torches to find the horse; but I found him the next morning at day-break, after a night made sleepless by the most vigorous fleas I have ever met. The poor brute was grazing quietly in the plain, and allowed himself to be caught without difficulty. Although his quarters and flanks were scored in every direction with claw-marks, only one wound had penetrated the flesh, and this to a depth of two inches, making as clean an incision as if cut with a razor. This I sewed up, and in a week the horse was as well as ever, though he bore the scars of his adventure for the rest of his life. It is, perhaps, worthy of remark, that the distance apart of the scratches made by the two outer claws of each stroke with the paws was between fourteen and fifteen inches."

When we met the caravans, whose noises we had heard upon the hill where Mr. Blanford had had this encounter, the difficulty of passing presented itself as serious. Our soldiers, after the manner of their kind, began to bully the poor muleteers, and to force the donkeys into the deep snow. The shouting was tremendous, and the mules and donkeys vied with each other in obstinacy, some of them resolving that, at all costs, their loads should graze my shins. Three or four times on the pass we had a battle of this sort, in which, at last, the inconvenience was arranged pretty equally, each caravan taking turn with the other in plunging through the deep snow. When we got clear of the jungle, we could look back over all the plain of Dashtiarjan; but the path ascended yet far higher to the top of Mount Perizan (the Old Woman); and when at last, after much toil, we gained that elevation, the sowars and gholams threw up their arms and screamed with delight. I had no need to ask the cause of their rejoicing. In a moment a strange transformation had taken place in the prospect. For weeks our eyes had found no repose from the glare of the snow; for weeks we had seen none but a snow-covered landscape. Here, in a moment, the scene was shifted as if by magic. From the top of the Perizan Mountain we looked upon valleys brown upon the sides and green upon the level plain. We had nearly done with frost; but we had the worst part of the road before us.

There is no portion of the way through Persia more picturesque than the half dozen miles from the Perizan to the caravanserai at Mian-kotul. This word "kotul" is only met with between Shiraz and Bushire. Between those two places there are three "kotuls"—of which the first is the Kotul Perizan. The word is one of terror to the traveler, for it appears to signify a road the most difficult and dangerous which it is possible to conceive—a path upon a mountain's side, sometimes upon the edge of a precipice, at others upon a descent so rapid as to render riding impossible. But always upon the kotuls the path is beset with stones, so numberless and awkward that horse and man pause at almost every footstep to consider where the next advance may be most safely made.

If one rides down a kotul, as we did at Perizan, a feeling of recklessness soon sets in. When at any step a fracture of the skull is not at all unlikely, one ceases after the first half-hour to think much of the danger. We passed corners where mule and merchandise are sometimes lost by a fall from the precipice into the stony valley beneath. But the beauty of the scene culminated at a point where a single peak of rock rises seven hundred feet from the centre of the valley, and stands, gray and jagged, with large birds flying about its summit. We might have thought it inaccessible but for the evidence of conquest upon the topmost rock, where a telegraph-post was fixed supporting wires, which at great height spanned the valley on each side of this precipitous elevation.

Another remarkable view, which in words can be but poorly painted, is that which meets the eye after passing this eyrie of the Indo-Persian Telegraph. We were slowly descending a deep, wide valley, from the hollow of which we were still raised three or four thousand feet. On the farthest side ran a chain of mountains, their summits appearing to cross the horizon in almost a level line. Like a great ridge or furrow, these mountains crossed our road from north to south; and about half-way down, in the slow descent we were making through the scrubby jungle which clothes the western side of Perizan, upon a projecting platform of rock, lay the caravanserai of Mian-kotul (the middle of the kotul). We were so high above it that we could see nothing but, as it were, the ground-plan of the building; the mules moving like specks from side to side of the yard, the roof of the surrounding stables like a line; the whole caravanserai but a spot in the immensity of the prospect.

CHAPTER XXV.

Mian-kotul Caravanserai. —Tofanghees on Guard. — Feuds between Villagers.—Kotul Dochter.—Traveling on the Kotul.—The Mushir-el-Mulk. —Lake Famoor.—Encampment of Eeliats.—Ruins of Ancient Persia.— Plain of Kazeroon.—Songs of Persian Soldiers.—Kazeroon.—Anniversary of Houssein's Death.—"Ah, Houssein!"—Fanatical Exercises.—Orange Gardens.—The Sheik of Kazeroon.—Plain of Kazeroon.—Attack on Major Napier's Caravan.—Village of Kamaridj.—Plain of Khan-i-Takhte.— Hospitality in Persia.—Kotul Maloo.—A Difficult Path.—Daliki River.— Arabs in Persia.—Palm-leaf Huts.—A Loop-holed Bedroom.—Petroleum at Daliki.—Barasjoon.—Rifle Practice.—Indian Officers in Persia.— Functions of Political Resident.—Sowars from Bushire.—Caravanserai at Ahmedy.—Arrival of Captain Fraser.—The Mashillah.—A Wet Day's Ride.—Bushire.

THE caravanserai at Mian-kotul was no better and no worse than others. A black arch ten feet by eight, with no windows, opening by a door-way in which a carpet was the only screen, upon a stone platform raised about three feet above a yard full of mules and asses, some of them knee-deep in the dirt of the place, is not a very charming residence. For the last time, the night was cold and frosty; the next day we were to descend more than five thousand feet into a land of palm-trees and orange groves, where the raggedness of the people would look less wretched and pitiful, and where poverty would lose much of its misery. Kazem was delighted at his own accomplishment, when, under my direction, he turned out a dish of eggs and bacon; but looking at the slices of the forbidden meat (which had been exported from the United Kingdom by a merchant of Shiraz), he laughed, and said, "No Irān mau eat." His bright eyes beamed with pleasure at the coming change of climate, though he grew more and more apprehensive as to the safety of the road. "Very bad robbers," he said, in an interval of cookery, pointing forward on our road to Bushire. Like a prudent man, he had turned the heap of silver which represented his wages and allowances into paper at Shiraz. Mr. Odling had kindly taken the silver, and telegraphed the amount to Kazem's credit in Teheran, so that of this money he could not be robbed. The transaction had given much ease to Kazem's mind.

Outside the caravanserai of Mian-kotul, the way to Bushire descends through a grove of trees to a small plain, also covered with stunted oaks and some growth of under-wood.

We had advanced about a quarter of a mile into this wood, when there suddenly appeared seven wild-looking men, each armed with a gun and a long knife. They might be robbers or friends; I really could not tell which, as we approached them. That they were waiting for us was quite clear. Without a word, they surrounded the caravan; and presently, without appearing curious as to their quality, I gathered from Kazem that they were men living in the neighborhood who proposed to accompany us through part of our way to Kazeroon as an extra guard for our greater security. Several of them went on before, dispersed like sharp-shooters, in the wood. Sometimes they fired at birds, but I think none fell to their aim. After walking about four miles to the centre of a small plain below the kotul, they gathered round me and made "salaam," at the same time asking for money.

It struck me that there could not be very great difference between declared robbery and a request which was so much like a demand, made by seven armed men, two of whom had their hands upon my saddle. However, they were satisfied with a small present, and, before dismissing them, I asked why they wished to leave us in a part of the plain where, if their presence was at all useful, it was certainly most desirable.

They told me they could not go any farther, because they were "at war" with the men of the next village. That led to another explanation, in which Kazem and the charvodar joined. From this it appeared that in the parts of Persia south of Shiraz there are, as a rule, feuds existing between village and village, arising in the first place from some dispute, agricultural or matrimonial, between two men, and having a fatal result. The friends of the murdered man have then to undertake the sacred duty of revenge. Any one of them will, at sight, shoot or stab in cold blood any one of the relations of the murderer, or, perhaps more correctly, the man-slayer. This homicidal disposition ultimately spreads to the villagers on each side, and the feud thus becomes a war between village and village.

In the South of Persia we never saw a man or a boy unarmed. The donkey-drivers carried long guns slung at their backs; the peasants who were scratching the earth in patches with wooden plows were armed in the same way, and most of them carried, in addition, a long sword-knife in their girdle. Every man, in fact, was a tofanghee; and one of the traveler's difficulties is to get rid of those men who spring up at the sight of a caravan from the bushes or stones, and are ready to be paid guards, or to remain in something very like the attitude of robbers if no money is forthcoming. If we had not had our two sowars, we should possibly have had trouble with these tofanghees of Mian-kotul.

At the end of the plain, a concealed outlet over a low elevation led us to the summit of the Kotul Dochter (the Daughter-kotul). Four tofanghees joined us at this point; and when we were obliged to dismount, owing to the difficulties of the road, we found them useful in getting our horses down the kotul. If they had really been robbers, instead of men with perhaps a tendency in that direction, they could have chosen no more satisfactory place for attack. No horse can make more than two miles an hour over a kotul. One might more easily try to trot or gallop over the lava of Vesuvius than upon the stones of a kotul; and of all the kotuls, the "Dochter" is by far the steepest and most difficult. No one attempts to ride upon the Kotul Dochter. It is a way, partly natural, partly built, and partly hewed, in the side of a precipitous rock about two thousand feet high.

Half an hour's labor by the small strength of our caravan would have closed it altogether. With stones alone a dozen strong men could defend the almost perpendicular zigzag against a host. Such "gates" are a security to a country; but what a high-road for the commerce of Persia! When one thinks that every piece of Manchester goods passing to the markets of Shiraz and Ispahan has to be carried upon a mule, stumbling and slipping, toiling up these rude stairs by a path so difficult that camels are not employed, it is easy to see the advantage of Russia, who sends her manufactures by way of Tabriz and Resht. The Mushir, the vizier of the Firman Firma, who has made himself rich by the subordinate government of the province of Fars, has, let it be said to his credit, done much, by the erection of retaining-walls, to render the Kotul Dochter less dangerous. Many were the loads of goods, and many the mules, which were dashed to pieces before the improvement of this ladder of stone by the Mushir.

But the Mushir-el-Mulk, as this functionary was called, has, I hear, since we left Persia, met the fate of all energetic rulers in that country. For alleged offenses, perhaps for the high crime of getting rich and failing to share his profits with the Shah and the Imperial Government, the Mushir-el-Mulk has, I am told upon high official authority, been summoned to Teheran, where he has received "the sticks," has been compelled to make a large disbursement, and has been formally deprived of the profitable position he held as Grand Farmer-general of the province of Shiraz.

Until we saw the Kotul Dochter, we had not fully realized why it was not possible for a takht-i-rawan to pass that way. In the corkscrew windings of the Kotul Dochter, there was at times scarcely room for the body of a mule; and though we followed closely, one almost upon the heels of the other, yet the leading horse of our caravan was sometimes a couple of hundred feet below the rear-guard. When we turned our eyes from the rock we were descending by a sort of irregular stone ladder, two thousand feet long, we looked over a fertile plain — a tender green, where there were patches of young wheat, set here and there with groves of palms, which seemed to be the only trees; and to the left lay the shallow, tranquil waters of Lake Famoor. It was the 5th of February; and the rose-bushes beside the stony path upon the spur of the mountain which led from the foot of the Kotul Dochter to the plain were gay with blossoms. These seemed to welcome our arrival from the snow, which for nearly fifty days had been always under our eyes. A river runs from the lake through the plain; and beside it on the greensward, the pasturage of which belonged to any man, was an encampment of the much dreaded Eeliats, their low tents of goat's-hair cloth stretched on sticks, in which only a year-old baby could stand upright — reminding us of the very similar abodes of Bedouin Arabs in Northern Africa.

At the point where the path to Kazeroon is at last level, and quite clear of the mountains, there are some interesting ruins of ancient Persia. By these we dismounted, and enjoyed our luncheon in a genial climate. The ruins are those of a tomb or a temple, and their interest centres in a large bass-relief carved upon the smoothed face of the overhanging rock. A monarch, heavily bewigged with false hair, in the fashion of ancient Persia, and as marvelously bearded, is seated with a lion before him, his chair of state encircled by attendants. In front of this work there are the ruins of an inclosure, in which we lingered until it was necessary to get on over the plain to the town of Kazeroon.

We had passed in three hours from winter to summer; my Cabul sheep-skin coat was no longer endurable. The way was level and grassy. Birds fluttered in the air; the graceful foliage of the palm-trees waved about us; the swarthy, Arab-like Eeliats, who had migrated from the plains of Ispahan and Shiraz on the coming of winter, were here tending their flocks, every one of them with a gun at his back and a knife in his belt; and in the far distance, where the palm-trees were congregated in dense groves, lay Kazeroon, in which there is an office of the Indo-Persian Telegraph, kept by an Armenian, who we knew was prepared to receive us. Hassan and Abdullah, our sowars, were singing in their own way, taking turns in the monotonous dirge, which is the only singing voice of the Mohammedan nations, when suddenly Abd-ullah shouted in Persian the word for "antelope." In the twinkling of an eye—to say a moment would seem an exaggeration—their horses were at a gallop, and they were chasing furiously over a patch of wheat. Away they galloped, so far as to be almost out of sight. First, Hassan fired without slackening speed; then Abd-ullah shot; but there were no results, and presently they returned, and resumed their doleful song, which was a somewhat stupid rhyme about the charms of an imaginary lady, repeated again and again, without the slightest apparent consciousness, interest, or weariness. Sometimes the songs of Persians, delivered all in the same tone, are in language highly indecorous. Among the Turks as well as the Persians, it is observed with surprise by Europeans, that, even in the superior classes, talk is habitually indecent, and that this immoral flow is not arrested by the presence of women and boys. The Vizier of the Zil-i-Sultan, who called upon me in Ispahan, a man of great position, and of an ability rare in Persia, invited me to an entertainment at his house, which I was too ill to attend. Mr. Bruce, the missionary, went, and told me on his return how he had been shocked at the filthiness of the general conversation carried on, especially by the host and father, in presence of his youthful sons—two boys whom I had seen riding in Ispahan, attended, after the manner of people of their class, by a dozen mounted servants.

It may be that Kazeroon appears more beautiful on approaching it from the snowy mountains than in coming from the greater heat of Bushire. To us it seemed the very ideal of an Oriental town. There were orange gardens with the golden fruit upon the dark-green leaves; there was scarcely a house which was not shaded by a palm-tree. The inhabitants live, for the most part, on dates. There were mosques with domes of mud, and minarets of sun-baked bricks. The poverty of the people, the squalor of their huts (many of them made of mats hung on poles), all this was as evident as on the higher and colder regions. But nobody shivered or looked pinched and hungry. Two pounds' weight of dates makes a good meal, and can be bought for about the value of a halfpenny in English money. We were delighted with the promise of rest as we rode into Kazeroon, and by no means sorry when the charvodar rode up with Kazem, and, salaaming, begged as a favor that we would not travel the next day, as it was the day of Houssein's death, and they wished to keep the solemn festival in Kazeroon.

A tofanghee from the telegraph-office had met us about a league from the town, and now ran forward to announce our arrival to his master, who received us very kindly, placed a large empty room at our disposal, and, having done this, set himself to telegraph the news of our arrival to north and south. We were out betimes in the morning, to see the doings of the people of Kazeroon in honor of the lamented Houssein. From the court-yard of the principal mosque we heard the continuous cry, "Ah, Houssein!" "Ah, Hous-

17*

sein!" arising, and, standing in the door-way, saw the whole place was full of men, the surrounding roofs crowded with women and children. In the centre, about fifty men had formed themselves into a ring, holding each other's hands. In this formation, they expanded and contracted the circle, advancing and retreating with the cry "Ah, Houssein!" uttered in the tone of profoundest grief. This was kept up with mechanical regularity for about an hour. Then, when every man's brain was reeling with the exercise and with watching it, at a word from their leader the men sat down, and each one beat his bare breast with his open palm, and then clapped his hand upon his thigh with the common cry. This, too, was done with the same precision. We left them at this work, and soon after it was understood that the two parties, one holding that day to be the proper anniversary and the other preferring the morrow, were disposed to fight over the difference. There was some tumult, and the governor ordered that there was not to be the usual procession in the streets, of which the leading feature is the slashing of their faces and persons with knives, and the consequent staining of their white garments with blood, by the most devoted mourners for Houssein. The telegraph clerk and I went into the streets to see how this order was obeyed, and had got into a narrow place, when we heard from a hundred voices the cry "Ah, Houssein!" coming toward us. We hurried to an outlet, and reached an open space just in time to avoid a rushing crowd of men, each one of whom leaped into the air as he shouted at every step "Ah, Houssein!" and at the same time beat his inflamed breast with his hand. Men in the condition of those forming this crowd were virtually insane with frantic exertion and the continuous exercise of the same movement. Had we met them in the narrow way, we should very likely have been knocked over and trodden to death. I felt that, looking on as we were, a single word of hatred for the infidel would have been sufficient for the sacrifice of our lives. This production of irresponsible fanaticism by shouts and oft-repeated movement, by exercises such as these, and such as those of dancing and howling dervishes, is as much a part of the recognized machinery of the Mohammedan Church as the celibacy of the clergy and the domestic fulcrum obtained in the confessional-box are of the Roman Church.

From this scene of noisy and dangerous fanaticism it was pleasant, when we were joined by my wife, to pass into the largest of the orange gardens, a grove of magnificent trees, most of them more than two hundred years old, and all loaded with fruit. The central path through this orange garden is a sight to be remembered. From the ruins of the tank in the centre, the surrounding orange-trees, the largest we have ever seen, presented a delicious appearance. Possibly there would not have been so much fruit remaining on the branches, had the oranges not been of the sour variety. We have not met with sweet oranges anywhere in Persia as a product of the country. They are imported from Baghdad and other places. I can hardly suppose that the deficiency of Persia in this respect is due to want of the proper climate or soil for ripening sweet oranges. No part of the world would seem better adapted for the growth of oranges than the region about Kazeroon. At Bushire it may be too hot; at Shiraz the winter may be too severe. But Kazeroon, though it is two thousand seven hundred feet above the sea, has the climate of Seville; the palms prove that the cold is not severe, and the corn-fields that there are abundant moisture and genial sunshine. On returning from the orange garden, we met a small crowd, in front of which walked an old man with beard dyed red. His dress was rich; he had a huge ring of silver upon his hand, and a heavy pair of spectacles upon his nose. He was the religious Sheik of Kazeroon—the Sheik-ul-

Islam he would have been called in a capital—the ecclesiastical mayor and judge of the place, and the crowd was composed of his retinue attendants. The telegraph clerk presented me to the old man, who shook hands, and welcomed us to Kazeroon with grave politeness.

The weather was showery, and there were signs that the half of the population which did not assent to the celebration of the previous day was preparing to realize its own idea of the anniversary of Houssein's death when we rode out of Kazeroon. I think Kazem favored the day of our departure, and the charvodar that after our arrival, as the proper date of this ceremony. However, no objection was made to our progress, though we passed through the plain of Kazeroon, of which only a few patches are cultivated, under a heavy shower of rain. There were abundant evidences of natural fertility in the soil, which seemed to need nothing but industry to be highly productive. At the end of the plain, the path mounted toward a small caravanserai, adjoining which was a hut built of palm-leaves. We had this swept out, and sat on the floor to eat a luncheon of eggs and dates, and then, still in the rain, rode up and down among the hill-tops —though some of the most favorite haunts of robbers—until we looked down upon another plain, that of Kamaridj, in the middle of which stood the white dome of some Mohammedan tomb, and at the farther end the village in which we were to pass the night. This was the place where the Honorable Major Napier's caravan was attacked and robbed—as pretty a plain as any in Persia. As we looked down upon it from the hills, there were two herds of long-haired goats, the only life upon the plain. The ground was sloppy with the rain; and the palm-trees, under which Kamaridj lay, were visible for two hours before we reached the village. That which in grander spheres would be called a reign of terror prevails always in Kamaridj and the villages of Southern

Fars. They are at all times liable to that which in higher latitudes would be dignified with the names of siege and sack. Their efforts to win prosperity are blighted by the musket of the tax-gatherer and the pistol of the robber. In good and bad years alike, for every one of their palm-trees and their bullocks the peasants must pay a heavy charge to the costly system of misrule dignified with the name of government, of which the Shah is the head; and, in bad years as in good, the robber urges his claim to maintenance at the expense of the only hard-working class in Persia. For such depredation the site of Kamaridj is most convenient, nestled under hills in which there is concealment for a troop from the eyes of an army.

Kamaridj was all alive with excitement at the sight of our caravan approaching over the plain. Two men, armed, of course, ran out about a mile to meet us; and when we entered not a few of the roofs were occupied with women. We found a fairly good room in Kamaridj; and on the morning of February 8th rode over the hills, in a climate which seemed perfection, through a country full of the budding luxuriance of a Southern spring, to the plain of Khan-i-Takhte, in which there were continuous groves of palm-trees, extending for miles an unbroken shade. Our soldiers and muleteers sung—not so sweetly as the birds—and the conductors of the two or three caravans we passed in the day's ride were smiling and talkative. Near a great patch of palm-trees stood the telegraph-office, which was to be our stopping-place for the night. It was, we knew, uninhabited, the clerk having recently suffered an attack of apoplexy, in consequence of which he had been removed by Mr. Odling to Shiraz. A tofanghee was in charge of the place. There was something very sad, on entering the rooms, to see the clock stopped, the instruments all dead and dusty, and the necessaries of a European's daily life lying about in disorder—evidences of the suddenness of the attack by which the greater part of the life of this man had been taken from him.

The simplicity of hospitality in such a country is fully experienced in a case of this sort. In the presence of the master of the house it is very much the same; the reception of visitors is devoid of nine-tenths of the difficulty with which it is encompassed at home. One finds an empty room; the carpets and furniture are taken from the mules' backs, the property of the traveler. For all the trouble they are at, he pays the servants of the house; his own servants prepare and cook his food, and in the morning he leaves not a trace of his sojourn.

We were still eighteen hundred feet above the sea. We were now to descend by the Kotul Maloo to Daliki, where we should be but two hundred feet above the line at which our ride was to end—the level of the Persian Gulf at Bushire. From the plain of Khan-i-Takhte we looked back on that high, serrated ridge of mountains, the other side of which we had seen from the caravanserai of Mian-kotul. Indeed, the plain appeared to be locked on all sides by mountains, but we rode on toward the southern end, where the path suddenly disclosed a steep descent upon the side of an almost perpendicular cliff. There has been no building at the Kotul Maloo. Somehow or other, in the course of years, the hoofs of mules and the feet of men have worn a track from one huge stone to another, and a zigzag has been formed, which descends at gradients of about one in three, but so unequally that every step is more or less of a climb. Looked at from the bottom, one would hardly suppose the piled-up rocks of the Kotul Maloo to be accessible. It is prudent to make some noise in the passage, so that, if a caravan is ascending, the mules may be made to stand aside in the few places where it is possible for one loaded animal to pass another with a similar burden. At the foot of the Kotul Maloo the ravine widens, and there is a splendid view in the valley beneath of a river, the waters of which were rushing when we saw them, and green with the nauseous salts which they contain. To the side of this river we gradually descended into a valley, through which it passed in a broad stream toward a bridge, which is certainly the finest in Persia—another work of the Mushir who then governed Fars in the name of the Firman Firma. Near this bridge, the stream, which is known as the Daliki River, turned abruptly round high rocks, through a southern outlet by which we also passed, after sitting a while near the bridge, in a thick growth of beautiful ferns, to eat our luncheon.

It would have been utterly impossible for an unguided stranger to have followed without error the path by which we accomplished the remainder of that day's journey. It lay, unmarked because of the hardness of the rocks, through a labyrinth of hills. Sometimes we forded the river, at others passed for a mile upon bowlders which seemed to bear no trace of a track. Then we left the stream, and, crossing a hill, entered upon an entirely new scene. No part of the way from Shiraz was more curious and fatiguing. At last our tired horses climbed a rounded hill, which was the final elevation. From this we had a prospect over a sandy plain of apparently illimitable extent. We could not see the gulf; but, in fact, had our sight been sufficient, and the Persian belief in the flatness of the earth established, we might have seen ships riding at anchor off the town of Bushire. Near the foot of this last hill lay the village of Daliki—a wild place, more Arab than Persian—the inhabitants living in huts made of mats or of palm-leaves. The general plan of Daliki, like that of all the villages upon the plains around the Persian Gulf, is very simple. A mud-bank about a foot high incloses the area of each hut, and upon this is made a frame-work of palm branches, covered or thatched with the broad fronds or leaves of the same tree, or with mats plaited with strips from the palm-leaves. Daliki is environed with palm-trees. The people of Daliki have terrible blood-feuds with neighboring villages, and suffer greatly from occasional raids by bands of robbers from the mountains. Major Champain, R.E., the Director of the Indo-Persian Telegraph, informs me that, in passing Daliki a month after we staid in that village, he saw two dead bodies lying exposed, those of men slain by robbers, who were still in sight, hastening, with their booty, into the fastnesses of those hills by which we approached the village. There are two huts in Daliki which have a bala-khanah. Of one of these we took possession. But the roofing over the mud-stairs was so very low that we were obliged to hoist up some things with a cord, and to throw up the smaller articles to one of the large holes intended for windows. The room was nine feet by twelve, and had loop-holes on all sides, twenty-four in number. The night was not cold; we could afford to laugh, and call this liberal provision of draughts "airy." At times in the night there came through some of the numerous holes in our room a smell which reminded me of Russian Baku, the Asiatic Petrolia on the Caspian—an odor of naphtha, from the natural springs which lay neglected, and running to waste, a little to the southward of the village.

By a slight détour we visited these springs in the morning, on our way to Barasjoon, the next station. There seems to be no doubt about the quality or quantity of the petroleum. All the streams around us were colored and covered with the outflow; but no one attempts to make use of it. There may be under-ground a practically inexhaustible supply, and doubtless Englishmen would be found ready to sink wells, and to engage in exportation, if it were safe to deal with the Persian Government. The wells would not be more than fifteen or sixteen miles from the waters of the Persian Gulf at Sheef, and the price of coal in India is certainly high enough to encourage enterprise of this sort.

The smell of petroleum was still on the plain when we were joined by a number of ruffianly-looking men, who, after walking with us for a mile, to my great relief departed in the direction of the mountains. The ground between Daliki and Barasjoon is unlevel, but not hilly. Cultivated patches, all unfenced, are few and far apart. In these, wheat was waving five inches high around bushes which the cultivators had not taken the trouble to remove. The sun shone very hotly on the 10th of February, as we approached Barasjoon, which consists of a telegraph-station, a caravanserai, and a village. Throughout the evening there was a continual noise of firing. The one amusement of the men of these villages seems to be rifle-shooting. They are always striving to improve themselves as marksmen, and as nothing else. Their agriculture is careless; their homes are miserable; their food, for the most part, dates; they are subject to the most cruel tyranny. The governor collects his taxes from them at the head of an irresistible force; their one delight is to be ready against their neighbors with their rifles. The head-man or sub-governor of Barasjoon, enthusiastic like the rest in this direction, was, we were told, taking shots one evening not long ago from the roof of his house, and was unable to resist the tempting mark offered by a harmless shepherd, upon whom he inflicted a wound from which the man died in two days. A resident at Barasjoon told me the story was quite true; that the head-man killed the shepherd only because he was seized with a cruel desire, at sight of the man, to have a living mark for his shot, and that no punishment whatever had followed this wanton murder.

On the morning following our arrival at Barasjoon we received a most welcome re-enforcement. We were really delighted to see the red uniforms and British accoutrements of two Bombay sowars, who had been sent to meet us with a letter of invitation and welcome by Colonel Ross, the political resident at Bushire. Perhaps this is as good a place as any in which to allude to the connection, amounting to something like co-ordinate authority, which has at one time existed in greater degree than at present, but which is still maintained on the part of the Foreign Office and the Government of British India, in Persia. At one time I believe the Legation in Teheran was a mission from the Indian Government, dispatched by and maintained solely at the cost of that Government. At present the Indian Government makes, I understand, a contribution to the cost of the Legation in Teheran, and maintains at Bushire a political resident, who is protector of the commerce of the gulf, and mediator-general (backed by a force of gun-boats) between the tribes upon the Arabian and Persian shores, the object being to secure safe and unrestricted intercourse between the towns of the gulf, and free communication from India and Great Britain with the inlet to the Tigris and Euphrates at Bussorah and up to Baghdad.

The political resident at Bushire is not subordinate to the minister in Teheran, and they are, I should suppose, sufficiently far removed to render their occasional intercourse free from embarrassment. The lines which separate their authority are probably not defined. In Shiraz, Mirza Hassan Ali Khan, the British agent, told me that in applying for leave of absence, he obtained permission both from Mr. Thomson and from Colonel Ross, though the latter has no connection with the Foreign Office, and is an Indian officer on special service, under the orders of the Bombay Government, reporting only to that Government.

The sowars he had kindly sent to meet us and to conduct us to the Residency were Sikhs; fine men on good horses, wearing scarlet turbans, and long tunics of the same British color, high jack-boots, and armed with short carbine and cavalry sword. I noticed they could not make themselves understood by our Persian sowars or servants. They had spent the night at Ahmedy, and, after some hours' rest, their horses were fresh enough to return with us to that caravanserai. It was a tedious ride upon almost a dead level of damp sand, with small groves of palm-trees each a few miles apart. In the last hour when we were in sight of the caravanserai of Ahmedy, rain fell very heavily, which made us arrive in great discomfort. But the caravanserai was strong and new; it was possible to have a fire; there was not more than one open hole in our room, and, when the sky cleared, we spread our wet clothes upon poles on the roof, and enjoyed the lookout from that place of vantage. The scene was one of life near the tropics with an arctic background. There were behind us the brown hills over Daliki, and above these the high snowy ranges we had passed through from Shiraz. All around in the immediate neighborhood of the caravanserai was a level of brown sand, which met the shallow waters of the gulf at an almost invisible distance. A stream beset with palm-trees ran near, and toward this our string of mules was being led out to water after the removal of their loads. In this sea of sand the rectangular walls of the caravanserai were the only interruption. It may strike the reader, as it did myself, that the panorama, though remarkable and thoroughly Oriental, was one which could be painted with little liability to error, even from these few and imperfect words of description.

Over the sand from the direction of Bushire there came galloping a group of white horses. The new arrival was Captain Fraser, assistant political resident at Bushire, who was out on a sporting expedition, attended by two sowars, comrades of those who had joined our caravan, and two servants. From his arch in the caravanserai he sent his card to our arch; and shortly afterward I paid him a visit. He had come out on a shooting expedition, and, when I left him, we received a present than which nothing could have seemed more delightful and acceptable. One of his soldiers brought us, with Captain Fraser's compliments, a small loaf of exquisitely white bread in a cloth of equal purity. We had been living upon a supply of Persian bread brought from Shiraz, now eleven days old. We had not seen white bread since we left Russia, five months ago; and this loaf, good as any in England, had for us, in its setting of snowy linen, a charm which it is not possible to describe. When Captain Fraser joined us afterward upon the roof, we were rejoicing in his thoughtful gift.

Between Ahmedy and Bushire there is an expanse of wet sand extending for about twenty miles, to the possession of which the sea on both sides makes pretensions. It connects the dry land about Bushire with the main-land of Persia. Sometimes the "Mashillah," as it is called, is dry, and even dusty, but after rain it is sloppy; sometimes worse even than when we crossed it. We rode over the Mashillah under a down-pour of almost continuous rain. At every step our horses sunk over the hoofs, and the muleteers were obliged to walk barefoot, lest they should lose their shoes in the wet sand. We were enveloped in mist; we could see nothing but the wet quagmire over which we were struggling. The clothes of our soldiers, Indian and Persian, were wet through, and the men looked as sulky and miserable as Asiatics always do in rainy weather. For half the way we were splashing through water, and the rest was swampy. The gholams, who had charge of the baggage, failed utterly to keep up with us, and I was obliged to send two soldiers to look after them, and to bring the mules forward. They were not very willing to go back through the rain, and an hour passed before they re-appeared with the baggage, but without the gholams, whom they left to plod on at their own pace.

At two miles from Bushire the ground became harder. There was a small bank, on which we found a caravanserai.

We made a fire, and had luncheon there in great discomfort; but it was advisable to wait for some time, in order to get the caravan together for our march into Bushire. To reach the town, we had to cross a level stretch of sand, a fine field for a gallop with better and less tired horses.

We can hardly express the joy with which we saw the union-jack flying on a high mast planted before the sea-front of the Residency. Colonel Ross's numerous guard of Bombay native infantry turned out to present arms on our arrival; and in the wide court-yard of his house the resident himself gave us a kindly welcome. Our ride through Persia was ended.

CHAPTER XXVI.

Bushire.—The Residency.—Arab Towers and Wooden "Guns."—Government in Persian Gulf.—The Arabian Shore.—Arabs and Arabs.—The Sultan's Power in Arabia.—Oman and the Ibadhis.—Pilgrims to Mecca.—Destiny of Rotten Steamships.—Pilgrims' Coffins.—Six Hundred Arabs Drowned.—Persian Land Revenue.—Collecting Customs Duties.—Trade and Population.—Commerce of Bushire.—Cultivation of Opium.—Opium and Cereals.—Export of Opium.—British Expedition in 1857.—Occupation of Persia.—Persian Army in 1857.—Interests of England.—The Indo-Persian Telegraph.—Persia Ripe for Conquest.—Persia and India.

AFTER the chapar-khanahs and caravanserais of the road, how Elysian seemed the apartments and the comforts of the Residency! We gladly parted company with all our traveling-baggage, and Kazem's eyes glistened with delight as we made him a present of bedsteads and bedding, fur coats and jackets, saddles and bridles, pots and pans, chairs and tables. We had a week to enjoy the hospitality of Colonel and Mrs. Ross before the next boat of the British Indian Company would sail for Kurrachee and Bombay.

The Residency is a large pile of buildings, with a great deal of court below, and a great deal of staircase and veranda above. On one of the flat roofs is a structure which is common to all the superior houses of Bushire—a room built like a cage, with poles and laths, in which the hot nights of summer are passed. The town lies behind the resident's house. In front, about fifty yards from the gate, there is a sea-side terrace, a quarter-deck, as it were, belonging to the Residency, but open to all comers; and below this the waters of the gulf ripple or beat upon the sand. At each end of this walk is the ruin of an Arab tower, a relic of the days of barbarism and piracy. In Arab fashion, timbers have been built into the rough masonry, and upon the outer side of the shell of these towers the weather-worn blocks of wood project, about three feet apart. I am precise about these timbers, because, by a curious chance, I had happened in Shiraz to meet with an old copy of a London newspaper, containing a letter from a traveling correspondent in the Persian Gulf. He was writing of Bushire, and assuming close acquaintance with a place which he had evidently seen only from three miles' distance—in fact, from the deck of a steamer, while passing down from Bussorah. He particularly drew attention to the "armament" of these Arab towers, which, he said, were encircled with an array of "guns." This is not the first time, perhaps, that wooden poles have been taken for cannon. But the fact is that Bushire is entirely without any remarkable defenses. The resident's gun-boat, a part of that unknown force, the Anglo-Indian Navy, is generally in the offing, and the military duties of the Persian Governor of Bushire are, as a rule, confined to oppression of the inland subjects of the Shah. Looking out from the front of the Residency, the gulf narrows to the right in the direction of Bussorah, and on the left, where the sand-bank (at the end of which is Bushire) rises rather higher than elsewhere, is the ground on which the British troops encamped in 1857. If the opposite shore were in range of sight, we might see to the south, Bahrein, the emporium of the pearl-fishery. The annual value of the pearls found in the Persian Gulf exceeds four hundred thousand pounds a year. The oyster-shells have a considerable value; for these are as large as a cheese-plate, and the inside is the best of that lustrous substance known as "mother-of-pearl."

Upon that—the Turkish-Arabian side of the gulf—slave-holding tribes are allowed by the Governments of the Empress of India and of the Sultan to engage in a moderate amount of fighting among themselves. On great occasions, the resident at Bushire and his subordinate, the resident at Muscat, interfere; and it is understood that the Indian Government permits no fighting on the water. On land a system of chieftainship prevails, and he who is strongest wins Bahrein. The Sultan of Turkey is nominally the sovereign ruler of this wild shore, and suzerain of the chief at Bahrein, and also of the petty Sultan of Muscat. But the Turkish Sultan's authority is never seen, and rarely heard of. Sir Lewis Pelly, who was the predecessor of Colonel Ross as resident at Bushire, in remarkable if somewhat unofficial language, reported to the Government of Bombay concerning these tribes: "The Arabs acknowledge the Turks as we do the Thirty-nine Articles—which all accept and none remember." I am inclined to think that even this is an exaggeration of the Turkish authority. I do not believe it is accepted by these lawless tribes, who seem to have but one rule of life, which is this: that a man's slaves are his own, and that the African is an amphibious creature, who, with the cruel alternative of a wire whip applied to his back, must live as long as possible under the waters of the Persian Gulf in search of pearls for the benefit of Arab masters. The reign of anarchy at Bahrein can not be more strikingly displayed than in the official report of the Bushire resident, that "Bahrein once hoisted in succession Turkish, Persian, and English flags." It is even added, "She has been known, when attacked, to hoist them all at once."

Farther to the south, still upon the Arabian shore, we come to Muscat and Oman; and all that is known of these regions goes further to show that the Sultan's writ does not run in the East of Arabia. Colonel Ross, who was for some time resident at Muscat, found the tribes divided under the general names of "Hinawi" and "Ghafiri." But it appears that this division is not ancient. At the beginning of the eighteenth century, in civil wars of unusual magnitude, one set of tribes ranged under Khalf, the Hinawi, and another under Mohammed, the Ghafiri, whose contentions established divisions which have since endured. In the native chronicles of these tribes, their historians, or writers, have divided all the tribes of Arabs into three classes: 1. *El Arab el Arabeh—i. e.*, pure Arabs—those whom they believe to have been created with a natural disposition for speaking Arabic; 2. *El Arab el Mota' arribeh*, those who have achieved the position of Arabs by acquiring command of the Arabic language; and, 3. *El Arab el Mosta' ribeh*, the naturalized Arabs.

Of these three classes, the teachers of to-day hold the first to have been lost or become extinct. But their devotion to the God of Mohammed, and to the great Meccan as the foremost and chiefest of the prophets and interpreters of God, endures, though it has become sectarian. For instance, the Ibadhis, a very numerous religious body on this coast, reject both the Turkish and the Persian doctrine as to the devolution of Mohammed's powers and functions. With the Turk it is a necessary article of faith to believe that the Sultan administers the Koran, as the rightful representative of the Prophet. He has no confidence in civil law, which differs from the code of Mohammed. The Sultan is the inheritor of Mohammed's authority, though not of his prophetic powers; yet probably millions would accept as the inspired word of God any pretended revelation he might make by way of addition to the Koran. These are not times favorable for promulgating supernatural revelations; but if a man gifted with as much original genius and power and capacity for leadership as Mohammed possessed were to arise in Turkey, he might add Suras to the Koran at his pleasure. But his revelations, unless enforced by the sword, would have no authority among tribes like the Ibadhis of Arabia, nor with the Persians. The latter have a belief, somewhat like that of

Christians, that their Imām, or head of their religion, will some day re-appear in likeness of the form he had on earth. But the Ibadhis have another belief: they have a visible successor of Mohammed, a true Imām, whom they select. They are much given to pilgrimages, which, living as they do in the Holy Land of Mohammedans, are for them comparatively easy.

In his "Annals of Oman," Colonel Ross says: "Among the Ibadhis, a man must have amassed sufficient for expenses, and one year's ordinary expenditure in addition, before he makes the pilgrimage to Mecca." The observances of pilgrims from this shore are not very different from those of other sections of Mohammedans. In the Mina valley they throw the three stones, typical of Abraham's conflict with Satan, when the Evil One sought to tempt the father of the faithful. They are taught to regard as essential the following five points of ritual: 1. The spirit or intention in which the pilgrimage is undertaken and carried out; 2. The duty and excellence of prayer on Mount Arafat; 3. Shaving in Mina valley; 4. The proper making of the circuit of the House of God; 5. Running seven times from Safa to Merwa. It is obligatory that, after putting on the *ihram*, or garment of pilgrimage (which Mr. Bicknell, who made the pilgrimage, says consists of only "two towels"), the pilgrim must hunt no game and take no life; he may not even hunt to death the vermin upon his body; and if, in a fit of natural irritation, a death of this sort should occur, he is liable, upon confession, to the payment of expiatory offerings.

The modern pilgrim, whether he is bound for Mecca or for Paray-le-Monial, does not select the most troublesome mode of travel; and even native-born Arabs prefer a British steamship to the perils and hardships of crossing the sandy, foodless, waterless desert, which lies between the shores of the Persian Gulf and the holy places of Mecca. At sea, it is true, they endure a maximum of the perils of navigation; but they are ignorant of the comparative safety with which Europeans are conveyed in well-appointed ships, and they may think that the annual sacrifice of life enhances the grandeur and importance and the glory of pilgrimage. Since the invention of steam navigation, the shores of Asia have been strewed with the bodies of Mohammedan pilgrims. Mr. Plimsoll once told me that the ship-breaker's trade is virtually extinct; that old ships are not broken up. He has found that our coasting-trade is to a great extent carried on in rotten ships; and I myself, while bathing, have seen one of these touch the sand, and fall to pieces in twenty minutes; so that, by the time I had dressed after my bath, there was not a trace upon the sea of a brig of three hundred tons burden which had stranded in ten feet of water. This, no doubt, is the general destiny of old sailing-ships of the smaller class. They are broken up by storms, and sometimes the crew are saved, and sometimes all hands are lost.

But it was not until I traveled in Asia that I became fully aware of what is done with rotten steamships; they are, in fact, the pilgrims' coffins. From Japan to the Red Sea, the superannuated and dangerous steam-vessels—useless in a supervised trade, in which it is not permitted to drown passengers and crew by glaring neglect in regard to the seaworthiness of the ship—are engaged in what is known as the native carrying and coasting trade. While we were at Bushire, news arrived of the complete loss (with the exception of two survivors of the crew) of a steamship on the well-known rocks outside the port of Jiddah, the landing-place for Mecca, in the Red Sea. Six hundred pilgrims were drowned, and a fortnight afterward we met the survivors as fellow-passengers in our voyage to Bombay. They were natives of India, and from them we learned that the ship, a very old one, had been bought by a native merchant in Bombay from an English firm, and chartered for the conveyance of pilgrims from the Persian Gulf to Jiddah. The men said she went to pieces the moment she touched the rocks, like a rotten shell. Though they were close to shore, there was no time to get a boat out, nor to make any effort to save the crowd of passengers. The thing—homicide is perhaps the fittest name for it—occurs frequently; and the difference between the drowning of Europeans and the drowning of Asiatics is graduated in the English newspapers just as it is in the ship-owner's mind. The destruction of six hundred Arabs is recorded in London in a single line of small print. If the original owner of the vessel had sent it to sea with half the number of his countrymen on board, with the same consequences, the largest prints, with an array of headings, would have signalized the natural result of his neglect. The parade of virtuous airs by ship-owners, who sell old vessels of this sort with the knowledge that they are to be engaged in the carrying-trade of Asia, while, for reasons which are obvious, they provide vessels for service at home which comply with reasonable demands for the assurance of safety, remind me of the old lady, widow of a Southern planter and owner of many slaves, who, professing a languid horror of slavery, said to an Abolitionist visitor, "I can not bear it; it goes against my conscience to keep slaves. *I* mean to *sell mine!*"

If an Arab of Bahrein or Muscat should produce a bag containing the smallest "seed pearls," and offer, in consideration of a hundred rupees, that a handful may be taken, my advice to any one receiving such a proposal would be, "Don't." There are no men in the world, not even the jewelers upon the Ponte Vecchio at Florence, who know the value of pearls better than these Oriental merchants. But they are not much seen at Bushire, which is engaged with the import of British manufactures and the export of Persian produce; the former consisting chiefly of cotton-piece goods, and the latter of raw cotton, wool, corn, opium, almonds, and raisins. The world, I think, can not furnish another example of a trade carried on under circumstances as deplorable as those which indisputably exist at Bushire. There is no security for the safe-conduct of commerce. The political resident has lately reported that "the district of Bushire, in common with all Southern Persia, has been infested with bands of robbers, whom the local authorities have proved wholly unable to repress." But this is only a part of the insecurity which extends to all the relations of Government. Take another remark by Colonel Ross: "The Government collects the land revenue, paying a fixed sum to the Central Government," which means that no inhabitant of the region is secure in his gains against the rapacity of the local Government. That Government is free to extort all that it can get, upon condition of making a certain annual payment at Teheran. The consequence is, that the entire province is kept in perpetual disorder by the demands of armed men, who plunder under the pretense of taxation, and who, by the peasantry, are scarcely preferred to robbers. Then with regard to customs. In describing a dinner party in Ispahan, I have mentioned the khan, to whom Colonel Ross alludes in his report to the Bombay Government, in which he states that "the Bushire customs were let to a person of Ispahan, in 1873, for 32,000 tomans, or rs. 1,28,000." A less civil but more correct mode of expressing the circumstances would be to say that a man with the reputation of an ex-brigand has amassed a fortune by purchasing from the Shah, for the above-mentioned sum, the power of extorting all that he can in any manner get, by way of customs, in or about the port or district of Bushire.

Imagine such a system of customs carried out by such "a person" under the following circumstances, for which the political resident may be quoted as the highest authority: "The farmer of customs employs his own servants to manage, Government officials not interfering. The transactions are kept secret, no returns being required by the Government." Colonel Ross, in language which I have already quoted, adds, "The system is felt to be inconvenient to traders." He is too able a man not to have experienced some difficulty in restraining his pen to such moderation in regard to a "system" which is indeed infamous — the repression of trade by the license of robbery.

To all this must be added the uncertain burden of export duties, which, in the article of raw cotton, "are so large as to prevent trade," and the difficulties of a road, nowhere good, which culminate in such places as the Kotul Maloo and the Kotul Dochter.

The trade, and I believe the population of Persia also, are declining. In transmitting to the Government of India the Trade Reports for the Persian Gulf and Muscat for the year 1874-'75, Colonel Ross states that "there has been a very marked falling-off in trade, as regards the Persian coast, during the year under report. At the port of Bushire the decrease is shown both in imports and exports, and amounts to an aggregate of over eighteen lacs of rupees. The decrease would have been still greater but for the removal of the prohibition on the export of grain and increased exportation of opium." The following shows the total value of the exports and imports from and into the port of Bushire for the years 1873 and 1874:

	1873.	1874.
IMPORTS—Total value	Rs. 39.85.820	Rs. 34.72.720
" Specie	6.17.405	1.25.000
	46.02.925	35.97.700

There is thus a decrease in the total value of imports, including specie, of more than ten lacs of rupees. The exports are:

	1873.	1874.
EXPORTS—Total value	Rs. 28.67.333	Rs. 26.45.775
" Specie	10.53.396	4.46.000
	39.20.729	30.91.775

The decrease in one year of the exports is thus shown to be considerably more than eight lacs of rupees. In this one year the demand of Persia for cotton goods of English manufacture declined in value to the extent of three lacs of rupees, while the value of her export of raw cotton declined only to the extent of one lac.

The two chief items in the port statistics of Bushire are the import of cotton goods and the export of opium. With regard to the former, although there has been the signal decline above referred to, it was the opinion of those most competent to judge that at the close of 1875 the market was overstocked, and that a further depression of trade was to be expected. With reference to opium, of which in 1874 there was exported from Bushire a quantity valued at more than fourteen and a half lacs of rupees (about two lacs more than the value of the export in the preceding year), an interesting report by Mr. Lucas, one of Colonel Ross's assistants at Bushire, has been presented to the Government of India, from which it appears that opium is cultivated principally in Yezd and Ispahan, and partly in the districts of Khorassan, Kerman, Fars, and Shuster. The opium grown in Yezd is considered to be of superior quality to that produced in Ispahan and elsewhere, owing to the climate and soil being better adapted for the production of the drug. But in the district of Yezd there can not be any considerable increase in the area devoted to the growth of poppies, owing to the utter insufficiency of the water supply. In the province of Ispahan water is more easily attainable, and there an increase in the production of opium would seem possible. Mr. Lucas appears to have made the discovery that the terrible famine which afflicted Persia in 1870-'71 was due, in no small degree, to the withdrawal of land from the production of cereals, owing to the temptation which the far greater profits of opium held out to the cultivators. He says that, a few years ago, the profits of the opium-trade having attracted the attention of Persians, almost all available or suitable ground in Yezd, Ispahan, and elsewhere was utilized for the cultivation of opium, to the exclusion of all cereals and other produce. It was then supposed by some that the cultivation of opium would be indefinitely extended in Persia. But the attempt of the natives to enrich themselves by cultivation and growth of a profitable article of trade, and their neglect to provide the necessaries of life, combined with drought and other circumstances, resulted in the famine. The costly experience thus gained has made the Persians more prudent; and although the cultivation has improved, and the yield from the same area has been greater, the export in 1874 was less by 600 cases than in 1869-'70.

The crop is harvested in May and June, manufactured and exported in the winter. Of the 2002 cases exported in 1874, nearly three-fourths were shipped for Hong-Kong, and the remaining 583 cases for London. In order to avoid the duty levied at British Indian ports, the opium intended for China is carried from the Persian Gulf to Suez, where it is transhipped into vessels of the Peninsular and Oriental Company. The Persian opium is, however, said to be not much liked in China, owing to its having a peculiar flavor, caused by the mixture of a large quantity of oil during the process of preparation, and also because it is not always free from adulterating matter. It is in greater favor with the wholesale druggists of London, inasmuch as it contains, on an average, a larger quantity of morphia than the opium produced in India.

Bushire (which is sometimes spelled Abushehr and Bushahr) is a collection of mud hovels, no better and no worse than other towns in Persia. The population is a mixture of Persians, Arabs, Indians, and Armenians. The rupee is current coin at Bushire. I have no doubt that the British expedition in 1857 did much to familiarize the people of the gulf with the coinage of India. But of that war in which Outram and Havelock were engaged, no traces are visible at Bushire. That it was ended by a satisfactory submission on the part of Persia, and that those gallant leaders were thus released from one of the most ineffective wars our country has ever waged, in time to give their aid and that of their forces in suppressing the Sepoy mutiny, was most fortunate.

If another difficulty should arise, Indian officers will know more about Persia than they did in 1857. They will understand that before any one of the great cities of Persia can be reached, there are for an army terrible obstacles to be surmounted in the mountainous paths, and in the extreme severity of the winter. Nothing that our expedition accomplished was calculated to strike the Persians with terror. The people of Tcheran, of Ispahan, and of Shiraz know little, and care little, for the towns of Mohammerah and Bushire, to which, together with the island of Karrack, our occupation was limited. The force tried the road to Shiraz, but found it inaccessible; and, in the small advance that was made, the sufferings of the troops from cold was very severe. We may some day be forced to occupy the province of Fars; but that is a policy which England does well, by all the means in her power, to avoid. It implies the abandonment of all that is most valuable in Persia to Russia, whether Russia annexes North Persia or not. Even now the manufactures of Russia compete with us, and successfully, as far south as Shiraz. A prolonged hostile occupation of Bushire and the coast by the British would make Ispahan wholly Russian; and the rich provinces upon the Caspian, including Tabriz, the most populous town in Persia, would be virtually, or in fact, part of the Russian Empire.

The occupation of Persia is for the Tsar a very much more easy matter than for the Empress of India. The year 1857 was well chosen for us to be at war with Persia, the year after the Treaty of Paris had been forced upon the young Tsar, who loves and longed for peace. Even then we might not have continued it with impunity; and such an occasion is not likely to recur. The Shah's power exists by favor of England and Russia; but the authority of England in Persia is probably inferior to that of Russia, because Russia is absolute in the Caspian, and thus, with a secure base of operations by land and water, can overrun Persia by passing her armies through the Caucasus, or down the Caspian, without fear of molestation. Though we met with no physical trace of the war of 1857, we heard an incident which is very characteristic of the Persian army. After the loss by the Persians of Mohammerah in that war, the officers of the Khelij regiment, which was thought to have behaved badly, were punished by having rings passed through their noses in the Shah's camp near Teheran; to these rings cords were attached, and the unhappy men, harnessed in this fashion, were then driven in disgrace through the lines. It was said that Prince Khunler, who was in command, especially deserved punishment; but that as he was able to pay a douceur of fifteen thousand tomans, he received, instead of disgrace, a sword and dress of honor.

The true interests of England in Persia are easily appreciated. It is our interest to promote reform in the Shah's Government, and to improve his army, in order to secure better government in Persia, which is impossible without a sufficient and well-trained military force. The Persian army would be a respectable force if it were well drilled, and led by men of competent education, sufficiently well paid to be removed from the paltry temptations which are now enough to lead Persian officers from the line of duty. As a rule, they are scandalously ignorant, greedy of bribes, vicious, and cruelly oppressive. Our interest in Persia is synonymous with that of the Persians. The present condition of Persia, fast becoming worse, invites foreign occupation. It is our interest that Persia should stand; prospering, improving, and independent; and to this end there are needed great intelligence and activity, together with the most complete knowledge of the policy of England, of India, and of Russia which it is possible to obtain, in the person of the minister accredited by the English Government to the Shah. This indispensable provision has not been duly regarded by the Foreign Office; and until it has been made, the first and most necessary step toward the promotion of British interests in Persia will not have been accomplished.

England has, however, planted in the Indo-European Telegraph an "institution" in Persia, which, though it adds nothing to her strength in the country, and does not in any degree fortify her position as against Russia, is a monument of her power and an emblem of her civilization. The Persian system of government must, indeed, be execrable, when we find that it has not benefited by this great addition to the power and resources of a wise administration. Nothing but the inherent badness of that Government could have led to this failure. The decline of Persia has not in any perceptible degree been arrested by this annihilation of space in the service of the Government, in a country where space is a chief obstacle to good government. I have often thought, when following these wires across salt deserts, where there was no sign of life, and in the mountains, where the iron cords were sometimes strained almost to breaking by the weight of frozen snow, that under the rule of the Marquis of Salisbury the government of an empire, compared with which that of Persia is insignificant, was passing there; and thus I have been led to reflect what a blessing it might prove to that most miserable land if conquest were to secure peace and order, and give to Persia, with those most precious gifts, the scientific discoveries of Europe.

CHAPTER XXVII.

The Province of Fars. — Memorandum by Colonel Ross. — Boundaries of Fars. — Government of Fars. — Six First-class Governments. — The Districts of Bushire. — Karagash River. — Eeliats. — Nomad Tribes of Fars. — Numbers of the Tribes. — Eel-Khanee and Eel-Begee. — Chief Routes in Fars. — Taxation and Revenue. — A Revenue Survey.

ENGLAND is more interested in the province of Fars than in any other part of Persia; and in a memorandum by Colonel Ross, lately communicated to the Government of Bombay, I have found so much valuable information upon the affairs of that province, which includes an area of not less than sixty thousand square miles, that I propose in this chapter to give the facts almost in the words of the political resident. Fars includes the whole of Southern Persia proper, Lar being considered one of its subordinate governments. On the Persian Gulf, Fars includes the sea-board belonging to Persia, from 50° to 58° east longitude — from Bunder Dilam to the boundary beyond Cape Jashk. The northern limit of Fars, identical with the jurisdiction of the Shiraz Government, I have mentioned in an earlier chapter, in describing our brief stay at the caravanserai of Ahminabad, which is certainly the most northerly house in Fars, between the thirty-first and thirty-second parallels of north latitude.

On the west, Fars is bounded by Khuzistan and Luristan; on the north-east, the district of Aberkah lies between Fars and Yezd, belonging to neither at present, and from the north-east comes to a point at no great distance north of Bunder Abbas; the frontier of Fars is identical with that of the Persian province of Kirman. The districts of Bunder Abbas lie in the strip between the gulf and Kirman and Bashkard, and are included in Fars in a political rather than a geographical sense.

The marked contrast of climate which I have shown as existing between that of the uplands from Ahminabad to Daliki, as compared with the region which we crossed in riding from Daliki to Bushire, has given rise to a division of Fars into the "Garmsir," or hot districts, and the "Sardsir," or cool districts; the former being the lowlands, and the latter the highlands.

Colonel Ross states that a great part of the province of Fars is still, as regards Europeans, *terra incognita;* and he adds that even the courses of the most important streams are matter of conjecture. Very much has been added to our knowledge of "Eastern Persia" by the work of Major St. John, R.E., in connection with the Boundary Commission, recently published by the authority of the Indian Government.

The Governor-general of Fars, who is also Governor of Shiraz, and whose seat of government is in that city, reigns in the name of the Shah over this extensive and important province. He is assisted by the Mushir, to whom I alluded as the builder of the excellent bridge over the Daliki River, at the foot of the Kotul Maloo, and the improver of the Kotul Dochter. The Mushir (whose full title is "Mushir-el-Mulk") is the person most feared in the province; but this does not appear to exempt him from the ordinary vexations of Persia; for a caravan conveying goods on his private account from Bushire was not long since pillaged near the Kotul Dochter.

For administrative and fiscal purposes, there are in Fars six subordinate governments of the first class, under subgovernors, who are responsible for the revenues and management of their districts. Of these we have met with one in the person of Mirza Réza Khan, Governor of Abadeh, whose letter to myself has been printed in an earlier chapter. Besides the divisions of the first class, there are considerable districts not administered by these six governments. The outlying districts are usually managed by a "head-man," directly responsible to the Government in Shiraz.

The six subordinate divisions of Fars are: 1. Bebehan; 2. Bushire; 3. Lar and Salia; 4. Bunder Abbas; 5. Darale; 6. Abadeh and Iklid, each of which is subdivided.

The district of Bebehan is ruled by the Ihtisham-el-Dowleh, Sultan Awiss Mirza, son of Ferhad Mirza, Motemid-el-Dowleh. The revenues of this Government are, in part, obtained from chiefs of Eeliat tribes. The political resident states that Bebehan is little known to Europeans, and he thinks the routes to Shiraz and Kazeroon require further surveying.

His Highness the Sipah Salar (commander-in-chief), who is really Sadr Azem (prime minister), gave us a vizierial letter to Houssein Kuli Khan, entitled Saad-ul-Mulk, the Governor of Bushire. But his excellency was out tax-gathering with a considerable force, and consequently we had not the honor of meeting with him. Formerly Bushire and the adjacent district were administered by a governor directly responsible to the Imperial Government in Teheran. The present governor is the subordinate of the Governor of Shiraz.

The Bushire districts are dependent almost entirely upon the rain-fall for the watering of their crops. The rivers of Khisht and Daliki, skirting the district of Dashtistan, unite and flow into the Rabillah Creek, some miles north of the town of Bushire. The lower part of Dashtee (a subdistrict of Bushire) is traversed by a river which flows into the creek called Khor Ziaret. It is supposed that this is the stream which, farther up the country, is known as the Karagash (the ancient Silakus), which Colonel Ross says is believed to rise near Shahpur, and to flow round to the eastward of Firozabad. He continues: "The Khor Ziaret can be entered by vessels of not exceeding six feet draught, and is navigable for such craft for some miles. I recently proceeded up the creek for about twelve miles, and the information elicited from the inhabitants of the district tended to confirm the conjecture that here is the embouchure of the Karagash River. It would be an interesting and useful undertaking to march up this river as far as possible."

We visited Lingah, in the Lar districts, on our way down the Persian Gulf. These districts, says Colonel Ross, "are little known to Europeans, and the geographical position of the town of Lar but vaguely known." We also landed in the districts of Bunder Abbas, to which we have made a reference in the notes of our passage from Bushire. In the Government of Darab, which we nowhere traversed, there are some interesting ruins, and Colonel Ross states that "iron mines exist in this part of Persia." In the sixth district—the Government of Abadeh and Iklid—we staid, in our ride between Ispahan and Shiraz, both at the chief town and at Zurmak, in the same district.

A very interesting portion of Colonel Ross's memorandum is that which relates to "The Eeliat or Nomad Tribes of Fars," races to which I have already made more than one allusion. He says:

"Some of the Eeliat tribes found in Bebehan have already been mentioned, and it was stated that they are Looree tribes. In other parts of Fars, the Eels are 'Toorks' and 'Arabs.' These pastoral people roam with their flocks from one pasturage to another, according to the seasons. In the winter they frequent the comparatively low lands; and when the increasing power of the sun commences to scorch the grass, they move off to the cooler uplands. The winter encampments are termed 'kishlak,' and the cool summer quarters 'zelak.' Each tribe usually frequents the same tract year after year. In the early part of summer, the Eeliats are on the move with their flocks, and robberies are then frequent. It is necessarily difficult to form any estimate of the number of those tribes, but they form an important part of the population of Fars, and contribute some twelve to fifteen thousand pounds of revenue yearly.

"The Eeliat population has greatly diminished of late years, as during the last famine many perished, with a large proportion of their cattle and flocks; others have of late abandoned the nomadic life, and become members of the settled population; and this has been particularly the case with the once noted 'Feelee' tribe.

"Of all the Eeliats of Fars, the Kashkaee are most numerous; and although the number has greatly diminished since the famine, they muster about eight thousand houses. This tribe have been great breeders of horses, but at present comparatively few are reared among them. The families (*teerah*) of Kashkaee are Ader-Ban, Chardeh, Chireek, and Lashnee.

"The Arab Eels have about three thousand houses (or rather tents), and roam from their kishlaks in Salia to the summer pastures, or zelak, in Bowânât. They claim descent from the Benu Sharban tribe of Arabia.

"The Basseree tribe, numbering about one thousand houses, are found in Mervdasht, Sirhadd-i-charhardongah, and Servistan.

"The Baharloo tribe, of about one thousand tents, inhabit Darab; others are the Arayâloo, the 'Napar' and 'Abu'lwardee,' the 'Tewalallee' and 'Amlah Shâhee;' the 'Mammasennee,' of about one thousand houses, inhabit Shoolistân.

"The following tribes are nearly extinct as nomads, having mostly settled in towns: 'Feelee,' 'Bujat,' 'Berkushadee.'

"The Eeliats are for the most part governed immediately by chiefs of their own, who are appointed by the Government of Persia, and held responsible for collection of revenue and the conduct of the tribes.

"The Kashkaee tribes have at their head an Eel-Khanee

and Eel-Begee. The former is the higher title, and the nominal Eel-Khanee now is the Sooltam Mohammed Khan; but as matters are, this personage's office is practically in abeyance, and is administered by a Persian officer, Nowzer Mirza.

"The present Eel-Begee is Dârâh Khan, brother of Sohrâh Khan, who was put to death by the Persian Government at Shiraz. The residence of the Eel-Khanee of Kashkaee has till lately been Firozabad, where the late Eel-Khanee, Mohammed Khoolee Khan, commenced to build a pretty villa, somewhat in European style."

It will also be interesting to quote what the political resident has to say in the current year as to the routes in the province of Fars:

"The chief caravan road traversing Fars is that which leads from Bushire to Shiraz by Kazeroon, and from Shiraz northward toward Ispahan.

"Another route from Bushire to Shiraz passes through Firozabad. This road is somewhat longer, but, from the gradients being greater, is considered more capable of being made practicable for wheeled conveyances or artillery. At present this road is not used as regards the sea-port traffic.

* * * * * * *

"The roads to the summer haunts of the Eeliats in the north-west of Fars, where the great mountain, Koh-i-Dana, or Koh-i-Pádána, rises to a height (according to Major St. John) of about seventeen or eighteen thousand feet, have, it is thought, never been explored by British travelers, though these districts are interesting enough to repay the toil of a journey through them.

"More accurate topographical information regarding the various districts of Fars (as of other provinces), and the roads traversing them, would be of great advantage to the Persian Government. In fact, the acquirement of such knowledge would evidently be one of the first steps, and an indispensable condition, to any real reform of the fiscal system and administration of the country generally. There are at the present extensive tracts and districts, the extent, capacity, and even position of which are but vaguely known at the seat of Government.

"Information regarding the resources of many districts is necessarily derived by the Government of the country from interested persons.

"In some cases—it is said that in one case, out of ten thousand pounds actually realized from a district—about two thousand pounds goes to the Government, and the remainder into the private purse of the official who farms the place. The Persian Government very frequently puts the leases up for sale to the highest bidder; and this system, though a partial safeguard against such extreme cases, has many unsatisfactory results. Be it remarked that it matters nothing to the peasantry what the assessment may be, as in any case they are taxed to the utmost. But the question is one immediately affecting the resources of the Government, and indirectly the whole well-being of the State.

"It would be difficult to suggest a measure calculated to have a more beneficial result to Persia than a well and honestly conducted revenue survey. There is reason to believe that the more enlightened of the Persian ministers are alive to these considerations, and disposed to adopt this measure; but so many are interested in perpetuating existing ignorance, that the scheme would have many powerful opposers. If adopted, however, not only would result a knowledge and increase of her resources to Persia, but justly and properly fixed assessments would tend to check the system of dishonesty and fraud, which, commencing at the sources, as at present, taints the whole stream of official life in Persia."

CHAPTER XXVIII.

British India Steam Navigation Company.—Crew of the *Euphrates*.—Pilgrims in Difficulty.—Streets of Bushire.—German Archæological Expedition.—Sermons in Bricks.—Leaving Bushire.—Slavery in the Persian Gulf.—Fugitive-slave Circulars.—The Parsee Engineer's Evidence.—Ships searched for Slaves.—Pearl-fisheries of Bahrein.—Anglo-Turkish Ideas.—Lingah in Laristan.—Bunder-Abbas.—Landing at Cape Jahsk.—"Pegs" and Pale Clerks.—A Master Mariner's Grievance.—The End of Persia.—Coast of Beloochistan.—Shooting Sleeping Turtles.—Harbor of Kurrachee.—Kurrachee Boat-wallahs.—The Orthodox Scinde Hat.—Faults of Indian Society.—English Ladies in India.—Intercourse with Natives.—Unmannerly Englishmen.—Exceptional Behavior.

A CHEERY, bright-eyed, broad-shouldered man, some way on the younger side of thirty, who could laugh louder than any, and beat most of us at a game upon the Residency billiard-table, was Captain George Stevenson, of the British India Company's steamship *Euphrates*, which on her arrival from Bussorah had cast anchor about three miles from Bushire. A vessel drawing seventeen feet of water can not with safety get much nearer. Captain Stevenson's gig had been pulled ashore by six Indian sailors—the crew of the *Euphrates* did not include a single European—neatly dressed in blue, and with blue caps surrounded with a scarlet turban. Another steamer had been lying for two days before the Residency under rather peculiar circumstances. She was loaded with pilgrims, who had received tickets for Bussorah; but the ship was chartered only to Bushire, and the captain professed to be ignorant that the pilgrims had shipped for the more distant port. The political resident was informed that the pilgrims would not allow the captain to come on shore in order to explain his difficulty; they held him, in terror for his life, a hostage and surety for the performance of the contract which had been made with them; and for my own part I was delighted to see Colonel Ross firmly on the side of the pilgrims. He sent off the assistant secretary to communicate to the captain his opinion, which was that he (the captain) would do well to fulfill the engagement declared upon the tickets, and carry the pilgrims on to Bussorah. It was, I think, owing to the praiseworthy firmness of the political resident that the British flag did not become, in the eyes of these two hundred Persians, a deception and a snare, and that they were not landed, many of them without food or money, upon a shore of which they knew nothing, and where they had no means of communication with their homes. Worse, indeed, might have happened; and in a fight between the pilgrims and the British officers of the vessel, the justly exasperated Moslems would probably have succeeded in making the ship their own at a terrible cost of life. We were all very glad to see the vessel steaming quietly around toward Bussorah.

After rain, the narrow streets of Bushire are in many places, sometimes from wall to wall, covered with green pools of stagnant filth, through which one may pass dry-shod on bricks or blocks, which have long been used as stepping-stones across these shallow cess-pools. These filthy places might be filled up by a hundred men in one day's labor; but throughout Persia there is no regard whatever for sanitary considerations. He will not fail to prefer the work of nature to that of man, who, after gazing over the blue waters of the gulf, plunges into the labyrinth of mud-walls and noisome passages, through the squalid bazaar, among the mud hovels of Bushire to the other side of the narrow peninsula on which the town stands. But when the horrors of this middle passage are overpassed, the view is even more beautiful than that from the front of the Residency, including the sweep of the sandy Mashillah, and the snowy highlands of Persia.

About four miles from Bushire, a scientific expedition, directed by Dr. Andreas, an Armenian, and carried on at the cost of the Berlin Government, has been for some time engaged in excavating a mound which evidently inclosed the ruins of an ancient temple. That the mound contained matter of interest appeared probable to some officers of the Indian navy, who examined it at the time of the British Military Expedition in 1856-'57. Architecturally, Dr. Andreas's discoveries do not appear to have been very significant. From the ruins he has unearthed, it seems that the building over which the mound had formed was used as a "fire-temple;" but the material of the walls included bricks which can be made to speak—bricks having one of the sides covered with cuneiform inscriptions. These bricks evidently formed part of some older work, from which they had been carried, and then built into this structure near Bushire. I have seen several of these bricks; they are rather longer than the common brick, and very hard; the cuneiform letters are raised on one side, and have endured twenty-five hundred years' wear and tear with surprising steadfastness. We had the pleasure of meeting Dr. Andreas and his colleague at the Residency before we embarked for Bombay. But in quitting Bushire, we were not to leave Persia. We had nearly six hundred miles to travel down the gulf, before passing the boundary which separates Persia from Beloochistan at the little promontory of Gwadur.

There is nothing in nature more delicious than the spring sunshine of southern latitudes; than the exhilarating air of such a morning as that on which Captain Stevenson took us off to the *Euphrates* in his gig, pulled by six Suratees of his crew. The first of those ill-advised slave circulars which the Government issued—and withdrew, from the storm of anger they evoked—had just reached us, and formed the subject of much talk. It was well known that the supposed difficulties of naval commanders in the Persian Gulf had been the cause of this movement. It was believed in the gulf that Sir Lewis Pelly was, more than any one else, responsible as the adviser of the Government in this unfortunate business. He had been political resident at Bushire, and had found, as all resident officers in such places must discover, that the real difficulty in the matter rests with officers on shore rather than with naval commanders. At Bushire, a considerable portion of the population is held in slavery; it is considered by those well acquainted with the facts that the proportion of slaves increases in descending the gulf. But I could find no one who wished for more definite instructions. The agent for the British India Company's line of steamers trading from Baghdad and Bussorah, through the whole length and breadth of the gulf, to Kurrachee and Bombay, told me he had had in seven years but one case brought to his knowledge. One of his captains informed him, on this occasion, that he had two fugitive slaves on board his ship, and asked what was to be done with them. This occurred six years ago, and the agent wrote to the then political resident, referring the matter to him. He acted as political residents are generally disposed to act; that is, with a leaning toward the slave-owner's claim for the restoration of his "property." He did not write a reply (British officers do not like to commit themselves to slavery in black and white); he sent a verbal message to the agent to the effect that he might give up the slaves if he pleased; but the agent found the captain not at all disposed to take this view of his duty. Sailors are generally opposed to the notion of surrendering slaves to the ignominy of their former life, and to the cruelty which they well know the attempt to escape will bring upon them by way of punishment. He declared that he should take the fugitives to Bombay, and so he did.

We had to row three miles from the shore at Bushire to where the *Euphrates* lay at anchor, and to pass the resident's gun-boat, which is supposed to be specially concerned with the suppression of the slave-traffic, and the maintenance of general peace upon the waters of the gulf. The chief-engineer, a Parsee, joined us as a fellow-passenger. He had been four years on this particular service, and could speak English. He said that, during those years, ten or a dozen slaves had come on board the gun-boat. Sometimes they had swum off from the shore at night; some had "come on board with the coals;" others had been found hiding in the ship. In no case, he said, was there, on the part of the captain, or officers, or crew, any desire to send them ashore. If a slave swum off at night, the men on watch were always ready to give the poor wretch a hand on to the deck; and if a fugitive slave were discovered when the vessel was at sea, it was just the same—every body was ready to pass him on to Bombay, or to some place where he would be free and safe. But it generally happened, said the Parsee engineer, that the owner on shore discovered his loss, and at once suspected the British ship. If the owner came off by himself, and even if he were permitted to look through the vessel, the probability was, said the engineer, that he would not find his missing slave. The slave-owners, however, are generally wiser than this, and succeed in clothing their claims with the authority of the Queen of the United Kingdom and the Empress of India. Wherever it is possible, they resort to the political resident, acquaint him with their loss and their suspicions, and obtain from him a letter to the commander of the vessel, requesting that, if the fugitive slave be on board, he may be given up.

In most cases, the political resident being the superior officer, this of course amounts to an order; and the engineer said this was the plan so generally adopted that it might be said that it was only when the slaves came from "foreign ground," which he explained to mean any part of the coast upon which there was neither resident, nor agent, nor consul, that they were taken on, or passed on, to Bombay. The fact appears to be, that, owing to the leaning of the resident British officers to the ideas and interests of the slave-owners among whom they dwell, there is a very small chance of escape for a fugitive slave where the British crown is represented, and a very good chance wherever the British flag is flying at sea, out of sight and out of reach of any British authority on shore. I met with a captain of one of the British Indian Company's vessels, who had twice allowed his ship to be searched by slave-owners upon a requisition from the political resident at Muscat. A first-class engineer in the same employ, a Scotchman, who had served in the gulf for three years, told me that he had seen but one fugitive slave on board his ship. He found this man hidden in the screw-tunnel (the casing in which the rod connecting the screw with the engines is placed), and allowed him to work his passage as a coal-trimmer to Bombay.

Of the large number of slaves upon the shores of the gulf, both on the Persian and the Arabian side, it is certain that but very few attempt escape. All the severe and dangerous work of the pearl-fisheries is sustained by slaves, the result of these fisheries being, as I have said, estimated as worth four hundred thousand pounds a year. There is abundant evidence that the pearl-divers prefer to risk the perils of the water, which swarms with sharks, rather than be flogged on shore; and I am surprised, hearing of the lashings with wire whips, and of other tortures to which they are subject, it so rarely happens that one or two swim off to any ship displaying the British flag.

That the difficulty, such as it is, culminates in the Persian Gulf, must be admitted. The numerous sovereign tribes which hold and rule the shores of the gulf are restrained from hostilities and piracy by the influence of the resident officers of the British Indian Government, who believe that the maintenance of their authority would be much more difficult if they appeared to acquiesce in that which is regarded as the confiscation, for the advantage of the British, of Arab or Persian "property." Most people find it easier to adopt a local opinion than to maintain the ideas of the higher society in which they have lived. I met lately with an account of "harem life in Turkey," written by an Englishwoman, who had lived as governess for six years in the house of a great pasha upon the Bosphorus. She appeared to see no degradation of her sex in the ceremonious "dinner-party," in which the pasha sat, surrounded with his three wives and their children, together with the children of his slave wives. These last performed the offices of the table; and, though not thought worthy to sit with their own children, were privileged to wait upon them. As to the pasha's property in his slaves, she appeared to think it quite right that the eunuchs should look closely after them, because it must be remembered that, in any attempt to get away, they were not only leaving a kind master, but were "thieving themselves," a feat which seemed, in her eyes, to be an act of most atrocious wickedness. With regard to the fugitive-slave question, which is for the present relegated to its former condition by the substitution of a colorless and indefinite circular, the result of my inquiries in the Persian Gulf was, that I could find no one who desired more precise instructions; and it appeared, from the evidence I could obtain, that a fugitive slave is rarely met with, and that when seen, his chances of escape are excellent, provided the British crown is not represented on the land from whence he has taken flight.

After staying a few hours before Lingah, in the province of Laristan, we steamed on to Bunder-Abbas (landing-place of Shah Abbas), the principal place of entry—for it is not a port—in the Persian province of Kirman. We had been two days at sea, and were glad to land upon the shelly beach at Bunder-Abbas. But the people, black and yellow, pressed upon us, in their eagerness to see an Englishwoman, and our progress in the squalid town and bazaar was slower than we desired. Many of the women bore upon their faces, by way of covering, a half-mask of stiffened cotton upon a bamboo frame, finished with a metal ornament upon the nose, and supported upon the face by a string passing over the head. The town looked like a sore upon the beauteous landscape. To have wandered on the shore strewed with pink shells, or inland among the palm-trees in sight of the mountains, would have been delightful. But the people of Bunder-Abbas would allow us neither pleasure. Where we walked they followed, laughing, screaming, "larking"—as English street-boys would say. If we stopped to pick up a shell, twenty hands were indiscriminately filled with shells, and the contents pressed upon us.

This is the "Gumberoon" of "Lalla Rookh;" and over the waters of the gulf we could see the pale coasts of the Island of Ormus, the commencement, now neglected, of our Indian Empire. Probably the most ancient traces of European occupation are to be found in this island, which was once the emporium of Portuguese, and subsequently of British commerce. Sailing up the coasts of India, this was the first detached land—the first spot in which those who were secure of the sea, but not of the land, could establish themselves with safety. Ormus is now the home of a mixed but very scanty population, engaged for the most part in fishery—catching sharks for the sake of trading in their fins and bones, and edible fish for sale along the coast. We had lovely weather in the Straits of Ormus, and anchored in smooth water under Cape Jahsk, where we soon obtained a number of beautiful shells. On the flat and feverish land of Jahsk there is a large station of the Indo-Persian Telegraph, inhabited by half a dozen young Englishmen, who are attracted by a salary which, to a youth, appears high, into a most unwholesome place, with little chance of promotion. The pale-faced lads whom we saw there assured us that in summer Jahsk was the hottest place in the world; and this is not far from its general reputation. We were touched by the sight of their faces; not bronzed with sunny health, as are those of many Anglo-Indians, but paler than those of Lombard Street clerks, who so very rarely see the sun. Most of the clerks at Jahsk were resolved to "give it up" at the end of their three years' engagement; but I suspect that when that time comes, and they have to face the alternative of recommencing life in England or India, they will settle into that state of acquiescence or chronic discontent, which, in those who survive, is so often the sequel to the first impressions of life in low latitudes.

Near the sand and rocks upon which we landed there was a village of bamboo huts, inhabited by the servants of the Telegraph staff; and about half a mile distant were the large, low buildings of the office, which included a billiard-room and comfortable quarters for the clerks. It was at Jahsk that I first heard of "pegging" as a familiar habit. Every one of the pale clerks whom I met with was full of kindness and hospitality, of which, however, his first notion seemed to be that I was in want of a "peg," upon which the peg-holder of the Anglo-Indian, the brandy-bottle, was produced. To see the thermometer at ninety degrees in the shade, and a pale youth—toward whom, as a fellow-countryman, in that far-distant island, one feels an indescribable tenderness—looking for support to a bottle of brandy, is a pitiful sight; and it is one which, even in the flying glimpses we had of Anglo-Indian life, appeared far too common.

A fresh wind was blowing, as we rounded Cape Jahsk, and

steamed out from the coast on to the broad bosom of the Indian Ocean. After dark, Captain Stevenson set out a grievance which certainly deserves, and I understand has since received, the attention of Government. He is one of a highly respectable class of British subjects who have obtained certificates as navigating officers from an Indian Board of Examiners. Possessed of a certificate as master from the Board in Bombay, he, and those in a similar position, are empowered to take charge of any vessel trading from or into any Indian port. If the Directors of the British India Company ask him to take charge of a homeward-bound ship, he can do so, and navigate her into the port of London or Liverpool, or to any port in or belonging to the United Kingdom. But there the validity of this certificate ends; and the commander, who is thought by uninsured owners trustworthy and competent for the navigation of their vessel into a British port, can not bring the same vessel out of port, unless he has been examined and has obtained a certificate in the United Kingdom. If he has this certificate his Indian diploma is worthless, because the British certificate is valid everywhere and the Indian certificate is not. Captain Stevenson had been placed in this position; he had been offered the command of a large steamship chartered for London; but he was obliged to decline the flattering proposal, because he would have to leave the port of London as a passenger only in the vessel which he was held competent to command on the homeward-bound voyage.

There seems, in these circumstances, to be a grievance demanding a remedy, which is surely simple and easy. Either the Indian boards are incompetent, or their certificates should be held valid throughout the dominions of the queen-empress. So far as I can learn from inquiry, I am led to believe that the Indian examiners at the chief ports of the three governments are highly competent, and that nothing but advantage would result from giving force to their certificates in the United Kingdom. Navigation demands education as well as experience, and charts are brought to such perfection that perhaps the more important work of the master of a ship is performed in his cabin. No well-trained captain finds difficulty along a surveyed and lighted coast which he sees for the first time; and if it be said that the man examined in London or Liverpool is likely to be better acquainted with the coasts of the British isles than one who seeks a certificate in Calcutta or Bombay, it is easy to reply that the candidate in London has perhaps the less valuable knowledge, for he is likely to find his danger upon the unlighted shores of Eastern Africa and Southern Asia, the rocks of which are probably known to the candidate in Bombay. I advised the preparation of a petition to Parliament, which I hope will now be needless.

Next day we approached the coast of Beloochistan, and, rounding the highland of Cape Gwadur, anchored before the town, where the shore is strewed with the bones of sharks, which are caught and killed for the value of their fins. The eastern boundary of Persia, as settled by Sir Frederick Goldsmid, and agreed to by the Shah, touches the sea at this point. The coast near the shore is generally flat and uncultivated—a sandy desert. We were there in the last days of February, and at that season there are, near the villages, a few patches of green, insignificant oases in the arid expanse. Beyond Gwadur we met with several large turtles asleep on the surface of the ocean; but though rifles were plentiful, and bullets whizzed about, we were not successful in securing the material for soup. Two bullets flew off from a turtle's back as though his shell had been the plates of an iron-clad. Twenty-four hours later, the projecting point of highland which marks the westernmost boundary of British India came in sight, and then a lower headland, over which we could see the topmasts of vessels in Kurrachee harbor.

What a change is marked in passing from the wretched shores of Persia, with no harbor in north or south, to the moorings at Kurrachee, surrounded by the most valuable results of the intelligent labor of Europe! The beacon in the white, English-looking light-house; the steam-dredges at work; the huge iron vessels, long and narrow, built for the Suez Canal, and locally known as "ditchers," are pouring out cargoes of railway iron for the Indus Railway; one steamship is coiling from the shore miles of telegraph-cable, for the repair of a disaster; another is steaming behind us with the mails from England. Order, activity, utility, nowhere seen by us for months past, appear here to be natural and constant. We are hardly at anchor before the *Euphrates* is boarded by a dozen boat-wallahs, merchants or peddlers, loaded with bundles of shawls from Cashmere, inlaid boxes and needle-work of Scinde, caps and trinkets of Kurrachee. They are proof against taunts and trouble. They will expose a hundred articles on the deck without promise of sale, and submit to the exposure of their petty knaveries with unruffled manner. New arrivals probably give a higher price for these goods than that for which the same articles could be purchased in Regent Street. It is easy to find a good carriage at the landing-stage, which is three or four miles from the town and cantonment of Kurrachee. We drove, in the first place, to the Travelers' Bungalow, intending to stay two nights on shore, but were repelled by the dirt of the place, by the sight of the nasty bedding, the grimy look of the heavy wooden furniture, and the general uncleanliness of the rooms.

The roads about Kurrachee are of unsurpassable excellence, wide (perhaps too wide for a tropical country, where the shade of the road-side is desired by all) and smooth, as well made as any in or out of London. This appears remarkable within a day's journey from the miserable tracks of

Beloochistan. One can never be more disposed to admit the material benefits which the English rule has conferred upon India than in passing quickly, as we did, from the countries of the Persian Gulf. From the landing-place to the cantonment of Kurrachee the ground is low and flat; from the waters of the harbor the roof of the Frere Hall, four or five miles distant, can be seen high above the surrounding houses. When we visited the hall, there were sixteen natives doing the work of two Europeans in waxing and polishing the floor preparatory to a ball, which was to take place in the evening. The narrow streets of the native town are full of interest. The costumes are mostly white: it is in their head-dress that the people of India are most fantastic, and perhaps they are nowhere more so than in Scinde. The orthodox Scinde hat, which is like an Englishman's hat inverted—the wide, straight brim being at the top, the head fitting into the brimless cylinder—is one of the most curious; but scarlet is the prevailing color in turbans.

The peculiar faults of Indian society had never occurred to me before I landed at Kurrachee: the weariness of a society in which the aims and hopes of all have one goal; in which all bear the same stamp of officialism; in which that very valuable element in society, the leisure class, which asks for nothing, and which has such a refining influence upon the views and sentiments of the employed classes, is conspicuously absent. I can fancy that in the Australian colonies there is already the nucleus of an established class, which is not engaged in money-making, nor in pushing its way to offices of the State, and which does not consider a return to England, loaded with accumulations of years of exile, to be the grandest hope of life. But it is quite certain that there is no such class in India. There is an intelligent, active, moving class, all, it may be said, of one rank and sort, in their origin from the great middle class of English people, existing in an unnatural manner, and dominated by two prepossessions—the hope of promotion on the line to which all belong, and the hope of return to the British islands, from which all have set out.

Even in such a hasty passing glance as we had at Indian life, it is easy to see that these men are part of the very flower of our nation, some of the best men of their time. But no men can be impervious to the influences which surround their every-day existence for the best part of their lives, and in Indian society there is not sufficient diversity to render it agreeable. It is the same with the women as with the men; but in their case, the faults of Indian society, due to its circumstances, are more marked, and even more perceptible. Robbed by the climate of their children; overcharged to the lips with the gabble of the station or cantonment; with a nice knowledge of the relative advantages of civil and military, covenanted and uncovenanted, service; their feminine hopes and delights and triumphs are all upon the same line—success in the ball-room, promotion for their masculine friends, the opening of a "Europe box," and a house in Kensington as the full and final reward of life.

Practically, there is no admixture of the ruling with the subject population. The Government of India is, in the main, just and liberal; occasionally, in its zeal, it attempts an impossible combination of despotic and constitutional forms. The younger officers are sometimes guilty of gross rudeness to natives of the higher classes, and of harsh treatment to the lower-class natives in their service. This injurious and detestable conduct is, as a rule, abandoned in the moment when an officer rises high enough, or becomes by accident so conspicuous as to be subject to public opinion at home. The great value of the influence of English opinion upon the Government of India is exhibited in the fact that the most responsible officials are invariably the most benign, considerate, and just in their dealings with the natives of India. Of the natives, many are now put high in place and authority, many are reputed friends of Englishmen. Yet if, as I believe, the few cases which have come under my observation are typical, this "friendship" is not friendship; it is nothing more than intercourse, regulated and sweetened by polite forms, of which none are greater masters than the high-class natives of India.

But if the intercourse of Indians with English must be that of a subject with a governing race, contumelious treatment of natives by Englishmen should be avoided, and, when possible, should be punished. During our stay at Kurrachee, I heard the particulars of a case which exhibited a gross instance of this misconduct. The Prince of Wales was then in India, and a native prince had chartered two British steamships for the conveyance of himself and suite to Bombay. Into the smaller vessel, his highness was accompanied by his ministers and personal attendants; the larger was destined for his escort, amounting to about two hundred armed men. When these last went on board, the English captain demanded the surrender of their arms, and he did this, as I was informed, in no very gracious manner. The men had not expected to be disarmed, and thought it implied degradation. To have explained fully and kindly to them that it was the necessary rule of the service, and applied to British as well as native troops, would have been easy and satisfactory. But the English captain not only offended the whole of the force by his manner in demanding their arms; he inflicted an unnecessary wound upon the commanding officer, a first-class passenger, in asking also for his sword. This was an outrage to which an English officer would not have been liable, and I was told by an eye-witness of the scene how pained he was to observe the emotion of the native officer in complying with this insulting demand. From all that one hears of the conduct of Englishmen in India, I most readily and gladly admit that behavior of this sort is exceptional.

CHAPTER XXIX.

Bombay.—The *Serapis* in Harbor.—Suburbs of Bombay.—Parsee Dead.—Towers of Silence.—Hindoo Cremation-ground.—Cotton Manufacture in India.—Report of Indian Commission.—Neglect of Indian Government.—A Bombay Cotton Factory.—Hours of Factory Labor.—Seven Weeks' Work.—Natives of India.—Expenditure of Indian Government.—The Great Absentee Landlord.—Grievance of Cultivators.—Their Enemies, the Money-lenders.—English and Native Equity.—The Suez Canal.—Landing at Ismailia.—English at the Pyramids.—Alexandria.—"Cleopatra's Needle."—Proposed Removal to England.—Condition of the Obelisk.—Recent Excavation.—Captain Methven's Plan.—Removal in an Iron Vessel.—Cost of Removal.—Egypt and the Khedive.—Preparing for Mr. Cave.—Sham Civilization.—The Horse-trampling Ceremony.—English *en voyage*.—Egypt and Persia.—Customs Officers at Alexandria.—Egypt and Turkey.

THE white *Serapis* and her iron-clad companions were lying at rest in the glistening waters of Bombay harbor when we entered upon that magnificent anchorage. Most people know the unimpressive aspect of the town from the harbor, with the salient angle of the Apollo Bunder, or wharf, for a centre-piece. But those who have never been in Bombay, who know that really handsome city only by pictures and photographs, will hardly believe how bad are the hotels, or how beautiful, on a March morning at sunrise, are the suburbs of Bombay. As to vehicles, there is novelty in the harnessed bullocks ambling through the streets; but the newest fashion of carriage, the tram-car, interested me more than all. A tram-car might be registered as one of the trade-marks of democracy. The tram-way will do great things in breaking down the barriers of caste among the natives, and of lordly prejudice on the part of Englishmen. To see the open benches of the Bombay tram-cars loaded with white-robed Parsees, with Hindoos, with Mussulmans, with one or two lightly clad Europeans; to see this equal representation of castes and classes in a carriage to which all are free to mount, with no distinction whatever—is a lesson in the ways of civilization. And there is no better plan of seeing the busy life and teeming population of the Hindoo quarter of Bombay than to ride through it upon the tram-way; but to see the suburbs of Bombay in their vernal beauty, drive in early morning to the Towers of Silence, where the dead of the Parsee community are exposed to the vultures. The road winds and undulates between gardens, in which plants such as in the temperate zone are regarded as the choicest and most splendid exotics, wave their grand foliage, and extend a most grateful shade, in the fullest luxuriance of tropical splendor.

There are villas belonging to the wealthy Parsees of Bombay as elegant in architecture, and as rich in their adornment, as any in the outskirts of London or Liverpool. Riding in this direction has another advantage. By a slight divergence, one may obtain practical experience for the guidance of choice in the disposition of the dead. With no great distance between them, there are the Towers of Silence, the Hindoo cremation-ground, and the European grave-yard. In the Parsee towers there is no exposure or exhibition of the dead, except to the vultures, which pounce upon the body. I asked a Parsee whether he did not shudder at the thought of such treatment of his own body after death. "Better than worms," he replied, pointing to the grave-yard.

But to unaccustomed eyes the sight of these winged destroyers, sitting expectant upon the topmost stone of the high towers, is most repulsive. When a corpse is brought in, the friends and mourners deliver the body to the guardians of the tower, by whom it is placed on a grating near the top, but entirely concealed from view. The remains of these bodies lie upon the grating until the whitened bones fall to the foot of the tower. One may almost tell by the action of the vultures when a body is being placed. There is a great flapping of wings, and a rising of the birds into view from their horrid feast, when the attendants of the tower mount to place the newly dead. While this is being done, the top of the tower is thickly surrounded with the foul birds, perched close together; and those who are a mile distant may know when the arrangement is ended, and the dead body left alone, by watching how the vultures flutter down and out of sight, to fasten on the corpse.

Europeans are not admitted to the walled inclosure in which the Hindoos of Bombay burn their dead. This cremation-ground is about a hundred yards long and thirty wide, bounded on one side by a high road. On the other side the soil of the adjoining grave-yard rises so high that, standing there, one can observe the processes of cremation. By the side of the wall next the road there is a long shed, in which the family and friends of the deceased range themselves. At one time I saw three bodies burning upon as many pyres. The attendants appeared to be very skillful in selecting and building up the fire-wood, with four strong timbers at the corners, of sufficient substance to hold the burning wood of the pyre together until the body is consumed and these sustaining posts are charred, and fall upon it in ashes. On the ground in front of the mourners' shed they build the pyres; the body is laid in a shroud upon wood, and covered with sufficient to insure complete destruction. The fires blaze away in the fierce sunlight, the attendants occasionally stepping forward to pull the logs together with a long staff, which each one carries in his hands; and in about two hours from the first cry of the mourners, when the body is first enveloped in flame, the pyre has crumbled into a deep bed of fiery ashes, which are scattered by the wind. I did not find that the operation was offensive; but, then, I was upon the windward side.

One of the most prominent and notable facts in Bombay is the increase and the character of the cotton manufacture. Familiar with that industry during my four years' residence in Lancashire as assistant commissioner, in the time of the Cotton Famine, I determined to look closely into the mode of conducting the manufacture without factory laws in Bombay; and, with that view, obtained permission to inspect one of the largest and best of the factories. I saw quite enough in one hour to convict the Government of India of culpable delay in regard to a subject which seems to me to call for immediate action.

A commission was appointed in 1875 to inquire into the application of the factory laws, as enforced in England, to India; and this commission reported in July of that year, the majority being hostile to any legislation. Yet the factory to which I am about to refer is, both in regard to the hours of infant labor and to construction, better than the average of those that must have come under the commissioners' notice. If gentlemen do not think that circumstances such as these betray neglect on the part of the Executive Government, it is not likely they will be converted by the under-secretary's promise of "further inquiries in Bromah and Surat." Judging from the conduct of these commissioners, and the tenor of this reply by Lord George Hamilton to a question put to him by Mr. Anderson in the House of Commons in February of the current year, the Indian Government appears to be playing into the hands of the party interested in opposing legislation, by adopting costly methods of delay and circumlocution.

The establishment I visited had about forty thousand

spindles, and, together with the loom-shed, employed about eight hundred people, including men, women, and children. The building was in no important respect dissimilar from the Lancashire factories, and the machinery, of Lancashire make, was of the best quality and construction. The hands were leaving the mill for their meagre midday rest of half an hour (the only rest they have in the whole of the working day), just as I was entering the counting-house. I had a very good opportunity for observing their physique. The path by which they passed me was so narrow that with my sun-umbrella I could have touched any one of them. Never have I seen such a wretched crowd of working-people—the men pale and haggard, the women and children drooping, and gray with cotton-dust. The men had been working continuously from a quarter-past 6 A.M. to 1 P.M., the time of my arrival; the women and children from 7 A.M. The hours of work are—for men, from a quarter-past 6 A.M. to a quarter past 6 P.M.; for women and children, from 7 A.M. to 5 P.M. They have only one half-hour for rest and food; and as I sat waiting for their return, the thirty minutes seemed very short.

At the door by my side, when they re-entered the mill, stood the superintendent, with a stick in his hand, "just," as he said, "to give a tap to them as comes late, for you must be master of 'em." The time was half-past one; and the little children, some of them not more than seven years old—exhausted with the previous six hours of continuous labor—were again at work in the terrible atmosphere of a Bombay factory for another three and a half hours. But this cruelty, involving, of course, the utter abandonment of education—a cruelty from which the British child is protected by law—is not the worst to which these Hindoo children are subjected. During a period of seven weeks, this factory had been closed only for three days. There is no observance of any regular day of rest; and for forty-six out of the forty-nine days preceding my visit, these children had toiled from 7 A.M. to 5 P.M. at their unhealthy and exhausting labor.

It is hardly necessary to state that on every floor of the mill the hands were exposed to many and great dangers from unprotected bands and wheels, and from insufficiently fenced shafting; these are the invariable features of factory labor without any official regulations. On the whole, I can not conceive a case more clear and simple; the Hindoo children are surely entitled to the same protection which the law has so long afforded to "young persons" in the United Kingdom.

With regard to the natives of India generally, I had of course, in a short stay at Kurrachee and Bombay, no opportunity of looking widely or deeply into their condition. But it appears that there is a strong disposition in the minds of leading men in the Government of India toward fair treatment, and even liberality, in official dealings with natives. There are, however, two grievances, both wide-spread, and both of the highest importance, which are heard of in every part of India, and which appear to baffle the wisest and most conscientious legislators.

"True," says the native subject of the Empress of India, "you have given us good government. You are mercilessly punctual and exacting in your demands, and the unfailing regularity and uniformity of these charges are, some say, almost perhaps as painful as would be the varying leniency and rapacity of native rulers. But, under your rule, that which we have, we possess in safety; where we lose, is in the fact that the expenditure of Government and of the governing body is not made in India, but in England." The complaint is, indeed, very much the same as that which comes with great force from Ireland. The crown of Great Britain, like a great absentee landlord, collects a vast rent-roll in India, which is expended in the savings of civil and military servants transmitted and retained in England—in their clothing, and in the many articles of food and luxury which are purchased in England. Even the trappings of state pageantry bear the mark of London. "In all this," say the natives, "we lose greatly. If we had native rulers, they would not be so invariably just, nor would peace and order be so secure; they perhaps would lavish money in fighting, and squander other sums in semi-barbaric display. But all their outlay would be with us, and among ourselves." It can not be denied that there is very much which is, to say the least, plausible in this line of argument.

For the other grievance the means of remedy or alleviation are less difficult. This relates to the land, and to the property of the cultivators. They borrow small sums at high rates of interest; they are ignorant; they are sometimes unfortunate; their simple agriculture is peculiarly at the mercy of the seasons. Principal and interest are added and re-added; the money-lenders are perhaps dishonest, and obtain acknowledgment of a document the real nature of the contents of which is unknown to the poor ignorant peasant. At last the debt, or alleged debt, with its quickly mounting interest, has become big enough to bear comparison with the value of the unhappy rayah's interest in the land, upon which the toil of his whole life has been bestowed. Then he is hurried by the money-lender before the English magistrate; the debt, or alleged debt, is proved. By what process this proof is accomplished the peasant is often profoundly ignorant. No account is taken of the circumstances; the inexorable logic of written evidence —the verdict of the British rule—is all against him; judgment is given, and in the end his little property is sold to the money-lender, who has from first to last made a very successful transaction. Meanwhile the peasant, with a heart full of bitterness, has gone to ruin, bearing with him, in his destitution, a miserable sense that he has been jostled out of his homestead with the sanction of an English judge.

The Englishman urges that, under native rule, things would be much the same. Men must pay their debts. "No," says the native, "it would not be so under native rule. Native justice is wilder, less terribly regular, less legal, but probably more equitable. The rayah, under native rule, would have a better chance against the money-lender." And in this conclusion the native objector is, no doubt, to some extent justified. Here, then, is one of the most difficult of legislative problems for the consideration of Indian legislators. Would it be judicious—we can not deny that it is possible—to give tenure which should be free from responsibility for debt—to give the cultivator something which the money-lender could not claim? Every man would like to be, if even to some extent only, invulnerable, so that in whichever direction "the slings and arrows of outrageous fortune" might fly, these could not wound him irreparably. Every one would like to have security against being stripped naked by creditors, and turned, helpless and shivering, upon the desert of utter and extreme poverty. Would not the end be, that the borrowing would continue with heightened rates of interest, and the rayah, under this coveted protection, would fall into poverty more extended and miserable than even he has yet known?

That which struck me most, in passing through the Suez Canal, is the seeming insignificance of the work. In some places, the water-surface is not more than ninety feet wide; and, standing upon the deck of a ship of three thousand tons burden, one must look almost perpendicularly over the vessel's side to see the water of the canal. We stuck fast for an hour in such a place, the head of our ship pressing upon one side, the stern upon the other, of the narrow channel. This, of course, involved a similar delay for the vessels which followed us. On gaining the inland waters of the wide expanse which is still called "the Bitter Lakes," ships are allowed to travel at full speed; and great efforts are made in order to obtain precedence in the succeeding narrows.

We landed at Ismailia, and proceeded by railway to Cairo, a town which resembles Algiers in that it is French in one part, and thoroughly Mussulman in another. A more or less accurate notion of the bright bazaars of Cairo is a common possession; and how the English go to the Pyramids, trotting through the dust upon sprightly donkeys, is well known.

At Alexandria I fulfilled a promise in writing the following letter to Lord Henry Lennox, then First Commissioner of Works, concerning the removal of "Cleopatra's Needle," a work which he had been urged to undertake:

"Hôtel Abbat, Alexandria, April 1st, 1876.

"Dear Lord Henry Lennox,—A long time has elapsed since our conversation in July last with reference to the removal of the obelisk commonly known as 'Cleopatra's Needle,' as proposed by General Sir James Alexander to the Metropolitan Board of Works. Detained in Persia by an attack of fever, and by unlooked-for difficulties in traveling, I have arrived in Egypt later by more than three months than I intended when I left England.

"The taking-away of the ancient monuments from a country which they were originally designed to adorn is a policy against which there is much to be said. It is almost pitiful to contemplate, upon the now carefully protected Acropolis of Athens, a Caryatid, rudely carved in wood, doing duty with her four lovely sisters of marble in bearing the entablature of the Erechtheum, while the original is in London, instructing the art-world, perhaps no better than would a plaster cast, in the beauty and grace of Greek sculpture. But these considerations do not apply, with any considerable force, to the prostrate obelisk now lying upon the shore of the new port of Alexandria. It forms no part of any structure; it is not protected, nor in any way cared for, by the Egyptians; and within fifty yards of the ground in which the 'English' column is lying, there is another, apparently of the same age and size, carved with hieroglyphics of similar character. It appears to me, therefore, that the English people could, if they please, appropriate this gift free from any fear or feeling that in doing so they would be 'spoiling the Egyptians.'

"The desirability of removing the obelisk resolves itself into two questions—the cost and the value and interest of the monument as compared with the necessary expenditure. There can be no doubt as to the feasibility of removal. An opinion has certainly prevailed in England that the obelisk is so much defaced and broken as to have lost all interest. But I will venture to say that this opinion has not been formed by any one who has seen the whole of three sides which have been exposed by the excavations recently made by Sir James Alexander. The opinion was formed when but very little more than the upper side of the base was visible—a valueless part which appears never to have been sculptured, and to have been intended for burial in the foundation when the obelisk was in position. The column, as at present exposed, is at once seen to be a monument of great value and interest, one which, not only from its antiquity, but also from its quality as a monolith, would be specially notable in London, which, unlike most of the capital cities of Europe, possesses no adornment of this character. The English people can not see in their own country a carved stone even approaching the dimensions of this colossal obelisk of red granite. As to the condition of the monument, I have examined three of the four sides, and there is no part of any one of the hieroglyphics the carving of which is not distinctly traceable. The edges of the carving are somewhat worn, and the angles of the obelisk rounded; but the interest of the monument is in no place substantially impaired, nor is there discernible any important fracture of the stone. The dimensions of the obelisk are: total length from extremity of base to apex, sixty-six feet; seven feet square at base, and four and a half feet square at base of apex. The weight is probably about two hundred and fifty tons.

"In considering the method and cost of removal to England, I have had the great advantage of the assistance, on the ground, of Captain Methven, the senior captain and commodore of the fleet of steamships belonging to the Peninsular and Oriental Company. The base of the obelisk is less than twenty yards from the waters of the Mediterranean; and within about a hundred yards there is a depth of two and a half fathoms of water. It has been suggested to float the obelisk by attaching to it a sufficient quantity of timber. But this is a very crude proposal, apart from the fact that no sufficient quantity of timber is obtainable in this almost treeless country. Undoubtedly it would be possible to remove and to ship the obelisk by constructing a railway on piles for such a distance as would admit of the approach of a vessel capable of carrying it securely to England. In this case, the obelisk would be suspended in slings from running-gear, and moved out to sea until it hung over its destined position in the vessel. But the shore is not the most suitable for this plan, which, moreover, would involve a very large expenditure.

"The position of the obelisk is favorable for the adoption of a third method, which appears both to Captain Methven and to myself to be the most easy, safe, and practicable, and, at the same time, the least costly, of any that have been suggested. The ground in which the obelisk now lies seems sufficiently firm (with proper supports at the sides of the necessary excavation) to sustain girders from which the column could be slung without any change in its position. To insure a proper distribution of the weight, it would be desirable that these girders should rest on iron plates, and that they should be of greater substance in the centre, where the weight of the obelisk would be borne. Captain Methven is confidently of opinion that the obelisk could be safely conveyed to England in an iron vessel not exceeding four hundred tons of builders' measurement, one hundred and twenty feet in length, and drawing, when loaded, not more than six feet of water. This decked iron vessel, or barge, would be constructed in England and sent in pieces to Alexandria, where it would be put together in the space to be excavated beneath the suspended obelisk, the channel necessary to get to deep water being at the same time formed by a steam-dredge, or, if the shore be rocky, by blasting—a method which has been very successfully adopted on a much larger scale than would be requisite here by the Peninsular and Oriental Company at Bombay. When the vessel was ready to receive the obelisk, the intervening walls of earth between the base of the stone and the sea would be thrown down, and the incoming water would raise the vessel to its burden. The iron barge could then be towed into the harbor, when it would be decked, and have so much freeboard added as appeared desirable. Captain Methven feels quite sure that by any competent steamship of her majesty's navy the vessel could be towed to England without danger of damage to the towing ship, or risk of losing the obelisk, regard being had to the season, and to the state of the barometer, on quitting this port and that of Gibraltar. Finally, I would say that Captain Methven seems to be of opinion that all this could be accomplished at a cost of about five thousand pounds. Yours, faithfully, ARTHUR ARNOLD.

"The Rt. Hon. Lord H. G. LENNOX, M. P."

In Egypt, we see Mohammedanism through a veneer of Parisian civilization. The Khedive, a Mussulman in *gants de Paris*, is in fact the *entrepreneur* of the country, concerning which his highness deals with the financiers of Europe. His personality as a ruler never appears to rise out of the business of entertaining, concessionizing, and loan-mongering, in which, to the outside world, his highness seems always to be engaged. Mr. Cave had just left Egypt when we arrived in the country; and during our railway journey between the two capitals, Cairo and Alexandria, an incident occurred, which I give for what it is worth, but which seemed to me to be very truly illustrative of the Government of Egypt. Certainly it displayed what Egyptians think practicable and probable in the way of government by ministers of the Khedive. A well-known banker of Alexandria, a European, was traveling in the same carriage with us, and, on the way, we had some conversation. At an unimportant station he was greeted by two men of the country, cultivators or corn-dealers of a superior class, Mohammedans, who at once engaged with him in earnest talk. On resuming the journey, I asked my fellow-traveler what had been the subject of discussion, so full, judging from the manner of those engaged, of interest and amusement.

"Oh!" he replied, "they were talking to me about Mr. Cave's report. They say that in anticipation of Mr. Cave's inquiry, the Khedive ordered the collection of a year and a half's taxes in one sum, and in advance, and that the amount was then set down as one year's payment, in order to deceive the British financier. And the worst of it is," he added, "the wretched fellahin expect that the tax-gatherers will come round all the same, and treat the payment, which was said to be for a year and a half, as an extraordinary affair—a sort of backshish for the Khedive."

In passing through Egypt, I looked with all the care I could command to find traces of that intelligent government which has been so often attributed in England to the Khedive. I compared what I observed with all that I have seen in Turkey and Persia; and though in this comparison there was a marked difference, with much advantage on the side of Egypt, I saw everywhere, in native hideousness, in the rural districts and in the towns, beneath the sham civilization of modern Egypt, the horrid features of slavery and its twin, polygamy, with the universal degradation which follows in the train of these institutions of Mohammedanism. The people of Egypt are far less civilized, less intelligent, incomparably more ignorant and cruel, than the most wretched of the Christian subjects of the Porte; and Egypt differs notably from European Turkey in the fact that the overwhelming majority of the people are Mussulmans. There are many in England who, in the devotion of their lives and language to horses, seem as much disposed to serve as to rule the four-footed animal; and that a horse can show itself superior to men is officially demonstrated at least once a year in Cairo, when the mounted Sheik-ul-Islam rides over the prostrate bodies of fanatics, or, as some say, of hirelings. The unwilling quadruped shoved forward by the hands of modern Egyptians, its brute nature revolting from a cruelty to men, while they, the bipeds, affect to regard the animal as the instrument of a miracle, is a spectacle the human degradation of which is perhaps deepened by the presence of cultivated Europeans as interested spectators. My impression is, that a good many English *en voyage* (and the French and Germans are very often no better) are attracted, rather than repelled, by disgusting exhibitions; and that if only a spurious halo of propriety were thrown over the scene by the name of religion, they would throng to observe circumcision, or human sacrifice, or even the culinary operations of cannibals. Yet as to the last I am perhaps wrong, for in that there would be an element of personal danger. It is then they shrink—it is then they show a surprising keenness of apprehension. "See how they run" when cholera has invaded their hotel, or the waves their steamboat. But they will stand, in seeming approval, while the people of the foreign country in which they are sojourners degrade and deface humanity; they will smile at the performance of horrid cruelties of which the law would take cognizance at home; they will flock to witness the performance of exercises associated with gross, and to them patent, superstitions; they will do all this, without a sign of disgust or disapproval.

From Persia, Egypt differs most obviously. Egypt proper is fertile, flat, and well watered by the Nile and its tributaries, and, above all, it is nearer to the civilization and to the highways of the commerce of Western Europe than are parts of that continent in the east of Russia. But in regard to the "poverty of the poor," or to their oppression in the name of the State, I doubt if there is much advantage on the side of the Egyptian. I was very much reminded of Persian officials when we were passing the ordeal—for it is an ordeal—of getting out of the port of Alexandria. While the Khedive's officer was examining our baggage, half a dozen porters and boatmen cried continually, "Give him something;" "Give him a rupee;" "Give him half a rupee;" "Give him a cup of coffee;" while the eyes of the customs officer twinkled with hope of the usual bribe. I have heard that a main obstacle to the success of Egyptian railways is the impossibility of preventing the officials from illicit trading in free passages, and I can well believe it. From the Khedive, who emulates the Padishah upon the Bosphorus, in multiplying his palaces at the cost of his miserable subjects and of deluded bondholders, to the murderous deeds of the semi-savages in his service upon the Nile, or in Abyssinia, or in Bulgaria, the Egyptian viceroyalty shows itself more prosperous, but not less marked with extravagance and excess, than the supreme and suzerain power in Constantinople.

CHAPTER XXX.

"From the Levant."—Sunnis and Shi'ahs.—Turkish Government and Turkish Debt.—Fuad and Midhat Pashas.—Not a "Sick Man."—"Best Police of the Bosphorus."—Religious Sanction for Decrees.—The Council of State.—"Qui est-ce qu'on trompe?"—Murad and Hamid.—Error of the West.—Precepts of the Cheri.—Authority of the Sultan.—Non-Mussulman Population.—Abd-ul-Hamid's Hatt.—A Foreign Garrison.—Hatt-y-houmayoun of 1856.—Failure of Promises.—Fetva of Sheik-ul-Islam.—Non-Mussulmans and the Army.—Firman of December, 1875.—Sir Henry Elliot and the Porte.—Conscription in Turkey.

A SERIES of letters,* published in 1868, contained our impressions of travel in Greece and in European Turkey. We then visited Thessaly, Roumelia, Constantinople and the Bosphorus, Bulgaria, Roumania, Belgrade, and Croatia. I have no intention of retracing this ground on paper, and my present reference to the affairs of Turkey will only be such as is necessary to exhibit the connection which exists between the Government of the Sultan and the Mohammedan religion.

I propose to devote the remaining space in this volume to a survey of the general condition of the Mohammedan peoples referred to in the preceding chapters, as affected by the doctrines of the founder of Islam set forth in the Koran. And in this survey the principal place must be given to the political circumstances of Turkey, which is the head-quarters of that larger division of Mohammedans known as Sunnis, as Persia is the head-quarters of the smaller, but still powerful, division known by the name of Shi'ahs.

---

* From the "Levant." By Arthur Arnold. Chapman & Hall, 1868.

The prestige of the Caliphate must have been greatly shaken by the catastrophe which ended in the suicide of Abd-ul-Aziz, and by the puppet reign of the unhappy Murad. But these events have called attention to the real position of the Sultan, which, during twenty years of peace, had been somewhat overlooked, possibly because in those years the conquests of the Turks have been, not territorial, but financial. The Turkish Government has been the most successful spendthrift of our time. But the day of reckoning arrived, and the Turk could no longer provide the bait with which for twenty years he had been catching a rich provision from Europe. General Ignatieff thought the bubble would have burst at least eighteen months before the declaration of insolvency actually occurred. But when, at last, it broke, this generation saw that which was for most of them a strange sight. They were enlightened as to the basis of the Sultan's power; they saw him regarded in that which is his true character, an acclaimed chief rather than an hereditary sovereign; the head of Islam, with power bestowed and established under the sanctions of the Koran.

If Fuad Pasha (whose disciple, Midhat, is striving for supremacy) had an ideal system of government, it was that which a man far greater than he, but with a mind of similar tendencies, had expounded in "Les Idées Napoléonniennes." To reconstruct the Caliphate, to reform it into a liberal despotism seated upon the heads of a dumb democracy—this was the thought of the great minister with whose death is supposed to have departed the glory of the reign of Abd-ul-Aziz. The revolution which cast that wretched Sultan from an eminence of power, awful in its solitude and responsibility to those who can conceive its full extent and authority, to a condition of restraint and imprisonment which rendered life unendurable, was proclaimed as a reversion to the policy of Fuad Pasha. Midhat Pasha was hailed as the political heir of the ex-medical student of Paris. Mahmoud Pasha, with his Russian leanings, was pushed away into outer darkness; in Besika Bay, England had congregated the largest fleet of ironclads that had ever been brought together under one flag; she was hailed as the friend, the inalienable ally, of Turkey, which the new ministers were prepared to show was not a "sick man," or, if sick, that, as Fuad himself said, "Turkey had no organic malady."

Then, in those tumultuous days when the power of Abd-ul-Aziz was passing away, were perpetrated the atrocities, the tearful and bloody record of which Europe has written upon pages that for all time will stand as a dreadful memorial of Turkish misrule. These are, it is now understood, wild fruits which grow by the wayside of the Mohammedan system. Never since 1868, when he became acquainted with the country, has the present writer consciously neglected an opportunity of denouncing the Turkish rule, of showing that the Turkish Empire has organic disease, and that her incurable malady grows ever more deadly as she is forced, by new arterial connections, closer and more closely into the light of the political ideas and civilization of Western Europe. It is not difficult to reduce the pleas for the maintenance of the Turkish Empire to that one plea of expediency, upon which, indeed, the greatest master of Turkish policy, Fuad Pasha, was content to rest its claim when he said, "We are the best police of the Bosphorus," nor to show that the validity of this plea is a reproachful testimony to the greed, and jealousy, and want of true civilization on the part of the great powers of Europe.

The Turkish power is a Mohammedan theocracy. No law is popularly accepted as valid unless it has religious sanction. The statute-book must run with the Koran. The neglect on the part of the Turkish power in regard to the fulfillment of the pledges inscribed in the hatt-y-houmayoun of 1856, of the due performance of which the other powers then felt themselves assured, does not vex the mind of a genuine Turk. Those promises were but wind—we will not, as Mr. Gladstone said, call them "air." The obligation to fulfill them was not to be found within the pages of the Koran. They were not, they have never been, indorsed with the *fetva* of the Sheik-ul-Islam. They had not the sanction of the Church. The *fetva* of the Sheik-ul-Islam—which is naught if it does not imply the consent of the whole body of Mussulman clergy — was needed before any could engage in the dethronement of Abd-ul-Aziz. It was needed to put an end to the three months' existence of Murad with the names of sultan and of padishah.

In the first chapter of this work, in regard to the Capitulation of 1675, we have seen that the outward manifestation of this theocratic basis can be suppressed. No grand vizier offering a treaty to England would now style his master "Emperor and Conqueror of the Earth with the assistance of the Omnipotent and the especial grace of God, the Prince of Emperors and the Dispenser of Crowns." Even in the Treaty of 1856 there is no trace of divine authority about the attributes of the Sultan. He is simply styled "Emperor of the Ottomans." This was the work of A'ali and Fuad, the great exemplars of the present time. It is not a final condemnation of the Turkish power to say that it is theocratic, for the possession of that quality and sanction has been the pretense of all powers, and is still the reputed basis of most of the powers of Europe. In his own dominions, the Tsar is just as much the "Shadow of God" as the Sultan. We must look to the ethics of the religion which is the ground upon which such authority is claimed. Mere forms of speech can be changed, and the language of Paris put into the mouth of the Padishah. When a great utterance was composed for Abd-ul-Aziz, the Napoleonic was the most approved form of composition. Had I been blind, I could have fancied myself at the Tuileries on the 10th of May, 1868, when, amidst hopes not less extravagant than those which encircled the first days of poor Murad's elevation, his predecessor, Abd-ul-Aziz announced the establishment of the Council of State and the High Court of Justice. He, the successor of sultans whose pretensions to divine direction had not been less declared than those of the infallible Pope; he who was the Pope of the Sunni Mohammedans—confessed that something was wrong, something rotten in his State, "because," said the master of greedy pashas, "if the principles and laws already established had answered to the exigencies of our country and our people, we ought to have found ourselves to-day in the same rank as the most civilized and best-administered states of Europe." With this naïve admission of failure, and "with a view to promote the rights of his subjects," Abd-ul-Aziz, the reformer, whose praise was then hymned in leading articles nowhere more loudly than in England, announced the establishment of the Council of State, "whose members are taken from all classes of our subjects without exception." "Another body," he continued, "instituted under the name of the High Court of Justice, has been charged to assure justice to our subjects in that which concerns the security of their persons, their honor, and their property."

No Christian could speak more fairly. To those who know something of the Turkish system, all this was "words," and nothing more. "Qui est-ce qu'on trompe?"* said Prince Gortschakoff to Lord Augustus Loftus concerning Turkish reports. But they did deceive England, for one reason—because we have always had a large party, composed of men of both sides in politics, who did not wish for an exposition of the true condition of Turkey, who were willing to be de-

---

* Correspondence respecting the Affairs of Turkey, No. 58.

ceived, and to deceive others. These were the bond-holders, who, whatever happened, feared to speak ill of Turkey, lest, in doing so, the value of their property should be depreciated. With regard to the Turkish Empire, the bond-holders have always been optimists, and they have had a very powerful influence upon public opinion. Men talked and wrote of Abd-ul-Aziz as they talked and wrote, for a few days, of Murad, and assumed then, as they were ready to assume in the case of Murad, and as they are now ready—though they are, it must be admitted, less confident, in the case of Abd-ul-Hamid—to assume that a man whose youth has been passed under suppression and surveillance, to whom education has been denied as dangerous, upon whom comparative continence and frugality have been enforced, would, when he acquired unlimited power and wealth—when he could indulge unchecked the favorite weaknesses of the Prophet—be a lover of liberty and law, a wise and liberal statesman, the husband of one wife, the master of no slaves, and in his private expenditure the delight of anxious bond-holders. It has been the inveterate error of the West to suppose that in Turkey figs grow from thistles—that beautiful women are produced by a life in rooms from which the glorious eye of the heavens, as well as the sight of man, is excluded; by walking out-of-doors in veils which prevent every breath of fresh air; in shoes and upon stones which render exercise a torture, and graceful carriage an impossibility; by a life of inanity, ignorance, and indulgence in unwholesome food. The error is not uncommon, nor its cause recondite. We have glanced at the self-delusion of the interested; but there are others who have made this error. Their mistake is akin to that of the dramatists of the Restoration, who, Lord Macaulay says, knew not that "drapery is more alluring than exposure." The mystery of the East has been their delusion; and this mystery, if it is faced closely and fairly, especially if it is regarded during moments when, in the political struggle, its veil is disarranged, is, as we shall see, a cover for evils which prefer darkness rather than light in social life—a despotism, with slavery for a domestic institution, and upon the throne of European Turkey, a misrepresentation founded upon force, upheld by oppression of those who are its subjects, and by the jealousies of the powers which are entitled its protectors.

The language of the present Sultan curiously resembles that which I have quoted from the proclamation of Abd-ul-Aziz. Abd-ul-Hamid declared that* "the critical condition of the empire arises from a bad application of the laws, based upon the precepts of the Cheri (a codification of the laws of the Koran); and hence have resulted financial discredit, defective working of the tribunals, and the non-development of trade, manufactures, and agriculture. To remedy these evils, a special council will be charged to guarantee the exact execution of existing laws, or those measures which may be promulgated in accordance with the Cheri. The council will also superintend the budget. Public functions will be intrusted to capable persons, who will be held responsible, and will no longer be dismissed without cause."

The same remedy, a "council," is proposed, but there is a more frank admission in the hatt of 1876 that the Government of Turkey is founded upon the precepts of the Koran. The Turkish Government has ceased to represent itself to foreign powers as theocratic, but, regarding its subjects, this is its truest title. When, in 1856, the Sultan appeared, as we have seen, to throw off, in deference to his Christian protectors of the Latin and Anglican churches, the assumption of divine authority, it was in fact asserted, though in language purely mundane. He was styled "Emperor of the Ottomans," that is, of the Othmans—of the followers of the

---

* *Daily News* report of imperial hatt, September, 1876.

conqueror whose sword Abd-ul-Hamid has girded on in the Mosque of Ey-yub, the leader, in fact, of three millions out of twelve millions of people in Europe, supreme ruler by no other right than that of possession, having no consent or true allegiance from the vast majority of the people of European Turkey; being, in fact, successor of Mohammed in the Caliphate, and of Othman in the Empire. Two facts I may mention which exhibit the true character of the Sultan's rule most clearly; the Mohammedan is to the Christian population in European Turkey as one to three; but the non-Mohammedan people are excluded from the army by which the Sultan's power is maintained. I have quoted the language in which the Council of State was announced. In its formation, the Council was a scandal, and in existence it has been the means of further enriching the oppressors of the country. The non-Mussulman population being as three to one, A'ali Pasha, the idol of the Softas, composed a council, which indeed exhibited this proportion, but with the figures reversed —three-fourths of its members being Mussulmans.

When Murad was put on the throne, the same farce was played, but the language was less grandiloquent. The grand vizier addressed himself, vià Murad (the hatt was addressed to "my illustrious vizier"), in phrases adapted from the failure of 1868.* "The domestic and foreign difficulties of the Government have brought about, in public opinion, a want of confidence, which, by disturbing the sense of security in every way, has entailed very material losses. It is necessary to put an end to this state of things, and to find a remedy for it; it is necessary to adopt a line of conduct which shall insure the welfare, as well as the material and moral prosperity, of all our subjects. The realization of these aspirations depends upon the establishment, upon a really sound basis,

---

* Imperial hatt, dated June 1st, 1876.

of the principles of Government administration, and this consummation is the ever-present object of my care."...."All our subjects, without exception, shall enjoy full and complete liberty;....and in order to carry out this project,....and with a view to this most essential result, it is both important and necessary that the Council of State....should be reorganized." Abd-ul-Hamid has said, or implied, at least as much; and we are thus brought to the position in which statesmen such as Fuad and Midhat Pashas find themselves when, after entering into promises in the French of Paris, they are surrounded with realities in the Arabic of Stamboul. They can make hatts, of course; but if these surpass the sanctions of the Koran, they must rest in the pigeon-holes of the Sublime Porte.

The Government of Turkey is unquestionably Mohammedan, and the course of this survey leads us now to inquire what are the inalienable essentials of Mohammedanism? what is its capacity for change, for re-interpretation, in accordance with modern ideas? The position of the Turkish Government, thus representing only one-fourth of the people in the European empire, and claiming sovereignty over other millions in Servia and Roumania, who have successfully repudiated any direct interference on the part of the Sultan with their internal affairs, is that of a foreign garrison, the soldiery having no connection with the mass of the people. This Government and garrison cohere by force of religious ties. Both are Mohammedan. It was long ago admitted by powerful friends of Turkey — that is to say, by the governments of England, France, and Italy — that the only safe path for the empire in the future lay in the abandonment of this exclusive mode of government; and it was A'ali Pasha who, in the famous hatt-y-houmayoun of 1856, promised the overthrow of the Mohammedan system. To make this assurance more certain, he consented, on behalf of his master, that the contracting powers of 1856 should be made parties to the execution of this hatt, by a special reference to it in the ninth article of the treaty. Of the thirty-five articles of this hatt-y-houmayoun, the most interesting and, from my point of view, the most important articles have, as Mr. Butler Johnstone, a friend to the Turkish power, writes, " remained dead letters." I will take his remarks upon this neglect, because there can be no doubt that he does not overstate the case. Referring to the promises of the hatt-y-houmayoun, Mr. Butler Johnstone says:

" (*a*) There were to be mixed tribunals of justice, codification of the law, translations of the codes into the different languages of the empire, settled modes of procedure: this has been translated, as we have seen, into mock courts, unpaid judges, arbitrary procedure, and corrupt decisions. (*b*) Farming the revenue was to be abolished, and a sounder fiscal system established: nothing of the kind has been done. (*c*) A solemn undertaking was entered into to grapple with the evil of corruption: at present the whole administration is corrupt. (*d*) Banks were to be established, to assist agriculture and come to the aid of commerce: nothing of the sort has been thought of. (*e*) Roads, canals, and railroads were to be pushed forward with vigor, so as to open up the resources of the country: the absence of roads and canals has prevented the relief of a famished population; and as to railroads, the only important line finished was a cloak for a most notorious scandal. (*f*) Foreign capital was to be invited and encouraged by every means, so as to develop the great resources of the country: such vexatious obstructions have been placed in the way of foreign capital that it has shunned the country; and men of integrity, like Scott Russell and T. Brassey, have had all their offers rejected. Unless the pashas catch a glimpse of backshish, foreign enterprise is an abomination in their eyes. (*g*) Christians were to be admitted into the army on the principles of general equality: nothing of the sort has taken place."

These promises, made by Abd-ul-Medjid, are in all important points identical with those made by Abd-ul-Aziz; they were implied in the hatt of Murad, from which I have quoted, and they were understood to be adopted by Abd-ul-Hamid. Midhat Pasha is, no doubt, prepared, if he gets opportunity, to follow Fuad and A'ali in the political dishonesty of manufacturing imperial edicts, made for show and not for use, which can not have operation in the Turkish Empire, because no law is there held valid which has not the *fetva* of the Sheik-ul-Islam and the general assent of the clergy. I shall contend that these promises are made without regard to the basis of Turkish law—the Koran; that they can not be executed without a complete surrender of Mohammedan principles, involving, ultimately, an overthrow of the Mohammedan Empire.

A Mohammedan government could not perform the promises of the hatt of 1856 without ceasing to be Mohammedan; because Mohammedanism, as a religious system, does not admit the followers of other creeds to administrative co-operation upon terms of equality. The Turkish Government promised codification of law, and independent tribunals of European pattern. How is it possible to put the laws of the Koran into a code acceptable to Christians? The Turkish Government promised to admit the whole population to the military service on the principle of equality. But this is equivalent to making the army three-fourths non-Mussulman, a situation in which Mohammedan supremacy in the Government could not endure for twenty-four hours. By a monstrous euphemism, the exclusion of the non-Mussulman population from the army is charged to them as "exemption," and they are made to pay about five shillings per man to establish their own degradation. The Christian peasants may, in some parts, be too ignorant to comprehend that in this exclusion their oppression is established. Yet the true character of the tax is very evident from the fact that it has been imposed, not only upon able-bodied men, but in respect of male infants from their birth, and old men long past military service.* This was one of the grievances of the Bulgarians, and by a firman of last December the Porte was pledged not to levy the tax upon infants and old men. But this promise, like all the promises of the Turkish Government, was worthless; and Sir Henry Elliot reported to Lord Derby that "unless the Turkish Government were to abandon a large proportion of the revenue derived from the tax, it became necessary greatly to raise the amount to be paid by each individual of an age to serve."† The Government, therefore, with no remonstrance from Sir Henry Elliot, declined to give the tax the appearance even of an exemption charge; and the British embassador has reported that this demand, even of an installment of justice, has led to a discussion of the liability of Christians to military service; for which he has said, "Some of them, and especially the Bulgarians, are showing themselves disposed to ask. They are aware that the conscription would, in many respects, press more heavily upon them than the exemption tax; but they know, likewise, that no firmans or regulations will do so much to bring about a real equality between Mussulman and Christian."‡ That which, of course, these poor people have not hitherto realized is that a conscription, fairly conducted among the population of Turkey in Europe, could only end in the substitution of Christian for Mohammedan supremacy in the empire.

Abd-ul-Aziz was Sultan when dispatch No. 33 was written; he was in his grave when Sir Henry Elliot returned to the subject on the 8th of June. His excellency has always

---

* Correspondence, No. 33. † Ibid. ‡ Ibid.

shown himself more solicitous for the preservation of the Turkish Empire than for the just administration of the Sultan's power; and, accordingly, though regarding the exclusion of the non-Mussulman people from the army as "the one great badge of distinction existing between the two races," admitting that "the Christians have become aware that until it is swept away their nominal equality with the Mussulmans can not be complete and real," he urges that "it is not necessary that the conscription should at once be put in force among the Christian population; but the military schools should at once be opened to them, and they might be received either as volunteers or as substitutes for Mussulmans drawn as conscripts." Of course the Christians would resist a conscription which sought to make them tools of the misgoverning rule to which they are subject, and from which they have at all times suffered grievous wrongs. They are unequal, and unable to appreciate the ultimate results of such a measure in the subversion of the Mohammedan power.

CHAPTER XXXI.

Islam in Persia.—Mohammedans of India.—Ali of the Shi'ahs.—Abu-Bekr Successor of Mohammed.—Imāms of the Shi'ahs.—Réza and Mehdee.—Religion in the East.—Mohammed as a Soldier.—War with Infidels.—Christianity of the Middle Ages.—Stretching the Koran.—Mohammed's Marriage Law.—Status of Mohammedan Women.—Women and Civilization.—Special Privilege of Mohammed.—Mormonism and Mohammedanism.—Consequences of Polygamy.—Protection of Polygamy.—Mohammed and Ayesha.—Scandal silenced by the Koran.—Mohammed's Domestic Difficulty.—Law for Men and Women.—Women in Mohammed's Heaven. — The Mohammedan Paradise. — Mohammed and the Jews. — Birth of Christ in the Koran.—Miracles of Christ.—English Leaning to Islam.—Mohammedanism and Christianity.—Christians of the East.—Moslem Intemperance.—Wine and the Koran.—Superiority of Christianity.

LET us now glance at the peculiarities of Persian Mohammedanism, which should have special interest for Englishmen, inasmuch as the dissent of the Persians shows the difference which exists in that large body of our Indian fellow-subjects, amounting to about 40,000,000, whose Mohammedanism is so often referred to as a matter which should rule our policy in Turkey, and as a danger to our empire in India.

Islam in India is divided into Shi'ahs and Sunnis—a distinction which separates the Mohammedans of Persia, who are Shi'ahs, from the Mohammedans of Turkey, who are Sunnis. In the Christian world, the Greek and Latin churches exhibit a similar point of union, and a somewhat similar difference. Both are united in Christ; yet in the world, and in the practice of the religion which they allege to be that of Christ, the Greek and the Roman churches live as theological enemies. As a rule, theological rancor increases between religious bodies in proportion as their tenets approximate; and, accordingly, in Constantinople we find that the bitterest sectarian enmities exist between the Armenian Catholics and the Armenian Orthodox, their difference seeming to outside observers to be merely that "'twixt tweedledum and tweedledee." In the Mohammedan Church, some animosity divides Shi'ahs and Sunnis, separating Persian and Turk—the Shi'ah of Northern, from the Sunni of Central and Southern, India. There are villages in Eastern Persia, and in Afghanistan, inhabited by a mixed population of Shi'ahs and Sunnis, and in some of these, in order to prevent disturbance, the Shi'ahs are confined to one side of a road, while the other side is exclusively devoted to Sunnis.

When Mohammed fought the "battles of God," Ali, his brave son-in-law, husband of the Prophet's only surviving daughter, Fatima, was ever in the thickest of the fight. He was the Ajax of the heroes of Medina in the warfare against Mecca. If there was single combat to be done, Ali was the man who stepped forward to slay the champion of idolatrous Arabia; it was the flashing vengeance of Ali's cimeter which brought back the tide of battle when it had ebbed away from the standard of the Prophet. But Ali was not the immediate successor of Mohammed in governing the Church Militant of Medina. Among the earliest of the followers of the Prophet, among the companions of his flight—that "Hegira" from which all Mohammedan people date their time, as all Europe (outside Turkey) does from the birth of Christ—was one Abu-Bekr, upon whom it is said Mohammed called, in the agonies of death, to take his place in the Mosque of Medina.

In a corner of the court-yard of this mosque stood the Prophet's home, including the apartments of his nine wives. It was in the room of his favorite wife, the beautiful and vivacious Ayesha, that he lay dying, when, according to Sunni belief, he summoned Abu-Bekr to the pulpit, and was held by this act to have indicated a preference as to his successor in the position of ruler, or caliph. After the Prophet's death, Abu-Bekr was acclaimed to this position—the spiritual and temporal headship of Islam. From that time to these days of the unhappy Abd-ul-Aziz, and Murad, and Hamid, the person acclaimed Caliph upon the death or deposition of his predecessor has been accepted by the Sunni Mohammedans as their chief. For ages this great title has remained with the descendants of Othman; and from him the Turks have acquired the name of Ottomans, or Osmanli. But this restriction to the line of Othman is an accident—a convenience; the line has become sacred by unbroken descent of the Caliphates; but that is all. Turks have become accustomed to hereditary descent of the superior power; but this form of succession is no fundamental principle of their system; and though their ruler is head of the Church and State, he is, as we have seen, liable to deposition by the authority of the Church. It was the *fetva* of the Sheik-ul-Islam which confirmed Houssein Avni and Midhat Pashas in their resolve to dethrone Abd-ul-Aziz. With the Sunni Mohammedans, the Sultan represents the power of the Prophet.

With the Shi'ahs it is otherwise. To the Shi'ahs of Persia the Shah is nothing but a supreme magistrate, whose office it is to govern in accordance with, and by the light of, the words of the Koran. With them, Imāms, that is, the full inheritors of the office of Mohammed, are too sublime to walk the earth in these degenerate days. Abu-Bekr was no Caliph of theirs; they repudiate him, and with him the title by which nearly all of his successors have reigned. To Ali, and to the descendants of Ali, especially to his son, the son of Fatima—to Houssein, murdered at Kerbela—is their homage given. They acknowledge but twelve Imāms; and it is long since they have seen the last of these holy impersonations. The first three Imāms of the Shi'ahs were Ali and his two sons, Hassan and Houssein. The eighth was the very holy Réza, whose shrine at Meshed is always crowded; the twelfth and last, known by the name of Mehdee, was born A.D. 868, and, according to Shi'ah belief, was taken from the sight of men when he was only nine years old. Mehdee is the invisible Imām of the Shi'ahs; he is to return to earth some day, bearing with him the complete and perfect Koran, which, in the Shi'ah doctrine, was intrusted to the hands of Ali. For the Shi'ahs, the humanity of religion, the link between God and man is found in Ali, and, to a greater extent, in Houssein; probably because the latter died a violent death.

Returning now to the general subject, I would say that observation of Mussulman authority in Europe, Asia, and Africa has convinced me of the truth of the following opinion, penned by a distinguished upholder of Mohammedan rule in Turkey: "Religion in the East," he most truly says, "has not the restricted meaning which it has with us. Every thing with them [the Mohammedan people] is religious. All those questions which with us would be termed matters of politics are with the Mohammedans matters of religion. Mohammedanism is, in fact, a religion, a code, and a civil polity, or, rather, these three things are different aspects of the same idea." Therefore, in order to master the internal springs of the Turkish system, we must go to the Koran.

Englishmen have been taken to the Koran by blind guides. Attempts like that of Mr. Bosworth Smith, in his "Mohammed and Mohammedanism," have been made to varnish the Koran with modern and unnatural coloring. Ill-judged and inaccurate as I shall show these to have been, such attempts are not, perhaps, surprising. It is the widely spreading revolt against certain dogmas attributed to Christianity which has led to this shallow delight in the Koran, of which the central doctrine is that of the unity of God. The Mohammedan service of the Grand Mosque, still known to Europe by its Christian name, Santa Sophia, is, in its outward aspect, lofty and sublime; it is ennobled by a comparison with the mean mummeries of the altars of Seville, or with the farthing tapers and picture-kissings of Moscow. But that outward form of worship is not Mohammedanism; and these things—the wooden dolls of Spain, "Our Ladies" of Montserrat and Atocha, and of this place and that (dolls endowed with revenues, and with sacristans for keepers of their wardrobes); the adored pictures of Moscow, devoid of beauty and of the charm of high and authentic antiquity—nor are these things Christianity.

We shall, however, be able better to appreciate the error of these apologists of Mohammedanism when we have glanced at the leading doctrines of Mohammed. The Prophet of Islam was a soldier, the Napoleon of his age. If the great Corsican had lived twelve hundred years before his time, it is not improbable that "Les Idées Napoléonniennes" would have taken the form of the Suras of the Koran. The sword of Mohammed was never long in its scabbard. He dictated a chapter of the Koran while his cheek streamed with blood from a wound sustained in the battle of Ohud. The Koran encourages Islam to war with the infidel in these words:*

"Fight on, therefore, till there be no temptation to idolatry, and the religion be God's."

"Fight for the religion of God against those who fight against you. Kill them wherever ye find them; and turn them out of that whereof they have dispossessed you; for temptation to idolatry is more grievous than slaughter."

"War is enjoined you against the infidel; but this is hateful unto you. Yet perchance ye hate a thing which is better for you; and perchance ye love a thing which is worse for you; but God knoweth, and ye know not."

"When ye encounter the unbelievers, strike off their heads,

---

* Sale's "Al Koran."

until ye have made a great slaughter among them..... And, as to those who fight in defense of God's true religion, God will not suffer their works to perish; he will guide them, and dispose their heart aright; and he will lead them into Paradise, of which he hath told them. Oh! true believers, if ye assist God by fighting for his religion, he will assist you against your enemies, and will set your feet fast; but, as for the infidels, let them perish..... This shall come to pass; for that God is the patron of the true believers; and for that the infidels have no protector."

Of course there is not in ordinary times an active desire to indulge in a crusade against overwhelming odds; the supreme teaching of utility is too strong for that. But every Moslem knows that the defeat of heresy by the sword is a cardinal point of Mohammed's teaching, and that Mohammed's Paradise is promised to those who fall in such conflict. It is no refutation of this to allege that the Christianity of the Middle Ages was no better; and to quote the Papal legate who put the edge of the Roman Catholic sword to all throats with the words "Kill all; God will know his own." Yet the error which is latent in this line of argument has to be exposed. It seems to some Englishmen to be a discovery, at once interesting and startling, that all systems of religion—those established before Christ as well as that of Mohammed—are inseparably related. They find not only ideas, but dogmas transmitted; they learn to infer that Christianity is not the Alpha and Omega of religion. Standing in regard to the orthodox interpretation of their own sacred books somewhat in the attitude of "the poor cat i' the adage, letting I dare not wait upon I would," they are overjoyed with the delicious *soupçon* of irrefragable heterodoxy thus imparted, and in their rapture fail to grasp the utilitarian chain which would lead them, link by link, to an invaluable test in this comparison.

They are not too careful how they deal with their own Bible when "the insuperable dogmatic character" of the Koran is in question. The member for Canterbury, who, I presume, is with Lord Beaconsfield upon the side of the angels in the matter of evolution, has argued that "the inspired character of the Christian sacred books has not prevented progress in religion in Europe, and for this reason, viz., that the inspired writings are sufficiently elastic in expression to admit of progressive developments and interpretations; otherwise religious thought, and with it civilization, would have been strangled in the Christian world. And so it is with the Koran."

These desperate friends of Mohammedan power are blind to facts as well as tendencies. Stretch the doctrines of the Koran to the length they desire, and the religion of Mohammed is gone; strain them politically, so as to establish a true equality of Mohammedan and non-Mohammedan population, and the empire of Othman must pass away. Of course, doctrines of the Koran may be amended by a revised interpretation—that is, some of them. Women need not be condemned to suffer ill health from want of fresh air because the Koran tells them "to discover not their ornaments," to conceal their charms from all but certain persons. Upon this matter, directly affecting the whole population, there are several interpretations now in sight among Mohammedans. The Persians include the eyes, the Turks do not; and the opinion of high society in Constantinople has ceased, in fact, to include any part of the face, the only difference from European custom being that, whereas the veils of English ladies fall from the head-dress, and are not always worn, those of the belles of Stamboul, not less diaphanous, but indispensable, mount from the chin to the nose.

The Koran says, "Take in marriage such women as please you—two, three, or four, and not more;" but the faithful may enter into temporary connubial arrangements with any number of "those women" whom they have "acquired" as "slaves." It will be said that there is nothing in these words to prevent the spread of monogamy, which is already the established rule of life with many Turks. Nothing whatever; indeed, we find these words in the Koran: "If ye fear ye can not act equitably toward so many, marry one only, or the slaves which ye shall have acquired." Moreover, it is obvious that time tends to encourage the decline of polygamy. The men of Constantinople who have but one wife have not lost confidence in the teaching of the Koran. They are coming to European ways, because, by increasing the individuality of women, civilization has surrounded polygamy with embarrassments. Some of them say they prefer to have but one wife because of the better enjoyment of her society, and the avoidance of jealousies and difficulty in regard to children. Others admit that expense sways their mind. The ladies of Stamboul have acquired by association tastes which are very costly: a liking for jeweled watches, for Paris fashions in dress, in carriages, in furniture. Each one of Mohammed's nine wives had but a mud-built shed, all grouped in one corner of the ground surrounding the mosque at Medina. Ayesha alone would have ruined him if, with his means, the Prophet had humored her extravagances in modern Stamboul.

Wherever Mohammedanism touches a higher civilization, the woman at once gains individuality, the veil becomes more transparent, and polygamy is less common. Why? Because the progress of civilization is synonymous with the advance of individuality, and individuality is both troublesome and costly in the persons of dependents. "There is nothing in the religion of Islam," said a writer of the highest authority in a recent article upon "The Situation Viewed from Constantinople," "which can fairly be called adverse to civilization." I shall abundantly expose the falsity of this proposition; but if the writer had said, "There is nothing in the religion of Islam which can withstand civilization," I should have agreed with him. The thinly veiled beauty of Constantinople has requirements unthought of by the secluded Persian lady, and thus the Turk is guided to the equitable law of monogamy. I will even admit that, in adopting this rule, the Moslem does not repudiate the sanctions of the Koran, and that, after a life spent in fidelity to one wife, he does not regard with scorn or contempt the "specially revealed" privileges of Mohammed in regard to polygamy. Yet it is hard to feel aught but disgust for Christian writers who degrade themselves by penning apologies for the rampant lust of Mohammed. He slaughtered a Jewish tribe, and selected a wife from those he had made widows. He coveted Zeinab, the wife of Zeid, his adopted son, and could not rest until he had compelled a divorce between Zeinab and Zeid, so that he might take Zeinab for himself. It was this last outrage which led Mohammed to perpetrate in the Koran his greatest offense. The lowest depths of historical imposture seem to contain nothing so foul as the deliberate admixture of special license for himself, in regard to polygamy, with sacred principles of justice in the Koran. Surely I have made a larger concession than truth will admit, in saying that the practice of monogamy, which the apologists of the Turk rightly declare to be extending in Turkey, is consistent with reverence for the man who, because he wished to take for himself the wife of another, and could not gain possession of her as a slave, put these words into the mouth of the Mohammedan God:

"O Prophet, we have allowed thee thy wives, unto whom thou hast given their dower, and also the slaves which thy right hand possesseth of the booty which God hath granted thee, and the daughters of thy uncles, and the daughters of thy aunts, both on thy father's side and on thy mother's side, who have fled with thee from Mecca, and any other believing woman, if she give herself unto the Prophet, in case the Prophet desireth to take her to wife. This is a peculiar privilege granted unto thee above the rest of true believers...... Thou mayest postpone the turn of such of thy wives as thou shalt please. God knoweth whatever is in your hearts, and God is knowing and gracious."*

Joe Smith and Brigham Young have not been without success in their humbler way, and in more rational times; but it may fairly be doubted if they would have had as large a following had their sacred books contained special privileges of this sort for the leaders of Mormonism.

Polygamy, which implies the unnatural appropriation of women by the rich of the male sex, is responsible for much of the vice of Eastern nations. The worst side, the lustful inspiration of the Koran, is nowhere more strikingly exhibited than in the laws relating to adultery and fornication. Against the traffic in the latter vice the Koran is most severe; and in throwing down the house which I observed in ruins in Kashan, the governor had only fulfilled the duties of a true Mussulman. The Koran says, "If any of your women are guilty, produce four witnesses from among you against them; and if they bear witness against them, imprison them in separate apartments till death release them, or God affordeth them a way to escape." In the days of Mohammed, women were imprisoned under this law till they died, and their death was often brought about by starvation, or some other cruel means. Later, this practice was mitigated by the Sonna; and while their male partners in crime were of course free, unmarried women guilty of unchastity were scourged with a hundred stripes, and married women were stoned. Women slaves, being held less accountable for their vices, received half the

---

* Sale's "Al Koran."

penalty to which free women were subject; and as stoning could not be done by halves, flogging was their punishment.

The polygamous households of Mohammed and his followers were protected by these laws; but for the crime of men against women the Koran has no punishment. " Compel not," says the Prophet, in the 24th Sura, " your maid-servants to prostitute themselves, if they be willing to live chastely, that ye may seek the casual advantage of this present life; but whoever will compel them thereto, verily God will be gracious and merciful unto such women after their compulsion." This particular passage in a book held sacred by millions of mankind was the " revealed " reply of Mohammed to the complaint of a woman, a slave in the household of Abd'allah Ebn Obba, who had six female slaves, on each of whom he laid a tax, and obliged them to pay it by the proceeds of an unchaste life. This suggestive rule of the Koran is still in operation, and we have had an opportunity of learning, upon official authority, how it works in Turkey. "A custom prevails here," Mr. Consul Abbott reported, " to exempt from military conscription a Mussulman young man who elopes with a Christian girl, and whom he converts to his faith. This being a meritorious act for his religion, it entitles him, as a reward, to be freed from military service."* Mr. Abbott's expression " elopes with " is an obvious euphemism for " abducts."

A difficulty which occurred in the household of Mohammed, and which nearly caused the cruel death of Ayesha, the most beautiful and engaging of his wives, led to the issue of a Sura specially " sent down from heaven," which did inflict some punishment upon men in their relations with women, the inspiration being obviously the jealousy of Mohammed. In the sixth year of the Hegira, when Mohammed was beginning his career of conquest, he undertook a military expedition against

---

* " Consular Reports on the Condition of Christians in Turkey."

the tribe of Mostalek, and on the march he was accompanied by his young wife Ayesha, who rode upon a camel, screened from all eyes in a curtained structure fastened upon the back of the animal. One night, when the forces of the Prophet were returning to Medina, Ayesha ordered the driver to stop her camel. The animal was stopped, and made to kneel. In the darkness Ayesha retired a little way into the desert. In returning, according to her own account, she discovered that she had lost a necklace of onyxes, a gift from her husband, the Prophet. She therefore retraced her steps, looking carefully for the lost treasure. If a well-trained camel is placed upon its knees, it is not difficult to step from the harness into a carriage, or howdah, upon the animal's back. The driver supposed, after some minutes had elapsed, that Ayesha was again in her place, and, taking this for certain, led the camel onward.

When Ayesha regained the track, she found the camel gone, and sat herself down by the way-side, thinking, so she said, that search would soon be made for her. She fell asleep, and in the early dawn of morning was awaked by one Safwan, who trembled as he recognized the favorite wife of the Prophet. He awoke her, Ayesha said, by softly murmuring twice in her uncovered ear the words, "We are God's, and unto him we must return." Ayesha's first instinct was to shroud herself from this man with her veil. She then allowed Safwan to set her upon his camel, and to lead her toward the army, in the rear of which Safwan had been one of the most distant stragglers. They overtook the forces of Mohammed when the soldiers were resting about the hour of noon. Immediately there was a great cry of scandal in the household of the Prophet, and Abd'allah Ebn Obba spread through the camp a charge of planned adultery with Safwan against Ayesha.

Mohammed was a terribly jealous husband; moreover, he

was thirty years older than this vivacious girl. His jealousy increased as he advanced in years; and, on one occasion, when the hand of a companion was thought to have touched that of Ayesha, the Prophet felt so much uneasiness that he was not comforted until he had settled the present and future of his wives by a revelation from heaven. And, accordingly, in the 33d Sura we read: "O true believers, enter not the houses of the Prophet, unless it be permitted you to eat meat with him, without waiting his convenient time: but when ye are invited, then enter..... And when ye ask of the Prophet's wives what ye have occasion for, ask it of them from behind a curtain. This will be more pure for your hearts, and for their hearts. Neither is it fit for you to give any uneasiness to the apostle of God, or to marry his wives after him forever; for this would be a grievous thing in the sight of God."*

When Ayesha returned, seated upon Safwan's camel, she won Mohammed's belief in her protestations of innocence. But the Prophet found that evil tongues were not stopped from speaking against the woman who, after the death of Khadijah, had the strongest and most enduring hold upon his affections. He resorted therefore, as was usual with him in any personal difficulty, to revelation; and in a Sura which, as I have before said, was introduced as specially "sent down from heaven," he promulgated a new law for the punishment of Ayesha's enemies. "Those," says the Koran, in the 24th Sura, "who accuse women, and produce not four witnesses of the fact, scourge them with fourscore stripes, and never more receive their testimony, for such are infamous prevaricators..... As to the party among you who have published the falsehood concerning Ayesha,....every man of them shall be punished according to the injustice of which he hath been

---

* Sale's "Al Koran."

guilty." And according to this *ex post facto* law, those who spread the scandal—Abd'allah Ebn Obba, Zeid Ebn Refaa, Hassan Ebn Thabet, Mesta Ebn Othatha, and Hanna Bint Jabash — all received fourscore stripes, except Abd'allah, who was too considerable a person to be beaten, even by the authority of the Koran. On this occasion Mohammed propounded, by way of the Koran, one of the very few laws which pretend to be equitable in the relations of polygamous husband and wife. "They," he dictated in the same Sura, "who shall accuse their wives of adultery, and shall have no witnesses thereof besides themselves; the testimony which shall be required of one of them shall be, that he swear four times by God that he speaketh the truth, and the fifth time that he imprecate the curse of God on him if he be a liar. And it shall avert the punishment from the wife, if she swear four times by God that he is a liar; and if the fifth time she imprecate the wrath of God on her if he speaketh the truth."*

Islam is adverse to civilization; the Koran is not "sufficiently elastic in expression to admit of progressive developments and interpretations," because it is a religion essentially opposed to the progress of humanity. It is a religion of force and of sex. "The true servants of God," says the Koran, concerning the Mohammedan heaven, will be rewarded with "delicious fruits, and the virgins of paradise withholding their countenance from any other than their spouses, having large black eyes, and skin like the eggs of an ostrich." The coarse materialism of this, and many other passages almost similar in words, together with other passages I have quoted bearing upon the relations of Islam with infidels, sustain Mr. Gladstone's description of the Turks, of whom, in his eloquent pamphlet, he says, "For the guide of this life they had a relentless fatalism; for its reward hereafter, a sensual paradise."

---

* Sale's "Al Koran."

This unspiritual, sexual language of the Koran has been dealt with by an English apologist in a very shallow argument. The writer of "Mohammed and Mohammedanism" clearly knows nothing whatever of Oriental people. He would probably be surprised, as well as shocked, to find that among the superior classes the conversation is of this character, even in the presence of women and children. It is a hard fact, that no higher ideal of supernatural life is given in the Koran; and the grossness of the picture is, we are told, explained by Mohammedans to be merely "Oriental imagery." This might seem plausible at a distance, if the programme of Mohammed's heaven included entertainments for women—if for them there were something more than bare admission. They are not even translated into the "black-eyed virgins" who are to share the fruits and the couches of paradise; for, says the Koran, "We have created the damsels of paradise by a peculiar creation."

It is not my purpose to contrast one religion with another. I am not engaged in the defense of Christianity, nor in the needless work of vindicating its superiority to Islam; yet it is with a feeling of offense that I find in the work above mentioned the heaven of Mohammed contrasted with the heaven of Christ, "where they neither marry, nor are given in marriage;" and the sensual hereafter of Mohammed condoned with the absurd apology, that "a polygamous people could hardly have pictured to themselves a heaven without polygamy." The *raison d'être* of women on earth, in the eyes of Mohammedans, has been translated so faithfully and truly into their heaven as to lead many to suppose that the Koran allows no future life to women. But evidently the denial of a share of paradise to women was not the idea of the dictator of the Koran. He constructed heaven as he observed the earth, and has therefore, not without show of reason, been held to have denied the immortality of women, while extolling that of men. If all the Turcophiles in the world tug together at the words of the Koran, they can not be expanded, or reasonably interpreted, so as to exhibit an equality of divine favor to men and women.

When Mohammed grew strong, he became the relentless persecutor, the cruel exterminator, of the Jewish tribes in the neighborhood of Medina. But the early Suras of the Koran suggest that there was a time when he labored to stand well with the Jews, and with those of them who had become Christians, or who honored Jesus Christ as a great prophet. Mohammed relieved the Jews from the crime of Christ's crucifixion. He caused this to be written in the Koran: "They have said, 'Verily we have slain Jesus, the Son of Mary, the apostle of God,' yet they slew him not, neither crucified him, but he was represented by one in his likeness. They did not really kill him, but God took him up to himself, and God is mighty and wise."* Christianity was becoming a considerable power in the time of Mohammed; and so far as he understood the doctrines of Christ, he adopted them. But it never occurred to Mohammed that Jesus Christ was God. He acknowledged the birth of Christ as miraculous. The version of the birth of Christ given in the Koran is said to have been obtained from the writings of the Apostle Barnabas. It is very curious: "We sent our spirit Gabriel unto her, and he appeared unto her in the shape of a perfect man. He said, 'Verily I am the messenger of thy Lord, and am sent to give thee a holy son.' The pains of childbirth came upon her near the trunk of an old palm-tree. She said, 'Would to God I had died before this, and had become a thing forgotten and lost in oblivion!' And a voice called to her: 'Be not grieved now that God hath provided a rivulet under thee; and do thou shake the body of the palm-tree,

---

* Sale's "Al Koran."

and it shall let fall ripe dates upon thee, and eat and drink, and calm thy mind.' And when she brought the child to her own people, and they said, 'Thou hast done a strange thing,' she made signs to the child to answer them; and they said, 'How shall we speak to him, who is an infant in the cradle?' Whereupon the child said, 'Verily I am the servant of God; he hath given me the book of the Gospel, and hath appointed me a prophet. And he hath made me blessed wheresoever I shall be, and hath commanded me to observe prayer and to give alms so long as I shall live. And he hath made me dutiful toward my mother, and hath not made me proud nor unhappy. And peace be on me the day whereon I was born, and the day whereon I shall die, and the day whereon I shall be raised to life. This was Jesus, the son of Mary." And again: "Verily Christ Jesus, the son of Mary, is the Apostle of God, and his word which he conveyed into Mary, and a spirit proceeding from him." "God" speaks again and again in the Koran of the "evident miracles" which he permitted Jesus to work; but the Koran never leans to the doctrine that Christ is God. "They are infidels who say, 'Verily God is Christ, the son of Mary.'" "And when God shall say unto Jesus at the last day, 'O Jesus, son of Mary, hast thou said unto men, Take me and my mother for two gods beside God?' he shall answer, 'I have not spoken unto them any other than what thou didst command me — namely, Worship God, my Lord and your Lord.'"*

An English school leans to Islam because it is monotheistic; they touch gently on its faults for the sake of its assertion of the unity of God. Perhaps we should have fewer exhibitions of this sort if it were generally known that, while denying the Godhead of Christ, the Koran accepts his miraculous conception and birth; and, denying that he was crucified, holds

---

* Sale's "Al Koran."

to his miracles, and declares that those miracles were an exhibition of divine powers. We must recognize the fact that to write upon the history and the influence of religions, one upon another, in a way to be of permanent value, something more is requisite than is displayed by any of the apologists of Mohammedanism whom we have met with. When one of these writes of an "elastic" Bible, and of "stretching" the Koran, toward what line is it that these sacred books are to be strained? Religion, it seems, is to be made to fit in with civilization.

If we want to understand whether there is any thing in Islam opposed to this union with civilization, we must know what we mean by one and by the other. We have now seen something of the doctrines of Islam. What, then, is civilization? If it were merely buying iron-clads, laying down telegraph-wires, borrowing money upon worthless paper, building with glass and iron, or arming men with breech-loaders, I should say, "Islam has done all these things." But I take civilization to be, in its briefest meaning, the extension of civil rights—the co-existence of the supremacy of law with the liberty of individuals to develop and employ their faculties for their own utmost happiness and advantage.

The sum of success in this endeavor is ever increasing. We know more truly than we can know any other thing that

"Through the ages one increasing purpose runs;"

and we have in this fact, in the increasing individuality of mankind, in what we call progress or civilization, a test by which to judge the doctrines of religion, whether they be transient or eternal. Of the facts which the history of the world has furnished, no one is more patent than the fact and the method of human progress, in which many religions have been, and will be, submerged. Mankind is outgrowing, or has outgrown, the practices of slavery and polygamy which are sanctioned by the Koran, and which did not seem hateful in the days of Christ. The experiences of life lead to the laws of life, which are necessarily more and more concerned with the rights of individuals. Of the Book of Mohammed, nothing is left, in the light of the present civilization, but the idea of God, supreme, omnipotent, impersonal. It is not so with the words of Christ. His standard—that of the brotherhood of mankind—is the banner of the time to come, and gives the largest prospect of progress which eyes can see upon the horizon of humanity.

The Christians of Turkey are often dishonest, not seldom drunken; and though not inferior to the people of Russia in political capacity, are in this respect far beneath the level of any other European people. But theirs are vices and deficiencies such as ages of oppression by a foreign soldiery (the Turks are such to them) would produce anywhere. They have had no instruction—no consolation, except from priests as ignorant as themselves. The extolled virtues of the Turk are those which have ever been exhibited by conquerors in the plenitude of supremacy above millions who toil to make their wealth, such as a foreigner would have seen in the Anglo-Normans eight hundred years ago.

In Mohammedan countries, where there is no interference by civilized powers, we have seen that a convert to Christianity forfeits his property upon application to the Sheik-ul-Islam by the next of kin. In the present year, an Armenian Christian of rank postponed his visit to a royal personage on account of wet weather. I asked him what connection the humidity of the atmosphere had with his intention, and he said that non-Mussulmans were not welcome; the tradition from the times when they were forbidden to walk the streets in wet weather—in order that Islam might avoid the superior power of contamination which their garments acquired by moisture—being not yet quite forgotten. It is not true that the non-Mussulman population has a monopoly of intemperance. I have never seen people drink ardent spirits in such large quantities as some Mohammedans of station whom I have met with in travel. A Moslem prince lately asked me why I drank wine. "It does not make you drunk. *I* take arrack," he added. English doctors in the East are frequently summoned to cases of delirium tremens, but

"Offense's gilded hand doth shove by justice."

The rich Moslem drinks privately, the non-Mussulman publicly. The Moslem drinks at night, the non-Mussulman at all times. Perhaps a majority of Mohammedans would refuse to drink intoxicating liquor; though in a troop of servants I have never seen more than a respectable minority of this mind; and it is possible—indeed it is probable—that of the poor, many believe the Koran to be as inexorable as our Good Templars. The belief is common throughout Europe that the use of intoxicating liquors is forbidden in the Koran. The author of "Mohammed and Mohammedanism" falls into this error. He says that Mohammed absolutely prohibited gambling and intoxicating liquors. The Prophet did nothing of the sort in the Koran. The words of the Moslem Bible are these: "They will ask thee concerning wine and lots [*al meiser*]. Answer, In both there is great sin, and also some things of use unto men; but their sinfulness is greater than their use."* I should suppose that even Mr. Bass would go as far as this. It is, however, the belief of pious Moslems that when Omar demanded from the Prophet direction more definite, in order that a better condition might be maintained among the then encompassed army of Islam, Mohammed did in some terms forbid gambling and the drinking of intoxicating liquors; but this prohibition was never

---

* Sale's "Al Koran."

made part of the Koran. In Mohammed's paradise we find the apotheosis of Bacchus. Youths in perpetual bloom are to attend the happy "with goblets, and beakers, and cups of flowing wine; their heads shall not ache by drinking the same, neither shall their reason be disturbed." The "black-eyed damsels" are again introduced, and the promise is given to the men in paradise, "They shall not hear vain discourse, or charge of sin, but only the salutation, 'Peace! peace!'" As to gambling, Mohammedans play cards upon the sands of the desert, as well as upon the decks of ships, and on the carpets and mats of their homes.

But I have made ill use of the present opportunity if I have induced upon the mind of the reader an impression very favorable to the Christians of Turkey and Persia. For this much I am always prepared to contend: they do possess, and their masters do not possess, a religion which admits of progressive developments and interpretations. The progress of humanity may for all time be illumined by the morals of the Gospel of Christ. It is nothing to show that Mohammedanism is more successful in proselytizing Eastern peoples than the harshly dogmatic, un-Christian "Christianity" of some dogmatic preachers. We may develop and interpret Christ's teaching as universal, for all sorts and conditions of men, and without distinction of sex. The purest doctrines of liberty entered the world by the mouth of Christ. Mohammedanism is a democracy for men — and not for all men, but only for such as are not slaves; and with these last and lowest the whole sex of women is placed. The religion of Islam is incompatible with progress, and must decline with

VALUABLE AND INTERESTING WORKS

FOR

PUBLIC AND PRIVATE LIBRARIES

PUBLISHED BY HARPER & BROTHERS, NEW YORK.

☞ *For a full List of Books suitable for Libraries, see* HARPER & BROTHERS' TRADE-LIST *and* CATALOGUE, *which may be had gratuitously on application to the Publishers personally, or by letter enclosing Ten Cents in Postage Stamps.*

☞ HARPER & BROTHERS *will send any of the following works by mail or express, postage or freight prepaid, to any part of the United States or Canada, on receipt of the price.*

ALISON'S HISTORY OF EUROPE. FIRST SERIES: From the Commencement of the French Revolution, in 1789, to the Restoration of the Bourbons in 1815. [In addition to the Notes on Chapter LXXVI., which correct the errors of the original work concerning the United States, a copious Analytical Index has been appended to this American Edition.] SECOND SERIES: From the Fall of Napoleon, in 1815, to the Accession of Louis Napoleon, in 1852. 8 vols., 8vo, Cloth, $16 00.

ABBOTT'S DICTIONARY OF RELIGIOUS KNOWLEDGE. A Dictionary of Religious Knowledge, for Popular and Professional Use; comprising full Information on Biblical, Theological, and Ecclesiastical Subjects. With nearly One Thousand Maps and Illustrations. Edited by the Rev. LYMAN ABBOTT, with the Co-operation of the Rev. T. C. CONANT, D.D. Royal 8vo, containing over 1000 pages, Cloth, $6 00; Sheep, $7 00; Half Morocco, $8 50.

ABBOTT'S FREDERICK THE GREAT. The History of Frederick the Second, called Frederick the Great. By JOHN S. C. ABBOTT. Illustrated. 8vo, Cloth, $5 00.

ABBOTT'S HISTORY OF THE FRENCH REVOLUTION. The French Revolution of 1789, as viewed in the Light of Republican Institutions. By JOHN S. C. ABBOTT. Illustrated. 8vo, Cloth, $5 00.

ABBOTT'S NAPOLEON BONAPARTE. The History of Napoleon Bonaparte. By JOHN S. C. ABBOTT. With Maps, Woodcuts, and Portraits on Steel. 2 vols., 8vo, Cloth, $10 00.

ABBOTT'S NAPOLEON AT ST. HELENA. Napoleon at St. Helena; or, Interesting Anecdotes and Remarkable Conversations of the Emperor during the Five and a Half Years of his Captivity. Collected from the Memorials of Las Casas, O'Meara, Montholon, Antommarchi, and others. By JOHN S. C. ABBOTT. Illustrated. 8vo, Cloth, $5 00.

ADDISON'S COMPLETE WORKS. The Works of Joseph Addison, embracing the whole of the *Spectator.* 3 vols., 8vo, Cloth, $6 00.

ANNUAL RECORD OF SCIENCE AND INDUSTRY. The Annual Record of Science and Industry. Edited by Professor SPENCER F. BAIRD, of the Smithsonian Institution, with the Assistance of Eminent Men of Science. The Yearly Volumes for 1871, 1872, 1873, 1874, and 1875 are ready. 12mo, Cloth, $2 00 per vol.

BAKER'S ISMAILÏA. Ismailïa: a Narrative of the Expedition to Central Africa for the Suppression of the Slave-Trade, organized by Ismail, Khedive of Egypt. By Sir SAMUEL WHITE BAKER, PASHA, F.R.S., F.R.G.S. With Maps, Portraits, and Illustrations. 8vo, Cloth, $5 00.

2 Valuable and Interesting Works for Public and Private Libraries.

BOSWELL'S JOHNSON. The Life of Samuel Johnson, LL.D., including a Journal of a Tour to the Hebrides. By JAMES BOSWELL, Esq. Edited by JOHN WILSON CROKER, LL.D., F.R.S. With a Portrait of Boswell. 2 vols., 8vo, Cloth, $4 00.

BOURNE'S LIFE OF JOHN LOCKE. The Life of John Locke. By H. R. Fox BOURNE. 2 vols., 8vo, Cloth, uncut edges and gilt tops, $5 00.

BROUGHAM'S AUTOBIOGRAPHY. Life and Times of Henry, Lord Brougham. Written by Himself. 3 vols., 12mo, Cloth, $6 00.

BULWER'S HORACE. The Odes and Epodes of Horace. A Metrical Translation into English. With Introduction and Commentaries. By LORD LYTTON. With Latin Text from the Editions of Orelli, Macleane, and Yonge. 12mo, Cloth, $1 75.

BULWER'S KING ARTHUR. King Arthur. A Poem. By LORD LYTTON. 12mo, Cloth, $1 75.

BULWER'S PROSE WORKS. Miscellaneous Prose Works of Edward Bulwer, Lord Lytton. 2 vols., 12mo, Cloth, $3 50. Also, in uniform style, *Caxtoniana*. 12mo, Cloth, $1 75.

CARLYLE'S FREDERICK THE GREAT. History of Friedrich II., called Frederick the Great. By THOMAS CARLYLE. Portraits, Maps, Plans, &c. 6 vols., 12mo, Cloth, $12 00.

CARLYLE'S FRENCH REVOLUTION. The French Revolution: a History. By THOMAS CARLYLE. 2 vols., 12mo, Cloth, $3 50.

CARLYLE'S OLIVER CROMWELL. Oliver Cromwell's Letters and Speeches, including the Supplement to the First Edition. With Elucidations. By THOMAS CARLYLE. 2 vols., 12mo, Cloth, $3 50.

COLERIDGE'S COMPLETE WORKS. The Complete Works of Samuel Taylor Coleridge. With an Introductory Essay upon his Philosophical and Theological Opinions. Edited by the Rev. W. G. T. SHEDD, D.D. With a Portrait. 7 vols., 12mo, Cloth, $10 50.

COLERIDGE'S (SARA) MEMOIR AND LETTERS. Memoir and Letters of Sara Coleridge. Edited by her Daughter. With Two Portraits on Steel. Crown 8vo, Cloth, $2 50.

DAVIS'S CARTHAGE. Carthage and her Remains: being an Account of the Excavations and Researches on the Site of the Phœnician Metropolis in Africa and other Adjacent Places. Conducted under the Auspices of Her Majesty's Government. By Dr. N. DAVIS, F.R.G.S. Profusely Illustrated with Maps, Woodcuts, Chromo-Lithographs, &c. 8vo, Cloth, $4 00.

DRAPER'S AMERICAN CIVIL POLICY. Thoughts on the Future Civil Policy of America. By JOHN W. DRAPER, M.D., LL.D., Professor of Chemistry and Physiology in the University of New York. Crown 8vo, Cloth, $2 00.

DRAPER'S CIVIL WAR. History of the American Civil War. By JOHN W. DRAPER, M.D., LL.D. 3 vols., 8vo, Cloth, Beveled Edges, $10 50; Sheep, $12 00; Half Calf, $17 25.

DRAPER'S INTELLECTUAL DEVELOPMENT OF EUROPE. A History of the Intellectual Development of Europe. By JOHN W. DRAPER, M.D., LL.D. New Edition, Revised. 2 vols., 12mo, Cloth, $3 00.

DU CHAILLU'S AFRICA. Explorations and Adventures in Equatorial Africa; with Accounts of the Manners and Customs of the People, and of the Chase of the Gorilla, the Crocodile, Leopard, Elephant, Hippopotamus, and other Animals. By PAUL B. DU CHAILLU. Illustrated. 8vo, Cloth, $5 00.

DU CHAILLU'S ASHANGO LAND. A Journey to Ashango Land: and Further Penetration into Equatorial Africa. By PAUL B. DU CHAILLU. Illustrated. 8vo, Cloth, $5 00.

FLAMMARION'S ATMOSPHERE. The Atmosphere. Translated from the French of CAMILLE FLAMMARION. Edited by JAMES GLAISHER, F.R.S., Superintendent of the Magnetical and Meteorological Department of the Royal Observatory at Greenwich. With 10 Chromo-Lithographs and 86 Woodcuts. 8vo, Cloth, $6 00.

Valuable and Interesting Works for Public and Private Libraries. 3

FIRST CENTURY OF THE REPUBLIC. A Review of American Progress. 8vo, Cloth, $5 00; Sheep, $5 50; Half Morocco, $7 25.

Contents.

Introduction: I. Colonial Progress. By EUGENE LAWRENCE.—II. Mechanical Progress. By EDWARD H. KNIGHT.—III. Progress in Manufacture. By the Hon. DAVID A. WELLS.—IV. Agricultural Progress. By Professor WM. H. BREWER.—V. The Development of our Mineral Resources. By Professor T. STERRY HUNT.—VI. Commercial Development. By EDWARD ATKINSON.—VII. Growth and Distribution of Population. By the Hon. FRANCIS A. WALKER.—VIII. Monetary Development. By Professor WILLIAM G. SUMNER.—IX. The Experiment of the Union, with its Preparations. By T. D. WOOLSEY, D.D., LL.D.—X. Educational Progress. By EUGENE LAWRENCE.—XI. Scientific Progress: 1. The Exact Sciences. By F. A. P. BARNARD, D.D., LL.D. 2. Natural Science. By Professor THEODORE GILL.—XII. A Century of American Literature. By EDWIN P. WHIPPLE.—XIII. Progress of the Fine Arts. By S. S. CONANT.—XIV. Medical and Sanitary Progress. By AUSTIN FLINT, M.D.—XV. American Jurisprudence. By BENJAMIN VAUGHAN ABBOTT.—XVI. Humanitarian Progress. By CHARLES L. BRACE.—XVII. Religious Development. By the Rev. JOHN F. HURST, D.D.

FORSTER'S LIFE OF DEAN SWIFT. The Early Life of Jonathan Swift (1667–1711). By JOHN FORSTER. With Portrait. 8vo, Cloth, $2 50.

GIBBON'S ROME. The History of the Decline and Fall of the Roman Empire. By EDWARD GIBBON. With Notes by Rev. H. H. MILMAN and M. GUIZOT. A new cheap Edition. With Index and a Portrait. 6 vols., 12mo, Cloth, $6 00.

GREEN'S SHORT HISTORY OF THE ENGLISH PEOPLE. A Short History of the English People. By J. R. GREEN, M.A., Examiner in the School of Modern History, Oxford. With Tables and Colored Maps. 8vo, Cloth, $1 75.

GROTE'S HISTORY OF GREECE. 12 vols., 12mo, Cloth, $18 00.

HALLAM'S CONSTITUTIONAL HISTORY OF ENGLAND. The Constitutional History of England, from the Accession of Henry VII. to the Death of George II. By HENRY HALLAM. 8vo, Cloth, $2 00.

HALLAM'S LITERATURE. Introduction to the Literature of Europe during the Fifteenth, Sixteenth, and Seventeenth Centuries. By HENRY HALLAM. 2 vols., 8vo, Cloth, $4 00.

HALLAM'S MIDDLE AGES. View of the State of Europe during the Middle Ages. By HENRY HALLAM. 8vo, Cloth, $2 00.

HARPER'S NEW CLASSICAL LIBRARY. Literal Translations.

The following Volumes are now ready. 12mo, Cloth, $1 50 each.

CÆSAR.—VIRGIL.—SALLUST.—HORACE.—CICERO'S ORATIONS.—CICERO'S OFFICES, &c.—CICERO ON ORATORY AND ORATORS.—TACITUS (2 vols.).—TERENCE.—SOPHOCLES.—JUVENAL.—XENOPHON.—HOMER'S ILIAD.—HOMER'S ODYSSEY.—HERODOTUS.—DEMOSTHENES.—THUCYDIDES.—ÆSCHYLUS.—EURIPIDES (2 vols.).—LIVY (2 vols.).—PLATO [Select Dialogues].

HAYDN'S DICTIONARY OF DATES, relating to all Ages and Nations. For Universal Reference. Edited by BENJAMIN VINCENT, Assistant Secretary and Keeper of the Library of the Royal Institution of Great Britain; and Revised for the Use of American Readers. 8vo, Cloth, $5 00; Sheep, $6 00.

HILDRETH'S UNITED STATES. History of the United States. FIRST SERIES: From the Discovery of the Continent to the Organization of the Government under the Federal Constitution. SECOND SERIES: From the Adoption of the Federal Constitution to the End of the Sixteenth Congress. By RICHARD HILDRETH. 6 vols., 8vo, Cloth, $18 00.

HUME'S HISTORY OF ENGLAND. The History of England, from the Invasion of Julius Cæsar to the Abdication of James II., 1688. By DAVID HUME. A new Edition, with the Author's Last Corrections and Improvements. To which is prefixed a short Account of his Life, written by himself. With a Portrait of the Author. 6 vols., 12mo, Cloth, $6 00.

HUDSON'S HISTORY OF JOURNALISM. Journalism in the United States, from 1690 to 1872. By Frederic Hudson. 8vo, Cloth, $5 00.

JEFFERSON'S DOMESTIC LIFE. The Domestic Life of Thomas Jefferson: compiled from Family Letters and Reminiscences, by his Great-Granddaughter, Sarah N. Randolph. Illustrated. Crown 8vo, Cloth, $2 50.

JOHNSON'S COMPLETE WORKS. The Works of Samuel Johnson, LL.D. With an Essay on his Life and Genius, by Arthur Murphy, Esq. With Portrait. 2 vols., 8vo, Cloth, $4 00.

KINGLAKE'S CRIMEAN WAR. The Invasion of the Crimea: its Origin, and an Account of its Progress down to the Death of Lord Raglan. By Alexander William Kinglake. With Maps and Plans. Three Volumes now ready. 12mo, Cloth, $2 00 per vol.

LAMB'S COMPLETE WORKS. The Works of Charles Lamb. Comprising his Letters, Poems, Essays of Elia, Essays upon Shakspeare, Hogarth, &c., and a Sketch of his Life, with the Final Memorials, by T. Noon Talfourd. With Portrait. 2 vols., 12mo, Cloth, $3 00.

LAWRENCE'S HISTORICAL STUDIES. Historical Studies. By Eugene Lawrence. Containing the following Essays: The Bishops of Rome.—Leo and Luther.—Loyola and the Jesuits.—Ecumenical Councils.—The Vaudois.—The Huguenots.—The Church of Jerusalem.—Dominic and the Inquisition.—The Conquest of Ireland.—The Greek Church. 8vo, Cloth, uncut edges and gilt tops, $3 00.

LEWIS'S HISTORY OF GERMANY. A History of Germany, from the Earliest Times. Founded on Dr. David Müller's "History of the German People." By Charlton T. Lewis. Illustrated. Crown 8vo, Cloth, $2 50.

LIVINGSTONE'S SOUTH AFRICA. Missionary Travels and Researches in South Africa; including a Sketch of Sixteen Years' Residence in the Interior of Africa, and a Journey from the Cape of Good Hope to Loando on the West Coast; thence across the Continent, down the River Zambesi, to the Eastern Ocean. By David Livingstone, LL.D., D.C.L. With Portrait, Maps, and Illustrations. 8vo, Cloth, $4 50.

LIVINGSTONE'S ZAMBESI. Narrative of an Expedition to the Zambesi and its Tributaries, and of the Discovery of the Lakes Shirwa and Nyassa, 1858-1864. By David and Charles Livingstone. With Map and Illustrations. 8vo, Cloth, $5 00.

LIVINGSTONE'S LAST JOURNALS. The Last Journals of David Livingstone, in Central Africa, from 1865 to his Death. Continued by a Narrative of his Last Moments and Sufferings, obtained from his Faithful Servants Chuma and Susi. By Horace Waller, F.R.G.S., Rector of Twywell, Northampton. With Portrait, Maps, and Illustrations. 8vo, Cloth, $5 00. Cheap Popular Edition, 8vo, Cloth, with Map and Illustrations, $2 50.

LOSSING'S FIELD-BOOK OF THE REVOLUTION. Pictorial Field-Book of the Revolution; or, Illustrations by Pen and Pencil of the History, Biography, Scenery, Relics, and Traditions of the War for Independence. By Benson J. Lossing. 2 vols., 8vo, Cloth, $14 00; Sheep, $15 00; Half Calf, $18 00; Full Turkey Morocco, $22 00.

LOSSING'S FIELD-BOOK OF THE WAR OF 1812. Pictorial Field-Book of the War of 1812; or, Illustrations by Pen and Pencil of the History, Biography, Scenery, Relics, and Traditions of the last War for American Independence. By Benson J. Lossing. With several hundred Engravings on Wood by Lossing and Barritt, chiefly from Original Sketches by the Author. 1088 pages, 8vo, Cloth, $7 00; Sheep, $8 50; Half Calf, $10 00.

MACAULAY'S HISTORY OF ENGLAND. The History of England from the Accession of James II. By Thomas Barington Macaulay. With Portrait. 5 vols., 8vo, Cloth, $10 00; 12mo, Cloth, $5 00.

MACAULAY'S LIFE AND LETTERS. The Life and Letters of Lord Macaulay. By his Nephew, G. Otto Trevelyan, M.P. With Portrait on Steel. Complete in 2 vols., 8vo, Cloth, uncut edges and gilt tops, $5 00; Sheep, $6 00; Half Calf, $9 50; Tree Calf, $15 00.

Valuable and Interesting Works for Public and Private Libraries. 5

M'CLINTOCK & STRONG'S CYCLOPÆDIA. Cyclopædia of Biblical, Theological, and Ecclesiastical Literature. Prepared by the Rev. JOHN M'CLINTOCK, D.D., and JAMES STRONG, S.T.D. 6 vols. now ready. Royal 8vo. Price per vol., Cloth, $5 00; Sheep, $6 00; Half Morocco, $8 00.

MOHAMMED AND MOHAMMEDANISM: Lectures Delivered at the Royal Institution of Great Britain in February and March, 1874. By R. BOSWORTH SMITH, M.A., Assistant Master in Harrow School; late Fellow of Trinity College, Oxford. With an Appendix containing Emanuel Deutsch's Article on "Islam." 12mo, Cloth, $1 50.

MOSHEIM'S ECCLESIASTICAL HISTORY, Ancient and Modern; in which the Rise, Progress, and Variation of Church Power are considered in their Connection with the State of Learning and Philosophy, and the Political History of Europe during that Period. Translated, with Notes, &c., by A. MACLAINE, D.D. A new Edition, continued to 1826, by C. COOTE, LL.D. 2 vols., 8vo, Cloth, $4 00.

MOTLEY'S DUTCH REPUBLIC. The Rise of the Dutch Republic. A History. By JOHN LOTHROP MOTLEY, LL.D., D.C.L. With a Portrait of William of Orange. 3 vols., 8vo, Cloth, $10 50.

MOTLEY'S UNITED NETHERLANDS. History of the United Netherlands: from the Death of William the Silent to the Twelve Years' Truce — 1609. With a full View of the English-Dutch Struggle against Spain, and of the Origin and Destruction of the Spanish Armada. By JOHN LOTHROP MOTLEY, LL.D., D.C.L. Portraits. 4 vols., 8vo, Cloth, $14 00.

MOTLEY'S LIFE AND DEATH OF JOHN OF BARNEVELD. The Life and Death of John of Barneveld, Advocate of Holland; with a View of the Primary Causes and Movements of "The Thirty-years' War." By JOHN LOTHROP MOTLEY, LL.D., D.C.L. Illustrated. In 2 vols., 8vo, Cloth, $7 00.

MYERS'S REMAINS OF LOST EMPIRES. Remains of Lost Empires: Sketches of the Ruins of Palmyra, Nineveh, Babylon, and Persepolis, with some Notes on India and the Cashmerian Himalayas. By P. V. N. MYERS. Illustrated. 8vo, Cloth, $3 50.

NORDHOFF'S COMMUNISTIC SOCIETIES OF THE UNITED STATES. The Communistic Societies of the United States, from Personal Visit and Observation; including Detailed Accounts of the Economists, Zoarites, Shakers, the Amana, Oneida, Bethel, Aurora, Icarian, and other existing Societies. With Particulars of their Religious Creeds and Practices, their Social Theories and Life, Numbers, Industries, and Present Condition. By CHARLES NORDHOFF. Illustrations. 8vo, Cloth, $4 00.

RAWLINSON'S MANUAL OF ANCIENT HISTORY. A Manual of Ancient History, from the Earliest Times to the Fall of the Western Empire. Comprising the History of Chaldæa, Assyria, Media, Babylonia, Lydia, Phœnicia, Syria, Judæa, Egypt, Carthage, Persia, Greece, Macedonia, Parthia, and Rome. By GEORGE RAWLINSON, M.A., Camden Professor of Ancient History in the University of Oxford. 12mo, Cloth, $1 75.

RECLUS'S EARTH. The Earth: a Descriptive History of the Phenomena of the Life of the Globe. By ÉLISÉE RECLUS. With 234 Maps and Illustrations, and 23 Page Maps printed in Colors. 8vo, Cloth, $5 00.

RECLUS'S OCEAN. The Ocean, Atmosphere, and Life. Being the Second Series of a Descriptive History of the Life of the Globe. By ÉLISÉE RECLUS. Profusely Illustrated with 250 Maps or Figures, and 27 Maps printed in Colors. 8vo, Cloth, $6 00.

SCHWEINFURTH'S HEART OF AFRICA. The Heart of Africa. Three Years' Travels and Adventures in the Unexplored Regions of the Centre of Africa. From 1868 to 1871. By Dr. GEORG SCHWEINFURTH. Translated by ELLEN E. FREWER. With an Introduction by WINWOOD READE. Illustrated by about 130 Woodcuts from Drawings made by the Author, and with two Maps. 2 vols., 8vo, Cloth, $8 00.

SHAKSPEARE. The Dramatic Works of William Shakspeare. With Corrections and Notes. Engravings. 6 vols., 12mo, Cloth, $9 00. 2 vols., 8vo, Cloth, $4 00.

6 *Valuable and Interesting Works for Public and Private Libraries.*

SMILES'S HISTORY OF THE HUGUENOTS. The Huguenots: their Settlements, Churches, and Industries in England and Ireland. By SAMUEL SMILES. With an Appendix relating to the Huguenots in America. Crown 8vo, Cloth, $2 00.

SMILES'S HUGUENOTS AFTER THE REVOCATION. The Huguenots in France after the Revocation of the Edict of Nantes; with a Visit to the Country of the Vaudois. By SAMUEL SMILES. Crown 8vo, Cloth, $2 00.

SMILES'S LIFE OF THE STEPHENSONS. The Life of George Stephenson, and of his Son, Robert Stephenson; comprising, also, a History of the Invention and Introduction of the Railway Locomotive. By SAMUEL SMILES. With Steel Portraits and numerous Illustrations. 8vo, Cloth, $3 00.

STRICKLAND'S (MISS) QUEENS OF SCOTLAND. Lives of the Queens of Scotland and English Princesses connected with the Regal Succession of Great Britain. By AGNES STRICKLAND. 8 vols., 12mo, Cloth, $12 00.

THE STUDENT'S SERIES. With Maps and Illustrations. 12mo, Cloth, $2 00 per volume.
FRANCE.—GIBBON.—GREECE.—HUME.—ROME (by LIDDELL).—OLD TESTAMENT HISTORY.—NEW TESTAMENT HISTORY.—STRICKLAND'S QUEENS OF ENGLAND (Abridged).—ANCIENT HISTORY OF THE EAST.—HALLAM'S MIDDLE AGES.—HALLAM'S CONSTITUTIONAL HISTORY OF ENGLAND.—LYELL'S ELEMENTS OF GEOLOGY.—MERIVALE'S GENERAL HISTORY OF ROME.—COX'S GENERAL HISTORY OF GREECE.—CLASSICAL DICTIONARY.

TENNYSON'S COMPLETE POEMS. The Poetical Works of Alfred Tennyson, Poet Laureate. With numerous Illustrations by Eminent Artists, and Three Characteristic Portraits. 8vo, Paper, $1 00; Cloth, $1 50.

THOMSON'S LAND AND THE BOOK. The Land and the Book; or, Biblical Illustrations drawn from the Manners and Customs, the Scenes and the Scenery of the Holy Land. By W. M. THOMSON, D.D., Twenty-five Years a Missionary of the A.B.C.F.M. in Syria and Palestine. With two elaborate Maps of Palestine, an accurate Plan of Jerusalem, and several hundred Engravings, representing the Scenery, Topography, and Productions of the Holy Land, and the Costumes, Manners, and Habits of the People. 2 vols., 12mo, Cloth, $5 00.

VAN-LENNEP'S BIBLE LANDS. Bible Lands: their Modern Customs and Manners Illustrative of Scripture. By the Rev. HENRY J. VAN-LENNEP, D.D. Illustrated with upward of 350 Wood Engravings and two Colored Maps. 838 pp., 8vo, Cloth, $5 00; Sheep, $6 00; Half Morocco, $8 00.

VINCENT'S LAND OF THE WHITE ELEPHANT. The Land of the White Elephant: Sights and Scenes in Southeastern Asia. A Personal Narrative of Travel and Adventure in Farther India, embracing the Countries of Burma, Siam, Cambodia, and Cochin-China (1871-2). By FRANK VINCENT, Jr. Illustrated with Maps, Plans, and Woodcuts. Crown 8vo, Cloth, $3 50.

WALLACE'S GEOGRAPHICAL DISTRIBUTION OF ANIMALS. The Geographical Distribution of Animals. With a Study of the Relations of Living and Extinct Faunas as Elucidating the Past Changes of the Earth's Surface. By ALFRED RUSSEL WALLACE. With Maps and Illustrations. In 2 vols., 8vo, Cloth, $10 00.

WALLACE'S MALAY ARCHIPELAGO. The Malay Archipelago: the Land of the Orang-Utan and the Bird of Paradise. A Narrative of Travel, 1854-1862. With Studies of Man and Nature. By ALFRED RUSSEL WALLACE. With Ten Maps and Fifty-one Elegant Illustrations. Crown 8vo, Cloth, $2 50.

WHITE'S MASSACRE OF ST. BARTHOLOMEW. The Massacre of St. Bartholomew: Preceded by a History of the Religions Wars in the Reign of Charles IX. By HENRY WHITE, M.A. With Illustrations. Crown 8vo, Cloth, $1 75.

WOOD'S HOMES WITHOUT HANDS. Homes Without Hands: being a Description of the Habitations of Animals, classed according to their Principle of Construction. By J. G. WOOD, M.A., F.L.S. Illustrated. 8vo, Cloth, $4 50.

YONGE'S LIFE OF MARIE ANTOINETTE. The Life of Marie Antoinette, Queen of France. By CHARLES DUKE YONGE, Regius Professor of Modern History and English Literature in Queen's College, Belfast. With Portrait. Crown 8vo, Cloth, $2 50.

TYERMAN'S WESLEY. The Life and Times of the Rev. John Wesley, M.A., Founder of the Methodists. By the Rev. LUKE TYERMAN. Portraits. 3 vols., 8vo, Cloth, $7 50.

TYERMAN'S OXFORD METHODISTS. The Oxford Methodists: Memoirs of the Rev. Messrs. Clayton, Ingham, Gambold, Hervey, and Broughton, with Biographical Notices of others. By the Rev. L. TYERMAN. With Portraits. 8vo, Cloth, $2 50.

VÁMBÉRY'S CENTRAL ASIA. Travels in Central Asia. Being the Account of a Journey from Teheren across the Turkoman Desert, on the Eastern Shore of the Caspian, to Khiva, Bokhara, and Samarcand, performed in the Year 1863. By ARMINIUS VÁMBÉRY, Member of the Hungarian Academy of Pesth, by whom he was sent on this Scientific Mission. With Map and Woodcuts. 8vo, Cloth, $4 50.

POETS OF THE NINETEENTH CENTURY. The Poets of the Nineteenth Century. Selected and Edited by the Rev. ROBERT ARIS WILLMOTT. With English and American Additions, arranged by EVERT A. DUYCKINCK, Editor of "Cyclopædia of American Literature." Comprising Selections from the Greatest Authors of the Age. Superbly Illustrated with 141 Engravings from Designs by the most Eminent Artists. In Elegant small 4to form, printed on Superfine Tinted Paper, richly bound in extra Cloth, Beveled, Gilt Edges, $5 00; Half Calf, $5 50; Full Turkey Morocco, $9 00.

THE REVISION OF THE ENGLISH VERSION OF THE NEW TESTAMENT. With an Introduction by the Rev. P. SCHAFF, D.D. 618 pp., Crown 8vo, Cloth, $3 00.

This work embraces in one volume:

I. ON A FRESH REVISION OF THE ENGLISH NEW TESTAMENT. By J. B. LIGHTFOOT, D.D., Canon of St. Paul's, and Hulsen Professor of Divinity, Cambridge. Second Edition, Revised. 196 pp.

II. ON THE AUTHORIZED VERSION OF THE NEW TESTAMENT in Connection with some Recent Proposals for its Revision. By RICHARD CHENEVIX TRENCH, D.D., Archbishop of Dublin. 194 pp.

III. CONSIDERATIONS ON THE REVISION OF THE ENGLISH VERSION OF THE NEW TESTAMENT. By C. J. ELLICOTT, D.D., Bishop of Gloucester and Bristol. 178 pp.

DRAKE'S NOOKS AND CORNERS OF THE NEW ENGLAND COAST. Nooks and Corners of the New England Coast. By SAMUEL ADAMS DRAKE, Author of "Old Landmarks of Boston," "Historic Fields and Mansions of Middlesex," &c. Illustrated. 8vo, Cloth, $3 50.

NORDHOFF'S CALIFORNIA. California: for Health, Pleasure, and Residence. A Book for Travellers and Settlers. Illustrated. 8vo, Cloth, $2 50.

NORDHOFF'S NORTHERN CALIFORNIA, OREGON, AND THE SANDWICH ISLANDS. Northern California, Oregon, and the Sandwich Islands. By CHARLES NORDHOFF. Illustrated. 8vo, Cloth, $2 50.

THE DESERT OF THE EXODUS. Journeys on Foot in the Wilderness of the Forty Years' ·Wanderings; undertaken in connection with the Ordnance Survey of Sinai and the Palestine Exploration Fund. By E. H. PALMER, M.A., Lord Almoner's Professor of Arabic, and Fellow of St. John's College, Cambridge. With Maps and numerous Illustrations from Photographs and Drawings taken on the spot by the Sinai Survey Expedition and C. F. Tyrwhitt Drake. Crown 8vo, Cloth, $3 00.

BARTH'S NORTH AND CENTRAL AFRICA. Travels and Discoveries in North and Central Africa: being a Journal of an Expedition undertaken under the Auspices of H.B.M.'s Government, in the Years 1849-1855. By HENRY BARTH, Ph.D., D.C.L. Illustrated. 3 vols., 8vo, Cloth, $12 00.

LYMAN BEECHER'S AUTOBIOGRAPHY, &c. Autobiography, Correspondence, &c., of Lyman Beecher, D.D. Edited by his Son, CHARLES BEECHER. With Three Steel Portraits, and Engravings on Wood. 2 vols., 12mo, Cloth, $5 00.

HARPER'S CATALOGUE.

Harper's Catalogue comprises a large proportion of the standard and most esteemed works in English and Classical Literature—COMPREHENDING OVER THREE THOUSAND VOLUMES—which are offered, in most instances, at less than one half the cost of similar productions in England.

To Librarians and others connected with Colleges, Schools, &c., who may not have access to a trustworthy guide in forming the true estimate of literary productions, it is believed this Catalogue, with its classified and analytical Index, will prove especially valuable for reference.

To prevent disappointment, it is suggested that, whenever books can not be obtained through a bookseller or local agent, applications with remittance should be addressed direct to Harper & Brothers, which will receive prompt attention.

Sent by mail on receipt of Ten Cents.

Address

HARPER & BROTHERS, Franklin Square, N. Y.

www.ingramcontent.com/pod-product-compliance
Lightning Source LLC
Chambersburg PA
CBHW020858020526
44116CB00029B/403